How Finance Is Shaping the Economies
of China, Japan, and Korea

AND
KOREA

EDITED BY YUNG CHUL PARK AND HUGH PATRICK
WITH LARRY MEISSNER

Columbia Business School
Publishing

Columbia University Press
Publishers Since 1893
New York   Chichester, West Sussex

Library of Congress Cataloging-in-Publication Data

How finance is shaping the economies of China, Japan, and Korea / edited by
Yung Chul Park and Hugh Patrick with Larry Meissner.
pages cm
Includes bibliographical references and index.
Summary: "A definitive historical record of financial development for three
countries, highlighting the centrality of the financial system in each country's
economic development and growth" — Provided by publisher.
ISBN 978-0-231-16526-6 (cloth : alk. paper) — ISBN 978-0-231-53646-2 (ebook)
1. Finance—China. 2. Finance—Japan. 3. Finance—Korea (South)

HG187.C6H69 2013
332.0951—dc23

2013015896

Columbia University Press books are printed on permanent
and durable acid-free paper.

This book is printed on paper with recycled content.
Printed in the United States of America

c 10 9 8 7 6 5 4 3 2 1

COVER DESIGN: Noah Arlow

Contents

Preface

THE CENTRAL theme of this book is in what ways, and to what degree, the financial system has mattered, and what roles it has played in the Japanese economy since about 1990, in the Korean economy since about 1980, and in the Chinese economy since its reform process began in 1978.

The purpose is to make definitive contributions to the financial histories of these countries available to a wide audience. Thus, the rigorous analysis essential for economists and financial specialists is written to be readily accessible to the nonspecialist curious about what are fascinating stories.

While these three economies are at different stages of development—and have distinct histories, institutions, political systems, and societal characteristics—their economies share basic commonalities in rapid catch-up development and in economic structure. Moreover, while financial development in each country has been driven by domestic forces, international short-term financial flows have been an opportunity and a challenge.

For all three countries, the nature and role of the financial system and its development and evolution in the process of real economic growth are integral, yet complex and nuanced. The result is a fascinating spectrum of experiences, and Japan's mediocre economic performance since 1990 relative to its potential provides a case study of the challenges of dealing with economic success as a mature, high-income advanced economy. The transition from an investment-led to a consumption-led growth model is not easy.

Policy makers in Japan, Korea, and China have certainly believed that finance matters. They have been deeply involved in the functioning, development, and, to one degree or another, control of their financial systems. They have learned, more in Korea and Japan than so far in China, that financial intermediation in the long run is best based on competitive financial markets, as well as control over inflation, macroeconomic stability, an appropriate institutional framework and structure, and effective prudential regulation for institution and system safety.

The introductory chapter provides a broad overview and explicit, comparative descriptions of the financial and economic development and growth of Japan, Korea, and China. It is not intended to summarize or synthesize the findings of the other chapters.

The final chapter, by Young-Hwa Seok and Hyun Song Shin, addresses the problems created by foreign short-term capital flows. These flows can and do create domestic liquidity conditions that result in housing (property) and other asset-market booms and exacerbate problems in the real economy when the bubbles burst. The authors stress the role of banks that seek loanable funds beyond their deposit base by borrowing short term to lend longer term, using Korea as a notable case. Korea engaged in the double mismatch of borrowing short term to lend long term and of borrowing in foreign currencies to lend in its domestic currency, during both the 1997–1998 Asian financial and 2007–2009 global crises. Importantly, the authors stress the importance of macro-prudential policies—that is, policies concerned with the resilience of the financial system as a whole—and review the tools available. In particular, they look at policies intended to neutralize the effects of capital inflows when monetary policy is constrained.

The country chapters, by Yiping Huang, Xun Wang, Bijun Wang, and Nian Lin (China, chapter 2), Edward Lincoln (Japan, chapter 3), and Yung Chul Park (Korea, chapter 4), are comprehensive and thorough descriptions and analyses that can be taken as definitive accounts of each country's financial development and evolution.

In principle, the cutoff date for the country studies is 2010 when the global financial crisis had receded and recovery was under way. Analysis for Japan begins in about 1990 and for Korea in about 1980. For China we start in 1978 when its reform process began. These time periods are selected because an extensive literature is available on the earlier postwar financial development of Japan and Korea. The literature on China's financial development is more limited.

Japan by 1990 was economically and financially developed, a high-income, mature industrial economy not unlike its Western high-income counterparts. At the other extreme, China began from a very low base and in 2010 was still far below where Japan and Korea had been in 1990. Korea is an intermediate case. It began its economic and financial development from a lower postwar base than Japan and now is far along in its catch-up process of real economic growth and financial development.

Each country has had to deal with burgeoning globalization from the 1980s, and especially with two major external shocks: the Asian financial crisis of 1997–1998; and the United States–generated global financial crisis of 2007–2009, symbolized for many by the "Lehman shock" of September 2008.

Nonetheless, the financial development and transformation of each country has been fundamentally a domestic story. Each began with strong controls over foreign capital inflows and outflows. With domestic financial development, the gradual easing of foreign capital controls was necessary, both for domestic reasons and in response to the deepening of the global economic and financial systems.

Each of the countries in this study has engaged in a somewhat different financial development as domestic circumstances evolved, and the global context has changed. Now the boom and bust that has begun the twenty-first century is causing a major rethinking of the role of finance. It is the hope of those involved in this project that an understanding of history and the methods of analysis presented here will help policy makers and provide both suitable reasonable hope and caution to those economies still on the doorstep of liberalization.

A note on terminology: this is a book on finance and economics, not international relations. We use Korea to refer to the Republic of Korea, which is sometimes referred to as South Korea. The official title of China is the People's Republic of China. And Japan is Japan.

Acknowledgments

THIS BOOK is the product of an international collaborative project initiated and organized by professors Yung Chul Park of Korea University and Hugh Patrick of Columbia Business School. Neither of us would have attempted the project without the other. We had learned how to work together through our experience some years ago in organizing a similar project, the fruits of which were published in *The Financial Development of Japan, Korea and Taiwan: Growth, Repression and Liberalization* (Oxford University Press 1994).

We were fortunate to attract outstanding specialists to join us in planning and carrying out the project, and to whom we are especially grateful: Yiping Huang of Peking University; Edward Lincoln, then at New York University's Stern School of Business; and Hyung Song Shin of Princeton University.

We all agreed it would be most productive to leave the determination of the major themes in each country chapter to the authors as experts. We further decided that each country chapter should be both comprehensive and detailed, with no particular limit on length, in order to provide the most thorough and updated analysis of the ongoing financial development. Preliminary drafts of the chapters were presented at a conference in Seoul in December 2010. The authors held a follow-up meeting at Columbia University in August 2011 to review the revised drafts before final, substantive revising and editing in spring and summer 2012.

All of us have benefited from the substantive comments of colleagues and administrative support from our respective institutions. We especially thank Larry Meissner for his careful reading and thorough, proactive editing of each chapter, working closely with the authors throughout. We are deeply grateful to him. And we thank three institutions that provided financial support for this project: the Center on Japanese Economy and Business at Columbia University, the Division of International Studies at Korea University, and the Center for Japan-US Business & Economic Studies at NYU Stern School of Business.

Hugh Patrick

How Finance Is Shaping the Economies
of China, Japan, and Korea

CHAPTER ONE

An Introductory Overview

HUGH PATRICK

THE ECONOMIC and financial systems of Japan, Korea, and China represent outstanding examples of very successful catch-up economic development and growth, major financial development, and gradual financial liberalization of initially highly repressed financial systems in an increasingly open global financial system. These are major achievements both for their citizens and for the world.

This book provides an analysis of that financial development process and how it has intertwined with the process of real economic growth in complex and nuanced, as well as obvious, ways.

The central theme is what role the financial system has played. That is, in what ways, and to what degree, has finance mattered? Each country is at a different stage of economic and financial development and has its own historical context. Nonetheless, the answers for each country have important similarities, as well as significant differences.

Three general implications for financial development can be derived from the experiences of these three countries:

First, financial development improves a country's resource allocation, but financial liberalization and increased financial intermediation do not necessarily result in a highly efficient allocation of financial resources, as the cases of Japan and Korea highlight.

Second, financial repression in the early stages of economic catch-up may not necessarily be negative, and may even be positive, as the Chinese case demonstrates.

Third, financial liberalization requires the development of good, prudential, market-supportive regulatory systems and their effective implementation. Financial regulatory failures or forbearance worsen economic performance, as shown on occasions in the Korean case and in Japan's lost decade of the 1990s. No regulatory model is perfect, nor is regulatory implementation. We cannot end boom-bust cycles, but potentially we can mitigate them.

The next three chapters provide definitive contributions to the literature on the modern history of the financial development of China, Japan, and Korea. The literature on Japan's postwar economic and financial development is extensive, so that chapter 3 by Edward Lincoln begins in 1990, when Japan had a well-developed financial system in which the bursting of major stock market and real estate bubbles heralded the end of the postwar era. Yung Chul Park's chapter 4 on Korea begins in 1980, as the country began to grapple with liberalization of a highly repressed financial system. It appropriately emphasizes the importance of the 1997–1998 Asian crisis and the reforms that directly ensued, and the effects of the 2007–2009 global financial crisis. Since the financial-system literature on China is limited, chapter 2 by Yiping Huang and his coauthors begins in 1978, when the reform process was launched, and provides considerable detail. In principle the cutoff date for these financial histories is 2010.

In the final and most explicitly policy-oriented chapter (chapter 5), Yong-Hwa Seok and Hyun Song Shin stress that financial globalization is prone to propagate and especially to amplify the boom-bust cycles, notably through the explosive growth of cross-country, short-term capital flows. They analyze Korea as an important case and consider the effects on European banks and their interactions with American financial institutions in the 2007–2009 financial crisis. Importantly, the authors address the global need for macro-prudential regulations and appropriate policy measures.

The basic purpose of this chapter is to provide comparisons of the similarities and differences among China, Japan, and Korea, both in their domestic dimensions and in their responses to the changing international economic and financial environment. The next section presents the context of the country studies, with particular attention to the 2007–2009 global financial crisis, which is an important part of the international context. Subsequent sections make explicit comparisons of the three countries regarding their economic development and growth, financial development, financial repression and liberalization, financial globalization, and the effectiveness and efficiency of fiscal development. The chapter concludes with a broad evaluation of the role of finance.

Demirgüç-Kunt and Levine (2008) provide a comprehensive survey of the general financial development literature, which also is discussed in the chapter by Huang and his coauthors (chapter 2). Voghouei et al. (2011) review the determinants of financial development; Kose et al. (2009) provide a perspective of the macroeconomic effects of financial globalization. Each of the country chapters provides relevant references to the literature on its financial and economic development.

Context

The broadest context for these country studies has been the unprecedented, good, sustained increases over the postwar period in global output, trade, and finance. This context is one of ongoing, dynamic change in long-run economic and political trends, increasing capital- and financial-market globalization, cyclical movements (booms and busts) in finance and economics, and shocks of varying degrees of severity. Three major groups of participants have been involved.

The first group is the economically advanced, high-income countries of the United States and Europe, which Japan joined in the 1980s. The second is economies that have developed rapidly over a sustained period and have now achieved quite high levels of per capita income. They are epitomized by the four Asian Tigers, led by Korea and Taiwan, Hong Kong, and Singapore. Third are the emerging countries that are rapidly growing from very low initial bases, epitomized by China.

The US-led, market-based, economic and financial world order has constantly evolved since its emergence from the depredations of World War II. In the 1980s the rise of Japan to being the world's second largest economy forced both it and the West to adjust and accommodate. This was significantly eased by Japan's close security and political

alliance with the United States. By 2010 China, now the world's second largest economy but still with low per capita income, was clearly
a major global power in political and security, as well as economic,
dimensions. The absolute and relative rise of China is a qualitatively
different challenge to all parties from that presented by Japan. Korea,
a staunch ally of the United States, because of its smaller size, was an
accepter of, rather than a challenger to, the world order. It has come to
play an important role as a middle power. Korea has important bilateral
economic relations with both Japan and China, albeit in different ways.

Japan has not dealt very well with success. Korea has been better
(though Park is less positive about Korea's performance than I am), and
China still has a long way to go. During the period covered, the three
countries have had to deal with two major shocks: the Asian financial
crisis of 1997–1998, which began in Thailand, and the global financial
crisis of 2007–2009, which began in the United States.

An extensive literature is available on the Asian financial crisis, and
each of the country chapters addresses its impact; sufficient time has
passed to have a good perspective. The financial impact was different
in each country, though in each case export growth declined and gross
domestic product (GDP) growth slowed. The Asian financial crisis had
a profound effect on Korea's financial system and its economy. Its banks
faced a double-mismatch problem: they had borrowed short term in
foreign currency, exchanged the funds into domestic currency, and lent
long term to Korean companies. In 1998 Korea's GDP contracted by 6.9
percent, an almost 12-percentage-point swing from 4.7 percent growth
the previous year. Korea had to seek an International Monetary Fund
(IMF) bailout. The IMF required it to carry out a wide range of major
financial and other economic reforms.

China had insulated itself from the direct financial effects of the
Asian crisis with foreign capital controls, as well as domestic controls
over its government-owned banks and other financial institutions.
Nonetheless, its growth slowed significantly, from 10 percent in 1996
to 7.6 percent in 1999, before accelerating again.

Japan was an international portfolio creditor and lender. Its banks,
like those elsewhere, engaged in a flight to safety, reducing foreign
lending. However, Japan was going through its own financial crisis for
domestic reasons, and the direct effects of the Asian crisis were limited.
Nonetheless, its domestic financial crisis choked a nascent recovery, sending Japan into a recession in 1998 with a GDP decline of 2.0 percent.

The global financial crisis of 2007–2009 profoundly affected banks and other financial institutions in the United States, the epicenter of the crisis, and in Europe. The direct financial impacts on Asia in general, and in Japan and China in particular, were much less severe. But, again, Korea was hard hit, though considerably less so than in 1997–1998. Even though Japan is a huge creditor nation, its banks had not invested heavily in US subprime or other securitized instruments, so their losses were modest and manageable. China's capital controls and domestic policies continued to effectively insulate its financial system from the global crisis, but it had to engage in massive macroeconomic stimulus. However, Korean banks were yet again caught in a double mismatch, depending excessively on foreign short-term loans to finance Korean company investment projects, as is well discussed in Park's chapter 4 on Korea and emphasized in chapter 5 by Seok and Shin.

The global financial crisis produced the Great Recession, which reached its bottom in 2009. The recession's impact was different in each country, as were the responses. The external shock in real terms was in the sharp drop in exports. Japan's exports slipped precipitously—from 8.7 percent growth in 2007 to a 24.2 percent contraction in 2009. As a consequence, GDP dropped 5.5 percent in 2009, its most severe decline in the postwar period. China's export shock was also very large, from 19.8 percent growth in 2007 to a 10.3 percent contraction in 2009. China's GDP growth slowed from a peak of 14.2 percent in 2007 to 9.2 percent in 2009, and then rose to 10.4 percent in 2010. Korea had to deal with both the direct effects of its financial system's double mismatch and a significant drop in exports, from 12.6 percent growth in 2007 to a 1.2 percent contraction in 2009. Korea's GDP growth dropped from 5.1 percent in 2007 to 0.3 percent in 2009, a decline about the same as China's and a bit less than Japan's. All three countries pursued macroeconomic stimulative policies, and as exports strongly expanded in 2010, their economies bounced back.

The 2007–2009 *Global Financial Crisis*

The global financial crisis of 2007–2009 has caused a rethinking of development strategies in general and the role of finance in particular. What began as an American financial crisis in summer 2007 became global with the dramatic collapse and bankruptcy of Lehman Brothers on September 15, 2008—an event termed by many in Asia and elsewhere as the "Lehman Shock." The immediate financial crisis was deemed under control by mid-2009, when the global real economy was reaching the bottom of a trough from which recovery has been slow. Difficulties have persisted into 2012 as the original crisis has morphed into a European debt crisis, with widespread trepidation about the future of the euro.

The fundamental causes of the crisis are all too familiar, but the scale was so much larger because of the nature (complexity) of globalized short-term financial markets. As with the Great Depression of the 1930s, there will never be an agreed, comprehensive, objective understanding of the crisis and its implications. Nonetheless the broad outlines are clear. Two *Journal of Economic Literature* articles are particularly useful: Andrew W. Lo's (2012) review of 21 books and Gary Gorton and Andrew Metrick's (2012) review of 16 documents.

The financial crisis began in the United States in August 2007, when problems in subprime housing mortgage markets spilled into short-term wholesale financial and money markets, affecting bank transactions with each other as counterparties. Although the trigger was losses in the imploding subprime mortgage market, it became a major crisis because of vulnerabilities that had accumulated in the overall financial system over a decade or more of institutional and financial innovation and development.

A shadow banking system had developed outside the regulated banking system. It involved mortgage originators, broker dealers, and investment banks participating in short-term money markets, especially markets for commercial paper and repurchase agreements (repos) between financial institutions. In addition to major US banks, European banks became deeply involved in US financial markets as major buyers of securitized mortgage packages, which they financed by borrowing in US short-term financial markets. For their own reasons financial institutions in Japan, Korea, and China were not deeply involved in this.

It is appropriate to fault the system, including both its participants and regulators, as well as politicians, policy makers, and their academic advisors. But it is impossible to determine who was most at fault. Groupthink and following the herd dominated behavior. Decision makers in many financial institutions, especially in the United States and Europe, made huge mistakes trusting flawed quantitative models and ignoring historical lessons (especially regarding leverage levels).

Very low-probability but calamitous risks (black swans and tail risks) were significantly underestimated.

The extraordinarily rapid growth and huge size of the originate-to-distribute model created collateralized debt obligations (CDOs) so convoluted that unwinding them has proven extraordinarily difficult and time-consuming. Mortgages of varying credit quality were pooled and then sliced into tranches. Slices of these packages often were repackaged and sold again or became the basis for derivatives. In the face of ever more complex, nontransparent financial instruments, the buyers performed little due diligence. And even the sellers had limited understanding of what they were creating.

Leverage was high, often more than 30 to 1, from the 1990s on. Incentives for executives and sales staff were misaligned, contributing to what can only be call appalling behavior. Optimism and hubris created bubbles far beyond the housing market as contagion spread.

The quest is now under way for more appropriate macro-prudential, as well as micro-prudential, regulation; better risk management methodologies; and better employee remuneration systems. Issues of appropriate regulation and institutional structure are taken up throughout the book, especially by Seok and Shin.

Catch-up Growth and Finance: An Overview

Because we are considering the three countries at different stages of their real and financial development, there are significant differences, as table 1.1 indicates.

China is an outlier in population and GDP size, and in its low level of development. Equally important, it began the period as a centrally planned command, socialist economy under Communist Party control, in strong contrast to the market economies of a democratic Japan and a Korea that (by 1987) had transitioned from an authoritarian regime to a democratic system.

Catch-up Growth

The most important similarity of the three economies is that they all have engaged in extraordinarily successful catch-up growth and development. Catch-up growth is a simple phrase for a complex, long-run

TABLE I.I

China, Japan, and Korea Indicators

China		Japan		Korea		Indicators
1990	2010	1990	2010	1990	2010	
1,135.2	1,338.3	123.5	127.4	42.9	48.9	Population, total (millions)
9,327.4	9,327.5	364.6	364.5	98.7	96.9	Land area (thousand sq km)
902	10,085	2,338	4,333	341	1,418	GDP, PPP (billion current intl $)
794	7,536	18,924	34,013	7,960	29,004	GDP per capita, PPP (current intl $)
69.8	167.9	184.1	224.2	34.1	70.8	M2 as percent of GDP
87.1	131.1	194.8	168.0	54.5	100.8	Domestic credit as percent of GDP
6.9	33.8	68.0	220.0	13.8	33.4	Government debt as percent of GDP

Note: Domestic credit is only to the private sector in Japan and Korea but includes state-owned enterprises in China.

process. The technology and productivity gaps between the world production frontier and the capabilities of a less-developed, poor country are huge. The gap is comprehensive in manufacturing and engineering technology, in business and management systems and skills, and in other forms of knowledge that together generate high productivity of labor, capital, land, and natural resources.

Catch-up essentially is based on disseminating better technologies, including effectively adapting foreign technologies to domestic factor endowments. This long-run supply-side approach has to be supplemented by adequate aggregate demand. Macroeconomic policies to hold down inflation, mitigate business cycle fluctuations, constrain bubbles, and shape the composition of domestic investment, consumption, and foreign trade are important. The following chapters consider the somewhat different circumstances in Japan, Korea, and China of the macroeconomic interactions between supply and demand.

Catch-up is achieved by high rates of new investment, generally utilizing existing foreign technology. The process requires incentives and institutions capable of seizing these opportunities (and eager to do so), businesses to carry out the investment, and educational systems to enhance human skills. Catch-up requires a government strongly committed to economic development and possessed of the ability to create a supportive environment.

The catch-up processes of our three countries have been fundamentally similar: rapid, relatively labor-intensive industrialization based both on high rates of fixed investment in factories, buildings, housing, and infrastructure, and on an increasing role of exports and imports in generating domestic demand and paying for imported resources and equipment. None of these countries is resource rich relative to its populations and development level. Each had an initially abundant labor force that over time has become increasingly educated, skilled, and absorbed into productive activities, with rising real wages. Agriculture has become a sector of increasing comparative disadvantage. With successful development, imports of oil, iron ore, and other natural resources are essential to sustain industrial production in all three economies.

One obvious major contrast among the three countries is that Japan and Korea have relied primarily on private-sector institutions and market forces, while in China the government and its state-owned enterprises initially were dominant, with the private sector gradually growing in importance.

Other contrasts are shown in table 1.2. Data on the United States are included for context. These measures are indicators of differences in economic and political systems, as well as differences in level of development.

The Role of Finance

In each case, but in quite different ways, with China the outlier, real economic development and growth have been deeply intertwined with the development of the domestic financial system and its financial intermediation process between savers and investors. All three countries have

TABLE 1.2

Perceptions of Japan, China, Korea, and the United States

China	Japan	Korea	United States	
				A. Governance Indicators (percentile ranking, 2010)[a]
5.2	82.5	69.2	87.2	Voice and accountability
24.1	76.9	50.0	56.6	Political stability and absence of violence/ terrorism
59.8	88.5	84.2	90.0	Government effectiveness
45.0	80.9	78.9	90.4	Regulatory quality
44.5	88.2	81.0	91.5	Rule of law
32.5	91.9	69.4	85.6	Control of corruption
				B. Other Surveys
3.6	8.0	5.4	7.1	Corruption perceptions index[b]
91	20	8	4	Ease of doing business[c]
6.24	7.37	7.37	7.58	Economic freedom[d]

Sources: Panel A, The World Bank Group Governance & Anti-Corruption Indicators; Corruption perceptions index; Transparency International; Ease of doing business, www. doingbusiness.org; Economic freedom, Fraser Institute, www.freetheworld.com.

[a]In Panel A, 0 is the lowest rank.

[b]The Corruption Perception Index is for 2011 and uses a scale of 0 to 10. New Zealand, at 9.5, had the highest rating.

[c]Ease of doing business ranks 183 countries. The source provides a variety of sub-indicators and data.

[d]Economic freedom are 2009 summary ratings, as published in the source's 2011 report. Each country's summary rating is compiled from forty-two distinct pieces of data, available in the source. Hong Kong had the highest rating, 9.01 out of 10. The average for the entire list of 141 countries was 6.64.

bank-based financial systems. In the early stages of their post–World War II financial and economic development, the financial systems in all three were subject to significant degrees of government controls and financial repression. This was particularly the case of China, with its controlled, planned economy and state ownership of the financial institutions.

Loan and deposit interest rates were regulated, entry was limited, and government policy and administration guidance were extensive. In other words, the financial systems in all three countries initially were significantly repressed. China was by far the most extreme in this regard: when it began reforms in 1978, its financial system barely existed. In all three countries, financial development was based both on the strong demand for funds and on the gradual but substantial liberalization of their supply.

Rapid catch-up growth in Japan, Korea, and China has been based on high rates of investment embodying new technologies and concomitantly high rates of saving, mostly done by households. Although the financial systems in all three countries successfully transferred the savings to the investors, inevitably the process of financial intermediation has been complex, imperfect, and, at times, messy. The process has involved financial institutions (primarily banks), government policy, the financial regulatory system, markets that operated far less than perfectly, and interactions and feedback among real and financial variables. Inevitably, all these changed over time, but not always smoothly.

Policy makers in Japan, Korea, and China have certainly believed that finance matters. They have been deeply involved in the development, functioning, and, to one degree or another, control of their financial systems. They have learned—much more in Korea and Japan than so far in China—that financial intermediation in the long run is best based on competitive financial markets, control over inflation, macroeconomic stability, an appropriate institutional framework and structure, and effective prudential regulation for institution and system safety.

They have also understood that finance can be a powerful instrument to achieve many specific objectives, and to one degree or another government policies in all three countries have channeled funds to finance investment in government-priority sectors and activities that were not a good use of funds. Starting with bank-based financial systems the governments have gradually encouraged development of domestic capital markets.

Economic Development and Growth

To provide a context for a broad comparative description of the financial development of Japan, Korea, and China, this section provides an overview of their economic growth (see table 1.3).

TABLE 1.3
Real Growth, Percentage Increase by Decade

	GDP			GDP per Capita		
	China	Japan	Korea	China	Japan	Korea
1980–1990	143.0	47.2	130.9	110.1	39.1	105.3
1990–2000	169.6	12.5	80.4	142.4	9.5	64.6
2000–2010	170.8	7.3	50.0	155.5	6.9	44.3

Sources: Calculated using World Bank and OECD national accounts data.

Note: GDP is in local currency. Base period varies by country.

Post–World War II Heritage

The post–World War II heritages of the countries are significantly different. Japan was a defeated, war-torn country, but with a substantial development history beginning in the late nineteenth century. It became a democratic, pacifist society. Japan allied itself closely to the United States with the 1952 US-Japan Security Treaty as its bedrock, and relied on the United States not only as its most important trading partner, but also as its patron in international affairs.

It concentrated its policy focus and corporate efforts on rapid growth as a market economy, though initially subject to major controls over imports and foreign capital flows. From its beginnings in 1975 at meetings of the finance ministers of the major advanced industrial nations, Japan has been the only non-Western member of the G-7. By the early 1980s Japan's rapid growth had made it the world's second largest economy. By 1990 it had a GDP per capita in purchasing power parity terms that was slightly above Germany, France, and the United Kingdom and 82 percent that of the United States. It had a well-developed financial system well along its liberalization process. It is at this point, just before the stock market and real estate bubbles burst, that Lincoln begins his analysis of Japan in this book.

Following World War II, Korea, a colony of Japan from 1910 to 1945, was divided into two countries, North Korea (DPRK) supported by the Soviet Union, and South Korea (Republic of Korea) supported by the United States. The Korean War, beginning in 1950 and ending in an armistice (but not a peace treaty) in 1953, created an ongoing hostile relationship between North and South. South Korea, referred to in this book and typically in many texts simply as Korea, began its rapid economic development in the mid-1960s under an authoritarian government combining markets with direct controls and incentives. Korea then made a remarkable, peaceful transition to a democratic political system in 1987. Park begins chapter 4 on Korea in 1980 in order to address the modest financial liberalization efforts in the 1980s.

Following a long civil war, as well as war with Japan, China was unified in 1949 under the Chinese Communist Party as the People's Republic of China. China adopted a planned economy model with direct ownership and controls over resource allocation under a highly centralized government. In 1978 under Deng Xiaoping's leadership, the government adopted a market-oriented economic development model. It is from this point that chapter 2 on China by Huang and his coauthors begins.

Postwar Japan was classified by the World Bank as a developing country until 1964 when it joined the Organisation for Economic Co-operation and Development (OECD), the club of advanced industrial countries. Its economy had "caught up" with the West technologically by the late 1970s and had become a high-income, technologically sophisticated, mature economy with many of the problems facing its US and European counterparts by the late 1980s. Korea has proceeded far along its catch-up growth process. It became an OECD member in 1996, perhaps prematurely. But, in most technological and many structural senses, Korea had caught up with the advanced economies by 2010, although on a per capita level it still has a way to go.

Despite very successful economic development since reforms began, China's per capita GDP and average technological (productivity) levels are still low. Official Chinese per capita GDP measures, especially in purchasing power parity (PPP) terms, may not be very accurate, but they are several orders of magnitude below those of Japan and Korea.

The sheer size of China matters in making comparisons—population even more than geographic size. China's population is more than 10 times that of Japan and 27 times that of Korea. Like Japan and Korea, China's development has to be based essentially on industrialization.

Catch-up Growth: The Data

Per capita GDP is generally taken as the best single measure of the level of economic performance. In 2010, Japan's was $30,920 in PPP constant 2005 dollars, Korea's was $27,027, and China's was $6,810. Korea's 2010 level slightly surpassed Japan's 1990 level, but the world productivity frontier had continued to rise. China's growth began from such a low base that despite 30 years of rapid catch-up growth, its per capita GDP in 2010 was still far below Japan's. China's future catch-up growth potential continues to be high.

A Note on the Data

In this chapter, comparable data from the databases of the World Bank, IMF, and United Nations are provided for each country. Comparisons of total and per capita GDP and rates of growth are fraught with measurement difficulties. The World Bank provides directly comparative data using international dollars at PPP rates. For all three countries the data on international trade and on finance are good, though inevitably they do not include transactions in informal financial markets. Other economic data for China are considerably less good than for Korea or Japan. This reflects its still much lower level of development. Expert opinion is that data on most economic variables for China are relatively good compared to other emerging economies at its same level of development.

Table 1.3 and figure 1.1 present data on growth in the three countries for 1980–2010. The differences are wide, reflecting the respective timing of the catch-up process. GDP growth has depended both on increases in the number of workers and rises in labor productivity. In all three countries the increases in labor input slow, and the growth gap between GDP and per capita GDP narrows, during the 1980–2010 period.

Japan's 1980 per capita GDP was 69 percent of the US level, increasing to a peak of 86 percent in 1991. Subsequent mediocre growth performance in the 1990s reduced this to 72 percent in 2000, where it has since more or less remained. Part of this decrease is because the share of the labor force in Japan's population decreased, unlike the United States.

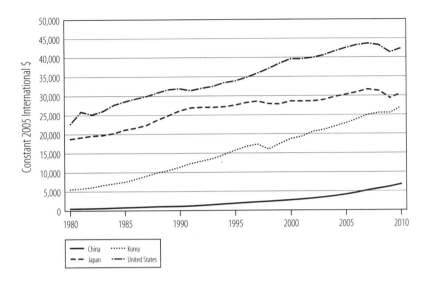

Figure 1.1 GDP per Capita. *Source*: World Bank, International Comparison Program database.

Note: GDP per capita here is based on purchasing power parity (PPP). PPP GDP is gross domestic product converted to international dollars using PPP rates. An international dollar has the same purchasing power over GDP as the US dollar has in the United States. GDP at purchaser's prices is the sum of gross value added by all resident producers in the economy plus any product taxes and minus any subsidies not included in the value of the products. It is calculated without making deductions for depreciation of fabricated assets or for depletion and degradation of natural resources. Data are in constant 2005 international dollars.

In contrast, Korea's per capita GDP was only 22 percent of the US level in 1980. It reached 64 percent of the higher US level by 2010.

China's story is one of very rapid growth in per capita GDP since 1980, but from only 2.1 percent of the US level, 3.0 percent of Japan, and 9.6 percent of Korea. By 2010 China's ratios were significantly increased, but still low: 16 percent of the US level, 22 percent of Japan, and 28 percent of Korea. Rapid catch-up growth has been due in substantial part to high rates of fixed investment.

The ratio of gross fixed capital formation to GDP in Japan peaked in the 1960s. In Korea it peaked at 40 percent in 1991, and in China at 46 percent in 2009, as shown in figure 1.2.

Even as investment increased dramatically in all three countries, so too did the domestic saving rate. Indeed, in all three, savings came to

Figure 1.2 Gross Fixed Capital Formation as a Percentage of GDP. *Sources*: World Bank and OECD national accounts data.

be larger than domestic investment, and the countries have become net lenders to the rest of the world. This is measured by their current account surplus in the balance of payments, as shown in figure 1.3.

Japan has continuously run current account surpluses since 1981, and by 1985 had become the world's largest net creditor. Korea turned its current account deficit to surplus by 1986, but as it liberalized its foreign capital flows it was able to borrow abroad and finance a current account deficit until the 1997–1998 Asian financial crisis shock. Since then, Korea has run current account surpluses, building up its foreign exchange reserves.

The China case is extraordinary; it has run a current account surplus every year since 1994 despite its low level of development. While investment increased dramatically, China's saving rate skyrocketed to half of GDP. The current account surplus increased dramatically from 2005, hitting a peak of 10.1 percent in 2007. That, together with the huge US current account deficit, has been the source of the global rebalancing problem facing both countries and the world economy. In 2006 China passed Japan to become the world's largest holder of official foreign exchange reserves.

The current account measures the net flow of a country's borrowing from, and lending to, the rest of the world over a period of time, often

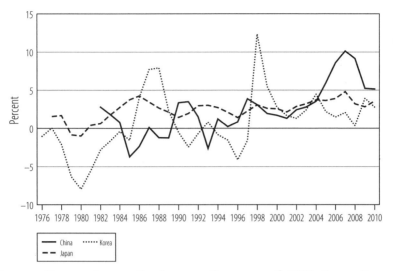

Figure 1.3 Current Account Surplus as a Percentage of GDP. *Source*: Current Account: International Monetary Fund, *Balance of Payments Statistics Yearbook* (various years) and data files; GDP: The World Bank and OECD estimates.

one year. Flows go both ways and so are much larger on a gross basis, even for short periods of time. Rather quietly, Japanese financial institutions became huge short-term foreign lenders. Korea's short-term foreign borrowing and running of current account deficits precipitated Korea's major difficulties in the Asian financial crisis. In the first decade of this century, despite Korea's current account surplus, its banks and companies once again significantly borrowed from foreign short-term sources since it was cheap, and Korea suffered a liquidity shock in 2008.

When Japan's catch-up growth began in the mid-1950s, investment demand outstripped rising domestic savings, but not only were foreign capital inflows and outflows restricted, global financial markets were not yet reestablished, and Japan's creditworthiness was not yet considered good. Nonetheless, as rapid catch-up growth proceeded, and the financial system developed, Japan engaged in a gradual process of deregulation and liberalization. By 1980 Japan's saving rate was high, and the global technological gap narrowed, so investment demand growth slowed.

Korea's early catch-up was in many respects similar to Japan's. However, the global economic system had extended significantly. External pressures and opportunities (joining the OECD and becoming classified as an advanced country) led Korea to liberalize capital flows in the early 1990s when the ex ante domestic investment-savings gap continued to be substantial.

As the chapters by Park on Korea (chapter 4) and on foreign capital flows by Seok and Shin well analyze (chapter 5), when global economic and financial conditions were good and markets were accommodating, foreign borrowing went well for Korea. But when the crisis of 1997 hit, Korea was badly exposed. This led to major economic reforms. In the 2008–2009 crisis, Korea was again hit, despite its large buildup of foreign exchange reserves. As these chapters discuss, Korea was able to deal with the 2008–2009 crisis substantially better than the 1997–1998 crisis in large part because of the reforms.

China, as a reforming but still command economy, has been able to fund its incredibly high gross investment rate by more than equal increases in domestic savings, both institutional and household. While generating current account surpluses, China continued to maintain significant controls over foreign capital flows in order to support its economic policy of competitive goods and services markets, regulated and underpriced factor markets, and a low exchange rate.

Evaluation of a country's catch-up growth potential is not easy, nor is a determination of when an economy is deemed to be mature. A reasonable measure of economic maturity is when the gap between a country's productivity and the global production frontier has become small—and that is a moving target. Using US per capita GDP as a proxy for the global production frontier, the ratio of Japan's per capita GDP to that of the United States peaked at 86 percent in 1991. In 2010 the Korea-US ratio was 63 percent, which suggests Korea still has considerable catch-up potential.

Demographics

Catch-up growth has brought major transformations of Japan, Korea, and China, as has long-run demographic transition. Although their population sizes are dramatically different, all are moving along the same demographic path. Japan is farthest along the transition from high birth and death rates and substantial population growth to low birth and death rates, long life expectancy, an aging population, and absolute population decline. The transition is less far along, but also rapid, in Korea and China.

Key demographic variables are the fertility rate, life expectancy, population growth, and share of the labor force in the total population. These measures changed substantially between 1980 and 2010 in all three countries. By 1980 all three had achieved quite high life expectancies at birth: 76.1 years in Japan, 65.9 in Korea, and a reported 66.0 in China. By 2009 life expectancies had increased to 83.0 in Japan, 80.3 in Korea, and 73.3 in China.

Fertility rates are key. Once total fertility becomes less than the replacement (stable-population) fertility rate, eventually the population will decline unless there is immigration. This is so even when life expectancy increases. The total fertility rate to maintain a stable population reflects several factors, especially female mortality rates, which means it varies across countries and through time within a country. The widely used 2.08 stable-population fertility rate is based on data for the United States.

Japan's total fertility rate dropped below its replacement rate in 1974 and was as low as 1.26 in 2005 before rising to 1.39 in 2010. As a consequence, Japan's population peaked in 2004 and has begun to decline. Korea's fertility drop has been even more precipitous, first declining below its replacement rate in the early 1980s: it was 1.81 in 1984; it fell to 1.08 in 2005; and it was 1.22 in 2010. Korea's population is projected to peak between 2025 and 2030.

Total fertility decreased in China to below its stable-population rate in the early 1990s at a much earlier stage of development than in most emerging economies. In 1993 the rate was 2.01 and by 2010 it was 1.60. China's population is projected to peak between 2025 and 2030, with a significantly lower per capita GDP than when Japan's and Korea's population peaked.

The labor force is a key variable in the growth of GDP, and in per capita GDP. An increasing ratio of the labor force in the total population, the "demographic dividend," means a relative, as well as an absolute, increase in the labor supply to produce GDP growth. An increase in labor supply made possible even more-rapid catch-up growth, especially once surplus agricultural labor had been absorbed into industrial production.

Measurement of a country's labor force combines age and labor force participation rates. The International Labour Organization defines the labor force as people 15 and older who are economically active; its October 2011 report provides population and labor force projections.

The labor force ratio peaked in Japan in 1997, and the absolute numbers of workers peaked in 1998. The absolute size of the labor force is projected to peak in Korea in the early 2020s, and in China in 2018.

Demographic maturity can be defined as when a country has zero or negative population growth, even allowing for immigration. Demographic maturity and economic maturity are interconnected, but the linkage is not tight. China's demographic projections are that population growth will cease before economic maturity (defined as a high per capita GDP) is achieved. Catch-up growth of per capita GDP presumably will continue even after population growth ends. Nonetheless, simply as a statistical matter, GDP per worker growth will translate into lower per capita GDP growth as the share of the labor force in the total population decreases in all three countries.

Incremental Capital-Output Ratios

Rates of return on investment, equity, and assets have declined in Japan and been low since 1990, and decreased somewhat in Korea but are still relatively good. In China, given the still large technological gap and rapid catch-up growth, returns on investment (capital) have been high. (The available numbers are not directly comparable across the three countries.)

One macroeconomic, albeit somewhat crude, measure of how productively an economy uses its new investment in combination with human resources, new technologies, and provision of financial services is the incremental capital-output ratio (ICOR). ICOR measures how much investment took place to achieve the increase in GDP. As the economy develops, ICOR is likely to rise even though the financial system may be allocating capital more efficiently, as the initially high marginal productivity of capital decreases.

The share of gross fixed capital formation in GDP in Japan peaked at 33.7 percent in 1970, was still a high 32.0 percent in 1990, but gradually declined to 25.2 percent in 2000 and 20.5 percent in 2010, as the mature economy's domestic investment opportunities had been mostly exploited. Moreover, GDP growth was particularly low since its potential rates were not even achieved. In Korea gross fixed capital formation was 25.6 percent of GDP in 1970, rising to 37.1 percent in 1990 but dropping with the 1998 sharp GDP decline to only 30.4 percent;

TABLE I.4
Incremental Capital-Output Ratios, Five-Year Averages

	China	Japan	Korea
1971–1975	6.17	6.75	2.64
1976–1980	5.72	6.23	4.39
1981–1985	3.57	8.21	3.66
1986–1990	5.31	6.20	3.67
1991–1995	3.48	20.80	5.25
1996–2000	4.70	28.24	7.86
2001–2005	4.33	18.29	7.08
2006–2010	4.30	177.53	7.57

Sources: Calculated using World Bank and OECD national accounts data.

Note: Five-year cumulative gross fixed capital formation divided by 5 year cumulative increase in GDP.

it subsequently stabilized in the 28–29 percent range, with a 2010 value of 28.6 percent. The ratio in China was 29.5 percent in 1978 and increased gradually and erratically to 36.3 percent in 2002, when it began its dramatic rise, reaching 45.5 percent in 2010. (These ratios on an annual basis are in fig. 1.2.)

The incremental capital-output ratios based on gross data appear in table 1.4. It is notable that the ICOR values have been so high for Japan since 1991. As Lincoln discusses in chapter 3, the results are a consequence of Japan's poor economic growth, compounded by business cycle phases of declines in GDP, while investment remained high. By the first decade of this century, Japan was engaged in too much investment and not enough consumption.

Not surprisingly, as the capital stock grew and deepened in Japan and Korea, ICOR rose. The low values for China suggest a high marginal productivity of capital; this persists since ICOR did not rise significantly. China's ICOR values are not surprising, given its sustained rapid rate of growth and its still low level of GDP per capita. At the same time, spending 45 percent of GDP on fixed capital formation probably cannot be sustained and has inevitably involved some poor projects with low returns.

Subtraction of capital consumption allowances from gross investment provides ICOR estimates based on net investment. It is difficult to estimate well the amount of fixed capital used in producing GDP.

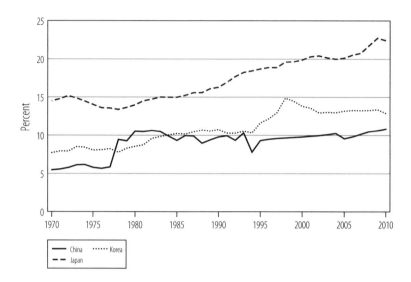

Figure 1.4 Consumption of Fixed Capital as a Percentage of GDP. *Sources*: China: World Bank estimates using United Nations Statistical Division, National Account Statistics data; Japan and Korea: *OECD National Account Statistics,* "National Accounts at a Glance: Capital" (online database).

Official measures of capital depreciation are shaped both by government tax policy and corporate strategy: when to replace older facilities, when to mothball them, when to keep them in operation, and when to take tax deductions. In the development process, capital stock increases over time more rapidly than GDP. Capital consumption will increase as development progresses and is expected to be a higher ratio in countries with a higher per capita GDP. Figure 1.4 shows these trends.

Japanese capital consumption allowances were high and rising, except for the sharp drop recorded for 2009 and 2010. Japan's higher ratios are due in part to its having larger capital stock relative to GDP than Korea and China, and to generous depreciation allowances for tax purposes. Indeed, Japan's consumption of fixed capital has constantly been among the highest of all OECD countries, substantially above OECD average ratios of 13–15 percent.

One of the data difficulties is that capital consumption allowances in national accounts are only in current prices. Net ICOR is estimated by subtracting the data in figure 1.4 from the ratio of gross fixed capital formation to GDP. This net ratio is then divided by real GDP growth.

TABLE 1.5
Decadal Incremental Capital = Output Ratios

	China	Japan	Korea
1971–1980	5.95	6.49	3.52
1981–1990	4.44	7.21	3.67
1991–2000	4.09	24.52	6.56
2001–2010	4.32	97.91	7.33

Sources: Calculated using World Bank and OECD national accounts data.

Note: Ten-year cumulative gross fixed capital formation divided by ten-year cumulative increase in GDP.

(I assume that the ratios of capital consumption allowance to GDP are not significantly different in current and constant prices.) The results are shown in table 1.5.

The net ICOR estimates are substantially lower than the gross ICOR data in table 1.4. On a net basis, ICOR rises modestly over time in both Korea and China, and not surprisingly is slightly higher in Korea. Japan is very different, since capital consumption allowances were high and rising (until 2009). While the investment share in GDP was decreasing, Japan's net ICOR estimates are much smaller than gross. As Lincoln cogently argues, using ICOR estimates for net nonresidential fixed investment, Japan's depreciation rates are higher than are economically justified. Moreover, because they have ample internally generated funds, Japanese corporations have been investing too much.

Financial Development

Catch-up growth and the demographic transition have been deeply intertwined with the process of financial development in all three countries. In the early stages of catch-up, technology and productivity gaps were so large that investment was very productive and highly profitable. Fixed investment rose and became a large share of GDP, particularly in China. Domestic saving rates rose concurrently. Domestic saving financed most of the investment; foreign borrowing was minor for Japan and China, though at times important for Korea.

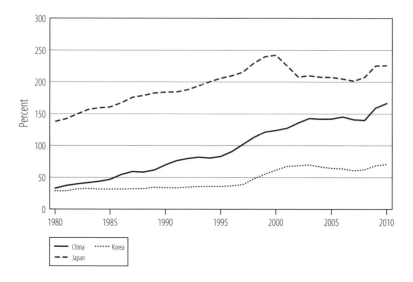

Figure 1.5 M2 (Money and Quasi-money) as a Percentage of GDP. *Sources*: M2 is from International Monetary Fund, *Financial Statistics*, and data files; GDP estimates are from the World Bank and OECD.

Financial intermediation between savers and investors was essential. Knowledge and information about good investment projects and about the capabilities of the potential investors were significant limitations. Access to credit, given the high profit opportunities, was probably as important as the cost of funds. From their beginnings, the financial systems in all three countries were fundamentally bank based, and they still are. The financial development process in all three countries brought about the development of other financial institutions. Capital markets gradually have come to play an increasing, but still relatively modest, role.

In all three countries, financial deepening was substantial—that is, finance grew even more rapidly than the economy. This process is shown, albeit in broad strokes, in increases in M2 and in domestic credit (figs. 1.5 and 1.6).

Japan's higher M2 is not surprising since its financial system was the most developed. That Korea's ratio is low relative to Japan's, despite its per capita GDP catching up with Japan, is noteworthy. Korean financial institutions have created a variety of relatively high-yield products, which have substantially replaced savings deposits. China's M2 growth

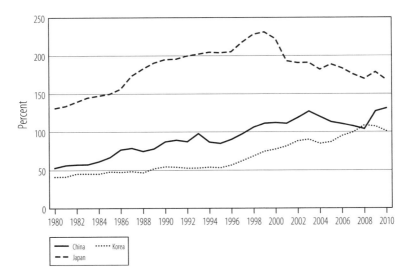

Figure 1.6 Domestic Credit as a Percentage of GDP. *Sources*: Domestic credit is from International Monetary Fund, *Financial Statistics*, and data files; GDP estimates are from the World Bank and OECD.

has been rapid, and by 2010 had slightly surpassed Japan's 1980 ratio. That is not so surprising, since China's per capita GDP in 2010 was roughly comparable to that of Japan in 1980.

The paths of domestic credit growth are broadly similar to M2, at least in terms of their respective ratios. Credit grew more rapidly than M2 in Korea, but less rapidly in China.

Banks are major lenders in all three countries. (Indeed, "domestic credit provided by the banking sector" is a higher percentage of GDP than "domestic credit" because of the way the World Bank defines the terms.) As discussed in chapter 3 by Lincoln, in Japan demand for bank loans decreased in the first decade of this century; firms built up internal reserves by retaining earnings, while new investment slowed. Japan was building foreign financial claims, including its foreign exchange reserves, over the period.

Banks

The banks in all three countries are mainly domestically owned and controlled, but with significant differences.

Japanese banks, as a result of postwar reforms, came to be owned by a highly diversified set of shareholders, mainly domestic, with no institutions holding a controlling share. Management has been in control; managers have been promoted internally, and have comprised most members of the boards of directors. Japan's 1997–1998 financial crisis led to the de facto insolvency of several major banks and government interventions. Two banks were nationalized and then purchased by foreign investors; they participate actively, but are not major players.

In Korea, ownership has also been market based, but it is a more complex story. The Asian financial crisis put the banks in jeopardy, and initially all the major private commercial banks were taken over by the government. Once their balance sheets had been cleaned up and some banks merged, government policy was to sell them off. Initially the only potential Korean buyers were business conglomerates (chaebol), so two were sold directly to foreign institutions. One of those was later sold to Korean investors at a huge profit. The resulting political controversy has significantly delayed the sale of the other. The government sold shares in several other banks through the stock market to highly dispersed shareholders. Over time, foreign holdings of several major banks in aggregate have become large, but with no single major foreign investor. Two banks remain in government hands.

Foreign entry into China's banking system has been more limited. All the banks, particularly the big four, were completely state owned at the beginning of the reform period. The government has sold substantial, but by no means controlling, stakes in the major banks to strategic foreign financial interests in order to better access foreign financial technologies, management skills, and markets. Three of the four main banks have been listed on the stock exchange. Nonetheless, the government maintains majority ownership, as well as control over senior management appointments and basic strategies.

Global banking institutions are represented in all three countries. These banks and their branches have played useful roles in providing access to information, foreign markets, and management skills. Only in Korea have foreign banks played a significant financing role, notably shown by the dependence on foreign short-term borrowing in the Asian financial and 2007–2009 crises.

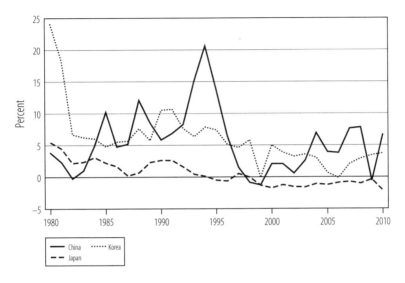

Figure 1.7 Inflation (GDP Deflator) (in percent per annum). *Sources*: World Bank and OECD national accounts data.

Inflation and Interest Rates

Inflation is a major obstacle in financial development. After dropping sharply from high levels in the early 1980s, Korea again experienced 10 percent inflation in 1990 and 1991, but the rate has been less than 5 percent since 2000. China's inflation pattern has been more erratic, with high inflation in 1993–1995 and above 5 percent in 2007–2008. Japan has had an entirely different problem—modest but persistent and pernicious deflation every year since 1998. Data are shown in figure 1.7.

In the early phases of financial development, policy makers controlled interest rates, notably bank deposit and loan rates, and set them low relative to inflation in order to provide incentives for investment. Given the lack of alternative financial assets and foreign capital controls, policy makers assumed correctly that the interest elasticity of demand for funds by investors would be greater than the elasticity of supply by savers. Bank deposits, including time and savings deposits, grew rapidly. As financial development progressed, interest rate controls were eased in Japan and then in Korea, but not much in China as of 2010.

Figure 1.8 shows the bank real interest rate on loans. The differences in volatility are indicative both of the levels of financial development and the

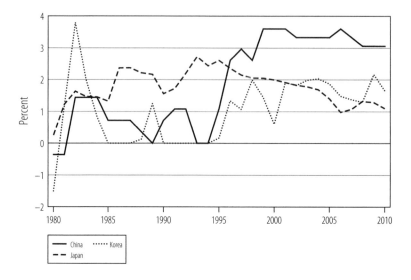

Figure 1.8 Real Interest Rate on Loans (in percent per annum). *Sources*: Nominal interest rates are from International Monetary Fund, *Financial Statistics*, and data files; GDP deflator is as estimated by the World Bank.

degree of control over inflation. As Lardy (2012) stresses, monetary policy in China deliberately reduced nominal lending and deposit rates, so that in real terms Chinese deposit rates were slightly negative during 2005–2010.

In principle, spreads between deposits and loans should be sufficiently wide for banks and other financial institutions to be profitable enough to ensure financial system stability. World Bank data provide a lower limit on spreads, since the average lending rates were typically higher than the prime rate, as figure 1.9 shows.

In Japan and Korea, banks typically required compensating deposit balances and high fees that are negotiated case by case. This makes the effective cost of a loan difficult to estimate, especially for smaller borrowers. Lending has been based on real collateral, and relationships have always been important in all three countries.

Capital Markets

Capital markets have gradually developed in all three countries and have somewhat reduced the dominance of banks. Stock markets developed earlier and further than bond and other fixed-income markets. By 1990

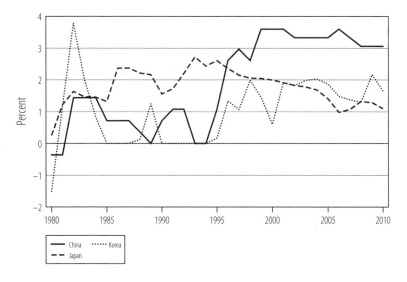

Figure 1.9 Interest Rate Spread (the lending rate minus the deposit rate, in percent per annum). *Sources*: International Monetary Fund, *Financial Statistics,* and data files.

both Japan and Korea had active, quite well-developed stock markets. Stock markets in China barely existed in 1990, but have grown rapidly as state-owned enterprises have listed.

The stock markets have been a source of funds, though usually not a predominant one, for Japanese and Korean companies. In all three countries stock markets have increased information available on companies and provided market assessments of company value. Chinese stock markets are considered quite speculative, Korea's less so, as reflected in the level and volatility of their turnover ratios. Share price volatility has been high, as indicated in figure 1.10.

The corporate bond market relative to GDP is substantially more developed in Korea than Japan and only nascent in China, as figure 1.11 indicates.

The requirements for bond issuance exemplify capital market requirements for adequate information, legal protection of creditors, objective credit analysis, transparency, and appropriate risk-based pricing. These requirements set higher standards for capital-market transactions because they are much more arm's length than bank lending. Almost all corporate bonds issued in all three countries have had high credit ratings; high-yield junk bond markets are not significant.

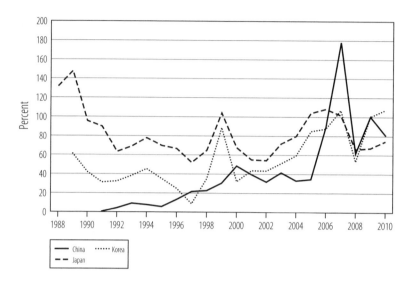

Figure 1.10 Market Capitalization of Listed Companies as a Percentage of GDP. *Sources*: Market capitalization: Standard & Poor's *Global Stock Markets Factbook* and supplemental data; GDP estimates are from the World Bank and OECD.

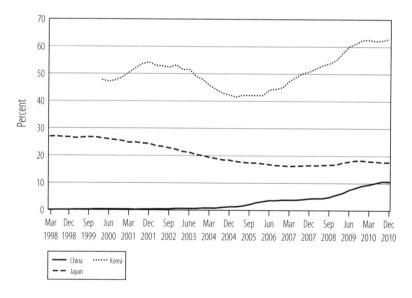

Figure 1.11 Corporate Bonds Outstanding as a Percentage of GDP. *Sources*: Bonds outstanding: Asian Development Bank, asianbondsonline.adb.org; GDP estimates are from the World Bank and OECD.

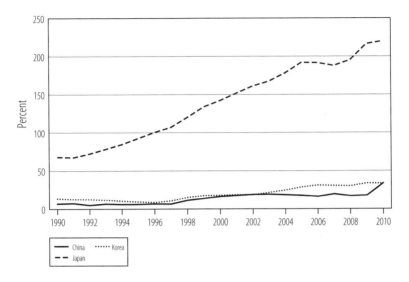

Figure 1.12 General Government Gross Debt as a Percentage of GDP. *Sources*: Government debt: International Monetary Fund, "World Economic Outlook Database," September 2011; GDP estimates are from the World Bank and OECD.

In Japan after 1990 it seemed large corporations would make a major shift from bank finance to commercial paper and bonds as major sources of external finance. Instead, particularly in the first decade of this century, companies were deleveraging, using profits to pay off debts and build cash reserves. Earlier, Korean banks guaranteed corporate three-year bonds rather than making longer-term loans. This guarantee system ended, but a market had developed, so large corporations have been able to continue to issue bonds to fund part of their fixed investments.

In both Korea and China, government bond issue has been modest; aggregate demand has been sufficiently strong that major fiscal stimulus has seldom been necessary. Japan is a completely different story, as figure 1.12 shows.

Japan's gross government debt as a percentage of GDP had gradually risen to a peak of 73.5 percent in 1987 before decreasing to 68.0 percent in 1990. Inadequate domestic demand has been Japan's most serious macroeconomic problem since 1990. Since 1991 Japan has pursued unprecedented macroeconomic policies of very easy monetary policy and fiscal stimulus. However, rather than new expenditures, fiscal stimulus and burgeoning budget deficits have been in significant part to offset reductions in tax revenues in what has been a deflationary, slow-growing economy with gradually increasing pension and other mandated welfare payments. The government's gross debt increased to 142 percent of GDP in 2000 and 220 percent in 2010, and its net debt of 120 percent was the highest of any OECD country.

Financial Repression and Liberalization

In the early stages of financial development, the financial system in each country was more or less severely repressed, with both domestic controls and restrictions on foreign capital inflows and outflows. Financial development required an ongoing process of financial liberalization in order to more effectively provide the capital allocation and financial services essential for rapid catch-up growth.

The role of the government in the financial system is always central. The government sets the rules and norms, as well as establishes the legal framework for the creation and operation of markets, institutions, and financial instruments. The central bank determines the money supply and seeks to achieve price stability, and provides prudential supervisions and oversight together with the other regulatory authorities.

In the early postwar period the Japanese and Korean governments went far beyond these basic tenets. They set bank deposit and loan interest rates, controlled institutions and markets, engaged in more or less direct allocations of credit to selected priority sectors, and took other measures that constrained the development of competitive financial markets. The governments have considered stability of the financial system to be the most important policy goal. This was used as a justification for interest rate and other controls even while in principle encouraging financial development.

The reformers in China in 1978 inherited a completely controlled financial system in a planned economy. There were no financial markets of substance. Government direct controls were exercised through ownership of all financial institutions.

With underdeveloped human and institutional resources, imperfect markets, limited competition, and inappropriate or ineffective incentive mechanisms, it is not surprising that Japan, Korea, and China engaged in substantial financial repression. However, as the catch-up development process proceeded, financial liberalization became more important in all three countries. The Japanese and Korean experiences of postwar financial repression are summarized in the chapters by Teranishi, Park, and Patrick in Patrick and Park (1994).

Financial liberalization had many ingredients. They included the replacing of administrative controls and guidance over the allocation of capital with free, competitive markets; market-determined prices (interest rates, asset price valuations); a relatively independent central bank; a pro-market prudential regulatory and supervisory system; and the introduction of an increasingly wide range of financial instruments.

By 1990, when the chapter on Japan begins (chapter 3), Japan had engaged in substantial reforms; its financial system was in most respects liberalized. As Lincoln analyzes, Japan's "Big Bang" financial deregulatory reforms in the 1990s succeeded in creating more favorable conditions for the development of capital markets. However, as he notes, the economy's poor growth performance has meant that Japanese companies have had little reason to take advantage of the reforms; they have yet to engage in significant bond and commercial paper issue.

Korea began to reduce its substantial restrictions on foreign capital flows in the mid-1980s, especially once it began to run a current account surplus in 1986. It continued global liberalization in the early 1990s, in preparation for joining the OECD in late 1996. Following its financial crisis in late 1997 and IMF-mandated reforms, Korea completed liberalization of capital flows, but once again became deeply involved in short-term foreign borrowing, causing the liquidity and foreign exchange difficulties of the 2007–2009 crisis. Still, as Park discusses, Korea had built a liberalized, quite well-developed financial system by the early years of this century.

China's case is completely different. A key finding of chapter 2 by Huang et al. is that over the course of 30 years of reform, China has moved almost half-way from a completely controlled, repressed financial system to a fully liberalized, market-based system.

Governments and their regulatory authorities repress financial systems in a variety of ways. Three of the most important restrictions have been controls over interest rates on bank deposits and loans, controls over foreign capital inflows and outflows, and government ownership and control of financial institutions. Regulated interest rates were set substantially below market rates, with spreads sufficiently large that banks could be profitable and safe. Given the paucity of good alternatives for holding savings, households have held most of their financial assets in bank deposits.

Low bank lending rates meant there was excessive demand for funds even by good, creditworthy borrowers with collateral. This made it easier for governments and bankers to use criteria in addition to profit maximization in allocating credit. Financial repression fit well with government efforts to assure adequate funding for industries and companies deemed priority—in China's case, especially those state owned.

The Japanese and Korean governments owned development banks and import-export banks, but government ownership of banking and financial institutions overall was modest. Government administrative guidance of bank lending to specific sectors, and even firms, played a smaller role in Japan than Korea, and by 1990 was no longer a factor in Japan.

Policy makers in all three countries pursued financially repressive policies for a variety of reasons, given their goals of investment-led rapid catch-up growth and maintenance of financial system stability. There were concerns that markets would not operate effectively; fully free markets were mistrusted. The institutional and legal structures in both finance and the real economy were weak. Certainly in China, but initially to some extent in the early stages of financial development in Japan and Korea as well, policy makers wanted the power that control over the financial system provided. The preferred borrowers—large firms and state-owned enterprises—were the beneficiaries of such restrictions, whereas private smaller enterprises and savers were the losers.

Financial Globalization

Controls over foreign capital inflows and outflows have been a major instrument of financial repression. They covered all types of foreign capital flows, from short-term and long-term portfolio capital to foreign direct investment. In the early postwar period, Japan, Korea, and China maintained direct controls over these flows, though with different approaches to each type of flow. The timing and the process of ending restrictions on, and engaging in, foreign capital inflows and outflows has differed significantly in each country. This reflected both the domestic situations and the global environment as they evolved.

From initially tight controls, Japan participated actively in the post-war capital market globalization process. Japan had removed most foreign exchange and capital controls by 1964, when it accepted IMF Article 8 status on foreign transactions and joined the OECD. Japan has had a floating exchange rate since the breakdown of the Bretton Woods system in 1973. From 1981 Japan has run an annual current account surplus, which undermined justifications for controls.

Korea began to reduce its substantial restrictions on foreign capital flows in the mid-1980s, especially once it began to run a current account surplus in 1986 (Park 1994, chapter 4). It continued global liberalization in the early 1990s in preparation for acceding to IMF Article 8 status and joining the OECD in late 1996. Following its financial crisis in late 1997 and IMF-mandated reforms, Korea largely completed its liberalization of capital flows.

China as of 2010 continued to maintain extensive controls on foreign capital inflows. Nonetheless, because of its sheer economic size, the development of its domestic financial system, and especially its current account surplus and huge foreign exchange reserves, it has become increasingly involved in financial globalization. Huang et al. provide a well-reasoned series of steps China can take to achieve basic capital account liberalization and a floating exchange rate.

In the early phases of catch-up growth, all three countries eagerly sought foreign technology, but only cautiously allowed foreign direct investment. In Japan and Korea, inward FDI restrictions gradually eased as the economy developed and domestic firms began to engage in significant direct investment and production abroad. Given the Chinese government's strong direct controls, FDI into China has been more difficult. During the first decade of this century, Chinese FDI abroad by state-owned enterprises began to increase rapidly, albeit from a very low base.

FDI has less direct impact on domestic financial markets than long-term, and especially short-term, foreign portfolio capital flows. Short-term flows into domestic banks, corporations, and money markets are by far the largest capital flows. And they are the most volatile since they can be reversed quickly. Gross flows, involving different institutions, are many multiples of the net positions at the end of each day, quarter, or year.

Japan's current account surplus and low domestic interest rates provided the incentives and opportunities for Japanese financial institutions to become major providers of short-term foreign loans, including to Korean institutions. In Korea, even though it had developed current account surpluses, foreign short-term funds were cheaper than domestic, which generated Korea's exposure in both the Asian and global financial crises. China has restricted both short-term capital inflows and outflows. As its current surplus account developed, particularly from 1995, it built up its foreign exchange reserves, held primarily in US dollar–denominated treasury securities and, to some extent, in similar euro-denominated assets. Although this has kept default risk low, it has exposed China to exchange rate risk and provided little return on the assets.

The two global financial centers are London and New York, whereas the major financial centers in Asia have long been Hong Kong and Singapore. Many Japanese policy makers have aspired to make Tokyo a global, or at least regional, financial center. For a range of reasons, including language, as Lincoln discusses, that has not transpired, and is unlikely to. Some Koreans have aspired to make Seoul a major regional center, but that also is unlikely. Chinese policy makers aspire to have Shanghai eventually become a major international financial center. That requires a major liberalization of foreign capital controls, a floating yuan exchange rate, and other substantial domestic financial and economic reforms, which means even the possibility is some years away. In any case, the sheer size of their domestic economies ensures Tokyo, Seoul, and Shanghai will be important centers of financial activity—albeit primarily domestically based.

Effectiveness and Efficiency of Financial Development

We know that finance is important. However, it is difficult to estimate empirically the comprehensive effects of finance on the real economy and its performance. Over time, it became clear to policy makers and market participants in all three countries that the efficiencies derived from a more market-based allocation of credit were so substantial that liberalization had to proceed, as Seok and Shin analyze. For Japan and Korea in the earlier postwar period, that process is addressed in Patrick and Park (1994).

Certainly, in broad terms the financial systems in Japan, Korea, and China have been very effective in supporting catch-up growth. Growth of GDP and per capita GDP were rapid. Savings were mobilized and allocated to investment. Investment rates were high, and most investments were productive. Price stability was achieved. Financial institutions and instruments developed and grew, and financial institutions and markets became more efficient in establishing values (prices) and handling transactions. Of course China's planned, command economy heritage is very different from the private ownership, market-based systems of Japan and Korea, and China is only part way along the process of catch-up growth and financial development. Nonetheless, rapid catch-up growth in each country is the best evidence that financial intermediation somehow has been successful.

Yet financial intermediation certainly was not especially efficient in allocating savings to the best investors. A comprehensive evaluation of just how efficient financial intermediation has been over time in each of the countries is difficult.

Small enterprises had less access to finance, and at higher costs even adjusted for actual risk. Even as capital markets developed, only highly rated commercial paper and corporate bonds were issued; markets for higher-risk fixed-interest rate instruments were still underdeveloped as of 2010. Venture capital markets have been nascent. Highly performing firms and growth industries have done well. But each country has had to deal with nonperforming loans, corporate bankruptcies, and zombie firms. Bank-client relationships generated information and trust, but they became less and less arm's length and, in extreme form, corrupt. Corruption has plagued finance in China considerably more than in Japan or Korea.

Since 1990 Japan's growth performance has been mediocre despite a well-developed financial system and the Big Bang reform to encourage capital markets. However, the financial system has not been the obstacle. Japan is a cautionary tale of a country that has had difficulty shifting from an investment-led growth model to consumption-led growth. It needs a new model.

Korea, even as it approaches economic maturity, still has relatively good growth prospects. At some point, the Korean economy will have caught up and have to shift to consumption-based demand. Its financial system functions reasonably well today, despite ownership and other problems, but will face new challenges as the economy becomes increasingly led by domestic consumption demand. For Japan and Korea, growth will depend more than ever on innovations to increase labor productivity.

The Chinese economy is still far from the global production frontier, so rapid increases in labor productivity will continue to drive growth. However, China's extraordinary increases in domestic investment and exports have become excessive. Consumption has become too low a share of GDP. Huang et al. sketch out the policy path to lower rates of investment, a smaller trade surplus, and a rising share of consumption. Nonetheless, even when these domestic rebalancings take place, for some time to come China's rapid growth will continue to be investment led. As they stress, further financial liberalization and development will be more essential than ever in the next 30 years of reform.

Financial Stability

Japan, Korea, and China have had different degrees of success in achieving and maintaining financial-system stability. Japan had a serious bout of domestically caused financial instability in the wake of its bubbles in the 1980s. Instability peaked in 1998 but persisted until the banking system was consolidated and the bank nonperforming loan overhang was brought to an end in 2002. Japan's major problem of macroeconomic financial stability since 1998 has been the persistence of mild but pernicious deflation.

Korea's two major financial crises originated abroad: the 1997–1998 Asian financial crisis and the 2007–2009 global financial crisis. As Park discusses, the financial system had a series of domestic financial problems, including credit card and loan excesses and the 2011 savings bank scandals.

In both Japan and Korea the government and regulatory authorities averted financial meltdown in times of crisis and engaged in substantial reforms; the financial systems emerged from each crisis in stronger shape. China, with government control over the financial system, has not had a major financial crisis either from domestic difficulties or foreign shocks.

In all three countries, banks and other financial institutions have been able to mobilize domestic saving reasonably well despite initial below-market deposit interest rates. Successful control of inflationary pressures was an important macroeconomic factor in making savings in financial form attractive. Indeed, despite very low interest rates on deposits, deflation in Japan since the mid-1990s, combined with mediocre growth, has made the real rate of return on deposits competitive. Japan's experience of mild but persistent deflation since the mid-1990s has strongly cautionary macroeconomic policy lessons.

Measuring Liberalization and Its Effects

One of the major contributors of the China chapter by Huang et al. (chapter 2) is their careful analysis of the increase in financial liberalization using a financial repression index they developed. Drawing on Stiglitz (1994 and 2000), they empirically demonstrate that for China in the first two decades after 1978, financial repression made a positive, if modest, contribution to GDP growth.

However, by the beginning of this century, remaining repression had become a negative, slowing GDP growth. One explanation is that financial repression in an economy moving from a command to a market system made it easier for the government to maintain macroeconomic stability. Given China's policies of controls over foreign capital flows and a pegged low exchange rate when the economy was booming, delaying financial liberalization and maintaining financial repression was one approach to try to contain inflationary pressures.

Park in chapter 4 makes a valuable contribution in the measurement of financial liberalization, using Korea in the period 1990–2007. He considers four indexes, ranging from single measures of financial liberalization to an index utilizing six variables. The latter suggests that Korea's financial system was quite repressed in 1990 but rapidly deregulated to about 80 percent of complete liberalization by 1998. The index then remains relatively flat until remaining deposit and loan interest rate controls were ended 2005, at which time it rose to about 90 percent of complete liberalization.

Park's analysis shows that financial liberalization, with the rising role of capital markets, contributed to improving the efficiency both of firms and industries. However, he does not find that financial liberalization increased total factor productivity. Park raises a further concern that Korean financial liberalization increased the inequality of the distribution of wealth, and thereby of income. Korean banks have tended to make loans based on existing real assets as collateral rather than on the projected profitability of projects. Property owners have been able to borrow in order to buy additional urban condominiums and other property. Lack of capability to evaluate new projects has been a major reason why strong venture capital firms and markets have not developed in Korea or Japan.

Conclusion

As the following chapters carefully and thoroughly consider, the financial systems in Japan, Korea, and China in the postwar period to 2010 have strongly supported their catch-up growth and overall economic performance. Financial markets, institutions, and instruments have developed, and over time financial systems have been more market oriented and liberalized, though there have been bumps in each country along the way. Of course, finance is not a panacea. The findings of this book are basically positive, but they have their disquieting elements.

For many policy makers throughout the world, the United States was considered the model of financial development and innovation. Temporary market failures or difficulties were believed to be self-correcting. The 2007–2009 crisis fundamentally undermined the US model of a highly liberalized financial system vigorously implementing financial innovations. The crisis has also brought to the forefront issues of macro-prudential financial regulation for each country and for the global financial system.

As Seok and Shin cogently argue, banks go beyond their own deposit base to finance major, and seemingly profitable, expansions of loans and investments by extensive borrowing in domestic and foreign short-term capital markets. The authors focus their analysis on the 2007–2009 crisis and its roots in US financial markets, institutions, and policies. They address its most important direct foreign effects, namely, on European banks and the global financial system. They develop viable policy proposals for macro-prudential reform for the United States, Europe, and by implication all market-based financial systems. As history informs us, to contain the development of major financial bubbles is one of the major challenges.

Huang et al. emphasize that control over foreign capital flows insulated China from both the Asian financial crisis and the 2007–2009 global financial crisis. Park notes that Korea's market-based system made possible excessive short-term capital flows, and, while the capital stock grew, financial intermediation contributed to greater income inequality and did not increase total factor productivity. Lincoln concludes that managerial control over Japanese corporations has meant those companies have engaged in barely profitable domestic capital formation in order to sustain firm size and jobs for their managers and other employees.

Due to poor risk management, for most of the first decade of the twenty-first century, credit was widely mispriced in capital markets and bank loan markets. Domestic financial systems became increasingly vulnerable as the bubbles inflated, leading to crisis. Governments and regulators have misdiagnosed the issues, including confusing liquidity with solvency difficulties, and promoted policies—such as encouraging home ownership with insufficient regard for ability to finance it—that exacerbated the bubble and the consequences of its bursting.

Following Shaw (1973) and McKinnon (1973), I earlier argued (Patrick 1994, chapter 8) that financial repression always had a negative effect but that, in the early phases of Japanese and probably Korean catch-up, growth was so rapid that it could not have been significantly faster even had there been less financial repression. Domestic human and institutional resources were fully utilized. In this era before financial globalization, Japan had only limited access to foreign credit; generating sufficient exports to pay for imports essential for rapid catch-up growth was the dominant constraint. The early stages in Korea are difficult to evaluate because the economy was plagued by inflationary pressures, negative real interest rates, and more financial repression than in Japan. However, the experience of China and the financial crisis of 2007–2009 have tempered this view.

Although there are important similarities, the financial development of Japan, Korea, and China have been somewhat different. At a given point in time, financial development was more advanced in Japan than Korea, and both much more than China. Over time both the domestic and global contexts have changed. The global financial boom and bust that has begun the twenty-first century is causing a major rethinking of the role of finance. It is the hope of those involved in this project that an understanding of history and the methods of analysis presented here will help policy makers in the rethinking process and provide both suitable caution and reasonable hope to those emerging economies still on the doorstep of liberalization.

Acknowledgments

I thank James Lee for his industrious research assistance and Tamaris Rivera both for typing this manuscript and for being my handler. And I particularly thank Larry Meissner, who restructured this chapter, reduced excessive repetition, and proactively thoroughly edited it.

References

Demirgüç-Kunt, Asli, and Ross Levine. 2008. "Finance, Financial Sector Policies, and Long-Run Growth." World Bank. Policy Research Working Papers 4469.

Gorton, Gary, and Andrew Metrick. 2012. "Getting Up to Speed on the Financial Crisis: A One-Weekend Reader's Guide." *Journal of Economic Literature* 2 (1) (Mar).

Gwartney, James D., Joshua C. Hall, and Robert Lawson. 2011. *Economic Freedom of the World: 2011 Annual Report*. Fraser Institute.

Huang, Yiping, and Xun Wang. 2011. "Does Financial Repression Inhibit or Facilitate Economic Growth? A Case Study of Chinese Reform Experience." *Oxford Bulletin of Economics and Statistics* 73 (6): 833–55.

IMF. 2009. "Frontiers Research on Financial Globalization." *IMF Staff Papers* 56 (1) (Apr).

Kose, M. Ayhan, Eswar Prasad, Kenneth Rogoff, and Shang-Jin Wei. 2009. "Financial Globalization: A Reappraisal." *IMF Staff Papers* 56 (1) (Apr): 8–62.

Lardy, Nicholas. 2012. *Sustaining China's Economic Growth after the Global Financial Crisis*. Peterson Institute of International Economics.

Lo, Andrew W. 2012. "Reading about the Financial Crisis: A Twenty-One Book Review." *Journal of Economic Literature* 50 (1) (Mar).

McKinnon, Ronald. 1973. *Money and Capital in Economic Development*. The Brookings Institution.

Park, Yung Chul. 1994. "Korea: Development and Structural Change of the Financial System." In Patrick and Park 1994.

Patrick, Hugh T. 1994. "Comparisons, Contrasts and Implications." In Patrick and Park 1994.

Patrick, Hugh T., and Yung Chul Park, eds. 1994. *The Financial Development of Japan, Korea and Taiwan: Growth, Repression, and Liberalization*. Oxford University Press.

Shaw, Edward S. 1973. *Financial Deepening in Economic Development*. Oxford University Press.

Stiglitz, Joseph E. 1994. "The Role of the State in Financial Markets." In M. Bruno and B. Pleskovic, eds., *Proceedings of the World Bank Annual Conference on Development Economics*, 1993, 41–46.

Stiglitz, Joseph E. 2000. "Capital Market Liberalization." *Economic Growth and Instability World Development* 28: 1075–86.

Teranishi, Juro. 1994. "Japan: Development and Structural Change of the Financial System." In Patrick and Park 1994.

Voghouei, Hatra, M. Avali, and Mohammed Ali Jenali. 2011. "A Survey of the Determinants of Financial Developments." *Asia Pacific Economic Literature* 25 (2): 1–20.

CHAPTER TWO

Financial Reform in China

Progress and Challenges

YIPING HUANG, XUN WANG, BIJUN WANG,
AND NIAN LIN

CHINA'S ECONOMIC reforms since 1978 probably have delivered as many puzzles as miracles. The Chinese economy has been extraordinarily successful in achieving strong growth. Yet it is different in many aspects from the typical set of "good economic institutions" prescribed by textbook economics. China does have a very open economy. But, rather than having private property rights, a well-developed legal system, and liberalized financial sector, it has a communist government, state monopoly in key economic sectors, and financial repression.

This can be recast as two interesting combinations relating to China's economic development and financial reform: (1) high levels of quantitative financial development have been achieved even though financial policies remain heavily repressive; and (2) financial repression did not prevent strong macroeconomic performance.

The primary purpose of our study is to understand the particular roles played by financial policies in China's economic reform and growth. We provide an extensive review of the progress of financial reforms and an assessment of their achievements and challenges. We find that the reforms have been generally strong in building the framework and expanding volumes, but weak in improving governance and liberalizing markets.

We explain the uniqueness of China's reform pattern by applying the framework of asymmetric market liberalization: rapid financial development and serious financial repression have both been means for the government to achieve the policy goal of the fastest growth possible. Quantitative assessment confirms that the government has been largely successful in achieving that goal.

In the 1980s and 1990s the growth impact of repressive financial policies was positive (the Stiglitz effect); by the late 1990s it had turned negative (the McKinnon effect). Risks of financial repression have grown substantially and become self-sustaining. We conclude it is time for China to complete its "unfinished revolution," and that this revolution may be best organized under a central theme of capital account convertibility.

The combination of widespread financial repression and strong economic growth raises the important question of just how desirable financial liberalization is, and addressing this issue is an important part of the chapter.

More specifically, in providing a realistic assessment of Chinese financial reform, this chapter explores these questions:

- What have been the main features of financial liberalization and financial development?
- Why did policy makers choose those financial policies?
- How did financial liberalization and financial repression affect China's macroeconomic performance?
- What are the potential costs of the remaining repressive financial policies?
- Should China push to complete financial liberalization and, if yes, when and how?

The chapter is organized as follows. The next section provides an overview of the reforms made so far and those that remain. We then review the theoretical and empirical literature on the relationship between finance and growth. Following is a detailed analysis of the development and reform of the banking system. Then, several sections look at the development, reform, and regulation of the capital (debt and equity) markets, including the role of foreigners. Focus next shifts to the establishment of the central bank, evolution of monetary policy, and development of the financial regulatory framework.

Reform of exchange rate policy and analysis of capital account controls are then taken up. Next, an overall assessment of financial liberalization in China—including its logic, impact, and risks—is provided. We conclude by presenting how China can take the last step of financial liberalization: achieving capital account convertibility of the currency.

Note that China's currency is formally known as the renminbi (RMB). It is also called the yuan. CNY is the ISO 4217 code. Throughout the chapter, dollars ($) are US dollars.

Overview of the Reform Period

In the cold winter of 1978, when Deng Xiaoping and his comrades decided to shift the policy priority from political struggle to economic construction, China was a poor, closed agrarian economy on the verge of collapse. Most farmers could hardly feed themselves, and there was a severe shortage of consumer goods. Urban industry churned out large volumes of low-quality heavy-industry products. Over the following decades, China achieved average GDP growth of 9.9 percent. By the end of 2010, China's GDP per capita had reached $4,270, and the economy had become the second largest in the world. The World Economic Outlook by the International Monetary Fund (IMF 2011) expects China to overtake the US economy in 2016, using its purchasing power parity (PPP) estimates of GDP.

There are various interpretations of the Chinese reform approach and explanations for its success. These include:

- Adoption of a comparative-advantage-conforming development strategy (Lin, Cai, and Li 1995). Replacing the previous, comparative-advantage-defying, development strategy significantly improved the efficiency of resource allocation and promoted productivity growth.
- Growing out of the central planning framework (Naughton 1995). Economic reforms focused on creating ever-greater breathing space for the non-state sector outside the central planning framework, while keeping the plan system unchanged initially.

- Convergence toward the East Asian market system (Sachs and Woo 2000). Chinese reforms have been, in essence, a repeat of the successful experience of the East Asian variant of the market economy rather than "institutional innovation."
- Use of an incremental dual-track reform approach (Fan 1994). The dual-track approach has effectively been a process of Pareto improvement without losers, which quickly rallied political support around the reformers.
- Asymmetric liberalization of product and factor markets (Huang 2010a, 2010b). Distortions in factor markets have repressed factor costs. This has contributed to extraordinary economic growth, but has caused structural imbalances.

These different mechanisms do not necessarily contradict one another. A common theme is the introduction of a free market system. All the explanations are relevant to understanding China's financial reform. Thus, free market mechanisms have played an increasingly important role in the financial sector, from allocation of funds to determination of asset prices. (For a comprehensive overview of China's economic development and general prospects, see Brandt and Rawski (2008), with 20 essays by leading students of China.)

What has been underappreciated in economic studies of the reforms is the role of policy distortions. One branch of standard economic theory predicts that distortions normally lead to losses of efficiency and welfare. However, Huang and his collaborators argue that despite causing economic imbalances, repressing costs of labor, land, capital, and energy through factor market distortions actually promoted economic growth (Huang 2010a, 2010b; Huang and Tao 2010; Huang and Wang 2010a).

Thus, interest rate and exchange rate distortions have been major forms of factor market distortion in China. Whether such distortions are good policies or bad policies depends on a comparison of their costs and benefits. Stiglitz (2000), for instance, has argued that financial repression might enable low-income countries to better deal with market failures.

Our interpretation of the Chinese experience centers around the government's asymmetric market liberalization approach.

General Aspects of Financial Reform

China had a mono-bank system when reform started. By the mid-1990s it had created a comprehensive financial system, including various types of banks and non-bank financial institutions, as well as equity, bond, and money markets (Huang 2001). Like Japan and many other East Asian economies, China's financial system is still dominated by the banking sector, with relatively smaller roles for direct financing.

Rapid financial deepening has been an important feature, evidenced by the rising proportion of broad money supply (M2) to GDP from 32 percent in 1978 to 181 percent in 2010. By 1990 the ratio of M2 to GDP was greater than that of the United States, even though China's economy was only 6 percent the size of the US economy at the time. The increase in M2 relative to GDP has not been unrelenting, as discussed later. Figure 2.1 illustrates China's financial deepening.

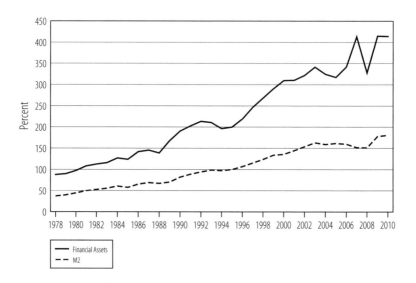

Figure 2.1 Money Supply and Financial Assets as a Percentage of GDP, 1978–2010.
Source: China Securities and Futures Statistical Yearbook.

Note: Financial assets are calculated as the sum of cash, deposits and loans, bonds outstanding, and the total value of stock markets.

Principal Types of Financial Repression

Repressive financial policies are still widespread and serious in China (Huang and Wang 2011). Following are four important examples:

The two key interest rates in China are the base deposit and base lending rates for commercial banks. These are set by the People's Bank of China (PBOC). Over the years commercial banks have come to enjoy greater freedom in deviating from the base rates. But, the regulations maintain floors for the lending rates and ceilings for the deposit rates. These prevent interest rate competition, guarantee a minimum interest spread, and thus help create large profits for the commercial banks. Negative real rates are also common (Lardy 2008).

A second example is that PBOC's monetary policy still relies more on quantitative measures than on price instruments. The most frequently used policy tool for liquidity management is the reserve requirement ratio (RRR) for commercial bank deposits. PBOC has not yet developed a policy rate like the Federal Reserve Bank's Fed funds rate.

Window guidance is another common practice: regulators influence the amount and composition of commercial bank loans by communicating directly with top bank executives. Window guidance is a legacy of the central planning system. It is sometimes effective in achieving results, but has the usual problems of administrative measures, such as overadjustment and inaccuracy.

Fourth, the authorities maintain important restrictions on cross-border capital flows. Despite steady liberalization of the capital account, the yuan is not yet freely convertible. Although there are almost no restrictions on inward foreign direct investment (FDI), outward direct investment (ODI) is often subject to a complicated approval procedure. Cross-border debt financing is highly restricted. Cross-border portfolio investment is governed by the "qualified foreign institutional investor" (QFII) and "qualified domestic institutional investor" (QDII) systems.

Summary of Findings

The findings of this study can be summarized in the following six observations:

First, Chinese financial reform has been generally strong in setting up the sector's framework and growing asset volumes, but it has been weak in improving governance and freeing markets.

In the review that follows, we group financial sector changes into four areas: (1) developing the financial framework, such as establishment of the central bank and stock exchanges; (2) expanding financial activities, such as increases in the number of financial institutions and sizes of financial assets; (3) restructuring financial institutions, such as reform of the state-owned commercial banks; and (4) liberalizing financial markets, such as removal of regulations on interest rates and opening to market competition. We may regard (1) and (2) as measures of quantitative development and (3) and (4) as measures of qualitative improvement.

Chinese financial reform has shown a very clear style of being strong on quantitative development but weak on qualitative improvement. Within a relatively short period, China developed a large, comprehensive financial system with all types of financial institutions and financial intermediation. But state intervention has remained widespread and serious. The government can assert strong influence on financial prices, institutional behavior, and market functions. Perhaps not unrelated, the volume of indirect financing (banks) grew much faster than that of direct financing (capital markets), as it is easier for the government to intervene in banking than in capital markets.

Second, the pattern of financial sector evolution is deeply rooted in the government's asymmetric market liberalization approach (Huang 2010a, 2010b). Thus, product markets have been almost completely liberalized by the reform, while factor markets, especially capital markets, have remained heavily distorted.

These distortions generally repress factor prices and lower production costs. They are like subsidies to producers, investors, and exporters. The purpose has been to achieve the fastest growth possible, although serious structural imbalances have resulted. In other words, the government adopted selected policy distortions to better achieve its policy objectives.

The same logic is applicable to China's financial reform. To achieve rapid economic growth, the government quickly expanded volumes of financial assets. Meanwhile, it has continued with repressive financial policies. There are several reasons for continued repression. For one, the government feared that complete liberalization might lead to greater market volatility and higher financial risks. Two, repressive policies have enabled the government to direct financial resources to priority areas identified by the policy. And, three, the repressed costs of capital, in forms of distorted interest rates and exchange rates, have promoted investment and exports, at least temporarily. Both financial development and repression are results of the government's direct promotion of economic growth, sometimes through state intervention.

Third, the combination of repressive financial policies and strong macroeconomic performance probably suggests that repression has not yet asserted serious damage on growth. Since reform began, China's economic and financial conditions have been much more stable than those in many other developing countries, which generally experienced more dramatic financial liberalization. This was, at least partly, attributable to the repressive financial policies (Stiglitz 2000; Li 2001).

Capital allocation was probably also reasonably effective under financial repression, especially given the government's clear objective of pursuing fast growth. At a minimum, the repressive financial policies did not erode China's growth dynamism.

Empirical analyses for this study, however, unveil two interesting findings: (1) a comprehensive index of financial repression suggests that China's financial reform is about half complete; and (2) although financial repression had a positive impact on economic growth (the Stiglitz effect) during the early years of economic reform, the impact is now clearly negative (the McKinnon effect) (Huang and Wang 2011).

These two points imply that the government was quite effective and successful in utilizing repressive financial policies to support economic growth. Continuation of repressive policies, however, may begin to affect growth performance, although this should not be regarded as evidence supporting the premature implementation of strong financial reform measures.

Fourth, the costs of financial repression have risen significantly. Although repressive financial policies probably helped maintain stability in the past, they are increasingly becoming a source of instability. Distorted interest rates and exchange rates already have caused serious structural imbalances, such as the unusually high investment share of GDP and very large current account surplus. During the global financial crisis, the closed capital markets in China also tolerated, if not encouraged, excessive borrowing by local governments and massive lending by the commercial banks. These likely increase risks of future fiscal and financial crises. More importantly, financial repression is becoming self-perpetuating: more repressive policies are needed to prevent the immediate blowup of the problems created by past repressive policies.

Repressive policies have also become obstacles for other important policy objectives. For instance, the rigid exchange rate regime, alongside the declining effectiveness of capital controls, has led to a gradual loss of monetary policy independence, evidenced by abundant liquidity conditions and growing inflationary pressures. Also, capital account controls are important hurdles for the government's ambitions of internationalizing the yuan and developing Shanghai into an international financial center before 2020 (Huang and Xie 2011).

Fifth, it is time for China to seriously consider completing what Lardy (1998) terms its "unfinished revolution" in the financial sector and the transition to a market economy. The costs of not doing so already have started to outweigh the benefits.

The key reform focus should be on capital account liberalization, which naturally requires further reforms of domestic financial institutions, interest rates, and exchange rates. Fortunately, China already possesses most of the necessary conditions for this last step: a liberalized real sector, a stable macroeconomic situation, healthy fiscal and financial systems, and a strong external account. Some of these conditions—especially the fiscal and financial systems, and the external account—may reverse in the future. Therefore, China should push forward with reforms within the next several years.

Sixth, overall, the Chinese experience of financial liberalization does appear to provide a good model for economic catch-up, provided the resultant risks do not amount to major disruptions of economic activities.

The essence of the Chinese reform approach is to let market mechanisms work wherever possible but to maintain repressive financial policy in order to overcome market failures by effectively allocating financing resources and maintaining financial stability. Over time, however, the risks may outweigh the benefits. Therefore, it is critical that governments keep pushing forward with financial reforms. The greatest risk of this strategy is the path-dependence of policy reforms. Repressive financial policies may help form powerful political-economic forces that may be difficult to do away with.

Summary of Remaining Reforms

The reform measures should take place in the following order: fiscal reform; financial and trade liberalization; exchange rate reform; and capital account liberalization.

Domestic financial liberalization probably requires the introduction of market-based interest rates, removal of state influences on fund allocation, and cessation of government intervention in the management of financial institutions. The exchange rate regime should shift toward a free float. And the authorities could abandon restrictions on cross-border capital flows.

However, as a developing country, China may prefer to retain certain mechanisms to support confidence and stability, such as a stabilization fund for the foreign exchange market, the qualified foreign and domestic institutional investors (QFII and QDII) schemes for portfolio flows, and a certain degree of state ownership of financial institutions.

The Financial Liberalization Literature

The literature on financial liberalization has grown significantly since the 1970s, alongside the worldwide wave of financial liberalization. Here we group both theoretical and empirical analyses into three categories: the general relationship between finance and growth; the roles of financial liberalization in transition and developing economies; and the Chinese experience of financial reform.

Several important lessons and observations relevant to China emerge from the literature review. First, in general, finance contributes positively to economic growth through functions such as channeling funds to efficient uses and overcoming problems of incomplete information. Second, the exact relationship between repressive financial policies and macroeconomic performance can vary depending on the stage of economic development and various institutional variables. Third, although financial repression probably helped China deal with problems of financial instability and market failure, it could become more costly, and even self-sustaining, over time. Fourth, further financial liberalization will yield positive results only if important prerequisites are in place and proper sequencing is followed.

Financial Intermediation and Economic Growth

That financial intermediation affects economic development has been recognized since at least Schumpeter (1911). Gurley and Shaw (1955) provided a theoretical basis, whereas Goldsmith (1969) was the first to confirm a relationship empirically. Merton and Bodie (1995) identified a number of important functions of the financial system that stimulated economic growth, such as clearing and settling of payments, pooling of saving, facilitating the allocation of resources across space and time, pooling risk, and reducing information costs.

Levine (1997) set out a theoretical framework illustrating the factors driving the formation of financial intermediaries and markets and their impact on economic growth. The central hypothesis is that acquiring information and making transactions are costly. Later, he summarized five main functions of the financial system: producing information ex ante about possible investment and capital allocation; monitoring investment and exerting corporate governance; facilitating trading, diversification, and management of risk; mobilizing and pooling savings; and easing exchange of goods and services (Levine 2005).

Some studies on endogenous growth also suggest that financial development can lead to higher long-term growth. For instance, Greenwood and Jovanovic (1990) demonstrate two essential functions of financial intermediaries in promoting growth. These are collecting and analyzing information on alternative investment projects and increasing investment efficiency through allocating funds to projects with higher expected returns. Bencivenga and Smith (1991) show that by enhancing liquidity and mitigating idiosyncratic risk through risk diversification and pooling, development of financial intermediaries resulted in reduction of households' unproductive holdings of liquid assets. Therefore, funds could be channeled toward illiquid but more productive activities.

Financial development appears to be a positive factor for economic development, yet financial repression is common in developing countries. Roubini and Sala-i-Martin (1992) set up an endogenous growth model to examine the effects of repressive financial policies on long-term growth. They argue that government might want to repress the financial sector because it is an "easy" source for financing the public budget. In order to increase revenue from money creation, governments that face large income tax evasion might choose to increase seigniorage by repressing the financial sector and increasing inflation. Financial repression would thus be associated with high tax evasion, low growth, and high inflation.

The positive relationship between finance and growth predicted by the literature has received considerable support from a large number of empirical studies. Applying data for 80 countries covering 1960–1989, King and Levine (1993a) find that higher levels of financial development are positively associated with faster current and future rates of economic growth, physical capital accumulation, and economic efficiency improvement. Rajan and Zingales (1998), using industry-level data in a large sample of countries over the 1980s, show that financial development facilitates economic growth by reducing the costs of external finance to firms and industrial sectors. Based on data for 63 countries covering 1960–1995, Beck et al. (2000) find that higher levels of financial intermediation produce faster economic and total factor productivity growth. Importantly, Beck et al. (2008) find that financial development exerted a disproportionately positive effect on small firms.

However, other studies cast doubt on the simple prediction that financial development boosts economic growth. Demetriades and Hussein (1996) highlight the danger of statistical inference in cross-sectional studies on the finance-growth nexus. They argue that countries with very different experiences in both economic growth and financial development probably have had different institutional characteristics, and thus should not be treated as homogeneous entities.

Based on a broad data set covering 95 countries, Ram (1999) finds that the predominant pattern indicates a negligible or weak negative association between financial development and economic growth. In addition, when the data sample is split into three groups by growth experience (low-, medium-, and high-growth countries), a huge parametric heterogeneity is observed for the finance-growth relationship. Similarly, Andersen and Tarp (2003) find that although a positive and significant relationship exists in their full-sample cross-sectional analyses, the correlation is negative for the poorest countries. In individual-country studies, they discovered different causal patterns between finance and growth.

This branch of the literature is useful for understanding the Chinese experience. Clearly, the generally positive finance-growth correlation was behind the Chinese government's push for financial liberalization, especially financial development, during the reform period. The exact effects of finance on growth, however, can vary significantly at different development stages and under different institutional arrangements. These insights might suggest that costs of financial repression in China would also change as income level grows and market environment improves.

Effects of Financial Liberalization

The finance-growth nexus highlights the important roles of financial reform in undeveloped economies and economies transitioning to a market system (Patrick 1966; Griffith-Jones 1995; IMF 1996; Hermes and Lensink 2000).

The term "financial repression" was coined by Ronald McKinnon (1973). He defined it as policies regulating interest rates, setting a high reserve requirement, and allocating resources. McKinnon argued that such policies impede financial deepening, hinder efficiency of the financial system, and lower economic growth. Following this argument, Pagano (1993) shows that financial policies such as interest rate controls and reserve requirement reduced the financial resources available for financial intermediating activities. Similarly, King and Levine (1993b) find that financial sector distortions reduce the rate of economic growth by lowering the rate of innovation.

Long and Sagari (1991) argue that mobilizing savings for investment, exerting effective corporate governance of state-owned enterprises, and selecting non-state firms to finance are all important elements of a successful transition to a market economy. Financial reform in transitional economies is more comprehensive than in most developing countries because it involves not only liberalization but also constructing the structure and framework of the financial system.

The experience of both transitional and developing economies highlights the difficulties in establishing successful commercial banking systems that can allocate financial resources efficiently (Bonin and Szekely 1994; Haggard and Lee 1995; Nissanke and Aryeetey 1998). Policy lending, barriers to interregional financing, distorted pricing, poor managerial incentives, and lack of prudential financial regulation can undermine financial performance.

The well-known McKinnon–Shaw hypothesis contends that common government interventions in the financial sector, such as repressing interest rates to below market-determined levels and directing credit, are fundamental stumbling blocks to economic growth (McKinnon 1973; Shaw 1973). The hypothesis asserts that interest rate repression has two primary negative effects. First, it reduces the incentive of economic agents to hold surpluses in the form of financial assets. Thus, the quantity of financial savings forthcoming is restricted, with negative implications for rates of investment and economic growth. Second, if interest rates are fixed at below-market levels, there is excess demand for credit and an administrative rationing process needs to be created. As a result, McKinnon–Shaw proponents argue that low-return investment might gain funding at the expense of high-return investments.

Arguments for financial liberalization have been questioned, initially by Diaz-Alejandro (1985). Fry (1997) argues that perverse reaction to higher interest rates by firms that are insolvent or not profit motivated is the primary reason for the failure of financial liberalization in some countries. The insolvent firms simply continue, if they can, to borrow whatever they need to finance their losses. Such firms bid up the interest rate until normally solvent, profit-motivated firms can no longer gain access to credit or became insolvent due to the high cost of borrowing.

This indicates there are prerequisites that must be met before successful financial liberalization can be implemented (Fry 1997). These normally include adequate prudential regulation and supervision of financial institutions and markets; a reasonable degree of price stability; fiscal discipline taking the form of sustainable government borrowing; a central bank that avoids inflationary expansion of reserve money; profit-maximizing, competitive behavior by financial institutions; and a tax system that does not impose discriminatory taxes on financial intermediation.

As many countries have yet to satisfy these conditions, a growing body of the literature argues that well-designed government intervention can be preferable to a fully liberalized financial system in terms of promoting economic development (Stiglitz 1994; Hellman et al. 1997). Stiglitz (2000) further argues that the increased frequency of financial crises in the 1990s was closely associated with financial market liberalization in developing countries.

Arestis and Demetriades (1999) point out that the conventional financial liberalization hypothesis is based on a set of strong assumptions, including perfect competition and complete information. These assumptions, however, often do not hold in many countries. Thus, these countries might be better able to deal with problems of market failure under financial repression.

Empirical findings are similarly inconclusive. Roubini and Sala-i-Martin (1992) demonstrate that part of the weak growth experience in Latin American countries can be explained by financially repressive policies. Using time series data for Malaysia, Ang and McKibbin

(2007) find that financial liberalization, through removal of repressive policies, has a favorable effect on stimulating financial development. On the other hand, Arestis and Demetriades (1997) and Demetriades and Luinte (2001) report that financial repression in South Korea had positive effects on its financial development.

One important lesson for China from these studies is that financial liberalization is a fundamental step toward more sustainable rapid economic growth. However, financial liberalization works well only if the country satisfies a set of prerequisites. Otherwise, it is much easier for the government to deal with problems of market failure, macroeconomic instability, and financial risks under financial repression. The implication is that, in order to derive maximum benefits and avoid financial crises, China must focus on the necessary conditions before pushing further liberalization.

Financial Reform in China

Financial liberalization in China generally has lagged reform in most other economic areas. Cheng et al. (1997) describe the Chinese financial sector as "essentially unreformed," while Lardy (1998) views Chinese financial reform as an "unfinished revolution." Despite major progress during the first decade of the twenty-first century, the government continues to exercise considerable control.

Some economists have argued that the apparent lack of financial reform represents a drain on an otherwise successful program of economic reform. For example, China kept a low interest rate ceiling for many years, which had detrimental effects. Typically, it encouraged inefficient investment and distorted financial efficiency. Similarly, Lardy (1998) suggests that setting lending rates below market-clearing levels ensured excess demand for loans. Political allocation of credit funds, including corruption, inevitably resulted.

The 1997–1998 Asian financial crisis has heightened scrutiny of China's state banking system, whose fragility stemmed from continued use of the financial system to support urban-based state-owned enterprises (Brandt and Zhu 2000; Bonin and Huang 2001; Huang 2002). Lardy (1998) estimates that, during the crisis, more than 25 percent of the loans of China's four major state-owned commercial banks (SOCBs) were nonperforming, which implies that these banks were technically insolvent.

Provincial data for 1997 reveal a striking inverse relationship between financial intermediation and GDP per capita that is at odds with the empirical regularity of positive correlation found in cross-country studies. This pattern suggests that allocation of financial resources across provinces was highly inefficient, with richer provinces being taxed relatively less than poorer provinces (Lardy 1998; Sehrt 1999). Park and Sehrt (2001) find that the importance of policy lending by state-owned commercial banks did not fall during the period 1991–1997, and that lending by financial institutions did not respond to economic fundamentals.

However, Maswana (2008) suggests that although repressive financial policies were bad for allocative efficiency, they probably created what he describes as "adaptive efficiency," an ability of the government to adapt quickly to a changing environment. Li (1994) argues that mild financial repression helped China maintain the financial stability needed for reform.

Financial repression can be considered an implicit tax. Lardy (2008) estimates that financial repression, mainly through negative real interest rates, costs Chinese households about 255 billion yuan ($36 billion), which is 4 percent of GDP, in addition to lowering overall economic efficiency. According to Lardy, corporations and banks each captured one-quarter of this, and the government took half.

Liu and Li (2001) also confirm a positive contribution of financial liberalization to economic growth during China's reform period.

These studies on the Chinese experiences reveal several important things. First, financial reform lags significantly in an otherwise impressive economic reform program. Second, repressive financial policies are still widespread and serious. Third, repressive measures probably helped the government to achieve some policy goals, while later on, their costs, in terms of investment inefficiency and income inequality, are rising rapidly.

Development and Reform of the Banking Sector

The banking sector is the most important component of the Chinese financial system. For some years it has accounted for more than 60 percent of total financial assets; total bank deposits were 180 percent of GDP in 2010. This section begins with a brief review of the development of banking. A detailed discussion then focuses on changes in two areas: reform of the state-owned commercial banks (SOCBs) and entry of foreign banks.

Since 2000 or so, China's SOCBs have experienced dramatic transformation, including resolution of nonperforming loans, adoption of a new accounting system, injection of public capital, introduction of foreign strategic investors, and stock listings in both domestic and foreign stock markets. They also have improved significantly in terms of asset quality and capital adequacy. And the SOCBs have risen to be among the largest banks in the world when ranked by stock market capitalization.

However, SOCB reform is far from complete. Most banks are still subject to important state interventions and operate more like state-owned entities than publicly listed companies. Massive loan expansion during the global financial crisis that began in 2007 was a testimony of the effectiveness of the policy but a failure of the risk-control mechanism.

Since reforms began, foreign banks have made critical contributions to the improvement of domestic banks by bringing competitive pressure, management skills, risk-control systems, quality services, new products, and a modern business model. Despite their high profile in the community and market, their share is very small, as discussed later. Foreign bank operation remains tightly constrained by regulations.

Early Evolution of the Banking System

During the pre-reform period, China had a mono-bank system, with the People's Bank of China (PBOC) serving both as the central bank and as a commercial bank. PBOC controlled 93 percent of the country's total financial assets at that time. It also had a separate license as the Bank of China (BOC) for international economic transactions. There was also the China People's Construction Bank (CPCB), which operated as a department within the Ministry of Finance (MOF).

These were not true commercial banks, something Deng Xiaoping (1979) pointed out: "Banks should perform all the functions of banks. Banks are not real banks. They are accountants and cashiers. They are currency issuers." This was not a major problem under the central planning system. However, when China began its transition toward a market economy, demand for proper financial intermediation increased significantly.

Therefore, the first major policy initiative in the banking sector was to establish a large number of commercial banks. This began in 1979

TABLE 2.1
Origins of the Big-Four Banks

Usually Referred to As	Full Formal Name (as of 2011)	Origins
ABC	Agricultural Bank of China Ltd (ABC)	1951 Agricultural Cooperative Bank; 1979 reestablished specialized rural business; 2009 became joint-stock company.
BOC	Bank of China Ltd (BOC)	Traces roots to central bank founded in 1912; from 1949 specialized foreign exchange and international trade bank; 1979 separated from PBOC; 1994 became a commercial bank; 2004 became joint-stock company.
CCB	China Construction Bank Corp (CCBC)	1954 as People's Construction Bank of China under MOF; 1979 State Council; 1994 policy lending separated; 1996 dropped "People's" from name; 2004 banking segments became joint-stock company.
ICBC	Industrial & Commercial Bank of China Ltd (ICBC)	1984 created from commercial banking segments of PBOC; 2005 became joint-stock company.

with the creation of the Agricultural Bank of China (ABC), specializing in rural business and leading to rural credit cooperatives; separation from PBOC of Bank of China (BOC) as the foreign trade bank; and removal from MOF of a renamed China Construction Bank (CCB). PBOC separated out its commercial transactions in 1984, forming the Industrial and Commercial Bank of China (ICBC). These four SOCBs are commonly referred to as the "big four." Table 2.1 provides further details on their origins.

In the 1980s the government also created many other banks and non-bank financial institutions. These included the China Orient Leasing Co Ltd in 1981, the People's Insurance Company in 1984, the Bank of Communications (BOCOMM) in 1986, and Citic Industrial Bank (now known as China CITIC Bank) in 1987.

TABLE 2.2

Distribution of Deposits, Loans, and Assets, 1978–2008, in Percent

1978–1995			1996–2008		
Deposits	Loans	Assets	Deposits	Loans	Category of Bank
81.98	91.07	65.11	64.64	64.22	Big four
1.47	1.22	14.88	15.37	15.80	12 joint-stock commercial banks and bank of communications
1.93	0.95	6.57	6.60	6.63	City commercial banks
18.12	6.34	11.73	11.66	11.60	Rural banks and cooperatives
0.18	0.43	1.71	1.74	1.76	Foreign banks

Source: Almanac of China's Finance and Banking; author's calculation.

Note: Excludes policy banks.

At the end of 2010, there were 3,749 banking financial institutions. These were: 3 policy banks, the big four banks, the Bank of Communications, 12 joint-stock commercial banks, 147 city commercial banks, and 2,646 rural credit cooperatives, as well as other institutions such as rural commercial banks, trust companies, financial leasing companies, and so on.

One very important feature of the banking system is that it is dominated by the big four. During 1996–2008, the big four accounted for more than 60 percent of the country's entire banking industry, whether measured by assets, deposits, or loans (table 2.2).

The Big Four and Banking Reforms

The big four are very important financial institutions for China's financial intermediation and financial stability. Over the years they probably have shouldered more policy responsibilities than any other financial institutions, including providing "social stability" loans to failing state-owned enterprises (SOEs).

By the time of the 1997–1998 Asian financial crisis, they had clearly become a major source of financial risk. The average nonperforming loan ratio was between one-quarter and one-third. They were judged to be technically insolvent by some international scholars (Lardy 1998; Bonin and Huang 2001). This was the result of policy intervention by the government, as well as poor management by the banks. Close to

90 percent of their loans at that time went to the SOEs. And SOEs as a group made a net loss in 1996 (Huang 2001).

In 1996 the government undertook new strategies for SOEs and state-owned commercial banks. The reform principle for SOEs, captured in the phrase "grasp the big, let go the small," was adopted in September 1997 at the 15th Communist Party Congress. This was the first major wave of privatization of SOEs. The intention was for the central government to be less involved with smaller SOEs while retaining and focusing on about 1,000 large SOEs affiliated with the central government. The smaller SOEs would be passed to local governments, which would then restructure, privatize, or shut them down.

By the end of 2010, the number considered "large" had been reduced to 100. Most are monopolies or near monopolies in industries such as telecommunication and oil. They are all profitable, which created a favorable external environment for banking reform.

The initial steps of banking reforms focused on capital adequacy and nonperforming loans. In 1998 the government issued 270 billion yuan of special treasury bonds to raise the capital adequacy ratios of the big four. In 1999, drawing on the US experience with the Resolution Trust Corporation (RTC), the government established four asset management companies (AMCs) to manage and dispose of the big four's nonperforming assets. These were China Cinda Asset Management Corporation (under CCB), China Huarong Asset Management Corporation (under ICBC), China Orient Asset Management Corporation (under BOC), and China Great Wall Asset Management Corporation (under ABC). The AMCs bought 1.4 trillion yuan (about $169 billion at the time, 21 percent of the loan balance of the SOCB at the end of 1998) of nonperforming assets from the big four in 1999.

The government encouraged banks to use their pretax profits, which were created in part by fat guaranteed interest spreads, to write off nonperforming loans (NPLs) remaining on the banks' books. The NPL ratio for state-owned banks dropped to an average of just over 19 percent in early 2004 and to 6 percent at the end of 2008, although it has remained consistently higher than for joint-stock banks. Data on NPLs are shown in figures 2.2 and 2.3.

Alongside NPL resolution, the authorities required commercial banks to change their loan-classification method from a backward-looking four-category system to a forward-looking, international-standard five-category system:

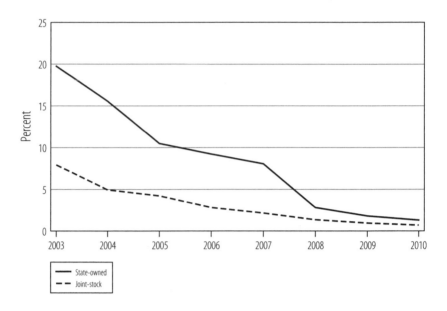

Figure 2.2 Nonperforming Loans as a Percentage of Total Loans, 2004–2008. *Source*: *Almanac of China's Finance and Banking*.

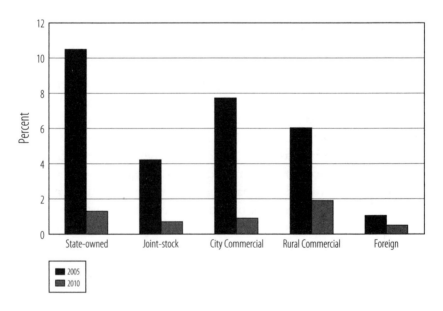

Figure 2.3 Nonperforming Loans of Commercial Banks as a Percentage of Total Loans, 2005 and 2010. *Source*: *Almanac of China's Finance and Banking*.

- Pass: Borrowers can honor the terms of their contracts, and there is no reason to doubt their ability to repay the principal and interest of loans in full and on a timely basis.
- Special mention: Borrowers are able to service the loans currently, but repayment might be adversely affected by some factors.
- Nonperforming
- Substandard: Borrowers' ability to service loans is apparently in question; cannot depend on their normal business revenues to pay back the principal and interest; losses might incur even when guarantees are executed.
- Doubtful: Borrowers cannot pay back principal and interest in full; significant losses will incur even when guarantees are executed.
- Loss: Principal and interest of loans cannot be recovered, or only a small portion can be recovered after taking all possible measures and resorting to necessary legal procedures.

The new system is forward-looking because it focuses on the ability of borrowers to repay the principal and interest. That is, it requires a risk assessment. According to a guideline issued by PBOC in December 2001, the new system was first introduced at the major branches of the big four and then officially adopted by all banks in 2002. This was an important step in aligning domestic banks with international banking practice.

To improve the transparency of bank operation and promote the more accurate classification of loans, in January 2002 MOF published "Accounting System for Financial Institutions." This reduced to 90 the number of days a loan was overdue before interest was no longer accrued, which is the international standard. From 1998 to 2001, interest continued to accrue until the loan was 180 or more days overdue. Before 1998, interest was accrued on loans whether they were sound or impaired, except when the government agreed to suspend the accrual on particular impaired loans.

Restructuring Bank Ownership Since 2001

China's accession to the World Trade Organization (WTO) in December 2001—in particular, the opening of the financial industry—called for urgent and fundamental reforms of the banking sector. In the following years, the government went directly to the heart of banking reform: restructuring of ownership.

At the end of 2003, policy makers picked BOC and ICBC as pilots for transformation into joint-stock commercial banks. In preparing for the IPOs, the authorities undertook four concrete steps to improve the banks' balance sheets: an official capital injection, approval of issuance of subordinated bonds to boost equity, disposal of NPLs through AMCs, and the introduction of foreign strategic investors (table 2.3).

As the first step of partial privatization, beginning in 2005 foreign banks took positions in the big four. The strategic investors were

TABLE 2.3
Restructuring Measures before IPOs of the Big Four Banks

BOC	CCB	ICBC	ABC	
Aug. 26, 2004	Sep. 17, 2004	Oct. 28, 2005	Jan. 5, 2009	Reorganization date
Dec. 2003	Dec. 2003	Apr. 2005	Nov. 2008	Capital injection date
186.4	186.2	124	130	Capital injection (RMB billion)
308.1	185.8	705	815.7	Disposal of NPLs[a] (RMB billion)
Sep. 2005	Jun. 2005	Jan. 2006	None	Foreign strategic investors, initial date
Temasek, Royal Bank of Scotland each 10%	Bank of America 9.0%, Temasek 5.1%	Goldman Sachs, Allianz Group, American Express 10% in total	None	Foreign strategic investors, percentage stake
43	32.8	30.5	None	Foreign strategic investment (RMB billion)
Jun. 2006	Oct. 2005	Oct. 2006	Jul. 2010	IPO date Hong Kong
Jul. 2006	Sep. 2007	Oct. 2006	Jul. 2010	IPO date Shanghai
110	74.6	173.2	149.9	IPO amount (RMB billion)

Source: Compiled by the authors from data in Okazaki (2007) and Huang et al. (2011).

[a]The Ministry of Finance gave receivables to ICBC (RMB 246.0 billion) and CCB (RMB 65.5 billion) and waived the paid-in capital of BOC (RMB 141.1 billion) and CCB (to doubtful NPLs). Simultaneously, MOF sold bills to the four banks in the amount of RMB 616.4 billion to offset the impact of the disposal.

required to lock up their shares for three years. The foreign investors brought to the Chinese banks not only capital but also staff training, risk-management assistance, guidance on internal control, corporate governance, and investor confidence (Berger et al. 2005).

In 2006 BOC became the first publicly listed Chinese bank, with Shanghai A-share and Hong Kong H-share listings. ICBC followed in 2006, CCB in 2007, and ABC in 2010. The state retains at least two-thirds ownership of each bank.

Public listings have brought significant changes to the big four in terms of ownership structure, corporate governance, information disclosure, and even financial performance.

The two principal profitability indicators, ROA (return on assets) and ROE (return on equity), have generally been improving at the big four since 2005. This trend continued despite the global financial crisis that began in 2007 (table 2.4).

TABLE 2.4
Bank Profitability Indicators, 2005–2010

	Return on Assets (percent)					
	2005	2006	2007	2008	2009	2010
ICBC	0.66	0.71	1.02	1.21	1.20	1.32
ABC	0.02	0.10	0.82	0.84	0.82	0.99
BOC	0.70	0.96	1.10	1.02	1.09	1.14
CCB	1.11	0.92	1.15	1.31	1.24	1.32
HSBC	1.56	1.62	1.99	1.34	1.18	1.35

	Return on Equity (percent)					
	2005	2006	2007	2008	2009	2010
ICBC	−27.92	13.65	16.21	19.34	20.13	22.13
ABC	1.32	6.40	−13.60	−23.55	20.52	21.44
BOC	13.06	14.44	14.37	14.01	16.60	17.96
CCB	19.49	14.99	18.38	20.82	20.81	21.44
HSBC	23.82	22.58	25.00	17.51	15.32	20.64

Source: BankScope. (Bankscope is an electronic global database of bank financial statements, ratings, and intelligence.)

Note: HSBC is included for comparison to China's big four. HSBC Holdings plc, parent of the Hong Kong and Shanghai Bank, is a global financial group with a significant presence in China.

TABLE 2.5
Composition of Bank Net Operating Profit, 2004–2010

	Net Interest						
	2004	2005	2006	2007	2008	2009	2010
ICBC	91	90	90	88	85	80	81
ABC	89	57	63	88	92	82	83
BOC	80	82	87	83	74	71	73
CCB	89	91	93	88	84	79	77
HSBC	54	57	58	52	53	47	47

	Net Fee and Commission						
	2004	2005	2006	2007	2008	2009	2010
ICBC	6	6	9	15	14	18	19
ABC	9	12	12	13	11	16	16
BOC	8	7	15	19	18	21	20
CCB	6	7	9	14	14	18	20
HSBC	23	22	23	26	23	24	26

Source: BankScope.

Note: Net interest and net fee and commission income as a percentage of net operating profits. HSBC is included for comparison to China's big four. HSBC Holdings plc, parent of the Hong Kong and Shanghai Bank, is a global financial group with a significant presence in China.

The composition of profits is shown in table 2.5. Profits are skewed heavily toward interest income; fee business is substantially underdeveloped compared with international counterparts. This illustrates important areas to improve in the big-four business model.

Despite significant and widespread improvement accompanying public listing, most Chinese banks, especially the big four, still operate more like SOCBs than listed banks. A good example is that the Chinese banks extended about 9.6 trillion yuan in new loans in 2009, more than twice the PBOC's original target for 2009 and twice the amount of new loans in 2008. Although it was good news for policy makers, it was bad news for investors. Dramatic lending expansion at a time of global recession says something about the influence of the state and the effectiveness of risk management. Therefore, the task of banking reform in China is far from accomplished.

Credit Cooperatives

Beginning in 1980, urban credit cooperative (UCC) were established to provide funding for small- and medium-private enterprises (SMEs), which were rapidly developing. At their peak in 1994–1995, there were about 5,000 UCCs.

Unfortunately, the UCCs were not properly run due to lack of expertise and interference by interest groups. This caused a long list of problems, including poorly regulated management, weak risk management capability, inefficient business operation, and—as a result—a high level of nonperforming loans (NPLs).

The PBOC decided to reform the UCCs by merging them into other banks. During the five years 1998 through 2002, more than 2,000 UCCs were absorbed by 111 newly established city commercial banks. At the end of 2008, only 22 UCCs were left. At the end of 2009 there were just 11, and at the end of 2010 there were none.

Transforming UCCs into city commercial banks has been rather successful because it significantly improved management quality and reduced financial risks. This is evidenced by continuous increases in profitability and declines in NPL ratios at the city commercial banks. However, the transformation brought a new problem: the new banks shifted focus from small enterprises to larger projects. This is unfortunate because a vibrant SME sector is important to the future of the Chinese economy.

Policy Banks

In the mid-1990s the government established three policy banks: China Development Bank (CDB), mainly in charge of large projects; Export-Import Bank of China (EIBC), handling external-related economic transactions; and Agricultural Development Bank of China (ADBC), tasked with facilitating rural development. Because all state-owned banks are burdened with policy lending, it is hard to judge the contribution of the policy banks. That is, if the intention of the policy banks was to allow state-owned commercial banks to shift away from policy lending, then creating the policy banks did not achieve that goal.

CDB is well run, judging from its asset quality. However, it went through a major transformation at the end of 2008, becoming a commercial bank, although it will continue to focus on medium- to long-term lending. This reveals a degree of confusion among policy makers about the future of policy banks. It is not clear which banks will take over from CCB the main responsibility for policy-oriented large projects.

EIBC has its hands full. Historically, its main task was to support China's exports. But now it is also required to promote imports. In addition, EIBC has an important mission in supporting China's "go global" strategy by financing outward direct investment, overseas project contracts, and economic and technological cooperation.

Foreign Banks

Foreign banks combined account for a tiny portion of Chinese banking assets, just 1.7 percent at the end of 2010. But their entrance has been of great significance to reform. For instance, without commitments to open domestic markets to foreign banks, the government would probably not have taken drastic reform measures at the big four. Also, foreign banks play a major role in terms of introducing new products and technology and improving services. This competition has spurred Chinese banks to improve their own practices and services.

Before 1949 Shanghai was an international financial center with a large number of foreign banks. After 1949, however, all but four foreign banks left China. The Hong Kong and Shanghai Bank, Standard Chartered Bank, Bank of East Asia (founded by Chinese in Hong Kong in 1918), and OCBC (Oversea-Chinese Banking Corp, based in Singapore) kept operating in Shanghai.

The history of foreign entry into the Chinese banking sector during the reform period can be divided into three periods: 1980–1993; 1993–2001; and post 2001.

During the 1980–1993 period, the predominant motive for a foreign bank to come to China was to provide services for foreign firms and so to create a better investment environment for attracting FDI to China. First came the Export-Import Bank of Japan, which set up a representative office in Beijing in 1979. By the end of 1981, 31 financial institutions had representative offices in China. Although useful, these offices were not commercially operational. In 1982 Nanyang Commercial Bank, headquartered in Hong Kong, became the first foreign bank to establish a branch in mainland China.

Foreign banks were initially allowed to conduct business only in the four Special Economic Zones (SEZs): Shenzhen, Xiamen, Zhuhai, and Shantou. Gradually, coastal cities and some central cities were opened. By the end of 1993, foreign banks had established 76 operation-type financial institutions in 13 cities. Total assets reached $8.9 billion. These banks mainly conducted foreign currency businesses for foreign enterprises and foreign residents.

During the second period, 1994–2001, foreign entry accelerated. The government enacted the first regulations governing foreign banks, detailing requirements for market access and regulatory standards. This was an important step in creating a more standardized and law-based environment for foreign banks. The entire country was opened. The government started to issue yuan business licenses to foreign banks in Shanghai, although clients were limited to foreign companies and foreign residents.

From 1993 to the end of 1997, the number of operating financial institutions established by foreign banks doubled to 173 and total assets tripled. The pace of foreign entry then slowed significantly, affected by the Asian financial crisis. In 1998 foreign banks accounted for 1.86 percent of the country's total banking assets. To promote foreign bank businesses, the authorities identified Shenzhen as the second city in which foreign banks could conduct yuan business. Foreign banks were allowed to enter the national interbank market to raise funds.

China's entry into the WTO in December 2001 was an important moment for the opening of China's banking sector. At the time there was pessimistic sentiment in the Chinese banking industry, worrying that foreign entry would destroy the Chinese banks. Such concerns, although understandable, were not realistic. Foreign banks faced many explicit and hidden constraints for business development. Also, as Bonin and Huang (2001) pointed out, foreign banks would not be able to compete fully because they would lack the scale of large domestic banks.

Foreign banks were to be allowed to conduct foreign-currency business with all domestic or foreign clients. Also, restrictions on yuan business were to be relaxed gradually over a five-year transition period, including, ultimately, being allowed to conduct yuan business throughout the country.

The five-year transition ended on December 11, 2006, at which time foreign banks could enter Chinese financial markets relatively more easily. By the end of 2006, the number of operating financial institutions established by foreign banks had increased to 312, composed of 14 wholly foreign-owned and joint-venture banking institutions registered in China and their associated 19 branches and subsidiaries; plus 200 branches and 79 subbranches established by 74 foreign banks from 22 countries and regions in 25 cities. In addition to these, 186 foreign banks from 42 countries and regions had set up 242 representative offices in 24 cities.

By the end of 2010, foreign banks from 14 countries and regions had set up 37 wholly foreign-owned and 2 joint-venture banks, while banks from 25 countries and regions had set up 90 branches. Further, 185 foreign banks from 45 countries and regions had set up 216 representative offices in China.

Foreign banks also entered the Chinese market in other forms, such as business collaboration and through equity cooperation. By the end of 2008, 9 strategic investors had interests in a big four bank; 34 foreign strategic investors had stakes in 24 small and medium commercial banks; and 3 foreign strategic investors had equity in 3 rural cooperative financial institutions. Combined, the 45 strategic investments represented $32.8 billion of foreign capital.

After 2001 the revenue of most foreign banks grew at an extraordinary pace. In particular, they garnered business from profitable companies and wealthy individuals. Nonetheless, between 1998 and 2010 their share in China's banking industry stagnated or even declined slightly. This clearly indicates the sector is not yet an open and competitive market. Regulations on new branches, ceilings for interbank market borrowing, and licenses for new products often have been hurdles for foreign bank business expansion.

Financial Markets

Influenced by ideology and constrained by the low level of economic development, there were almost no capital or financial markets before the reforms. In their early stages, these markets took an extremely decentralized and disordered form. In the years that followed, the central government worked to standardize and centralize the capital markets. This section outlines the money and bond markets. Stocks and derivatives are treated in subsequent sections.

Money Market

Repos are the main component of China's money market, and the interbank lending market is an element in establishing China's benchmark interest rate. Hence, discussion focuses on these two markets. There also is a notes market.

The interbank lending market was the first of these three to be established. In 1984 PBOC encouraged financial institutions to take advantage of different funding costs in various institutions, places, and times and to conduct interbank lending. A formal regulation was formulated in 1986, and the market began to develop. Initially, irregular behavior, such as speculation, was quite common. In response, the PBOC set up a national unified interbank lending market in 1996. The rates used in the interbank market are Shibor and Chibor. The monthly trading volume of the interbank lending market increased by about 100 times (fig. 2.4).

The repo business started in 1991 when the Shanghai Stock Exchange and National Securities Trading Automated Quotation System (STAQ) were launched. The first repo transaction was conducted between

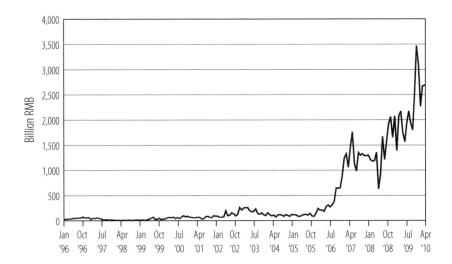

Figure 2.4 Interbank Lending Market, Monthly Trading Volume, 1996–2010, in Billion RMB. *Source*: Wind Info. (Wind Info is a leading provider of financial data and information on China in electronic form. It is based in Shanghai.)

Chibor and Shibor

The China interbank offered rate (Chibor) was established in 1996 as an important step in liberalizing interest rates. It is the average interest rate at which term deposits are offered between prime banks in China's interbank market. As such, it is a benchmark interest rate, and the interbank market's breadth and depth directly influence its quality. However, the calculation method is congenitally deficient. Although it was calculated based on actual interbank trading, there were very few trades.

The Shanghai interbank offered rate (Shibor) was created on January 4, 2007, to address problems with Chibor. Shibor uses the same calculation method as the London interbank offered rate (Libor) (that is, it is an arithmetic mean calculated from the interbank offer rate quoted by a group consisting of many of the banks with high credit ratings). Shibor is thus a more appropriate indicator for China's money market.

Currently, the varieties of Shibor publicly offered are overnight, 1 week, 2 weeks, 1 month, 3 months, 6 months, 9 months, and 1 year.

two members of STAQ in September that year. SSE introduced repo transactions in 1993. After that the market expanded rapidly, with the Shenzhen Stock Exchange also becoming a trading venue. Trading volume reached 300 billion yuan in 1994. In 1997 PBOC required all repo transactions to be conducted in the national unified interbank market. This meant commercial banks had to stop conducting repo business through the two stock exchanges.

To build formal channels between money capital markets, qualified securities companies and fund management companies were allowed to enter the interbank market after 2000. Most repo transactions take place in the interbank market.

Bond Market

China's modern bond market dates from 1981 when the government restarted issuance of treasury bonds. Trading is done interbank, on exchanges, and over the counter. The interbank bond market is the largest; since 2005 it has had a 90 percent market share in both trading volume and value. Transactions are by bilateral negotiations and settle trade by trade. The interbank market was set up in 1997 when all the commercial banks exited the exchange market, as required by PBOC.

The types of bonds are treasuries issued by MOF and guaranteed by the state, financial bonds issued by financial institutions, firm bonds issued mainly by state-owned enterprises, corporate bonds issued by joint stock corporations, mid-term bills issued by firms or corporations with a term of 3 to 5 years, central bank bills, and short-term financing bills issued by firms in the interbank bond market with terms of no more than one year.

Treasury bonds, financial bonds, and central bank bills are the largest groups, together accounting for an average of 96 percent of all bonds in each of the years 1991–2009. Treasury bonds were the earliest, as well as the main, form of bonds before 1995. Financial bonds then developed gradually. More than half of financial bonds are policy financial bonds. Because of the central bank's intervention in foreign exchange markets, starting from 2003 central bank bills quickly became the predominant bond and now account for more than half of total bonds, as shown in table 2.6.

Firm bonds are underdeveloped and the financing channels for issuance are not smooth. Such underdevelopment is a common phenomenon and problem throughout Asia, reflecting the significant role played by governments. It also reflects the lack of sound accounting and auditing practices and of high-quality independent raters, as well as a low level of creditor protection.

Development of Equity Markets

Stock exchanges were originally set up with a very heavy "central plan" color: the government dominated the entire process. The first stock was issued in 1983 in Shenzhen by a collective-owned enterprise in agriculture, followed by issuance by several other small state- and collective-owned enterprises. These were a type of redeemable preference shares: they were issued at par, had guaranteed principal and dividends, and were repaid when due—that is, they were more like bonds than ordinary (common) equity shares.

During the second half of the 1980s, various financing and fund-raising activities emerged as fiscal and bank resources fell short of

TABLE 2.6
Bond Issuance, Distribution by Types, 1991–2010

	Total in Billion Yuan	Distribution by Type, in Percent				
		Government Bonds	Financial Paper	Central Bank Bills	Corporate Bonds	Other
1991	35.2	100	0	0	0	0
1992	40.6	99	0	0	0	1
1993	52.8	100	0	0	0	0
1994	113.8	100	0	0	0	0
1995	144.9	74	26	0	0	0
1996	231.0	63	37	0	0	0
1997	245.7	55	43	0	1	0
1998	906.9	81	18	0	1	0
1999	425.6	69	28	0	3	0
2000	442.0	71	27	0	2	0
2001	468.4	63	35	0	2	0
2002	606.1	63	34	0	3	0
2003	39.2	42	23	32	2	1
2004	721.4	26	18	54	1	1
2005	802.8	18	16	61	1	3
2006	985.0	16	16	61	2	5
2007	2,356	29	15	50	2	5
2008	861.5	12	16	59	4	10
2009	1,642	19	16	44	6	16
2010	204.0	11	13	60	5	11

Source: Wind Info.

financing needs. State- and collective-owned small and medium enterprises (SMEs), in particular, were in a constant quest for funding. In 1986 the Trust and Investment Corporation of Shenyang began to act as an agency trading stocks and bonds, although the trading market was very small.

In response, during 1986–1988, the central government started pilot experiments transferring and distributing securities. There were strict controls, especially regarding the IPO process. Initially, the IPO process was almost completely controlled by the government. Local governments recommended companies for listing. Central-government authorities then examined the quality and future prospect of the recommended companies and made detailed arrangements for issue sizes, prices, and forms of issuance. There was great demand for listing, and local governments all pushed in favor of their own companies, especially SOEs.

The authorities then established the Shanghai Stock Exchange (SSE) in 1990 and the Shenzhen Stock Exchange (SZSE) in 1991. The markets, however, were particularly premature. The 8–10 incident is an example. In August 1992 potential investors poured into the city of Shenzhen to get shares in a new issue, which was heavily oversubscribed. There were allegations of corruption in allocating shares, and on August 10 those who had not been able to subscribe rioted. This caused serious social and political disruption.

This was not an isolated incident. After Deng Xiaoping's Southern tour in 1992, many small and large companies rushed to issue stock and bonds. There was an illusion that enterprises adopting the joint-stock system would be invigorated, and that investors buying stock could make a fortune. Unfortunately, regulation, which was initially the responsibility of local governments, did not keep pace.

The SME board was opened in June 2004 within the main board of SZSE to provide lower entry barriers for SMEs. By the end of 2010, 531 firms were listed. In 2008 the growth enterprise board (GEB) was officially launched, mainly for newly established firms in high-tech industries. By the end of 2010, there were 153 listed companies. A third-tier market (ASTS, Agency Share Transfer System) was established in 2001 to deal primarily with delisted firms and other over-the-counter (OTC) transactions. After 2001 some firms that no longer meet SSE or SZSE listing standards have been delisted, with trading of their shares shifting to ASTS.

The number of listed companies increased from only 10 in 1990 to 2,342 at the end of 2011. The increase in listings on the SZSE was particularly large in 2010 (41 percent) and 2011 (another 21 percent), due to the opening of the second board. As a result, SZSE now has far more companies listed than the SSE (1,411 vs. 938 at the end of 2011).

Total stock market capitalization increased from less than 500 billion yuan in 1993 to 32.7 trillion yuan at the peak in 2007. Trading value went up even faster; after a brief decline in 2008, it reached a new high of 53.3 trillion yuan in 2009. However, China's total market capitalization, at 67 percent of GDP in 2010, was still relatively low compared with other major economies (fig. 2.5).

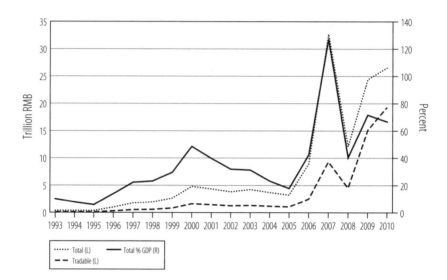

Figure 2.5 Stock Market Capitalization: Total, Tradable, and Share of GDP, 1993–2010 (in trillion RMB [left axis] and percent of GDP [right axis]). *Source*: *China Securities and Futures Statistical Yearbook.*

Note: Includes the Shanghai and Senzhen stock exchanges.

Regulation of Stock Markets

In November 1992, in the wake of the 8–10 incident, the China Securities Regulatory Commission (CSRC) was established. Over the years, the CSRC has adopted a wide range of reforms to improve the quality of the markets, most notably concerning the IPO process, information disclosure, independent directors, non-tradable shares, and fraud.

In March 2000 the CSRC promulgated a new policy: "Verification and Approval of Share Issue Procedures." As a result, the quota system was abolished. A new lead underwriter recommendation system and verification and approval system of stock issuing were put into place. The central idea was to increase the responsibilities of intermediary institutions, to enforce information disclosure, to exert the independent verification role of the Issue Review Committee (IRC), and to determine the issuing price by negotiations between the issuer and underwriter.

Information disclosure regulation was quite weak in the early stages of the markets. It was common that listed companies did not report important information regularly. There were several scandals where companies reported false results to mislead investors. To change this, CSRC issued "Administrative Measures on Information Disclosure by Listed Companies" on February 1, 2007. This aimed at enhancing information disclosure, protecting legitimate investor rights and interests, improving the quality of listed companies, and promoting the development of stock markets.

In June 2008 the CSRC took formal steps to regulate information disclosure of listed companies and reduce insider dealing. The policy was intended to strengthen corporate governance of listed companies by focusing on three key aspects:

1. Regulate substantial shareholders and the actions of their real controllers in order to enhance the independence of listed companies;
2. Strengthen the investigation of, and punishment for, the misappropriation of company funds by large shareholders;
3. Strengthen the mechanisms by which companies investigate, collect, and reveal information on their own.

The stock markets initially did not have rules for delisting. In 1998 regulators made special arrangements for adding "ST" to the names of listed companies that suffered losses for two successive years. ST stocks are still tradable. However, the maximum price change in one day was reduced to 5 percent; it is 10 percent for non-ST stocks. In 2001 the CSRC issued "Suspending and Terminating the Listings of Loss-Making Listed Companies Implementing Procedures," which marked the official establishment of a delisting system. It applied to listed companies suffering losses for three consecutive years. PT Shuixian became the first delisted stock on April 4, 2001.

Fraud by listed companies was once a common phenomenon. It was even more common for large shareholders to take advantage of their control to hurt small shareholders (Chen and Wang 2005). To protect investors, the CSRC introduced an independent director system in August 2001. This required that listed companies give full play to independent directors and emphasized that there should be at least one professional accountant among the independent directors.

Although all listed companies have nominally complied with this regulation, the effectiveness of the independent director system remains an open question. In some cases, independent directors have not had the necessary power to influence decision making. Also, many independent directors have not performed their duties diligently. Moreover, the functions of independent directors and supervisory boards often overlap, which can cause conflict between the two groups to the detriment of their effectiveness.

Equity Division

A special feature of Chinese stock issuance is "equity division." This is similar to multiple share classes. The types of shares are state owned, legal person, employee, and common (traded) shares. In order to ensure state control of the company, state-owned shares and legal-person shares originally could not be traded. This reduced shares available in the markets, which provides opportunities for price manipulation.

In 1999, and again in 2001, the authorities attempted to reform this situation by making state-owned and legal-person shares tradable. Such efforts seriously damped stock prices, as it meant doubling or even tripling the number of available shares.

At the end of 2004, total market capitalization was 371 billion yuan, of which non-tradable shares accounted for 68 percent. State-owned shares accounted for 74 percent of the non-tradable shares, just over half of the total market.

A reform of the equity division structure was started on April 29, 2005, with the purpose of transforming all non-tradable shares into tradable ones. By December 31, 2006, 1,303 listed companies had completed reform or started the process, representing 98.55 percent of the total market capitalization of the Shenzhen and Shanghai exchanges. At that point, equity division reform was accomplished. This was truly a remarkable achievement.

Foreign Investors

To attract more international capital, China launched RMB Special Shares (B shares) at the end of 1991. The B shares were listed on mainland exchanges, which proved inconvenient for the intended investors. In response, in 1993, the first mainland entity listed in Hong Kong, using what are called H shares. Listings on US and other foreign exchanges soon followed. (Table 2.7 provides further details of the various types of shares. Figure 2.6 provides data on B and H share issues.)

TABLE 2.7
Chinese Equity Division (Share Types)

Share Type	Date Introduced[a]	Where Traded	Trading Currency	Who May Own
A	1990 1991	SSE SZSE	RMB	Chinese domestic investors
B	1992	SSE, SZSE	US dollar Hong Kong dollar	Foreign legal or natural person[b]
H	1993	Hong Kong	Hong Kong dollar	Hong Kong local or any international investor
L	1997	London	Sterling	Local or any international investor
N	1994	United States (New York)	US dollar	Local or any international investor
S	1997	Singapore	Singapore dollar	Local or any international investor

Note: See box Chinese Equity Division (Share Types) for additional details. SSE = Shanghai Stock Exchange, established in 1990. SZSE = Shenzhen Stock Exchange, established in 1991.

[a]"Date Introduced" refers to when trading began.

[b]From 2001 Chinese domestic residents may also own B shares.

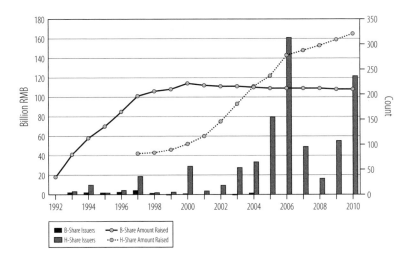

Figure 2.6 B and H Shares, Number of Companies and Capital Raised (in billion RMB), 1992–2010. *Source*: *Almanac of China's Finance and Banking*, various years.

Note: The figure shows the number of companies that, at the end of the year, had B shares or H shares outstanding, as well as the amount raised each year from newly issued shares.

Chinese Equity Division (Share Types)

For all share types, par value is in yuan, but shares are floated and traded in the currency of where the shares are listed, except B shares (see below).

Dividends are declared in yuan but paid in the currency of where the shares are listed, again with the exception of B shares.

A SHARES
A shares are one of the four classes of shares based on who may own them (see previous section). Called (Domestic) Individual Shares, they may be owned only by Chinese residents (including domestic institutions). They are like traditional common stock, and may trade freely on domestic markets.

B SHARES
RMB Special Shares, also called domestically listed foreign investment shares, are another of the four classes of shares based on who may own them.

B shares have a par value in yuan but are floated and traded in US dollars if listed on the Shanghai Stock Exchange, or in Hong Kong dollars if listed on the Shenzhen Stock Exchange. Investors are foreign legal or natural persons.

Because B share are listed on mainland exchanges, the original intended investors—that is, foreigners—found them inconvenient to trade. As a result, mainland entities began to list overseas, which largely reduced the function of B shares. Therefore, B-share issuance was suspended in 2000. However, the market was restored in 2001 when domestic residents were allowed to open B-share accounts using their legal holdings of foreign exchange. For a time, large quantities of money flocked into the B-share market. But, after a while, trading in B shares subsided.

H SHARES
H shares are listed on the Hong Kong Stock Exchange. H shares can be purchased and traded by Hong Kong local investors and other international investors.

L SHARES
L shares are based on an October 1986 "memo of understanding" between UK and Chinese authorities. Trading began in 1987.

All L shares are issued by corporations based outside China, but their main business operations are in China.

L shares are listed on the London Stock Exchange.

N SHARES

Most N shares are issued by corporations based outside China, but their main business operations are in China.

Many N shares were issued and trade as American Depository Receipts (ADRs). There are N shares listed on the New York Stock Exchange, American Stock Exchange, and NASDAQ.

S SHARES

S shares are issued by corporations based outside China (in Singapore and some British possessions), but their main business operations are in China.

Red Chips and P Chips

Besides the formal share types resulting from equity division, followers of Chinese stocks use two terms to group Chinese companies: red chip and P chip. These are explained here.

RED CHIP

"Red chip" is a term coined by Hong Kong economist Alex Tang in 1992 rather than a regulator-recognized category. The term initially was used for shares of Chinese government-controlled companies doing business primarily in China, but incorporated outside the mainland and listed on the Hong Kong Stock Exchange. Central, provincial, and municipal governments may be the controlling entity, either directly or indirectly.

By the early 2000s the term was also being used to include some of the more well-known private companies traded outside mainland China. The reason for this definition creep is the analogy to "blue chip" stocks: red chips are generally considered better-quality Chinese stocks.

A key difference between H shares and red chips is that H shares are Chinese domestic companies listed in Hong Kong, whereas red chips are foreign-based companies. This means Chinese officials have far less regulatory authority over red chips.

Initially, being foreign meant red-chip companies could not issue A shares, as Chinese regulations forbade foreign companies from going public on the A-share market. In mid-2007 the China Securities Regulatory Commission (CSRC) set experimental rules for red chips to issue A shares. But as of the end of 2010, the plan to allow red chips to issue A shares has not been implemented.

The new rules apply only to companies listed in Hong Kong for at least a year. There are size and profitability requirements as well. Companies that have a parent or subsidiary already listed on the domestic market can also apply to issue A shares.

The rule change was intended to increase the supply of shares available to domestic mainland investors, and thus cool what was seen as a frothy market. Still, A shares often have premiums compared to B shares of the same companies.

As of January 31, 2012, the Hong Kong Stock Exchange identified 102 companies as red chips. The market is tracked by the Hang Seng China-Affiliated Corporations Index, composed in early 2012 of 26 stocks.

P CHIPS
A "P chip" is a private-sector company incorporated in certain British Caribbean possessions that has operations in mainland China and is listed on the Hong Kong Stock Exchange. However, some people use the term to mean any Chinese private-sector company trading outside the mainland. In a further example of definition creep, some firms that have issued P-chip shares are considered "red chips"— meaning better-quality Chinese stocks, in an analogy to "blue chips."

Derivatives Market

Derivatives were introduced for commodity transactions earlier than for financial products. There are three varieties of financial derivatives in China: foreign exchange rate, interest rate, and stock. Foreign exchange and interest rate derivatives trade interbank, commodity, and stock derivatives on exchanges.

Commodities

On October 12, 1990, China Zhengzhou Grain Wholesale Market became the first commodities spot (cash) trading market in China.

In March 1991 it introduced forward contracts. The Futures Trading Regulations of China Zhengzhou Commodity Exchange, the first futures regulations in China, were completed in October 1992. On May 28, 1993, China Zhengzhou Commodity Exchange (CZCE) launched futures contracts, including wheat, corn, soybean, mung bean, and sesame. By the end of 1993, there were more than 50 futures trading markets (including both exchanges and wholesale markets) and nearly 1,000 futures brokerage institutions.

At the end of 1993, the State Council started a clean-up and rectification movement. As a result, 15 futures markets were allowed. Even then, they were deemed "experimental."

In 1998 a second clean-up and rectification movement was started. The 15 futures trading markets were merged into 3: Shanghai Futures Exchange (SHFE), Zhengzhou Commodity Exchange (ZCE), and Dalian Commodity Exchange (DCE). The varieties of commodity futures trading were reduced from 35 to 12.

Trading volume has enjoyed rapid growth since China's entry into WTO (fig. 2.7). Volume in 2003 was three times that of 2002. SHFE is

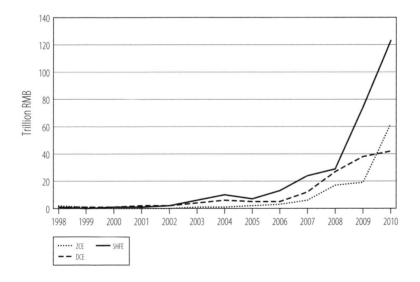

Figure 2.7 Commodity Futures Trading Volume by Exchange, 1998–2010, in Trillion RMB. *Source*: Wind Info.

Note: ZCE is the Zhengzhou Commodity Exchange, DCE is the Dalian Commodity Exchange, and SHFE is the Shanghai Futures Exchange.

one of three price centers for copper futures (with LME and COMEX). By the end of 2009, DCE was the world's second largest agricultural products futures market. (The Chicago Mercantile Exchange [CME] is first.)

Exchange Rate Derivatives

The introduction of exchange rate derivatives in China was in response to the exchange rate policy reform in mid-2005. In August that year, PBOC formally introduced yuan foreign exchange forward transactions to satisfy the need for economic agents to mitigate foreign exchange risk.

On April 24, 2006, yuan foreign exchange swap transactions were formally introduced by the China Foreign Exchange Trade System (also known as the National Inter-Bank Funding Center). The first order was signed between Bank of China and Export-Import Bank of China.

Volume in yuan foreign exchange swap transactions jumped to $443 billion in 2008, 37 percent above the 2007 level. Volume in 2010 was $1,283 billion, 190 percent above 2008. There are yuan swaps against the US dollar, the Hong Kong dollar, the Japanese yen, and the euro. Terms are concentrated on contracts of less than 3 months (including overnight).

Interest Rate Derivatives

As for interest rate derivatives, on October 8, 2007, PBOC issued a public notice to introduce FRAs (Forward Rate Agreements) in the interbank bond market. Following experiments, regular bond forward trading began in June 2005, and yuan swap trading began in February 2006. These steps improved the risk-sharing function of the market and sped the process of interest rate liberalization.

In the wake of PBOC's action, trading in financial derivatives increased significantly. Turnover of forward bonds in 2008 was 500.3 billion yuan, 98.8 percent more than in 2007. As to term, the 7-day future was most active, accounting for 75 percent of total turnover value. As to instrument, central bank bills and policy financial bonds dominated, together accounting for 94 percent of the total.

The notional amount of all yuan interest rate swap transactions in 2010 reached 1.5 trillion yuan. One-year and less-than-one–year transactions were relatively more active, accounting for 57.2 percent of the notional value of all swaps. By far the most common reference rate at the floating end of yuan interest rate swaps is the 7-day repo rate (54 percent in 2010). The next most common is Shibor (40 percent in 2010). A small percentage of swaps use the one-year term deposit rate (5.2 percent in 2010).

Stock Index Futures

The China Financial Futures Exchange (CFFEX) was established in September 2006 in Shanghai. Stock index futures contracts were revised in February 2010. Volumes have been significant. Table 2.8

TABLE 2.8
Principal Chinese Stock Indexes and Related Futures

Index	Date Introduced[a]	Number of Stocks	Composition	Futures Date Introduced[b]	Futures Where Traded
CSI 300	Apr. 2005	300	Largest, most traded A shares listed on SSE and SZSE	Apr. 2010	CFFEX
Hang Seng China-Affiliated Corp	Aug. 1994	25[e]	Selected Red Chips	Dec. 2003	HKEX (Hong Kong)
Shanghai Composite[c]	July 1991	About 1700[f]	All A and B shares listed on SSE	None	
Shenzhen Composite[d]	Apr. 1991	1453[g]	All A and B shares listed on SZSE	None	

[a]The base date of the index is generally earlier, and some indexes have been computed back to before their base date.

[b]When trading began.

[c]Subsequently, many indexes based on subgroups of SSE stocks have been introduced. Some of these have futures.

[d]Separate indexes for A and B shares were introduced at about the same time as the Composite index. Subsequently, many indexes based on subgroups of SZSE stocks have been introduced, including by sector and size. Some of these have futures.

[e]Since August 2010. Before then there were 33.

[f]As of December 2011, representing 938 companies.

[g]As of December 2011, representing 1,411 companies.

shows the principal stock indexes and when futures trading began in the index.

Warrants

Warrants were introduced in 1992. But at the end of June 1996, trading was halted because the government could not put up with the enthusiasm of speculators. No new warrants were issued for nine years. Then, in 2005 Bao Steel was allowed to issue warrants, and the market marked a new beginning. However, warrants quickly again became notorious as speculators participated with great passion. After a rush of issues in 2006 and 2007, the number of warrants decreased from a high of 27 in 2006 to just 1 by the end of 2010. Market capitalization peaked in late 2007.

Foreign Investors

When China entered the WTO, the commitments made in opening the securities industry included the following:

- Foreign securities institutions could conduct B-share transactions directly.
- Resident offices in China of foreign securities institutions could become special members of all the Chinese stock exchanges. (China's two stock exchanges use a membership system. To engage in brokering, a firm must be a member of the exchange. Special members [foreign brokers] are regulated differently, and have fewer rights, compared to ordinary [domestic] members.)
- Foreign financial institutions are allowed to establish joint-venture fund management companies. However, a foreign investor initially can own no more than one-third, and after three years can own no more than 49 percent.
- Foreign financial institutions would be allowed to set up joint-venture security companies within three years. However, the foreign ownership cannot exceed one-third.
- Joint venture companies can underwrite A shares, underwrite and trade B and H shares, and offer managed accounts.

By the end of 2006, China had fulfilled all of these commitments.

Foreign Financial Firms in China

The first Sino-foreign fund management joint venture, China Merchants Fund Management Co Ltd, was established in December 2002 with ING Asset Management BV as the foreign partner. The first Sino-foreign securities joint venture, China Euro Securities Ltd, also was approved in December 2002.

By the end of 2009, there were 9 Sino-foreign securities joint ventures and 34 Sino-foreign fund management joint ventures. Foreign ownership had reached 49 percent for 16 fund-management joint ventures. SSE had 3 special members and 38 foreign securities institutions conducting B-share transactions directly. Comparable numbers for SZSE are 3 special members and 22 foreign securities institutions.

In addition, 8 foreign exchanges have representative offices in China, and 160 foreign securities institutions have been allowed to open representative offices.

Qualified Foreign Institutional Investors

To achieve an orderly, secure opening of securities markets, effective from December 1, 2002, China introduced the Qualified Foreign Institutional Investors (QFII) system. QFII requires foreign institutional investors to use domestic commercial banks as custodians of their assets and to use domestic securities companies to execute trading operations in China. It also imposes quotas on the percentage of a listed firm foreigners may own. The requirements to be QFII are in table 2.9.

UBS AG and Nomura Securities Co Ltd became the first QFII in May 2003. By the end of that year, 10 QFII and $1.9 billion had been approved. By the end of 2009, 94 QFII had been approved, including 49 fund managers, 21 commercial banks, 11 securities companies, 2 insurance companies, and 11 others. Their assets totaled 289.9 billion yuan, 82 percent in securities. QFII float capitalization accounted for 1.4 percent of total A-share capitalization.

Qualified Domestic Institutional Investors

Even as the authorities were bringing in foreign investors, they began to open the way for domestic financial institutions to seek nondomestic

TABLE 2.9
Requirements for Participating in QFII

Foreign Investor	Requirements
Commercial banks	Total assets among top 100 in the world
	Security assets managed of not less than $10 billion
Mutual funds	More than 5 years' experience as asset manager
	Security assets managed of not less than $5 billion
Insurance companies	Established more than 5 years
	Security assets managed of not less than $5 billion
Security companies	More than 5 years' experience in security business
	Paid-up capital not less than $10 billion
	Security assets managed of not less than $10 billion
Other	Established more than 5 years.
	Security assets managed of not less than $5 billion

Source: CSRC (China Securities Regulatory Commission).

Note: The requirements apply to the foreign investor's most recent fiscal year.

opportunities. In April 2006 PBOC announced the Qualified Domestic Institutional Investors (QDII) system. QDIIs are allowed to raise RMB funds from domestic institutions and residents to invest in financial products overseas. The quota, denominated in US dollars, is granted by State Administration of Foreign Exchange (SAFE).

The first QDII products for individual investors, Hua An International Balanced Fund, launched in September 2006, raising some $197 million. By the end of 2010, 90 QDII had been approved, including 25 commercial banks, 37 securities and fund companies, 25 insurance companies, and 3 others. The approved investment quota was $72.98 billion.

Monetary Policy and Financial Supervision

The People's Bank of China (PBOC) was established on December 1, 1948. During the pre-reform period it did not act like a real central bank. It did issue currency on behalf of the government, but its main function was to distribute funds according to government directives. Even this function was supplementary, as collection and distribution of funds were mainly determined and handled by the central plans at that time.

There were calls to transform the PBOC into a proper central bank as early as 1978 when economic reform was launched. The State Council decided in September 1983 to split PBOC into two parts, effective the beginning of 1984. One part became a specialized central bank, which retained the PBOC name. The other part became a commercial bank, Industrial and Commercial Bank of China Ltd (ICBC).

In the following years, the authorities made important efforts to create a proper modern central bank. However, PBOC continues to rely mainly on quantitative measures such as reserve requirement and credit quotas to manage liquidity conditions.

In March 1995 the National People's Congress (NPC) passed the first Law of PBOC, which granted the PBOC legal authority to make and implement the country's monetary policy. The law also underscored the central bank's "independence," especially from MOF and local governments. Eventually, in late 1998 PBOC was transformed into a vertical system with nine branches across the country, independent of provincial administration.

PBOC has reduced direct intervention in commercial bank operation. For instance, the credit quota was abolished in 1998. Over the years financial supervision of the banking, security, and insurance industries has also been separated from PBOC.

Despite the 1995 law, PBOC is not an independent central bank. It is a part of the State Council, and its governor reports to the premier. Most importantly, PBOC is not a decision maker on monetary policies. The usual process is as follows. PBOC's Monetary Policy Committee (MPC) meets quarterly to discuss policy adjustments. Then, the PBOC governors' meeting makes policy recommendations to the State Council. (PBOC has a governor, five vice governors, and two assistant governors as of August 2012.) Finally, the State Council reaches a decision. Such a process implies that it often takes time for the top leaders to reach a consensus and make a decision. More importantly, if the leaders are more concerned with other policy objectives, such as GDP growth, then it can affect monetary policy.

Objectives

When the new PBOC was established in 1984, there was no clearly identified monetary policy objective. In 1986 the government issued the "Regulation on Administration of Banks," which defined the roles of financial institutions as "developing the economy, stabilizing the currency, and promoting socioeconomic performance." In 1993 the State Council for the first time identified a set of monetary policy objectives: maintaining a stable monetary environment and promoting economic growth. Later, the Law of PBOC passed by the NPC in 1995 refined the roles of PBOC as "stabilizing the currency and developing the economy," which sometimes were expressed as "promoting growth, supporting full employment, maintaining currency stability, and achieving balanced external accounts."

The various statements of objectives can be placed in three groups:

- Promoting growth and supporting full employment.
- Maintaining currency stability (and controlling inflation).
- Achieving balanced external accounts (and rebalancing the domestic economy).

The experience of Chinese policy making suggests these objectives are not equal. Policy makers often are most concerned about jobs and growth. When inflation risks rise, they often become deeply worried about price instability. And, although the government repeatedly vows to resolve internal and external imbalance problems, it has not taken any serious actions to achieve this.

The period after PBOC became a specialized central bank may be divided into three subperiods according to the primary monetary policy tasks. During 1984–1996, fighting inflation was a regular task. Then, during 1997–2002, deflation haunted the economy. Since 2003 maintaining a stable currency value and controlling inflation have been the top policy priorities (Yi 2009).

A critical change happened in 1996 when PBOC began to emphasize base money as a key policy target in order to fulfill its ultimate monetary objectives. From then on, PBOC has been monitoring more closely various measures of money supply (M_0, M_1, and M_2), which have shown great volatility in their growth rates (fig. 2.8).

Instruments of Monetary Policy

This section discusses the evolution of policy instruments during the reform period. Like the central bank, monetary policy is a new phenomenon. At the initial stage of reform, PBOC mainly relied on

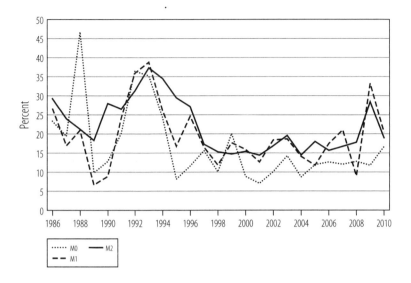

Figure 2.8 Annual Growth Rate of Money Supply: M0, M1, and M2, 1986–2010 (in percent). *Source*: Wind Info.

administrative measures such as a credit quota to control liquidity. Gradually, especially from 1998, indirect quantitative measures such as the bank reserve requirement ratio (RRR), open market operations, and central bank credit became more important. Additionally, PBOC started to focus on price instruments such as deposit and lending rates and the rediscount rate. But China's monetary policy remains very different from those in market economies, as it does not target a market interest rate, such as the Fed funds rate in the United States.

The main monetary policy tools currently include:

- Credit quota: a quantitative target the central bank set for individual commercial banks or other financial institutions.
- Window guidance: an instruction approach to directly influence financial institution behavior.
- Required reserve ratio (RRR): an indirect method regulating liquidity conditions.
- Open market operation: purchase and sale of securities to affect liquidity conditions.
- Central bank credit and rediscount business: policy tools for the central bank to inject or withdraw liquidity.

- Deposit and lending rates: base rates set by the central bank constrain the range of commercial bank interest rates.

Credit quotas were probably the most frequently used liquidity management instrument in the 1980s. At that time, the central bank set not only the total amount but also the composition of lending for individual commercial banks. From a monetary policy standpoint this was often quite effective due to its administrative nature. For instance, when inflation soared in 1988, PBOC sharply reduced the credit quota. This brought inflation down quickly. But such an approach has problems, such as inaccuracy and overadjustment.

Alongside financial development and deepening, such intermediate targets as credit quotas became increasingly inappropriate. For instance, the share of state-owned commercial banks (SOCBs) in newly extended loans dropped from 78 percent in 1990 to 51 percent in 1996. The growing portion of loans extended by non-SOCBs implies that direct controls over total credit became less effective over time. The development of direct financing channels such as stock and bond markets, and increasing interventions in foreign exchange markets, also made it more difficult for PBOC simply to focus on credit control.

In 1994 PBOC abolished credit quotas for most loan-making institutions. Only the big four SOCBs and three policy banks were still subject to quotas. By 1998 they too were free of quotas. This, however, does not mean that PBOC no longer manages loan volume. For example, in 2007 when inflation was rising steadily, PBOC undertook several measures, especially during the fourth quarter. One measure was reinstatement of credit quotas.

Window guidance, in which regulators provide advice to financial institutions through direct communication, is a very effective policy tool for controlling loan growth. Even though the commercial banks have undergone significant transformation, including introducing foreign strategic investors and public listing, most banks remain majority owned by the state, and their top managers are still appointed by the party.

The main problem with window guidance is its stop-go consequences. Use has declined significantly since 2000, but it is revived from time to time when the authorities face tough macroeconomic challenges. It was invoked in late 2007 for controlling liquidity and inflation, and in early 2009 for supporting stimulation policy.

The reserve requirement ratio (RRR) has been one of the more frequently used tools. In the mid-1990s, in order to influence commercial bank lending, PBOC began to adjust the RRR regularly, as an alternative to the past practice of directly setting credit quotas.

The deposit reserve system started in 1984. At that time the RRR was 20 percent for corporate deposits, 40 percent for household deposits, and 25 percent for agricultural deposits. In 1985 PBOC unified the ratios, initially at 10 percent. In 1998 PBOC combined required reserves and excess reserves into one account. Meanwhile, it lowered the RRR from its then level of 13 percent to 8 percent. In 1999 RRR was reduced to 6 percent. Most banks have maintained excess reserves.

It should be noted that, unlike in market economies, PBOC pays interest on both required and excess reserves, although at rates much lower than rates paid by commercial banks to their depositors.

A new policy, "differentiated required reserve ratio for different financial institutions," was introduced on April 25, 2004. Under this adjustment, the minimum reserve requirement was linked to financial performance indicators such as the capital adequacy ratio and nonperforming loan ratio. This change provided an incentive for financial institutions to behave more prudently and helped suppress the overexpanded loan market at that time.

From 2006 on, the RRR has become one of the most frequently applied monetary policy tools in China. During 2007, for instance, the RRR was increased on 10 occasions to absorb excessive liquidity, much of which had been injected by intervention in the foreign exchange market. When the global crisis hit China in late 2008, PBOC began to lower the RRR. From the second half of 2008 to the end of 2009 the ratio was lowered six times.

Additionally, the RRR imposed on small and medium financial institutions was set independently from the level applied to large financial institutions, beginning September 25, 2008. This difference remains in effect so as to lessen the burden of macro adjustments on smaller institutions.

Open market operations were started in foreign exchange markets in 1994. In April 1996 PBOC began to transact treasury bonds issued by MOF. By way of repos and reverse repos, PBOC realized decreases or increases in the money supply. But soon the authorities came to understand that open market operations could not function properly without proper institutional support, such as an interbank bond market, as well as relatively loose market conditions. So this initial trial was suspended except for limited forays. Thus, the total amount was less than 5 billion yuan in 1996.

After more than a year's preparation, open market operations on bonds were resumed in May 1998. Soon it became a major policy instrument. Not only did it help the central bank control base money and the money supply, open market operations in the interbank market have also aided the development of a national bond market.

The instruments used in open market operations expanded gradually. From 2003 PBOC has issued central bank bills to affect base money. Maturities are 3 months, 6 months, 1 year, and 3 years. In 2007 PBOC introduced repurchase agreements based on special treasury bonds. As of 2010 treasury bonds, central bank bills, and financial bonds from policy banks were all traded by PBOC in the form of either repurchases or outright operations.

During 1984–1996 the amount of central bank credit was the most important policy tool for managing liquidity conditions, replacing credit quotas. Unlike the credit quota, central bank credit was used by PBOC as a temporary important instrument to inject base money into the economy when growth of foreign reserves decelerated. The importance of central bank credit declined dramatically after 1994 when unsterilized foreign exchange market intervention became an important channel of liquidity injection.

Rediscounting was introduced alongside the development of commercial paper, and it officially became a policy tool at the end of 1995. Before 1998, the rediscount rate was set somewhere within a range of 5 percent to 10 percent below the lending rate, with just what level within the range depending on what the authorities thought was appropriate to achieve policy goals. In March 1998 the authorities experimented with the rediscount rate being determined by the market, de-pegging it from the PBOC lending rate.

Interest Rates

The most important interest rates are summarized in table 2.10. Perhaps the most visible rates are the base deposit and lending rates, which are illustrated in figure 2.9. (Interbank rates have already been discussed.)

Interest rate liberalization was formally launched by the State Council in 1993. The plan proposed starting with money market rates and bond yields and then freeing deposit and lending rates. Between

TABLE 2.10
China's Most Important Interest Rates

Rates	Explanation	Set By
Base deposit rate	Sets the ceiling for bank deposit rates and	PBOC
Base lending rate	Sets the floor for bank lending rates	PBOC
Shibor, Chibor	Interbank money market	Market
Treasury bond yields	Bonds trade in both an interbank market and on stock exchanges	Market

1996 and 2007, about 120 types of interest rates underwent reform. For some, this meant relaxed controls. Others were merged or completely eliminated.

The sequence followed for reforming deposit and lending rates has been:

- Foreign currency rates before local currency rates. Lending rates before deposit rates.
- Long-term, large-quantity rates before short-term, small-quantity rates.

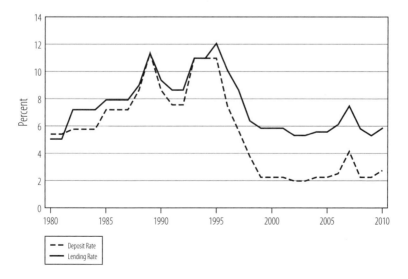

Figure 2.9 Base Deposit and Lending Rates, 1980–2010 (in percent). *Source:* DRCNET statistical database.

In the early years of the reform period, commercial banks still had to strictly adhere to the base rates. PBOC did not take the first step in liberalizing yuan lending rates until 1987. Commercial banks were allowed to float the lending rates of working capital loans up by a maximum of 20 percent of the base rate. In September 1988 not only did most types of loans enjoy the right of upward floating, commercial banks could also increase the rate by as much as 30 percent. This band was adjusted from time to time in the following years.

Beginning in August 2003 rural credit cooperatives in pilot districts could raise their lending rates up to twice the base rates. In 2004 PBOC allowed commercial banks and urban credit cooperatives to set their lending rates in a band 0.9 times to 1.7 times the base rate. The range for rural credit cooperatives was 0.9 to 2.0 times.

On October 29, 2004, PBOC abolished the ceilings on lending rates for all commercial banks but not for urban and rural credit cooperatives. The upper boundary for the cooperatives was raised to 2.3 times the base rates. The lower limit remained unchanged at 0.9 the base rate.

Deposit rates have remained highly regulated. On October 29, 2004, PBOC removed the floors for deposit rates, but retained ceilings, typically at 1.2 times the base deposit rate.

Remaining regulations on deposit and lending rates generate at least two types of consequences. First, ceilings for deposit rates combined with floors for lending rates sets a minimum interest spread for the banks. The spread is sufficiently large for the banks to capture high returns. This has been helpful in offsetting the bad assets created in previous decades. Second, real interest rates, especially deposit rates, have been negative from time to time (fig. 2.10). This is what McKinnon describes as a symptom of financial repression.

Regulatory Framework

Initially, almost all responsibility for financial supervision fell to PBOC. Then, beginning in the 1990s, a model spinning off supervision by sector was gradually adopted. "One central bank, three regulatory commissions" formed the core. The commissions and the dates they were established are China Securities Regulatory Commission (CSRC) 1992, China Insurance Regulatory Commission (CIRC) 1998,

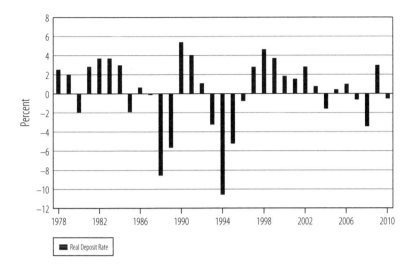

Figure 2.10 Real Deposit Rates, 1978–2010 (in percent). *Source*: Wind Info and calculations by the author.

and China Banking Regulatory Commission (CBRC) 2003. PBOC is mainly responsible for macro-prudential regulation, and the three commissions are in charge of supervision of their respective industries and markets.

This segregation-by-business regulatory model has worked reasonably well. However, there are often demands for allowing cross-sector businesses, especially as domestic financial institutions have faced competition from global comprehensive financial institutions.

From 2005 the State Council authorized Pudong New Area in Shanghai to carry out experiments with a comprehensive-supervision model. Similar authorization was given the Binhai New Area in Tianjin from 2006. A number of large financial institutions have made cross-sector mergers and investment, primarily in leasing and asset management. These, however, should be viewed more as pilot projects.

The question of whether China's financial regulatory system should stay segregated or go comprehensive remains open. Officials and experts are still assessing the costs and benefits of the different models. In the near term, it is most likely that the segregated model will continue, although calls for closer collaboration among the central bank and three regulatory commissions have grown loud.

Supervision of the Banking Industry

Given the dominance of banks, banking regulation has always been a very important part of China's overall financial regulatory system. In 1985 the State Council issued a directive that assigned responsibility for supervision of any activities related to money and banking to PBOC. PBOC has unveiled a series of regulations and rules to promote the healthy development of banking. A formal auditing system was introduced to monitor financial risk and policy implementation. After 1994 PBOC took further steps to improve supervision. It defined procedures and requirements for setting up new branches. It strengthened off-site surveillance of banks. And it demanded that commercial banks improve their risk controls.

With the 1997–1998 Asian financial crisis, PBOC devoted more effort to risk monitoring and controls. These included experimenting with the international standard five-category loan classification system in Guangdong in 1998, and then nationwide adoption of the system between 2002 and 2006. The authorities also emphasized the importance of rule-based regulation and an independent regulatory body. In 2003 the China Banking Regulatory Commission (CBRC) was separated from PBOC. The following year the National People's Congress passed the Banking Regulatory Law and revised the Commercial Bank Law.

Some observers feel that in the wake of the 2007–2008 global financial crisis, CBRC has become more powerful than PBOC in influencing some monetary variables, such as money supply.

Currently, CBRC bank regulation focuses on four ratios: capital, liquidity, loan-loss provision, and leverage. It also looks at risk controls and internal management in order to control financial risks.

From 1994 China began to implement adherence to the capital adequacy ratio requirement of the 1988 Basel Accord (Basel I). The Commercial Bank Law in 1995 explicitly stated that the capital adequacy ratio of commercial banks should not fall below 8 percent, the Basel standard at the time.

Overall, the basic method of banking supervision has improved gradually. From the initial ex post regulation, CBRC has shifted to ex ante risk detection. It has made serious efforts to improve the corporate governance of banks. In addition, CBRC pays close attention to international standards. Thus, CBRC was actively preparing implementation of Basel II when the global financial crisis struck. In the wake of the crisis, China is likely to move swiftly in implementing Basel III.

Supervision of the Security Industry

When stock exchanges in Shanghai and Shenzhen were established in the early 1990s, the Shanghai and Shenzhen municipal governments took responsibility for regulation and supervision. There were no unified national rules or policies. In this vacuum some local governments even set up their own stock exchanges (Wu 2008). These caused a brief period of chaos, as the local governments lacked the necessary experience, and often based actions with an eye on local political and economic concerns.

As a response, in 1992 the central government set up the China Securities Regulatory Commission (CSRC). It took over some regulatory responsibilities from both PBOC and local governments. In 1995 CSRC also assumed the power of nominating the top managers of the two stock exchanges. In 1998 CSRC took over the supervisory responsibilities for securities companies from PBOC. To strengthen the effectiveness and independence of supervision, CSRC started to reinforce its vertical leadership. By 1999 CSRC had 36 branches in major cities in China.

Although CSRC was useful for unifying the supervisory system, it focused more on controlling administrative approvals than on punishing irregular behavior. For instance, insider trading and market manipulation have been two very common phenomena in China. However, between 1992 and 2002, market manipulation cases accounted for only 5.5 percent of total cases penalized by CSRC; insider trading cases were a mere 2.6 percent of the total (Hu 2008).

CSRC has made tremendous strides in improving the quality of market infrastructure and the governance and accountability of listed companies. The most noticeable examples include the independent director system, mandatory information disclosure requirements, improvements in the initial public listing (IPO) selection process, and implementation of the qualified foreign institutional investor system (QFII).

CSRC has used its supervisory powers to improve the quality of security companies. Most early security companies were, explicitly or implicitly, owned by a government. Given lack of proper regulations—the same government often was the regulator—some company executives engaged in illegal behavior. In 2003 the authorities realized the industry required a comprehensive inspection and, possibly, reorganization.

Among the steps taken by CSRC to prevent companies from appropriating client deposits and assets, and more generally clean up the industry, were implementation of the "Third-Party Deposit" system and other firewalls, as well as increasing the harshness of penalties. Also, the China Securities Investor Protection Fund Corporation (SIPF) was established.

In the following three years, the authorities restructured 27 security companies through capital injection and merger. They forced 19 firms out of business and withdrew 4 companies' business licenses. By August 2007 the remaining 104 security companies all met the risk management requirements set by CSRC.

But CSRC's mission is far from accomplished. Cases of violating information disclosure and insider trading rules are still common. The stock markets still resemble a casino more than a financial market. Interventions by various levels of government are evident. Industry observers also point out the movement of CSRC officials to top manager positions at security and fund management firms. Therefore, CSRC and the industry are effectively run by the same group of professionals. And these professionals, from time to time, swap places with one another—the revolving door phenomenon that plagues regulatory bodies and legislatures throughout the world.

Supervision of the Insurance Industry

Regulation of the insurance industry was relatively easy during the early years when a number of state-owned companies dominated the sector. This is no longer the case, although the main players are still state owned. Promulgation of the Insurance Law in 1995 provided the legal foundation for regulation and supervision. The system has gradually shifted from passive to active monitoring and to risk-based, as well as compliance-based, supervision.

The China Insurance Regulatory Commission (CIRC) was established in 1998, replacing PBOC as the supervisor of the insurance industry. With the development of the insurance market, the supervisory framework adopted by CIRC evolved from concentrating only on market behavior to consisting of "three pillars": market behavior, solvency, and corporate governance structure.

Market behavior regulation focuses mainly on compliance with laws and provisions, whether interests of insured parties are compromised, and whether the behavior hinders development of the industry.

Solvency regulation is the core of insurance market supervision because it relates closely to the protection of the insured's benefits. The idea of solvency regulation was initially raised in the 1995 Insurance Law. After 2000 CIRC devised specific standards for regulation, and international practices were introduced. An insurance protection fund system was set up to safeguard against bankruptcy or liquidation.

Corporate governance structure regulation is a critical regulatory element, especially in maintaining solvency. For instance, CIRC has adopted several measures to ensure auditing independence.

Assessment of the Supervisory System

Thanks to restrictions on capital flows, China did not suffer serious damages compared with other emerging market economies. However, this does not mean China's supervisory system is sound; it still has a long way to go. The 2007–2008 global crisis has raised doubt about financial supervision systems in the advanced economies, so what path to follow is not as clear as it might be.

China's current system, with one central bank and three regulatory bodies as the core, was the product of the reforms of the two decades after 1990. So far the system is functioning well, judging from the overall stability of the financial system, although stability might also be helped by the closed capital account and state ownership of major financial institutions. But the regulatory system requires further substantial improvement because financial activities have become very complicated, and the domestic markets are becoming more open. Whether or not China continues with the existing segregated model or adopts a comprehensive model, there are important questions about boundary drawing and collaboration mechanisms among PBOC, CSRC, CIRC, and CBRC.

As China continues to open its financial markets and capital account, Chinese regulators will face a new range of issues—issues currently facing regulators in the other countries. These include:

- How to deal with the moral hazard problem of "too big to fail."
- How to control the risks of financial innovation and derivative products.
- How to devise counter-cyclical mechanisms in the capital adequacy requirement.
- How to discipline rating agency behavior.
- How to incorporate asset bubbles into monetary policy.

External Financial Liberalization

External financial liberalization—financial opening—can be defined as the removal of barriers to the flow of capital between countries (Eichengreen et al. 1999). Although conventional theory predicts that financial opening has positive effects on investment returns, economic growth, and risk diversification, the experience in many developing countries has shown that these benefits do not come automatically. Openness often coincided with an unsustainable increase in foreign debt and domestic consumption, a rash of unproductive investment, and sharp fluctuations in exchange rates, equity indexes, and asset prices (Diaz-Alejandro 1985; McKinnon and Pill 1996).

The analysis here focuses on two important aspects of financial opening: exchange rate policy and capital account controls. Compared to many other emerging market economies, Chinese policy makers have been extremely cautious in liberalizing restrictions on exchange rate and capital flows.

In 1978, as China first opened, a dual-track currency system was established: the yuan could only be used domestically, and foreigners used foreign exchange certificates. The exchange rates were set at unrealistic levels, which created a black market in currency.

In early 1994 the dual-track system was abolished. In its place, China adopted a managed float. However, currency appreciation, especially in terms of the real effective exchange rate, has remained limited, as the government worried about exports, jobs, and GDP growth. Most assessments suggest that the yuan has continued to be significantly undervalued, evidenced by large current account surpluses, rapid accumulation of foreign exchange reserves, and strong growth performance. The gradual appreciation approach adopted by the government sometimes causes massive speculative inflows and tensions with trading partners.

Despite steady liberalization, China is the globally most important economy without capital-account convertibility. With an increasingly open economy, the effectiveness of the controls undoubtedly has declined over time. This is unfortunate to the extent declining effectiveness has generated disturbances in domestic financial markets, as well as caused loss of monetary policy independence. These consequences are evidenced by massive liquidity and high inflation. However much controls helped maintain domestic financial stability in the past, the remaining controls are becoming a source of instability.

Exchange Rate Policy

When economic reforms began in 1978, the yuan was officially valued at 1.5 per dollar. However, the government estimated it cost at least 2.5 yuan to make $1 in export revenue. So, to encourage exports, it set an internal settlement rate of 2.5 yuan/dollar alongside the official rate.

In the following 15 years, there were different forms of a dual-track system, with an official rate and a secondary (black market) rate. Both rates depreciated sharply. Between 1988 and 1993, a new dual exchange rate system emerged, whereby the official fixed exchange rate coexisted with a market-determined rate in special foreign exchange markets called swap centers.

At the beginning of 1994, the authorities unified the dual rates at 8.7 yuan/dollar. At the same time, exchange rate policy was officially changed to a managed float. The nominal yuan to dollar exchange rate appreciated to 8.3 per dollar—about 5 percent—between the beginning of 1994 and 1997 when the Asian financial crisis was at its worst. To prevent further contagion of the crisis and help preserve economic and financial stability in Asia, China announced that the yuan would be kept stable around 8.28 per dollar, thereby effectively abandoning managed float.

Soon after the end of the crisis, China faced WTO accession and the sluggish global economic growth that followed the 9–11 attack. Concerned about exports, jobs, and economic growth, China continued with a stable exchange rate of 8.28 yuan/dollar.

Over the years there were increasing calls for the yuan to appreciate. Continued strong economic growth, large current account surpluses, and rapid accumulation of foreign reserves all supported the assessment of an undervalued currency. It also became a contentious issue in China's economic relations with the United States and Europe.

On July 21, 2005, PBOC announced three important changes to exchange rate policy. First, the yuan was immediately revalued by 2.1 percent against the US dollar. Second, the exchange rate regime returned to a managed float. And, third, the reference for policy shifted from the US dollar to a basket of currencies. This new basket included the currencies of China's other major trading partners, primarily the euro, Japanese yen, and South Korean won, with smaller representation of the Singaporean dollar, British pound, Malaysian Ringgit, Russian ruble, Australian dollar, Thai baht, and Canadian dollar.

In the following three years, the yuan appreciated 22 percent against the US dollar—about 16 percent in real effective exchange rate terms. In mid-2008 the world economy was seriously hit by the subprime crisis, leading PBOC to narrow the yuan trading band. But, on June 19, 2010, it announced increased exchange rate flexibility.

In retrospect, exchange rate policy during the reform period can be divided into two subperiods. Pre-1994 policy can be summarized as steady devaluation, often accompanied by faster movement in the secondary market rate. Post-1994 policy was basically a managed float, with disruptions during the Asian and global financial crises. The trend has generally been an appreciation, although the pace has remained cautious. Therefore, pressure for appreciation, and associated hot money inflows and large external surpluses, have persisted.

Over the years market supply and demand started to play increasing roles in exchange rate determination, with a steady reduction in restrictions on cross-border transactions and holding of foreign exchange. Meanwhile the foreign exchange market mechanism has improved. Before 1994 one exchange rate was determined by the authorities, another by the swap market. Now a unified rate within a band set by the authorities is determined in the interbank foreign exchange market through OTC transactions supported by market makers. Figure 2.11 shows exchange rates.

Despite repeated vows to adopt managed float and to increase flexibility, rate movements have remained quite limited. Between July 2005 and May 2011, the yuan appreciated from 8.28 to 6.50 yuan/dollar. During the same period, the real effective exchange rate strengthened 20 percent. This is clearly much less than China's main trading partners have been expecting since China joined the WTO in December

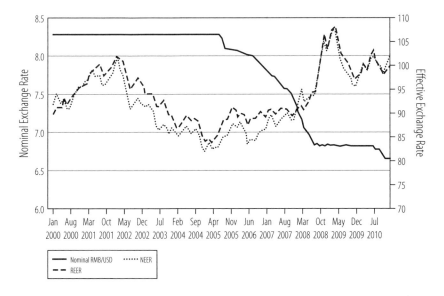

Figure 2.11 RMB per US Dollar, 2000–2010. *Source*: CEIC China Premium Database. (CEIC China Premium Database is an electronic economic time-series database, focused exclusively on the Chinese market that contains historical data back to 1949. The provider is part of ISI Emerging Markets, which is part of Euromoney Institutional Investor plc, an international publishing, events, and electronic information group.)

Note: The effective rates are indicated on the right axis by an index based to Jan 2000 = 100. REER = real effective exchange rate. NEER = nominal effective exchange rate.

2001. It is now a major source of economic policy conflict between China and the other major economies, especially the United States and European Union. Table 2.11 shows the growth of China's foreign exchange reserves and the role trade has played.

APPRECIATING THE YUAN   Given China's strong economic growth, massive current account surpluses, huge foreign exchange reserves, and large short-term capital inflows, the yuan is undervalued, whatever the method applied. However, the extent of undervaluation is contested, with estimates ranging from 5 percent to 50 percent (Goldstein and Lardy 2008). Most Chinese officials and scholars agree, at least implicitly, that the yuan needs to appreciate to reduce distortions in the economy. There are two ways an appreciation can take place: a one-step adjustment or a gradual appreciation.

TABLE 2.11

Chinese Foreign Exchange Reserves and Trade Balance, 1992–2010

Year	Foreign Exchange Reserves (FER)			Trade Balance[a]	
	Billion $	Absolute Change	Percent Change	Billion $	Percent of Change in FER
1992	19.4	—	—	4.35	—
1995	73.6	—	—	16.7	—
2000	165.6	—	—	24.1	—
2001	212.2	46.6	28.1	22.6	9.1
2002	286.1	73.9	34.8	30.4	12
2003	403.3	117.2	41.0	25.5	10
2004	609.9	206.6	51.2	32.1	13
2005	818.9	209.0	34.3	102.0	41
2006	1066.3	247.4	30.2	177.5	72
2007	1528.2	461.9	43.3	261.8	57
2008	1946.0	417.8	27.3	298.1	71
2009	2399.2	453.2	23.3	195.7	43
2010	2847.3	448.1	18.7	183.1	41

Sources: Foreign Exchange Reserves: State Administration of Foreign Exchange (SAFE) http://www.safe.gov.cn/model_safe_en/index.jsp?id=6; Trade Balance: PRC National Bureau of Statistics as reported at https://www.uschina.org/statistics/tradetable.html for 2001–2010; and China's Customs Statistics as reported at https://www.uschina.org/statistics/tradetable.html for years before 2000. The authors thank James Lee for assistance in constructing this table.

[a] Trade Balance: Exports reported on a free-on-board (FOB) basis; imports on a cost, insurance, and freight (CIF) basis.

A one-step adjustment is probably more efficient, but it is very hard to determine the right step. If the step is not big enough, pressure for appreciation would continue, if not escalate. If the step is too big, it could have serious negative effects on the real economy. More importantly, the ultimate goal of exchange rate reform is to establish a market demand-supply mechanism for determining the exchange rate. The one-step approach does not help with that objective.

Some senior leaders often argue that rapid appreciation would likely lead to a weaker export sector, fewer job opportunities, slower economic growth, and unstable social and political conditions. Thus, in both early 2005 and early 2010, there were warnings that appreciation by more than 3 percent a year could lead to devastating economic consequences within China. However, such pessimism is unwarranted. Between mid-2005 and mid-2008, the yuan appreciated against the dollar by an average of 7 percent a year. Yet, during those years, exports continued to expand rapidly, the job market was strong, and GDP growth stayed robust.

The experience of China and other developing countries suggests that economic activity can be resilient even in the face of exchange rate volatility. More importantly for China, if the yuan's peg to the dollar provided some anchor in the past, it now is more likely to bring more uncertainty and instability (Obstfeld 2006). Indeed, when China allowed only narrow bands, or when the currency appreciated gradually, hot money inflows increased significantly, encouraged by the market's expectation for further appreciation.

Perhaps it is time for Chinese policy makers to reconsider their strategy. For years the government has vowed to let market demand and supply determine the exchange rate. It also has hoped to encourage two-way fluctuations. These, however, have not happened. Rates are still controlled, and expectations for exchange rate movement remain one-directional.

The central bank still heavily intervenes in foreign exchange markets, evidenced by the continued growth of foreign reserves. And despite the announced use of a basket of currency, the central bank clearly still manages the exchange rate around the US dollar.

Capital Account Controls

China's capital account liberalization lags reforms in most other economic areas. Still, restrictions on cross-border capital flows have declined steadily.

In December 1996 the PBOC announced yuan convertibility under the current account. The original plan was to take another 5 to 10 years to completely liberalize the capital account. Unfortunately, that plan has been repeatedly delayed. Successive reasons have been the Asian financial crisis of 1997–1998, the 9–11 terrorist attack, severe acute respiratory syndrome (SARS) in Beijing and Hong Kong (2003), and so on.

During the global crisis that began in 2007, the Chinese economy has performed much better than the rest of the world. This has been at least in part because of capital account controls, which helped shield the domestic economy from external shocks. However, by 2009 as developed-country economic stagnation and deflation became a focus of attention, capital account liberalization became a hot topic again.

Subsequently, China has advocated including the yuan in the IMF's SDR basket and pushed plans to develop Shanghai into an international financial center. Neither of these is possible without a freely convertible yuan and an open capital account.

EVOLUTION OF CAPITAL CONTROLS When China started economic reform in the late 1970s, China's capital account was tightly controlled. Tight controls were imposed directly on cross-border transactions. In fact, there were almost no cross-border capital flows. And, through the State Administration of Foreign Exchange (SAFE), there were controls on certain aspects of foreign exchange transactions related to transactions such as remittances and repatriation of earnings.

As reform has progressed, the government has loosened controls, following the general strategy of "long term first, short term later; inflow first, outflow later; equity investment first, portfolio investment later."

Inward foreign direct investment (FDI) has experienced the most complete liberalization. FDI inflows started in the early 1980s when investors from Hong Kong, Korea, and Taiwan moved textile and clothing factories to the Pearl River delta. The Chinese government enthusiastically welcomed them. In fact, many local governments competed to attract FDI by offering preferential policy treatment, including reduced land use fees, discounted lending rates, and tax holidays. From the mid-1990s there was no longer any policy restriction on FDI other than the usual industry policy. During the first three decades of economic reform, China attracted more than $1 trillion in FDI (see table 2.12).

Liberalization of capital flows accelerated in the wake of China's WTO entry in December 2001. In addition to tariff cuts, China promised to eliminate, over the following five years, most restrictions on foreign entry and ownership. This meant the financial sector was to be opened to foreign competition. As an example of how this was implemented, foreign banks initially were allowed to engage in yuan business only in Shanghai, and then Shenzhen was added. Within five years, all geographical restrictions on foreign banks had been removed.

The authorities have also encouraged Chinese companies to raise funds from international capital markets through public listing, with

TABLE 2.12
Utilized Foreign Direct Investment, 1991–2010 (in billion dollars)

Year	Amount	Year	Amount	Year	Amount
1991	4.4	1998	45.5	2005	60.3
1992	11.0	1999	40.4	2006	63.0
1993	27.5	2000	42.1	2007	74.8
1994	33.8	2001	48.8	2008	92.2
1995	37.5	2002	55.0	2009	90.0
1996	41.7	2003	53.5	2010	105.7
1997	45.3	2004	60.6		

Source: CEIC.

Note: Utilized FDI refers to investment actually made, as distinguished from "contracted FDI," which are (often conditional) commitments that may take place over a period of years.

the first H-share (Hong Kong) listing in 1993. By 1997 Chinese-related companies were trading in New York, London, and Singapore. Overseas IPOs reduced the demand for B shares, which are settled in US dollars or Hong Kong dollars but denominated in yuan and traded domestically. In 2001 the regulators allowed domestic residents to open B-share accounts using their legal holdings of foreign exchange.

REMAINING CAPITAL CONTROLS Capital account controls remain in three broad areas. There are restrictions on both foreign and domestic investors, external borrowing, and direct investment.

Restrictions on foreign and domestic investors: in opening the securities market to foreigners, the government is pursuing a strategy of "fragmenting the market with separate investors." This means foreign investors may only buy shares and debt instruments denominated in a foreign currency. Further, Chinese residents are largely prohibited from buying, selling, or issuing capital or money market instruments in overseas markets.

Restrictions on external borrowing: although foreign-funded enterprises are free from any restrictions on raising short- or long-term debt in overseas markets, other domestic entities need to obtain approval from the relevant authorities as to the proposed borrowing amount and terms. This includes review and approval by SAFE. In addition, domestic financial institutions can only make external loans in line with the rules on foreign exchange liability/asset ratio management, and with prior approval by the relevant authorities. Domestic nonfinancial enterprises are strictly prohibited from extending any external loans.

Restrictions on direct investment: foreign direct investment is required to follow industrial policy guidance given by the government. Otherwise, there are no formal restrictions. Outward direct investment by domestic entities needs to be approved by the relevant government departments. Further, the necessary foreign exchange sources, and the associated risks of such outward direct investment, need to be assessed and verified by SAFE.

Capital Control Effectiveness

Here we review three methods to gauge the effectiveness of capital account controls. The first is a capital account control index (CACI). However, it provides only a legal measure of capital account controls. It is common in emerging market economies for this to differ significantly from actual controls. Therefore we also apply two other methods. One is a calculation of cross-border short-term capital flows, as these are subject to the most severe policy restrictions. The other is covered interest rate parity (CIRP).

CAPITAL ACCOUNT CONTROL INDEX   To quantify capital account controls, especially changes over time, Gou et al. (2011) constructed a capital account control index (CACI) for China. They plowed through some 144 policy documents issued by the State Administration of Foreign Exchange (SAFE) between 1977 and 2010 to trace the historical evolution of the controls.

The index divides transactions into 11 categories. These are capital market securities; money market instruments; collective investment securities; derivatives and other instruments; commercial and financial credits; guarantees, sureties, and financial backup facilities; outward direct investment; foreign (inward) direct investment; liquidation of direct investment; real estate transactions; and personal capital movement.

These are somewhat different from the 11 categories usually referred to in the literature. Thus, following Jin (2004), they combined commercial credit and financial credit into one category, but split foreign direct investment and outward direct investment into separate categories, given their different policy frameworks in China.

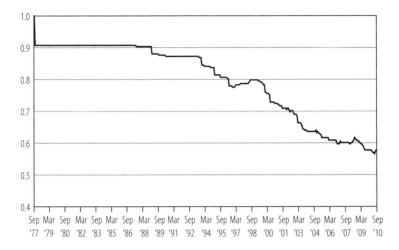

Figure 2.12 The Capital Account Control Index (CACI), 1977–2010. *Source*: State Administration of Foreign Exchange; CEIC China Premium Database.

Note: Computed using a methodology established by Gou et al. (2011).

Each category was given a value of 3 for the years before 1978, meaning strict control. For subsequent periods, a 2 was given for heavy control, 1 for light control, and 0 for liberalized. They assigned equal weight to the seven major categories. The final CACI is normalized to be in the range 0 to 1.

As shown in figure 2.12, CACI indicates liberalization since the late 1980s. Starting at 1 in 1977, suggesting almost complete controls, the index almost immediately dropped to 0.88 when the government loosened controls on commercial and financial credits, foreign direct investment, and liquidation of direct investment. Exchange rate policy reform in 1994, realization of current account convertibility in late 1996, and WTO accession in December 2001 all contributed to further decline. The 1997–1998 Asian and 2007–2008 global financial crises caused brief upticks. In 2010 CACI stood at 0.5.

RESIDUAL METHOD Gou et al. (2011), as a second approach, used an indirect method, also known as the residual method, to estimate short-term capital flows. They essentially subtracted three things—trade surplus, net FDI inflows, and net incremental debt—from funds

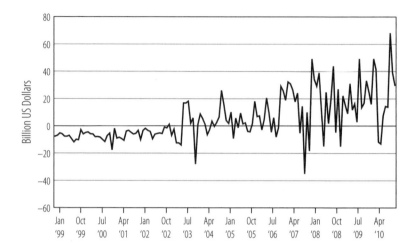

Figure 2.13 Short-Term Capital Flows: 1999–2010 (US$ billion). *Source*: State Administration of Foreign Exchange, Ministry of Commerce of PRC, Wind Info, and authors' calculation.

Note: A net figure is a capital outflow. Computed using a methodology established by Gou et al. (2011).

outstanding for foreign exchange, and added estimates of false reports in trade (over-invoiced exports and underreported imports). The only tricky item is the hot money related to false reports of trade.

As shown in figure 2.13, by their results, China generally had net short-term outflows until 2003–2004. Subsequently, both volatility and the volume of flows have increased significantly, with the suggestion of inflows being in a rising trend since late 2007. The data may be taken as evidence of either loosening capital controls or declining effectiveness. Large, volatile short-term flows probably have made PBOC's monetary policy making much more difficult.

Gou and her coauthor looked at the effectiveness of controls by regressing short-term flows on CACI. The results suggest controls did have an important effect on flows during the past decade. The estimation results, however, did not reveal whether the restrictions were completely or only partially effective.

COVERED INTEREST RATE PARITY A third approach for examining the effectiveness of capital account controls is covered interest rate parity (CIRP). CIRP is the condition where an investor cannot make a positive return by borrowing the home or base currency to invest the commensurate amount in a foreign currency on a covered basis. That is, CIRP posits that under perfect capital movement, onshore and offshore yields are equal. In short, there are no profitable arbitrage possibilities. Note that the proposition contains a number of very strong assumptions.

To avoid some of the problems with standard CIPR analysis, Huang and Wang (2010b) looked at the long-run and short-run relationships between domestic and foreign asset prices. If capital controls are partially ineffective, arbitrage is possible. If there exists a stable equilibrium in the long run between the offshore rate and the onshore rate, then one can conclude that the capital controls are ineffective in the long run. And, if changes in one yield lead to changes in the other, then capital controls are at least partially ineffective in the short run.

Huang and Wang assembled daily data for interbank rates (Chibor, Shibor) and PBOC bill rates as proxies for domestic onshore yields. They then used US dollar Libor and treasury bond rates to calculate offshore yields that ensure the establishment of covered interest rate parity. Having conducted the unit root test, they used a co-integration test to explore the long-run equilibrium relationship between onshore and offshore yield. Based on a vector error correction model, they used the Granger Causality test to explore the short-run dynamics between the two rates (see table 2.13).

They found a co-integration relationship between onshore yield and offshore yield. This implies that the arbitrage mechanism squeezes out the profitable opportunities in the long run, and speculative capital

TABLE 2.13
Estimation Results from Covered Interest Rate Parity

	Offshore	Onshore	Frequency	Long Run	Short Run
1	Libor	Chibor	Daily	Yes	No
2	Libor	Shibor	Daily	Yes	Yes
3	Libor	Chibor	Monthly	Yes	No
4	US Treasury	PBC Bill rate	Monthly	Yes	Yes

Source: Huang and Wang (2010b).

Note: The offshore yields or rates were adjusted for exchange risk.

movement makes capital controls at least partially ineffective. In the short run, it was found that Shibor as the proxy of domestic onshore yield Grangerly causes the offshore yield.

The Role of Financial Repression

Financial repression in China in the early 2010s is probably much broader and more extensive than in most other emerging market economies. Despite more than three decades of successful reform, the economy still exhibits all the typical features of repressive financial policies. First, PBOC still sets base interest rates for commercial banks and intervenes heavily in foreign exchange markets. Second, the state influences allocation of capital, with the majority of funds raised still going to state-owned enterprises. Third, PBOC frequently adjusts the reserve requirement ratio for commercial banks, with the ratio exceeding 20 percent at end 2011. And, fourth, the authorities still maintain strict capital account controls, especially over portfolio investment, debt financing, personal investment, and overseas direct investment.

But this has not stopped rapid financial development. The financial sector has grown from a mono-bank system in the late 1970s to a very comprehensive system, with all types of institutions, clients, markets, and assets. Many Chinese commercial banks are among the world's top 10 ranked by market capitalization.

Still, the financial system is heavily tilted toward the banking system. Total bank deposits accounted for 190 percent of GDP at end 2011. Stock market capitalization was 80 percent of GDP, whereas bond market capitalization was only 40 percent.

Financial repression has not prevented China from being the most dynamic emerging market economy, with average annual GDP growth of 10 percent. Moreover, with the exception of only a few years, macroeconomic conditions during the reform period have been very stable, with CPI inflation staying mostly around 3 percent.

Changes in the Financial Sector

Changes in China's financial sector can be classified into four types: construction of a financial framework; promotion of quantitative financial development; reform of the governance structure of financial institutions and a change in their behavior; and liberalization of the financial industry and markets.

As China decided to move toward a market economy, development of a suitable framework—a modern financial industry—became necessary. For instance, in the mid-1980s the authorities made serious efforts to make PBOC a true central bank. They reconstructed the objectives and tools for monetary policy. They created many new financial institutions such as large and small banks, insurance companies, and security firms. In the 1990s the government developed stock exchanges in Shanghai and Shenzhen and an interbank money market. Clearly, when policy makers took these actions, they had the financial systems in advanced market economies in mind as models.

The promotion of quantitative financial development is reflected in phenomena such as the rising proportion of broad money supply (M2) to GDP, the growth of total outstanding loans and total banking assets, and the growing importance of capital markets in total financing. On the other hand, intermediation still relies disproportionately on the banking sector.

Reform of the governance structure of financial institutions and a change in their behavior has been an ongoing process. A typical example is bank ownership reform. After a large and comprehensive banking industry was built in the mid-1990s, China faced serious challenges regarding financial risks because many banks did not allocate funds efficiently or control risks effectively. In part this was backward banking practice. But more importantly, it was related to the nature of state ownership of most banks. From the beginning of the twenty-first century, the authorities started to change the governance structure of banks. This has been done through the introduction of foreign strategic investors and public listing on stock markets. Today most major Chinese banks are listed on domestic or overseas stock markets and have a relatively diversified ownership structure. Most financial institutions also have independent directors, as well as better accounting systems, risk control mechanisms, and information disclosure practices.

Liberalization of the financial industry and markets can refer to many things. One aspect is increases in market competition. Another is freeing prices in financial markets. And, finally, there is lifting controls over domestic markets and the capital account. China has made significant strides in all three of these. Thus, during the reform period, the market share of state-owned commercial banks has declined from above 80 percent to close to 50 percent. The government has abandoned most restrictions on interest rates (although the regulation of commercial bank deposit and lending rates continues). And, from the early years of reform, the authorities have opened channels for cross-border capital flows in areas related to inward direct investment.

China has made remarkable progress in putting into place the basic framework of a financial system and growing the size of financial assets. The system now resembles the financial sectors of advanced economies. But important quality differences remain. China lags significantly in freeing key financial market prices, especially interest rates and exchange rates. Although it has made important improvement in the behavior of financial institutions and allocation of financial resources, most commercial banks still behave more like state-owned enterprises than listed companies. A simple characterization may be that the Chinese government has made serious efforts to build a modern financial sector but was not willing to give up all the controls.

The Logic of China's Financial Reforms

Why did reform show a pattern of being strong on framework and quantity but weak on price and quality? We seek to explain the logic of China's financial reform by applying the framework identified by Huang in a series of Chinese-language studies on asymmetric liberalization of product and factor markets (Huang 2010a and 2010b).

Huang noticed that since China's reforms began, product markets have been almost completely liberalized, with prices freely determined by demand and supply. But factor market distortions have remained widespread and serious. For instance, the government still intervenes in the prices of important energy products. It also influences key interest rates and exchange rates. Some of these distortions are legacies of the central planning system, and others were introduced during the reform period.

Such distortions have a common feature: they lower production costs by repressing factor prices. For instance, when international crude prices were at their peak around $150 per barrel in mid-2008, the domestic equivalent price was about $80. And real deposit rates frequently have been negative. Such distortions are subsidies to producers, exporters, and investors. They raise profits of production, returns to investment, and the competitiveness of Chinese exports. They promote economic growth but also cause serious internal and external imbalances (Huang and Tao 2010; Huang and Wang 2010a).

Huang and his collaborators argue that the main rationale behind the asymmetric liberalization approach was the government's objective of achieving the fastest possible economic growth. In a typical market economy, the government's main function is to provide public goods such as social and legal protection. In China, however, promoting economic growth is a top government priority. Deng Xiaoping in 1992 said that development is the absolute principle.

Economists have found that GDP growth was the single most important economic indicator determining local officials' chances of promotion (Li and Zhou 2005). This is, perhaps, why mayors in China act more like corporate CEOs than heads of local governments. And the Chinese government is sometimes described as a production- or development-oriented government. Therefore, given its policy objective, asymmetric liberalization is a rational choice for the government.

Factor price distortion has been used before by China to support growth—more specifically, urban industrialization. In the mid-1950s the government devised the "unified purchase and marketing system" for agricultural products. It bought food from farmers and sold it to urban residents, both at below-market prices. This enabled urban industry to generate extraordinary profits, which were reinvested (Song 1994).

From the beginning of economic reform, policy makers have recognized the importance of finance for growth. Therefore, the government immediately got on with the task of building a modern financial system, which it had to do from scratch. This resulted in rapid growth of financial infrastructure and financial assets. Rapid financial development is consistent with the general style of market-oriented reform (Lin et al. 1995; Sachs and Woo 2000).

Policy makers probably also understood the benefits of financial liberalization, highlighted in the oft-cited analyses by McKinnon, Shaw, and others. Therefore, the government continuously expanded the roles of the market mechanism in the financial system. It introduced joint-stock and foreign banks to promote competition. It gradually allowed market-determined interbank market rates and treasury bond yields, and increased flexibility in exchange rates. It even slowly reduced restrictions on certain types of cross-border capital flows, especially inward foreign direct investment.

But government continues to play an important role in the operation of the financial system, such as controls of interest rates and exchange rates, interventions in capital allocation, and restrictions on cross-border capital flows.

Reasons for Financial Repression

Why did the government choose to retain substantial financial repression instead of implement full liberalization during the reform period?

First, repressive financial policies were consistent with the general asymmetric liberalization approach of supporting growth through repressed factor costs. Specifically, depressed interest rates and exchange rates are like subsidies to investors and exporters and, therefore, are favorable for boosting investment and exports (Huang 2010a, 2010b). An undervalued currency promotes exports and discourages imports. This was particularly true during the years following the 2007–2008 Asian financial crises, as the government pursued both strong economic growth and large current account surpluses. Similarly, very low real interest rates encouraged investment, which has contributed to the very high share of investment in GDP.

Second, repressive policies allowed the government to use the financial sector as a major means supporting economic policy. During the global financial crisis, for instance, the government adopted a 4 trillion yuan stimulus package to boost growth. At the same time, it mobilized massive bank loans, which would not have been possible without the majority-ownership stakes the government had in many financial institutions. Similarly, in the late 1990s, the government had called on banks to support its "go west" policy of developing interior areas of the country.

Third, repressive policies can reinforce each other. Thus, some form of administrative capital allocation is necessary when interest rates are kept below market levels, as there is an excess demand for funds. This means continuing repressive policies has been necessary for the gradual, "dual-track" reform approach China has adopted (Naughton 1995). A key feature of Chinese reform has been to let economic activities grow outside the planning system, without initially hurting the planned economy (Fan 1994). This implies the government needed to continuously support state-owned enterprises (SOEs), even if they were not profitable. During the 1990s, many banks provided "stability loans" (policy loans) to failing SOEs. Eventually the government had to abandon this practice due to the burden it placed on the banking system. But the initial support, which was made possible under repressive policy, was critical for ensuring the smooth progress of economic reforms.

Fourth, repressive financial policies might be critical for maintaining financial stability during early stages of economic development. The general prediction that a fully liberalized financial system promotes efficiency and growth is dependent on a number of important assumptions, such as perfect competition and complete information. It is argued (for example, by Hellman et al. 1997; Stiglitz 1994, 2000), that when these assumptions are not satisfied, it probably is easier for the government to deal with problems of market failure and financial instability. China's own experiences provide some support for this argument. China would probably have suffered a major banking crisis during the Asian financial crisis, and a recession during the 2008–2009 global financial crisis, had there not been majority state ownership of the major commercial banks and a still relatively tightly controlled capital account.

The Effects of Financial Repression on Growth

Our earlier review of the literature suggests that economists are divided on the effects financial repression has on economic performance. In theoretical work, McKinnon (1973) concluded the effects are negative, whereas Stiglitz (1994) suggested possible positive effects under some circumstances. In empirical analyses, Ang and McKibbin (2007) found a negative impact for Malaysia, and Arestis and Demetriades (1997) found a positive impact for Korea.

Judging from the performance of the Chinese economy, we may tentatively argue that financial repression did not exert serious damages. But it is not clear if the Chinese experiences support the "McKinnon camp" or the "Stiglitz camp." There are several possible explanations for the combination of widespread repressive financial policies and strong macroeconomic performance in China:

- The comprehensive economic reforms unlocked such strong growth momentum that it dominated any effects of financial repression.

- The government allocated capital effectively under repressive policies.
- Financial repression actually raised the growth rate because it enabled the government to better deal with problems of market failure and financial instability.
- The degree of financial repression declined steadily during the reform period, which generated positive growth momentum.

It is very difficult to determine the relative importance of each of these effects.

Aggregate Financial Repression Index

This section provides a measure of the effects of financial repression on China's growth. We report our analyses in two steps. First, we construct an aggregate financial repression index (FREP). This should provide a picture of how repressive financial policies evolved during the reform period. Second, we analyze the exact impact of FREP on economic growth. In particular, we are interested to know if this impact varied over time. (This section draws on Huang and Wang [2010a] and Wang [2011].)

An aggregate measure of financial repression covers a list of policy variables. Thus, in empirical studies, different economists might use different approaches to measure financial repression. The easiest indicator is negative real interest rates (see, for instance, Roubini and Sala-i-Martin 1992; Lardy 2008). Others use a simple or weighted average of the policy variables. Here we follow Ang and McKibbin (2007) by applying the principal component analysis (PCA) approach, which was originally adopted by Demetriades and Luintel (1998; 2001). The advantage of PCA is that it deals with problems of both multicollinearity and over-parameterization.

We adopt a relatively broad definition of financial repression. There are indicators for six areas: negative real interest rate; interest rate controls; capital account regulations; reserve requirement ratio (RRR); lending by state-owned commercial banks (SOCBs); and state-owned enterprises' (SOEs) share of outstanding loans.

We calculate the real interest rate (RID) by subtracting CPI from the base deposit rate. Following Agarwala (1983) and Roubini and Sala-i-Martin (1992), we set RID to 0 if the real interest rate is positive, to

0.5 if it is negative but higher than minus 5 percent, and to 1 if lower than minus 5 percent. Thus, a higher index indicates a greater degree of repression.

Interest rate control (ICI) is the proportion of the total number of types of interest rates subject to government controls. At the start of the reform, there were 63 types of interest rates under controls. Of the total, 47 were domestic currency interest rates (14 deposit rates, 14 lending rates, 19 preferred lending rates) and 16 were foreign currency interest rates (10 deposit rates and 6 lending rates). Taking domestic and foreign currency rates together, there were 24 deposit rates and 39 lending rates.

Each category is set to 1 if there was control and to 0 otherwise. Because foreign currency rates are relatively less significant, we assign them only half the weight of local currency rates. As a result, the total calculated number of types of interest rates is 55.

The indicator capital account control (CACI) has been described previously.

The reserve requirement ratio (RRR) is set by PBOC. However, there was no reserve requirement policy before 1984. So, for years before 1984, we set the RRR equal to the ratio of the deposits held by PBOC as a commercial bank that it could not dispense by itself, such as fiscal deposits, basic construction deposits, and the deposits of non-profit institutions.

The share of the big four state-owned commercial banks and three policy banks (SBL) in total outstanding loans and the share of SOEs in total outstanding loans (SSL) reveal the importance of the state sector in loan allocation from the lender and the borrower sides.

Principal component analysis (PCA) derives common statistical components from all six variables to compute an aggregate index. This avoids the usual issues of multicolinearity among different variables and double counting of the key components. It involves three steps. First, we apply various statistical tests to determine the appropriateness of PCA for the sample. Next, by examining the total variance explained by principal components, we decide the number of principal components that should be extracted. Third, we set the formula according to the results on total variance explained in order to compute the aggregate FREP. The technical procedures and results are explained in detail in Huang and Wang (2011) and Wang (2011). Results are in Figure 2.14. FREP has generally trended down during the reform period. The

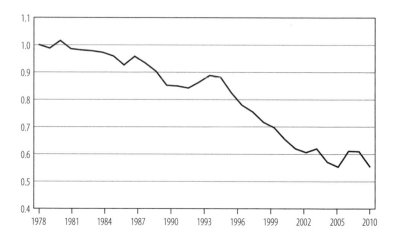

Figure 2.14 Financial Repression Index, 1978–2008 (1978 = 1.0). *Source*: Huang and Wang (2010a) and Wang (2011).

Note: According to the derived raw data series, –7.4 represents the state of no financial repression. However, to make the results easier to read, we have normalized the FREP series by setting the reading for a completely liberalized financial system to 0 and setting the start of the sample period (1978) to 1.

lowest reading, 0.516, was in 2006. The index rebounded in the following years, probably a result of responses to the global financial crisis.

FREP reveals at least two important results: (1) the reform period has witnessed a significant reduction in financial repression; and (2) financial liberalization had been less than half achieved at the end of 2008.

Quantifying the Effects

To examine the exact impact of financial repression on economic growth during the reform period, we ran several regressions of real GDP growth on FREP and a group of control variables: $RGDP_i = \alpha + \beta FREP_i + \Sigma_i \gamma X + \varepsilon_i$, where $PGDP_i$ is the real GDP growth rate, $FREP_i$ is the financial repression index, and X_i is a set of control variables. The control variables are investment share of GDP (inv_i), share of college students in total population (edu_i), trade openness ($trade_i$), government expenditure as share of GDP (gov_i), and share of SOEs in GDP ($state_i$). We use a provincial panel data set for the years between 1978 and 2008 (for details of the data set, see Huang and Wang 2010a).

TABLE 2.14
Estimation Results: Impact of Financial Repression on Economic Growth

	Full Sample	1979–1989	1990–1999	2000–2008
FREP	0.167***	0.787***	0.313***	−0.132***
	(0.041)	(0.132)	(0.073)	(0.037)
INV	0.133***	0.068	0.191***	0.100***
	(0.022)	(0.069)	(0.047)	(0.021)
TRADE	0.010	0.025	0.010	0.007
	(0.008)	(0.034)	(0.014)	(0.012)
EDU	2.361	1.934	0.561	0.438
	(0.539)	(6.445)	(0.627)	(0.745)
GOV	−0.189***	−0.225	−0.518***	−0.169**
	(0.055)	(0.141)	(0.191)	(0.083)
SOE	−0.039*	−0.048***	−0.119***	−0.039*
	(0.020)	(0.011)	(0.031)	(0.023)
Time trend	0.002***	0.008***	0.003***	0.002
	(0.0008)	(0.002)	(0.002)	(0.014)
Year-specific effect	YES	YES	YES	YES
Province-specific effect	YES	YES	YES	YES
Observations	750	275	250	225
R^2	0.179	0.138	0.326	0.187

Sources: Huang and Wang (2011) and Wang (2011).

Note: Year-specific effect refers to certain years when there were special events such as the Asian financial crisis and the global financial crisis. Numbers in parentheses beneath the coefficient estimates are related standard errors; * indicates statistical significance at the 10% level, ** at 5%, and *** at 1%.

THE RESULTS Here we report the results of four regressions: the entire period 1979–2008, and three subperiods, 1979–1988, 1989–1998, and 1999–2008 (see table 2.14).

Surprisingly, the coefficient estimate for FREP is positive in the regression covering the entire period 1979–2008. The estimation results for the three subperiods are even more interesting. Although the growth impact of financial repression was found positive in the 1980s and the 1990s, it turned negative during the first decade of the twenty-first century. Specifically, if there had been full liberalization (FREP = 0), real GDP growth would have been reduced by 0.79 percentage points in the 1979–1989 period and by 0.31 percentage points in the 1990–1999 period. But growth would have been increased by 0.13 percentage points in the 2000–2008 period.

This provides important support for the Stiglitz thesis. In the early stages of development, financial markets often are underdeveloped and might not be able to channel savings to investments effectively. Also, financial institutions often are immature and vulnerable to fluctuations in capital flows and investor confidence. Therefore, state intervention through repressive financial policies can actually support financial stability and promote economic growth.

At the same time, the results for the most recent period suggest that repressive policies now lower economic growth. This is consistent with the McKinnon thesis. State intervention in capital allocation, for instance, might prevent funds from flowing to the most efficient uses. Protection of financial institutions and financial markets might encourage excessive risk taking due to the typical moral hazard problem, without the benefits of free market discipline. Therefore, repressive financial policies would eventually slow financial development, increase financial risks, lower investment efficiency, and reduce economic growth.

Bridging the McKinnon and Stiglitz Theses

The Chinese experience of financial reform offers a bridge between the McKinnon thesis and the Stiglitz thesis. Repressive financial policies can have both positive and negative effects on macroeconomic performance. The net impact depends on the relative importance of the various effects. In the early stages of development, when financial markets are underdeveloped, financial repression might help mobilize resources, support financial stability, and, therefore, support economic growth. As the financial system matures, financial repression is more likely to reduce capital efficiency, increase financial risks, and, therefore, slow economic growth.

We should not take the Chinese experience as evidence that financial repression definitely raises economic growth. The effects of financial repression on economic growth are always combinations of the McKinnon effect and the Stiglitz effect. Which dominates during a particular period depends on many factors. For instance, the positive impact on economic growth during the early stage of Chinese reform probably is because of the government's effective allocation of capital and its capability of controlling financial risks. Otherwise, financial repression might still have been a negative factor for growth.

Completing the Unfinished Revolution

As the twenty-first century progresses, there are increasing signs in the Chinese economy that repressive financial policies are causing a range of financial and economic problems. These include growing financial and fiscal risks, inefficient capital allocation, worsening economic imbalances, and loss of monetary policy independence. Continuation of these problems could potentially derail China's macroeconomic performance. In addition, the repressive policies have become obstacles for other government policy objectives such as internationalizing the currency and developing Shanghai into an international financial center before 2020. Therefore, China should now seriously contemplate its task of completing financial liberalization. Indeed, in September 2012 PBOC unveiled the financial 12th Five-Year Program (2011–2015) focusing on liberalization of interest rates and exchange rates, reform of financial institutions, improvement of foreign reserve management, and promotion of capital account convertibility.

It is possible to organize the remaining reform tasks around capital account liberalization. Achieving capital account convertibility has a number of prerequisites, including strong macroeconomic performance, healthy fiscal and financial systems, a prudent financial regulatory framework, and strong external accounts.

We think that China already possesses favorable conditions in most of these areas. But the government still needs to establish market-based interest rates, introduce free-floating exchange rates, improve governance of financial institutions, and strengthen financial regulation. It is possible for China to complete its unfinished revolution by achieving basic convertibility of the yuan under the capital account within the 12th Five-Year Program period (2011–2015).

Growing Financial and Economic Risks

The finding that the overall growth impact of financial repression was positive in the 1980s and 1990s but is now negative has very important policy implications. Clearly, repressive financial policies have become burdens for macroeconomic performance. However, the effect looks small. Therefore, we should not anticipate a sharp acceleration of economic growth following removal of the remaining repressive policies.

However, other important risk factors are growing rapidly in China. Here we discuss several important problems that contribute increasingly to macroeconomic and financial risks.

The first relates to the behavior of financial institutions. Many Chinese financial institutions have undertaken market-oriented reforms. Nevertheless, most still behave more like state-owned enterprises (SOEs) than market entities.

For instance, state-owned commercial banks (SOCBs) went through a major transformation during the 2000s, involving writing off non-performing loans, receiving injections of public capital, gaining foreign strategic investors, and listing their stock. Despite adoption of a modern corporate structure, these banks remain tightly controlled by the state. The senior executives of the banks, including their chairs and presidents, are still appointed by the Party.

Important business and personnel decisions are still made by Party Committees, not by Boards of Directors. A striking example was that when prudence indicated that financial institutions should turn cautious during the global financial crisis, the banks all increased lending aggressively to support government policy. If the financial institutions continue to act on government instruction rather than market conditions, then serious financial risks could result.

The second problem is that state intervention has become an important constraint on the efficiency of capital allocation. Small and medium enterprises (SMEs) now play a much greater role in driving growth, but bank lending still heavily favors the state sector. Thus, SOEs account for less than 30 percent of industrial output but receive more than 50 percent of total loans. If borrowing by local government entities is included, the proportion is even higher.

Even dynamic SMEs find it extremely difficult to obtain loans from banks. In 2009 in Zhejiang province, where SME financing is better developed, only about 20 percent of SMEs obtained loans. Others had to meet their finance requirements through other channels, including borrowing from the curb market. But while the one-year base lending rate was 6.25 percent in June 2011, the lending rate in the curb market in Zhejiang was 24 percent. This points to an important aspect of inefficiency in capital allocation.

The third problem includes significantly distorted interest rates and exchange rates, which cause serious economic imbalances such as over-investment, underconsumption, and large external account surpluses. Initially the government repressed interest rates and exchange rates to promote investment and exports. But in 2010 the investment share of GDP was 48.5 percent, while the current account surplus was above 5 percent of GDP.

Real negative deposit rates were behind speculative activities in asset markets in 2010. When the possibility of further stock and housing price appreciation diminished, people rushed to speculate on commodities. Prices of these products skyrocketed. The undervalued currency has been the main cause of massive hot money inflows. This added significant liquidity to the domestic system and at the same time undermined the independence of monetary policy. All these factors risk the stability of macroeconomic condition and the sustainability of economic growth.

The fourth problem is the declining effectiveness of capital account controls, as shown by empirical analyses in this study. The result is that short-term cross-border capital flows have become much larger and more volatile. This can threaten the stability of the financial system. According to the Mundell Trilemma, a country can achieve only two of the following three international economic policy objectives: free flow of capital, stable exchange rate, and independent monetary policy. Weakening capital restrictions reduces PBOC's ability to control the domestic liquidity condition and interest rates. In a normal year, PBOC sterilizes only about 80 percent of the yuan liquidity injected by foreign exchange market intervention. This increases inflationary pressure.

The growing risks were evident during the global financial crisis. In the second half of 2008, when international capital markets experienced significant destabilization and the world economy suffered great recession, most financial institutions adopted cautious business strategies in order to control their risks. In China it was completely the opposite. In late 2008 the government announced a 4 trillion yuan stimulus package.

To further support growth, the government mobilized the banks to accelerate lending. Newly extended loans reached almost 10 trillion yuan in 2009 and 7.6 trillion yuan in 2010, compared with the PBOC's original plan of 5 trillion yuan for 2009. In addition, PBOC revealed that about one-third of the country's total outstanding loans were to various financing platforms of the government at different levels.

This probably implies excessive borrowing by government entities and reckless lending by commercial banks. It would not have happened if the financial institutions were not majority owned by the state and if both the governments and the financial institutions had to borrow and lend in an open capital market. This is worrisome. Despite substantial reforms, these institutions behave like traditional SOEs in some respects.

Such behavior successfully supported the government policy of pursuing strong GDP growth as a countercyclical policy during the global financial crisis. But it also planted the seeds of future financial risks. For instance, if a quarter of the government's borrowing from the banks turns bad, a not unreasonable possibility according to conservative estimation, the banking sector's average nonperforming loan ratio could rise by over 8 percentage points. And this does not take into account potential problems with the other two-thirds of bank loans.

More importantly, repressive financial policies are often self-sustaining. During the global financial crisis, the government adopted whatever measures were available to support economic growth. Some of those probably created important risks. Unfortunately, the government has not been able to withdraw the measures since the crisis abated. This is because any significant economic slowdown might expose the risks created earlier. To avoid an immediate blowup of the problems, the government has chosen to continue the repressive policies. This may continue for a while, until it is no longer possible to sustain. Then major crises could follow.

Repressive financial policies have become obstacles for other important policy objectives. For instance, the government has been promoting the internationalization of the yuan, inclusion of the yuan in the IMF's special drawing right (SDR) basket, and making Shanghai an international financial center by 2020. Already, yuan are used for trade settlement with some neighboring countries, yuan-denominated assets are issued in Hong Kong ("dim-sum bonds"), and several central banks hold yuan in their foreign exchange reserves. But internationalization of the currency cannot go very far if it is not freely convertible.

A quite worrying development following the global financial crisis has been the emergence of complacency and confidence among many Chinese financial-sector professionals, experts, and officials. Some even speak of the success of the "China model." This is unfortunate. China escaped the major crisis because of capital account controls, not because of sound domestic financial institutions. The fact that many Chinese financial institutions now have some of the largest stock market capitalizations in the world is not due to their quality but because of the collapse of the stock prices of their foreign counterparts. The global financial crisis may have proven that the Western system has its deficiencies. But the Chinese financial industry still has a long way to go to catch up in terms of reform and liberalization.

Capital Account Convertibility as the Organizing Theme

Lardy (1998) described Chinese banking reform as an "unfinished revolution." In the 2010s financial reform remains unfinished. The negative growth effect found for the period since 2000, and the growing risks discussed herein, imply that it is time to seriously consider completing China's financial liberalization. To achieve that goal, the government faces a wide range of tasks. These include establishing an independent central bank, introducing market-based interest rates, giving up intervention in capital allocation, improving governance of financial institutions, developing capital market institutions, increasing exchange rate flexibility, and liberalizing the capital account.

The best strategy is to organize reforms in all these areas around the central theme of achieving capital account convertibility. This is because capital account liberalization is the ultimate step in financial liberalization, and taking this step requires reforms in all the areas mentioned.

China implemented current account convertibility of the yuan in December 1996. The original plan was to take another 5 to 10 years to achieve capital account convertibility. That plan, however, has been repeatedly delayed. Fortuitously, the remaining restrictions helped shield the Chinese economy from external shocks and thereby supported domestic stability. But the restrictions are both increasingly costly for the economy and increasingly difficult to enforce.

An open capital account can bring volatility, and in some countries liberalization was followed by financial crisis. It is, therefore, important to emphasize the necessary conditions for liberalizations and the proper order of reform.

PREREQUISITES During the reform period, China has achieved unusual macroeconomic stability, a healthy fiscal position, good financial asset quality, a large current account surplus, gigantic foreign reserves, and improved financial regulations. These prerequisites for capital account liberalization are probably much better than those of other developing countries when they undertook liberalization.

First, macroeconomic conditions are quite stable. China has maintained an average 10 percent GDP growth during the reform period. Inflation was kept low, generally around 3 percent, with the exceptions of 1988, 1994, and 2004. Unfortunately, however, such an environment may not last forever. For instance, strong growth and low inflation during past decades was at least in part the result of low factor costs, including labor cost. These are rising, which is likely to lead to somewhat slower growth but higher inflation pressure in the coming years (Huang and Jiang 2010).

Second, the fiscal system is sound. In the late 1970s fiscal revenues accounted for above 30 percent of GDP. This dropped to around 11 percent in the early 1990s as a result of market-oriented reform and fiscal decentralization. Subsequently, the central government gradually has raised revenues through improved tax collection. Its share was 21 percent of GDP in 2010. Public debt is only about 18 percent of GDP in 2010. Even if we add all contingent liabilities, including nonperforming financial assets, deficits of pension funds, and local government liabilities, the total debt burden is only around 50 percent of GDP. Although the fiscal condition is very healthy now, this may change. For instance, borrowing by some local financing platforms and aggressive lending by state-owned commercial banks could add significant amounts of potential liabilities.

Third, banks have very low nonperforming loans and high capital adequacy. From the 1990s, the Chinese government has focused on banking reforms, including reducing nonperforming loans, adopting modern risk-controlling mechanisms, injecting state capital, introducing foreign strategic investors, and listing banks on domestic and foreign stock markets. Over the years the sector's quality improved significantly. For instance, the average nonperforming loan ratio declined from 44 percent in 1999 to about 2.4 percent in 2010. Banks are adequately capitalized and highly liquid. Some of these features may change, although in magnitudes that are likely to be limited. For instance, the massive lending during the global financial crisis and a possible correction of housing prices might generate nonperforming loans.

Fourth, the currency is under pressure to appreciate. China has run a large current account surplus. And the market expects the yuan to appreciate significantly in coming years. Therefore, in the near term, we are not likely to see massive capital outflows even if all restrictions are removed. More importantly, at year-end 2011 China held more than $3 trillion in foreign exchange reserves. This likely is sufficient to stabilize the financial markets even if uncertainty arises. Over time, however, the current account surplus may narrow as China and other countries work on global rebalancing. Pressures for currency appreciation may also eventually disappear.

All these factors suggest that China has already met the necessary conditions for capital account liberalization. Of course, not all the conditions are perfect. Some, such as regulatory capability, have to be developed in the process of liberalization. More importantly, an open capital account may also enforce market disciplines on domestic institutions and reduce risks. In an open capital market, for instance, the commercial banks will probably be more reluctant to follow the government directives on credit extension. An international market could also help discipline the spending behavior of local governments.

The Key Steps

What key steps should China take to achieve the ultimate goal of capital account liberalization? McKinnon (1994) proposed the following order of reform for developing countries: (1) fiscal reform; (2) financial and trade liberalization; (3) exchange rate reform; and (4) capital account liberalization. This is a useful sequencing for China to follow, although some steps could take place simultaneously.

China's overall fiscal position is strong, but there is significant room to improve. One is to shift the focus of budget expenditure from investment projects to public goods and services. The government also should reduce its intervention in bank lending decisions. Another area is operation of the state sector. The government still intervenes in prices of inputs such as energy. Therefore, it has to subsidize energy companies for operating losses. Further, it is important to discipline local government spending and limit their deficits. Local government borrowing has gotten out of control and could result in serious fiscal consequences.

FURTHER REFORMS Further substantial reforms are needed in the financial sector. First, China needs an independent central bank. PBOC has always been an integral part of the State Council, which is the ultimate decision maker for monetary policies. The government, obsessed with economic growth, undermines price and financial stability from time to time. An independent PBOC, ideally reporting to the National People's Congress, is critical for improving the quality of monetary policy and gaining the confidence of international investors.

Second, it is critical to introduce market-based interest rates. The government's key interest rate tools are still the officially determined base lending and deposit rates. These rates do not necessarily reflect market conditions. Negative real interest rates, for instance, contributed to persistent overinvestment and price bubbles. China already has the other two key types of interest rates: interbank and risk-free bond yield. But these markets need to be developed further in order to serve as benchmarks for pricing capital. This would allow PBOC eventually to shift to directly targeting interbank lending rates (Shibor) through various indirect policy tools.

Third, the government must completely give up intervention in credit allocation and promote competition in the financial industry. Policy-related lending should be the responsibility of the policy banks. The other banks should make lending decisions entirely based on commercial considerations. In any case, it is illogical for the state sector to continue to garner a disproportionate amount of capital. The government should redefine its role to being a majority owner, but not the direct operator, of most large financial institutions. Competition should also be increased in the financial industry. This can be done by allowing access to other financial institutions, such as small banks and foreign security companies, and lifting other restrictions.

Fourth, the government should make more effort to develop capital markets, especially for corporate bonds. Although banks are useful for economic development, direct financing plays a supplemental role in return- and risk-sharing between borrowers and investors. Capital market institutions need to be improved significantly. The stock markets, in particular, exhibit strong symptoms of immaturity. Participants are highly speculative and show very strong herding behavior. Incorrect information, insider trading, and manipulation are common.

FLOATING THE EXCHANGE RATE One of the most important tasks is to achieve conditional free float of the exchange rate. China adopted a managed float in early 1994. After disruptions during the

East Asian and global financial crises, the government reintroduced a managed float in June 2010. The exchange rate, however, remains rigid. The strategy of letting the currency appreciate only gradually has some serious consequences. These include encouraging the expectation of further appreciation, hot money inflows, a large current account surplus, massive liquidity, high inflationary pressures, and rapid accumulation of foreign exchange reserves.

It is, therefore, advisable that the authorities achieve a free float of the exchange rate by reducing central bank intervention in the foreign exchange market. Allowing fluctuations based on changing demand and supply may be possible after a period of rapid currency appreciation. However, the government may wish to intervene in the market to avoid excessive volatility, such as through a stabilization fund. But such intervention should be two-directional and different from PBOC's current intervention, which is only to hold down the value of the yuan.

Achieving the Goal

Capital account liberalization can then take place alongside floating the exchange rate. Capital account convertibility does not mean absolutely no restriction on capital flows. Given China's financial situation and regulatory capability, it is probably better for the country to first aim at basic convertibility. In particular, China should probably retain restrictions on certain types of volatile short-term capital flows, at least initially. This should help avoid excessive shocks to the financial system. It is also consistent with the IMF's decision to allow the temporary use of restrictive measures on cross-border short-term capital flows.

Our capital account control index suggests China has been liberalizing its capital account, especially since the Asian financial crisis. The State Administration for Foreign Exchange (SAFE) estimates that about 75 percent of 40 control measures monitored by the IMF have been partially, basically, or completely liberalized. Restrictions exist mainly on portfolio investment in bond and stock markets, derivatives and money markets, mutual fund investment, real estate transactions, debt financing, and outward direct investment (ODI).

It should be relatively easy to lift restrictions on debt financing and ODI. Cross-border bond issuance can be monitored through the debt-equity ratios of individual institutions and short-term debt proportions. ODI projects need to acquire approvals from SAFE, the

National Development and Reform Commission, and the Ministry of Commerce. The approval procedures have become simpler as the government encourages capital outflows through direct investment. Therefore, liberalization in these two areas can be implemented quickly.

Should China also immediately remove restrictions on cross-border portfolio investment? The experiences of India, Indonesia, and Korea during the global financial crisis suggest that volatile portfolio flows could become an important source of financial market instability. Therefore, it might be useful to retain some restrictions to avoid excessive volatility. Fortunately, China has already introduced the qualified foreign institutional investor (QFII) and qualified domestic institutional investor (QDII) schemes to allow cross-border portfolio flows. One option is to significantly increase the quotas under these schemes, and at the same time substantially weaken the restrictions, such as the number of days required for fund repatriation.

If China pushes ahead with these reforms carefully but forcefully, it may realize capital account convertibility within the period of the 12th Five-Year Program. The intermediate goal should be to achieve basic, rather than full, capital account convertibility.

Until the financial system is well developed and mature, some precautionary measures may still be useful. Such measures in three important areas deserve serious consideration. First, although the exchange rate regime should transition to free float as quickly as possible, the government may want to devise a stabilization fund to avoid excessive market volatility. Second, it is possible for the government to retain certain types of capital controls to avoid disruptive short-term speculative flows. And, finally, although state ownership of financial institutions should be reduced as a general part of financial reform, the government may want to maintain stakes in major financial institutions to support investor confidence in case of market uncertainty.

Conclusion

This chapter has analyzed China's financial system and reforms to it since the late 1970s. China has progressed quite far along a path of liberalization. We have investigated the logic behind Chinese policy makers' choice of liberalization path and provided quantitative, as well as qualitative, assessments of reform policies. Although probably helpful to China's growth during the first two decades of reform, continued financial repression is now deleterious to growth and other important Chinese policies. Thus, we offer a map of the path forward to a level of liberalization appropriate for China.

References

Agarwala, Ramgopal. 1983. *Price Distortions and Growth in Developing Countries.* The World Bank.

Andersen, Thomas, and Finn Tarp. 2003. "Financial Liberalization, Financial Development and Economic Growth in LDCs." *Journal of International Development* 15: 189–209.

Ang, James B., and Warwick J. McKibbin. 2007. "Financial Liberalization, Financial Sector Development and Growth: Evidence from Malaysia." *Journal of Development Economics* 84: 215–33.

Arestis, Philip, and Panicos O. Demetriades. 1997. "Financial Development and Economic Growth: Assessing the Evidence." *Economic Journal* 107: 783–99.

Arestis, Philip, and Panicos O. Demetriades. 1999. "Finance Liberalization: The Experience of Developing Countries." Eastern Economic Journal 25: 441–57.

Beck, Thorsten, Ross Levine, and Norman Loayza. 2000. "Finance and the Sources of Growth." *Journal of Financial Economics* 58 (1): 261–300.

Beck, Thorsten, A. Demirgüç-Kunt, and V. Maksimovic. 2008. "Financing Patterns Around the World: Are Small Firms Different?" *Journal of Financial Economics* 89: 467–87.

Bencivenga, Valerie R., and Bruce D. Smith. 1991. "Financial Intermediation and Endogenous Growth." *Review of Economic Studies* 58 (2): 195–209.

Berger, Allen, George R.G. Clarke, Robert Cull, Leora Klapper, and Gregory F. Udell. 2005. "Corporate Governance and Bank Performance: A Joint Analysis of the Static, Selection, and Dynamic Effects of Domestic, Foreign, and State Ownership." *Journal of Banking and Finance* 29: 2179–221.

Bonin, John P., and Yiping Huang. 2001. "Dealing with the Bad Loans of the Chinese Banks." *Journal of Asian Economics* 12 (2): 197–214.

Bonin, John P., and Istvan P. Szekely, eds. 1994. *The Development and Reform of Financial Systems in Central and Eastern Europe.* Edward Elgar Publishing Ltd.

Brandt, Loren, and Thomas G. Rawski, eds. 2008. *China's Great Economic Transformation.* Cambridge University Press.

Brandt, Loren, and Xiaodong Zhu. 2000. "Redistribution in a Decentralizing Economy: Growth and Inflation in China under Reform." *Journal of Political Economy* 108 (2): 422–39.

Chen Guojin, Hui Lin, and Lei Wang, 2005. "Corporate Governance, Reputation Mechanism and the Behavior of Listed Firms in Committing in Fraud," *Nankai Business Review.*

Cheng, Hang-Shen, H. Gifford Fong, and Thomas Mayer. 1997. "China's Financial Reform and Monetary Policy: Issues and Strategies." In Joint Economic Committee, Congress of the United States, *China's Economic Future*, 203–20. ME Sharpe.

China Banking Regulatory Commission. 2007. "Report on China's Banking Sector Opening-Up." http://www.cbrc.gov.cn/ 03/22/2007.

Demetriades, Panicos O., and Khaled Hussein. 1996. "Does Financial Development Cause Economic Growth? Evidence for 16 Countries." *Journal of Development Economics* 51: 387–411.

Demetriades, Panicos O., and Kul B. Luintel. 1998. "The Direct Costs of Financial Repression: Evidence from India." *Review of Economics and Statistics*, 79 (2): 311–320.

Demetriades, Panicos O., and Kul B. Luintel. 2001. "Financial Restraints in the South Korean Miracle." *Journal of Development Economics* 64: 459–79.

Deng Xiaoping. 1979, October 4. Speech at the meeting of the First Secretaries of Provinces.

Diaz-Alejandro, Carlos. 1985. "Good-Bye Financial Repression, Hello Financial Crash." *Journal of Development Economics* 19 (1–2): 1–24.

Eichengreen, Barry, Michael Mussa, Giovanni Dell'Ariccia, Enrica Detragiache, Gian Milesi-Ferretti, and Andrew Tweddie. 1999. "Liberalizing Capital Movements: Some Analytical Issues." *IMF Economic Issues* 17.

Fan, Gang. 1994. "Incremental Changes and Dual Track Transition: Understanding the Case of China." *Economic Policy* 19 supplement (December): 99–122.

Fry, Maxwell. 1997. "In Favour of Financial Liberalisation." *Economic Journal* 107: 754–70.

Goldsmith, Raymond. 1969. *Financial Structure and Development.* Yale University Press.

Goldstein, Morris, and Nicholas Lardy, eds. 2008. *Debating China's Exchange Rate Policy.* Peterson Institute for International Economics.

Gou, Qin, Daili Wang, Ping Yan, and Yiping Huang. 2011. "Effectiveness of Capital Account Control and Short-Term Capital Flow." Paper presented at Tsinghua University-Columbia University Symposium on International Economics, June 26–28, 2011, Tsinghua University, Beijing.

Greenwood, Jeremy, and Boyan Jovanovic. 1990. "Financial Development, Growth and the Distribution of Income." *Journal of Political Economy* 98 (5): 1076–107.

Griffith-Jones, Stephany, 1995. "Introductory Framework." In Stephany Griffith-Jones and Zoenek Drabek, eds., *Financial Reform in Central and Eastern Europe*, 3–16. St. Martin's Press.

Gurley, John G., and E.S. Shaw. 1955. "Financial Aspects of Economic Development." *American Economic Review* 45 (4): 515–38.

Haggard, Stephan, and Chung H. Lee. 1995. *Financial Systems and Economic Policy in Developing Countries*. Cornell University Press.

Hellmann, Thomas, Kevin Murdock, and Joseph Stiglitz. 1997. "Financial Restraint: Toward a New Paradigm." In Masahiko Aoki, H.K. Kim, and M. Okuno-Fujuwara, eds., *The Role of Government in East Asian Economic Development: Comparative Institutional Analysis*, 163–207. Clarendon Press.

Hermes, Niels, and Robert Lensink. 2000. "Financial System Development in Transition Economies." *Journal of Banking and Finance* 24 (4): 507–24.

Hu, Ruyin. 2008. *The Development and Transition of Chinese Capital Market*. Renmin Press.

Huang, Yiping. 2001. *Last Steps Across the River: Enterprise and Banking Reform in China*. Asia Pacific Press.

Huang, Yiping. 2002. "Is Meltdown of the Chinese Banks Inevitable?" *China Economic Review* 13(4) (December): 382–87.

Huang, Yiping. 2010a. "China's Great Ascendancy and Structural Risks: Consequences of Asymmetric Liberalization." *Asian-Pacific Economic Literature* 24 (1): 65–85.

Huang, Yiping. 2010b. "Dissecting the China Puzzle: Asymmetric Liberalization and Cost Distortion." *Asian Economic Policy Review* 5 (2): 281–95.

Huang, Yiping, and Tingsong Jiang. 2010. "What Does the Lewis Turning Point Mean for China? A Computable General Equilibrium Analysis." *China Economic Journal* 2 (3): 191–207.

Huang, Yiping, and Kunyu Tao. 2010. "Factor Market Distortion and Current Account Surplus in China." *Asian Economic Papers* 3 (9): 1–36.

Huang, Yiping, and Bijun Wang. 2010a. "Cost Distortion and Structural Imbalances in China." *China & World Economy* 18 (4) (July–August): 1–17.

Huang, Yiping, and Xun Wang. 2010b. "Effectiveness of the Capital Account Controls in China." *Financial Development Review*, issue 6. (In Chinese.)

Huang, Yiping, and Xun Wang. 2011. "Does Financial Repression Inhibit or Facilitate Economic Growth? A Case Study of Chinese Reform Experience." *Oxford Bulletin of Economics and Statistics* 73 (6): 833–55.

Huang, Yiping, and Peichu Xie. 2011. "Conditions, Timing and Progress of the Capital Account Liberalization in China." *China Finance*, issue 14. (In Chinese.)

IMF = International Monetary Fund. 2006. "World Economic Outlook 2006." International Monetary Fund.

IMF = International Monetary Fund. 2011 April. "World Economic Outlook 2011." International Monetary Fund.

Jin, L. 2004. "Research on the Intensity of Capital Control in China." *Journal of Financial Research* (Jin Rong Yan Jiu) 294: 9–23. (In Chinese.)

King, R.G., and R. Levine. 1993a. "Finance and Growth: Schumpeter Might Be Right." *Quarterly Journal of Economics* 108: 717–37.

King, Robert G., and Ross Levine. 1993b. "Finance, Entrepreneurship, and Growth: Theory and Evidence." *Journal of Monetary Economics* 32: 513–42.

Lardy, Nicholas. 1998. *China's Unfinished Economic Revolution*. The Brookings Institution Press.

Lardy, Nicholas. 2008. "Financial Repression in China." Policy Brief, Peterson Institute of International Economics.

Levine, Ross. 1997. "Financial Development and Economic Growth: View and Agenda." *Journal of Economic Literature* 35: 688–726.

Levine, Ross. 2005. "Finance and Growth: Theory, Mechanisms and Evidence." In P. Aghion and S.N. Durlauf, eds., *Handbook of Economic Growth*. Elsevier.

Li, David. 2001. "Beating the Trap of Financial Repression in China." *Cato Journal* 21 (1): 77–90.

Li, Hongbin, and Li-an Zhou. 2005. "Political Turnover and Economic Performance: The Incentive Role of Personnel Control in China." *Journal of Public Economics* 89 (9–10): 1743–62.

Li, Kui-Wai. 1994. *Financial Repression and Economic Reform in China*. Praeger Publishers.

Lin, Justin Yifu, Fang Cai, and Zhou Li. 1995. *The China Miracle: Development Strategy and Economic Reform*. The Chinese University of Hong Kong Press. (A 2003 revised edition is in print.)

Liu, Tung, and Kui-Wai Li. 2001. "Impact of Liberalization of Financial Resources in China's Economic Growth: Evidence from Provinces." *Journal of Asian Economics* 12: 245–262.

Long, Millard, and Silvia Sagari. 1991. "Financial Reform in European Economies in Transition." In P. Marer and S. Zecchini, eds., *The Transition to a Market Economy* vol. 2, 430–42. OECD.

Maswana, Jean-Claude. 2008. "China's Financial Development and Economic Growth: Exploring the Contradictions." *International Research Journal of Finance and Economics* 19: 89–101.

McKinnon, Ronald. 1973. *The Order of Economic Liberalization: Financial Control in the Transition to a Market Economy*. Johns Hopkins Press.

McKinnon, Ronald. 1994. "Financial Growth and Macroeconomic Stability in China, 1978–1992: Implications for Russia and Other Transitional Economies." *Journal of Comparative Economics* 18 (3): 438–69.

McKinnon, Ronald, and Huw Pill. 1996. "Credible Liberalizations and International Capital Flows: The 'Overborrowing Sydrome.'" In T. Ito and A. Krueger, eds., *Financial Deregulation and Integration in East Asia*, 7–37. University of Chicago Press.

Merton, Robert C., and Zvi Bodie. 1995. "A Conceptual Framework for Analyzing the Financial Environment." In D.B. Crane et al., eds., *The Global Financial System, a Functional Perspective*, 12–16. Harvard Business School Press.

Naughton, Barry, 1995. *Growing Out of the Plan: Chinese Economic Reform, 1978–1993*. Cambridge University Press.

Nissanke, Machiko, and Ernest Aryeetey. 1998. *Financial Integration and Development—Liberalization and Reform in Sub-Saharan Africa*. Routledge.

Obstfeld, Maurice. 2006. "Pricing-to-Market, the Interest-Rate Rule, and the Exchange Rate." NBER Working Papers 12699. National Bureau of Economic Research.

Pagano, Marco. 1993. "Financial Markets and Growth: An Overview." *European Economic Review* 37: 613–22.

Park, Albert, and Kaja Sehrt. 2001. Testing of Financial Intermediation and Banking Reform in China." *Journal of Comparative Economics* 29: 608–44.

Patrick, Hugh T. 1966. "Financial Development and Economic Growth in Undeveloped Countries." *Economic Development and Cultural Change* 14: 174–89.

Rajan, Raghuram, and Luigi Zingales. 1998. "Financial Development and Growth." *American Economic Review* 88 (3): 559–86.

Ram, Rati. 1999. "Financial Development and Economic Growth: Additional Evidence." *Journal of Development Studies* 35 (4): 164–74.

Roubini, Nouriel, and Xavier Sala-i-Martin. 1992. "Financial Repression and Economic Growth." *Journal of Development Economics* 39: 5–30.

Sachs, Jeffrey D., and Wing Thye Woo. 2000. "Understanding China's Economic Performance." *Journal of Policy Reform* 4 (1): 1–50.

Schumpter, Joseph A. 1911. *A Theory of Economic Development*. Harvard University Press.

Sehrt, Kaja. 1999. "Banks Versus Budgets: Credit Allocation in the People's Republic of China, 1984–1997." PhD dissertation, Department of Political Science, University of Michigan.

Shaw, Edward S. 1973. *Financial Deepening in Economic Development*. Oxford University Press.

Song, Guoqing. 1994. "From Unified Purchase and Marketing System to Land Tax." In Qiren Zhou, ed., *Rural Change and Chinese Development: 1978–1989* (II). Oxford University Press, Hong Kong. (In Chinese.)

Stiglitz, Joseph E. 1994. "The Role of the State in Financial Markets." In M. Bruno and B. Pleskovic, eds., *Proceedings of the World Bank Annual Conference on Development Economics, 1993: Supplement to the World Bank Economic Review and the World Bank Research Observer*, 19–52. World Bank.

Stiglitz, Joseph E. 2000. "Capital Market Liberalization, Economic Growth and Instability." *World Development* 28: 1075–86.

Wang, Xun. 2011. "Financial Repression, Financial Development and Economic Growth in China, 1978–2008." PhD dissertation, National School of Development, Peking University.

Wu, Xiaoling. 2008. *30 Years' Retrospect and Prospect on the Financial Institution Reform in China*. People's Publishing House.

Yi, Gang. 2009. *On the Financial Reform of China*. The Commercial Press.

CHAPTER THREE

Japan

Ongoing Financial Deregulation, Structural Change, and Performance, 1990–2010

EDWARD J. LINCOLN

FINANCIAL SECTOR evolution in Japan provides a different story than that of Korea or China during the 1990–2010 period. By 1990 Japan had already experienced considerable deregulation in financial markets. Although Japan had a period of considerable financial repression after World War II, that era was over before 1990. With deregulation, the way was open to gradually shift away from a bank-centered financial system toward one with greater reliance on capital markets. In addition, as the largest and most advanced economy and financial sector in East Asia, expectations were high that Tokyo would become a regional, even international, financial center.

The story of this chapter is that neither of these occurred. Japan retains a bank-centered financial system, and neither Tokyo nor Japanese financial institutions have become as international as many expected they would as the 1980s ended.

Parts of the story are well studied, including the asset price bubble of the second half of the 1980s and its collapse beginning in the early 1990s, the near collapse of the banking system under the weight of nonperforming loans in 1997–1998, and the slow resolution of the banking crisis. (See, for example, Patrick and Park 1994; Aoki and Patrick 1994; Hoshi and Patrick 2000; Tett 2003; Hamada, Kashyap, and Weinstein 2011.) Sufficient time has passed since the severe problems of the 1990s that it is possible to take a new look at what happened and what the consequences have been.

Although there has been a lack of fundamental change in the character of the financial system, change has occurred. This chapter details a number of structural changes, including a major consolidation of the banking industry, partial reform of the direct government role in the financial sector, and a rise in foreign ownership of corporate equity. Nonetheless, even with these changes, the system remains bank centered and there are issues of misallocation of financial resources.

Japan provides a cautionary tale for Korea and China, where there are similar beliefs that the economy should evolve toward a less-bank-centered financial system. Although Japan's initial bank-centered structure was a product of government regulation, the lack of substantial movement away from that system is the result of other factors considered in this chapter, such as a high level of risk aversion in Japanese society.

The financial turmoil in the United States and Europe in 2008–2009 that resulted from a real estate bubble and risky behavior by financial institutions might suggest that Japan was better off not converging on an American model. Some aspects of US deregulation led to imprudent and unethical behavior by some financial institutions, while innovation led to new, complex asset-backed financial instruments that were poorly understood even by market participants.

The view that US financial markets represent global best practice on which other nations ought to converge is, at best, rather tarnished. And Japanese financial institutions were lucky (due to their reluctance to take on risk following their domestic problems in the 1990s) to have avoided becoming enmeshed in the toxic asset problem in the United States, unlike a number of European banks.

However, a conclusion that Japan need not, or should not, change is not justified either. This chapter argues that misallocation of financial resources is a problem in Japan. Unlike China, where misallocation results from the heavy hand of the government, misallocation in Japan results from lack of market pressure on nonfinancial corporations to maximize returns. The consequence has been excess fixed investment in the corporate sector and low rates of return on capital.

The implication is that, although Japan need not converge on an American model, it has problems that need further change. Fixing these problems would push the system somewhat closer to the American model in the broadest sense. That is, Japan need not encourage complex financial instruments or risk-taking hedge funds, but it does need a financial system that puts greater pressure on the nonfinancial corporate sector to behave efficiently.

The problems still exist despite considerable legal and regulatory change during the 1990–2010 period. A wider array of financial instruments became available, and the financial sector underwent reconfiguration and consolidation. All of these changes occurred in the context of a major domestic financial crisis caused by the late 1980s bubble and its collapse in the 1990s. Falling real estate and stock market prices brought the financial sector to the brink of disaster by 1997, but the problems in the financial sector were eventually resolved. Today the system appears to be in little danger of a renewed crisis, having come through the 2008–2009 global financial crisis with few problems.

Nonetheless, the continued overinvestment in fixed capital and low rates of return are a concern for the future prosperity of the economy, especially given the demands on the system stemming from a falling and rapidly aging population. Financing an expanding share of retirees in the population will be more difficult without more efficient capital allocation.

Japan also provides a cautionary tale regarding international finance. Having a large economy, huge pool of domestic savings, and large financial institutions was not sufficient to turn the major domestic financial center (Tokyo) into a leading international financial center.

Since the 1950s Japanese manufacturers in a number of industries have taken the world by storm. Japanese financial institutions—unleashed on global financial markets as a result of deregulation in the 1970s and early 1980s—by 1990 appeared poised to replicate this global advance. But, this chapter concludes, Tokyo in 2010 was no more of an international financial center than 20 years earlier. A variety of constraints, such as language, risk aversion, and management decision-making structures, have hindered the role of Tokyo and Japanese financial firms in global markets.

The following sections provide a brief background on changes before 1990, the macroeconomic context in which the financial system evolved in the 1990–2010 period, analysis of the various components of the financial system, some observations on why Tokyo and Japanese financial firms are internationally less important than once expected, and an assessment of performance.

Most of the data in this chapter are for fiscal years that, in Japan, end with March of the following calendar year (fiscal 2010 ends March 31, 2011).

Economic Setting to 1990

The setting for the financial sector in postwar Japan was an extraordinary period of rapid growth, bringing Japan into the ranks of the advanced industrial nations by the 1970s. From 1955 to 1973 the economy grew at the extraordinary average annual real rate of 9.1 percent, with only modest inflation and in the context of a rather interventionist government that used extensive price controls, restrictions on competitions, and an active industrial policy to encourage favored industries.

This period of high growth was also characterized by continuous political dominance by the Liberal Democratic Party (LDP) and an "iron triangle" among the LDP, big business, and a strong career bureaucracy. After catching up by the mid-1970s, growth moderated but continued to be higher than other advanced industrialized economies until the early 1990s.

Until 1971 Japan operated on a fixed exchange rate within the Bretton Woods System. Despite deep concerns about negative effects on economic performance when that system collapsed, Japan continued its superior performance in the 1970s and 1980s under a floating rate, and the burst of high growth in the second half of the 1980s occurred despite a doubling of the value of the yen against the dollar from 1985 to 1987.

The financial sector was tightly regulated. The controls were part of the broader set of price controls and regulation that pervaded many sectors of the economy.

Most funds flowed through banks. Very few corporations were permitted by the Ministry of Finance to issue bonds, and for a variety of reasons, raising funds through new issues of equity was relatively unattractive. These included the custom of issuing new shares to existing stockholders at par value, inevitably far below market price. The stock market was active, but it played a very secondary role in raising new funds for corporations, and it was not an arena for contesting corporate control.

Banks were separated by size and function (including city banks, two categories of regional banks, long-term credit banks, trust banks, institutions specializing in the agricultural sector, and institutions serving small business). Virtually no entry or exit occurred in the commercial banking sector until the 1990s. Most interest rates were controlled, including both deposit rates and loan rates (with the sole exception of the short-term interbank market, called the call market), although banks found imaginative ways to partially evade the restrictions (such as compensating balances on loans to increase the de facto interest rate).

International transactions were limited. Few Japanese financial institutions were given permission by the government to operate abroad. For example, in the 1960s, the only Japanese bank with an office in New York was the Bank of Tokyo, which was a specialized foreign-exchange bank.

Government played an indirect role in directing the allocation of capital through indicative lending by government-owned banks and informal pressure on the commercial banking sector, although how significant these efforts were in affecting the allocation of capital across industries has been debated by academics for decades. (The market-based explanation of growth is exemplified by Trezise 1976. Emphasizing the positive role of government is Johnson 1982. Okimoto 1989 provides a more nuanced view of the government's role.)

This simple repressed system worked well, at least on the surface. Households (net savers) placed their savings in banks, and the banks lent to the corporate sector (net borrowers). The fact that the economy grew at an average annual rate close to 10 percent from the 1950s until the early 1970s suggests that the financial sector did a reasonably good job allocating financial resources to productive uses (although high overall economic growth masks mistakes and misallocation).

Would a less-repressed financial system have enabled even higher growth? The answer is unclear, although in some cases the misallocations of credit in these years created problems later, such as having to scale back an electricity-intensive aluminum refining industry in the 1980s that should never have been built in Japan in the first place.

The initial impetus for deregulation and reform began when the pace of economic growth diminished in the 1970s after Japan had largely caught up with the level of per capita income in the advanced industrial nations. This deceleration of growth created important changes in financial flows.

Two major developments were the emergence of government deficits and a persistent current account surplus (with the tendency for current account surpluses partially masked by the impact of the two oil crises in the 1970s, but emerging strongly after 1980). Conflict between the Ministry of Finance and financial institutions over conditions for issuing larger volumes of government bonds led to a gradual process of deregulating interest rates. The need to recycle current account surpluses in the form of net capital flow abroad led to a gradual decontrol of international financial transactions. (For an analysis of these early years of deregulation, see Lincoln 1988, especially chapters 4 and 5.)

The second half of the 1980s was a heady time in Japan. The Nikkei Average (the most widely followed stock index) tripled from 1985 to a peak on the final trading day of 1989. Urban real estate prices also tripled, though they peaked later, in 1991. Economic growth accelerated from an annual average of 3.5 percent in the first half of the decade to 4.9 percent from 1986 to 1991.

By 1990 considerable deregulation and reform had occurred in many parts of the economy, generally reducing the role of government. In the financial sector, interest rate controls were eliminated, although formal separation of financial institutions by function continued. Over the course of the 1980s, increasingly deregulated Japanese financial institutions also established an international presence, with penetration of international lending markets aided by their ability to obtain deposits at home at low interest rates. Meanwhile, deregulation and a rapidly rising stock market made equity financing more attractive, and deregulation enabled more firms to issue bonds. Government officials talked of Tokyo becoming a major international financial center and encouraged foreign firms to list on the Tokyo Stock Exchange.

Japanese government officials and corporate executives were proud and confident that they had created a market-based economic system that was better than those in the United States or Europe, capable of producing more-rapid growth with lower unemployment over the long run.

The reality was quite different. The late 1980s are now called the "Bubble Era." How deregulation led to problematic developments in the financial sector during this period is covered in the chapter by Seok and Shin (chapter 5).

The period since 1990 has been one of stock market and real estate prices far below their bubble-era peaks, mediocre economic growth (well below potential growth), weak labor markets, extreme distress in the banking sector, and deflation. Against that background, deregulation and structural change in the financial structure were driven by financial crisis and angst over poor economic performance.

1990–2010: Basic Contours

The period from 1990 through 2010 has been characterized by a series of economic problems causing underperformance of the economy. The proximate cause of these troubles lay in the rise of an asset bubble in the stock market and real estate market in the second half of the 1980s, and the collapse of that bubble in the 1990s. The bubble is illustrated in figure 3.1.

From 1985 to the beginning of the 1990s, both the stock market and the urban real estate market tripled. Since then (from an end-of-1989

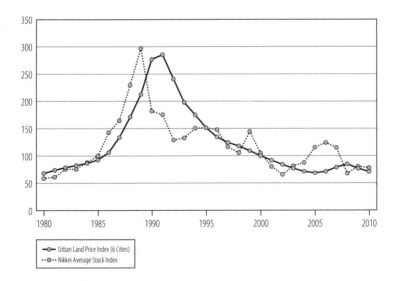

Figure 3.1 Real Estate and Stock Price Indexes (1985 = 100). *Sources*: The urban land (real estate) price index is from Cabinet Office, *Japan Statistical Yearbook*. The Nikkei Average is from Bank of Japan, "Long Term Data Series," and *Businessweek* ("Japan's Stocks Fall," December 31, 2010).

peak for the stock market and 1991 peak for the real estate market) all those gains have been lost. At the end of 2010, despite real GDP growth, both the stock market and urban real estate were trading below their levels of 25 years earlier. The Nikkei was 74 percent below its 1989 peak, and the official urban real estate price index was 75 percent below its 1991 peak. These data paint an almost unbelievable picture of dismal asset price performance over a quarter of a century.

As should be expected, the rise and loss of wealth had a major impact on the economy, compounded by a series of policy errors by the government. The collapse of asset prices had an obvious impact on the banking sector (rising amounts of nonperforming loans and an evaporation of unrealized capital gains on bank holdings of corporate equity), but the government responded slowly to this problem (this is explored later in this chapter). Fiscal stimulus to cushion the blow to the real economy was applied in a sporadic manner, undermining its impact. Monetary policy was slow to respond to the collapse of asset prices, so by the time the Bank of Japan had cut interest rates to a sufficiently low level, deflation had set in.

Figure 3.2 shows what has happened to economic growth since 1985. During the Bubble Era, when asset prices had been rising, defined loosely here as from 1985 through 1991 (even though the stock market was falling from 1990), the economy averaged 4.9 percent annual growth. This was higher than in other industrialized countries over

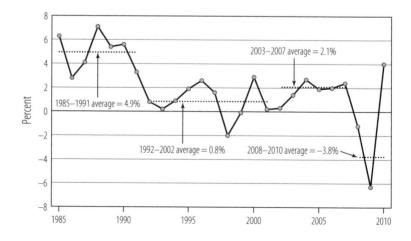

Figure 3.2 Real GDP Growth (calendar year, percent). *Source*: Economic and Social Research Institute, Cabinet Office.

the same period and resulted in considerable self-confidence among Japanese officials and corporate executives that their version of a market economy functioned better than those in the West. However, once the stock market and real estate market began declining, growth dwindled. From 1992 through 2002, an 11-year period, annual real GDP growth averaged only 0.8 percent. This period is commonly referred to as the "Lost Decade."

A recovery began during 2002, with growth from 2003 through 2007 averaging 2.1 percent. Since population was virtually stagnant, GDP per capita was also growing at 2.1 percent, a respectable performance for a mature economy. Despite the recovery in the context of a falling working-age population, labor markets remained weak with stagnant wages and high (for Japan) unemployment of around 5 percent.

The recovery was abruptly interrupted by the severe global recession, transmitted to Japan in late 2008 through a sudden drop in exports. Average growth for 2008–2010 was –3.8 percent, although the sharp drop was partially offset by 4 percent positive growth in 2010. As in other industrialized countries, the enduring strength of this most recent recovery was in some doubt (even before the negative impact of the March 11, 2011, earthquake and tsunami).

The Asian financial crisis of 1997–1998 had an effect on a number of the economies in the region, but not much on Japan. Japan's economy shrank 2 percent in 1998, but the cause of recession in that year lay largely in domestic factors rather than the Asian crisis (though exports to the crisis countries in Asia did decline). Principal among these was a decision to increase the national consumption tax from 3 percent to 5 percent in the second quarter of 1997, as well as the expiration of income tax cuts that had been put in place in 1994. Total tax increases were on the order of 2 percentage points of GDP, a large amount.

The economy began to experience low but persistent deflation as the pace of economic growth diminished in the 1990s. As a result, even though nominal GDP in 2010 was only about the same as in 1991, real GDP was 20 percent higher.

Figure 3.3 tracks the GDP deflator, which is the broadest measure of prices in the economy. It turned negative in mid-1994, returned temporarily to positive inflation in 1997–1998 (due to the increase in the national consumption tax) and again very briefly in 2008 (due to the increase in global commodity prices just prior to the global recession). Otherwise, prices have been falling, with the average year-on-year

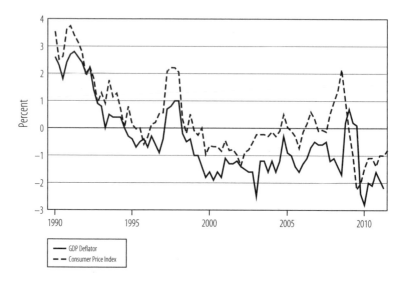

Figure 3.3 Price Deflators (quarterly, year-on-year comparison, percent). *Sources*: Economic and Social Research Institute, Cabinet Office; and International Monetary Fund, *International Financial Statistics*.

decline from mid-1994 through the second quarter of 2011 running at −1.0 percent. Compared to the devastating deflation that hit the United States and Japan in the early 1930s, this rate of decline has been mild, but it has been more persistent.

The consumer price index (CPI) is not quite so persistently negative. The average quarterly year-on-year drop in the CPI was only 0.13 percent from mid-1994 through the second quarter of 2011.

Implications

This macroeconomic background had two important implications for the evolution of the financial sector. First, the collapse of asset prices created a large nonperforming loan problem for the commercial banks, as well as problems for some securities firms and insurance companies. Second, the sense of malaise about the economy led to a mood in favor of deregulation (or at least change in the nature of regulation) of all kinds, including the financial sector.

Arguably, the major problems of the 1990s were macroeconomic in nature: excessively low interest rates in the second half of the 1980s;

rates kept too high for too long in the first half of the 1990s as asset prices fell; and inconsistency in fiscal policy. (For an analysis of the problems of the 1990s that focuses on these causes, see Posen 1998.)

Overall, Japan can be characterized as having weak or insufficient growth of domestic demand from the early 1990s to the present. Neither macroeconomic policy nor deregulation and structural change succeeded in unleashing stronger demand growth. The recovery of 2002–2007 was caused by (net) export growth, not acceleration of domestic demand. With household consumption representing 55 percent of GDP, the key ingredient in weak domestic demand growth has been flat or falling household income.

Nonetheless, a number of structural problems also contributed to the economic malaise of the 1990s, so the reassessment of regulation was clearly justified, especially for the financial sector. (For an analysis of the structural problems building in Japan during the 1980s that contributed to the economic troubles of the 1990s, see Katz 1998.)

Structural weaknesses contributed to the asset price bubble of the 1980s, as well as to the slow and flawed response to distress in the financial sector when the bubble collapsed in the 1990s. Eventual recognition of these problems, as well as a sense that the economy could perform better in the long run if the overall legal and regulatory framework for the financial and nonfinancial corporate sectors were changed, led to a period of regulatory change. These regulatory issues are considered in the following sections.

Financial Sector Structure and Evolution

Japan's bank-centered financial system was hard hit by the collapse of asset prices in the 1990s, as borrowers were increasingly unable to repay their loans. Overall, the financial sector was also affected by legal changes that permitted financial holding companies, a regulatory change discussed in the next section. The question here is how much the structure of the sector has changed since 1990.

The chapter by Seok and Shin (chapter 5) emphasizes a shift in the second half of the 1980s in which earlier rounds of deregulation enabled large nonfinancial corporations to raise money from capital markets rather than from banks, a change that caused banks to seek other, riskier borrowers. That shift appears to have contributed to the bubble and its collapse.

The broad story of the 1990–2010 period is one of coping with the consequences of the collapse of asset prices. This section looks at how the structure and behavior of the various component segments of the financial sector evolved over this period, concluding with a look at the broader picture of how households allocate their financial portfolios and how the corporate sector raises funds.

Banks

The banking sector was badly hit by the collapse of stock and real estate prices in the 1990s, with the amount of nonperforming loans rising rapidly as construction and real estate development firms ran into financial difficulty.

The initial response was to deny that problems existed, which was relatively easy because of lax accounting rules and the implicit agreement of the Ministry of Finance (MOF) that it was best if the public not know about these problems. The government reported nonperforming loan statistics, but these were generally not believable.

The trigger for policy change came in November 1997 with a series of failures. First, a mid-sized securities firm (Sanyo Securities) suspended some operations and then filed for bankruptcy. Next, a major bank, Hokkaido Takushoku Bank, collapsed. Then the fourth largest security firm (Yamaichi Securities) collapsed.

The Hokkaido Takushoku collapse was handled in the traditional manner, with MOF browbeating two other banks into absorbing it. However, the collapse and the difficulty MOF faced in resolving the matter raised anxiety levels. Rumors swirled through financial markets that soon one or more of the three specialized long-term credit banks also would fail. (For more detail on the buildup to the crisis in 1998, see Lincoln 1998; Ito 2000, especially 93–94.)

As banks appeared to be increasingly shaky in 1998, the government finally responded with new legislation. In early 1998 the government approved a recapitalization of major banks. Two new laws were enacted in October. One established a procedure to handle failed banks, and the other provided another round of capital infusion for those deemed salvageable. (The first round of capital infusion was in February 1998, but banks requested only a small portion of the ¥13 trillion made available at that time, so a further recapitalization was deemed necessary [Kashyap and Hoshi 2009].) The year

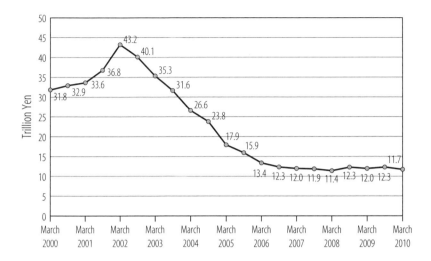

Figure 3.4 Nonperforming Loans (trillion yen). *Source*: Financial Services A, "Table 1: Transition of Loans Based on the Financial Reconstruction Act."

1998 also marked the start of the Financial Services Agency (FSA), as discussed later.

After the crisis and policy response of 1998, and with a more activist FSA from 2001, three important changes occurred in the banking sector. First, the nonperforming loan problem was gradually resolved as the FSA forced banks to write off their bad loans. Second, banks came under pressure from the FSA in 2002–2003 to increase their capital bases, which they did. Third, the banking industry underwent a major consolidation. With these changes, the banking sector was financially stable by the mid-2000s.

Figure 3.4 indicates what has happened to officially declared nonperforming loans (beginning 2000, by which time the numbers were relatively believable). From a peak of ¥43 trillion ($342 billion at then-current exchange rates) in March 2002, the amount declined to only ¥12 trillion ($103 billion) in September 2006. By this time, nonperforming loans were no longer considered a threat to the stability of the banking sector. From 1993 to March of 2010, banks declared losses associated with writing off nonperforming loans of just over ¥100 trillion, a bit less than $1 trillion at exchange rates prevailing over this time period (FSA 2010 and 2011b).

Banks that received government funds in 1997 and 1998 came under pressure in 2002–2003 to increase their capital bases. By March 2003 all four of the major bank groups showed a Bank for International Settlements (BIS) total risk-based capital ratio of roughly 10 percent, well above the BIS requirement of 8 percent (Japan Center for Economic Research [JCER] 2003). These ratios continued to rise, with the average capital adequacy ratio for all major banks reaching 11.6 percent in March 2005 and 15.8 percent by 2010 (FSA 2005, 2011a). ("Major banks" are those that make up the four major financial groups.)

BANK CONSOLIDATION Consolidation was the third major change: 15 large banks and a host of other financial service companies combined into 4 major financial holding companies. A key change enabling this consolidation was a 1997 law permitting financial holding companies that could include banks of various kinds and securities firms. As a further result, some of the holding companies also acquired securities firms and some smaller regional banks.

Consolidation began in the 1990s, but most of it took place in 2001–2005, a major restructuring of the industry in a short period of time. Most of the banks involved were the former city banks (the large nationwide commercial banks).

Aside from the permission for holding companies in 1997, a major motive for this rapid consolidation was the desire to create "too-big-to-fail" banks. A law passed in 1998 established a process for handling failed banks, involving temporary nationalization, government assumption of nonperforming loans, and liquidation or sale of the remaining institution to the private sector. Fear of being swept into this process, which would include dismissal of senior managers and major (or complete) losses for the shareholders, provided a powerful motive for consolidation. The government was more likely to be lenient and avoid the formal nationalization step in dealing with a huge troubled bank.

The principal banks nationalized under the new law were two long-term credit banks. Among the categories of banks in the earlier postwar period were three long-term credit banks: Industrial Bank of Japan (IBJ), Long-Term Credit Bank of Japan (LTCB), and Nippon Credit Bank (NCB).

Rather than collecting deposits, they raised funds by issuing bonds (bank debentures), although the bonds were somewhat like certificates of deposit. Further, these were bearer bonds, which made them popular with individuals desiring to shield assets from tax authorities (enabling, for example, intergenerational transfers without payment of inheritance tax). With longer-term liabilities than regular commercial banks, the long-term credit banks made long-term loans, mostly to the heavy industries favored by the government's postwar industrial policy (such as steel, electric power, chemicals, and shipbuilding).

By the 1980s the need for these specialized banks was fading. Some of the industries they financed were no longer growing rapidly or could now issue bonds rather than borrowing long term. Meanwhile, commercial banks were permitted to issue certificates of deposit, somewhat diminishing the distinctiveness of the bank debentures offered by the long-term credit banks. As a consequence, the long-term credit banks were in the forefront of those plagued with nonperforming loans. With traditional loan clients needing less money, they had moved into unfamiliar areas such as real estate.

Faced with imminent collapse, in October 1998 LTCB became the first to be temporarily under the new law. In early 1999 NCB was also nationalized. The viable remains of these two banks were eventually sold to private investors as regular commercial banks. LTCB became Shinsei Bank Ltd, controlled by Ripplewood Holdings LLC, an American private equity firm. NCB became Azora Bank Ltd, purchased by an investor group led by SOFTBANK Corp (which later sold its stake to the American private equity group Cerberus Capital Management LP). IBJ escaped nationalization; it was absorbed in a 2003 merger with Fuji Bank and Dai-Ichi Kangyo bank that created Mizuho Bank within the new Mizuho Financial Group. Thus, specialized banks raising long-term funds to make longer-term loans disappeared from the financial sector.

More generally, blurring the boundaries among the different kinds of banks provided another motive for consolidation. In addition to the long-term credit banks, the postwar structure included trust banks and several categories of commercial banks, ranging from the large nationwide city banks that were supposed to lend to large corporations and two tiers of regional banks that did not operate nationwide and lent to smaller regional and local firms. The even-smaller credit cooperatives (*shinkin* and *shin'yo kumiai*) also serviced small local businesses, while the well-established agriculture cooperatives ran their own credit cooperatives for farmers.

Over the course of the 1970s, changes in loan demand led the various kinds of banks to penetrate one another's markets. With the rationale for separation fading, creation of large general-purpose banks made sense, a reality reflected in the law permitting financial holding companies.

Some consolidation also occurred among smaller banks. From 1980 to 2005, the number of regional banks declined from 132 to 107, with most of that due to mergers (a few went bankrupt). Over the same period, *shinkin* declined in number from 451 to 298, also the result of a wave of mergers, especially after 2000 (Hosono, Sakai, and Tsuru 2009).

Bank consolidation opened the opportunity to rationalize operations by closing branch banks. From the 1950s through the 1970s, one of the features of commercial bank competition had been a race to build branches to collect deposits.

In an environment of controlled interest rates for both deposits and loans, plus excess demand for loans at the controlled interest rates, the logical competitive path for banks was to establish more local branches to collect more deposits. Even this competition was regulated by MOF, through its power to restrict the number of new branches opened each year by each bank.

Since the mid-1970s, however, this model has changed, with the emergence of a persistent excess of commercial bank deposits to private-sector loan demand. In this environment it was no longer advantageous to build more branches. Combined with a more mobile population due to the spread of automobile ownership and ATM machines, banks needed to reduce the number of physical branches. One of the possibilities from the wave of bank mergers that occurred from the late 1990s, therefore, was the ability to shut redundant branches.

Table 3.1 shows a sizable contraction in the number of commercial bank branches since 1990, beginning before the major bank consolidation. Overall, total branches declined by almost 19 percent. Over the 20-year period, a third or more of branches closed in all categories but one. First-tier regional banks actually increased branches in the early 1990s and had almost as many branches in 2010 as in 1990.

The government-owned Post Bank is a huge exception to the trend in diminishing the number of branches. It had slightly more branches in 2010 than in 1990. In 2010 Japan Post Bank had 80 percent more branches than all the other types of banks combined.

TABLE 3.1
Number of Bank Branches

End of Fiscal Year	Commercial Banks						Japan Post Bank[b]
	All Banks	City Banks	Regional Banks	Regional Banks II	Trust Banks	Other[a]	
1990	16,596	3,737	7,598	4,732	430	99	24,103
1995	16,954	3,732	8,042	4,632	432	116	24,583
2000	15,315	2,928	7,904	4,000	443	40	24,774
2005	13,617	2,470	7,464	3,229	277	57	24,123
2010	13,322	2,479	7,478	3,138	268	60	24,185
Change (%):							
1990–2000	−7.7	−21.6	4	−15.5	3	−59.6	2.8
2000–2010	−13.0	−15.3	−5.4	−21.6	−39.5	50.0	−2.4
1990–2010	−19.7	−33.7	−1.6	−33.7	−37.7	−39.4	0.3

Sources: *Japan Statistical Yearbook 2012;* Japan Post Bank, Selected Financial Information (under Japanese GAAP) for the fiscal year ended March 31, 2010, p 15.

[a]Data for "Other" listed as 2010 is March 31, 2009.

[b]Japan Post Bank was "privatized" in 2007, but the government continues to own 100% of the equity.

There was a considerable reduction in the number of bank branches in the years from 1990 to 2010. However, judging from the number of branches seen as one walks the streets of Tokyo, this reduction is not yet complete. Still, overall, the drop is significant.

BANK ASSETS Table 3.2 shows that domestic commercial banks have altered their investment portfolios. These banks show a substantial decline in the share of loans in total assets and a substantial increase in holdings of government securities. From 1990 to 2010 holdings of government bonds expanded from 4.0 percent of total assets to 18.0 percent, while loans dropped from 58.5 percent to 51.6 percent.

For the banking sector as a whole (including institutions for small business, for agriculture, and foreign banks in Japan), low-of-funds data tell essentially the same story, although the categories of assets are slightly different.

The data in table 3.3 indicate a somewhat more dramatic shift from 1991 to 2009. Loans declined from 76 percent of total assets to only

TABLE 3.2

Distribution of Assets of Domestic Commercial Banks (percentage of total assets)

	Total (billion yen)	Cash	Call Loans	Securities Sub-total	Govt Bonds	Corp Bonds	Corp Equity	Loans	Foreign Exchange	Other
1985	420,239	6.8	3.3	15.2	4.2	4.1	6.8	63.7	1.6	9.4
1990	757,299	10.2	2.3	16.4	4.0	3.3	9.1	58.5	1.3	11.4
1995	750,356	6.0	1.7	16.6	3.8	3.1	9.7	64.8	0.5	10.4
2000	759,138	3.8	1.6	21.6	9.0	2.4	10.1	61.1	0.4	11.5
2005	747,994	4.8	1.6	26.4	12.9	4.0	9.5	54.6	0.4	12.1
2010	814,772	3.0	1.9	26.1	18.0	3.9	7.5	51.6	0.3	17.1

Source: Japan Statistical Yearbook 2011.

Note: The data exclude specialized institutions for small business, those for agriculture, and foreign banks in Japan. Nonetheless, they represent a large share of the total banking market.

TABLE 3.3

Distribution of Assets of All Banks (percentage of total assets)

1992	2009	
781,209	1,505,453	Total (billion yen)
0.5	0.6	Cash
2.4	10.2	Deposits
78.6	43.0	Loans
18.2	31.2	Debt securities (total)
9.1	*26.0*	Government debt
3.6	*5.2*	Corporate debt
5.8	2.8	Equity
0.0	3.8	Derivatives
0.0	6.3	Foreign investments
0.0	2.2	Other

Sources: Bank of Japan, *Economic Statistics Annual*, 1991, 209–210; Bank of Japan, "Flow of Funds."

43 percent, while holdings of government securities (including those of all levels of government plus government-owned enterprises) expanded from 8.5 percent to 26 percent.

The differences in the percentage shifts between the two tables indicate that small financial institutions were even more active than commercial banks in acquiring government bonds. The rising desire to hold bonds did not extend to corporate bonds, which shrank from 9.4 percent of assets of all banks to 5.2 percent over the 1991–2009 period.

Based on data in the two tables, the conventional wisdom that Japanese banks have been bulking up on government bonds is correct. With corporate-sector loan demand shrinking, banks need an alternative investment opportunity.

One alternative is overseas investment. However, Japanese banks made costly mistakes when they expanded rapidly overseas in the 1980s, in both developed and developing countries. (Japanese banks were major lenders to Mexico and Thailand, among others, just before financial crises hit those countries.) Some banks also fell short of BIS capital adequacy standards for participation in international lending, preventing them from even considering this option.

Therefore, government bonds were attractive to commercial banks, offering a safe way to earn at least a low profit. Interest rates on government bonds have been low, but deposit rates at banks have been even lower. As of November 2010, interest rates on 10-year government bonds were just over 0.9 percent and the average interest rate on savings deposits (an average of deposits of all durations) was less than 0.1 percent.

If interest rates rise, banks would suffer a capital loss on their bond holdings, but rates remained very low from the late 1990s through 2010, and there is little prospect of any rise for some time to come.

Insurance

The insurance sector in Japan is separated into life and non-life segments. Technically, the barrier between the two segments was eliminated in 1996, but the form of entry has been to establish a wholly owned subsidiary in the other segment of the industry (mostly life insurers establishing non-life subsidiaries).

NON-LIFE INSURANCE The domestic non-life insurance market is large, ranking fourth in the world in terms of premium revenue in 2008 (at ¥11 trillion). Japan's market is only 14 percent the size of the market in the United States, but only slightly behind those of the United Kingdom and Germany (General Insurance Association of Japan [GIA] 2010, 16).

Measured by total assets, the industry has been relatively stagnant for the entire 1990–2010 period. In 1990 total assets were ¥26 trillion, and in 2010 ¥31 trillion. This was a meager 19 percent gain for the 20-year period, all from 1990 to 2001 (when assets peaked at ¥33 trillion). This stagnation should not be surprising given the stagnation in nominal GDP (and, therefore, the probable size of insurable risks associated with economic activity). (Data in this paragraph are from Bank of Japan [BOJ] 1991, 92; GIA 1998, 8; GIA 2003, 9; GIA 2010, 7.)

In the 1970s foreign insurance firms were allowed into Japan under an agreement that defined a third sector of insurance (in addition to life insurance and traditional non-life insurance) that included new products such as cancer insurance (providing for medical expenses not covered in the national health insurance system, as well as income support). A few foreign firms, including Aflac and AIG, managed a small but profitable business in Japan in this niche third-sector market.

Successive rounds of negotiations between the Japanese and US governments led to gradual decontrol of the industry, finally eliminating the distinction of the third sector in the mid-1990s. As a result, the role of foreign firms has undergone a modest but noticeable increase, including acquisition of four Japanese non-life insurance companies by 2010. Such acquired firms are counted by the industry association as domestic firms; foreign non-life insurance firms with branch offices in Japan (that is, those without equity ownership of a Japanese firm) actually declined from 29 in 1998 to 22 in 2010 (GIA 2010, 20; GIA 1998, 7, 25).

Because firms purchased by foreign firms are counted as domestic in the statistics, the available numbers underestimate the role of foreign firms, but it appears to remain somewhat limited. This is true even though Aflac Japan is the largest insurance company in Japan in terms of individual policies in force, helped by having gotten an early start in Japan in the 1970s by offering cancer insurance. In fiscal 1997 foreign insurance companies had ¥290 billion in premiums, just 2.7 percent of what domestic firms did. By fiscal 2009, this had risen to ¥391 billion, 5.6 percent of domestic firms' premiums (GIA 2010, 13, 16; GIA 1998, 7, 25).

Japanese insurers have been cautious about entering global markets. Premium income from insurance contracts written abroad actually fell from fiscal 1997 (¥78 billion) to 2010 (¥61 billion), and this income was only 1.0 percent of premium income at home. The industry remains thoroughly domestic (GIA 2010, 10, 13; GIA 1998, 7, 26).

TABLE 3.4

Life Insurance Industry Data (billion yen)

Fiscal Year	Premium Income	Value of Policies in Force	Total Assets
1990	27,321	1,605,338	131,619
1995	30,762	2,153,467	187,492
2000	26,941	1,802,075	191,731
2005	28,333	1,531,583	209,879
2010	34,454	1,379,409	320,691

Sources: Japan Statistical Yearbook 2010, Table 14–32, "Policies in Force and Management of Assets of Life and Non-Life Insurance Companies (Fiscal Years 1990–2007)"; Life Insurance Association of Japan, "Monthly Statistics."

Note: Data for 2010 are not comparable to earlier years as they include, for the first time, Postal Life. Postal Life was "privatized" in 2007. However, the government owns 100% of the equity.

LIFE INSURANCE As shown in table 3.4, the life insurance industry shows much the same pattern as non-life. The domestic market is large; the face value of total policies in force in 2010 was ¥1.4 quadrillion ($15 trillion at 2010 exchange rates). However, in terms of both value of policies in force and premium income, this industry has been stagnant since 1990. The apparent increase in total assets is due to the inclusion of Postal Life Insurance in the data for 2010.

With deregulation and some acquisitions, foreign insurance firms have made some inroads. At the end of 2009, 14 foreign firms had partially or wholly purchased domestic life insurance companies, and 4 others had branch office status (Life Insurance Association of Japan [LIA] 2009). Unfortunately, data on the market share of foreign life insurance companies in Japan are not available.

INSURANCE COMPANY INVESTMENTS Domestic non-life and life insurance have historically shown considerable deference to government policy. The 1997–1998 report of the non-life industry association even includes a paragraph about the "fairly substantial amount of funds" that was "set aside to fulfill the insurers' public responsibilities, to underwrite national government bonds, government-guaranteed bonds, and local government bonds" (GIA 1998, 10). Even without a policy motive, it is conceivable that insurance firms (just like commercial

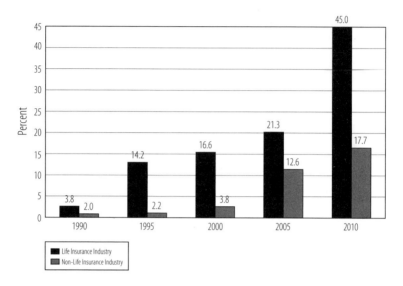

Figure 3.5 Government Bonds as a Share of Total Assets in the Insurance Industry (in percent). *Sources*: GIA, *Fact Book 2009–2010*, p 7; LIA, *Life Insurance Business in Japan*, 2003/2004 edition, p 4; and LIA, "Monthly Statistics."

Note: All data are for the end of the fiscal year (March 31 of the next calendar year). In the life insurance industry, the leap to 45% in 2010 is an artifact of the inclusion of Postal Life data after 2007.

banks) saw government bonds as a zero-credit-risk, modest-return investment.

Figure 3.5 shows that insurance firms have substantially increased their holdings of government bonds over time. (In the life insurance industry, the leap to 45 percent in 2010 is an artifact of the inclusion of Postal Life.)

Insurance firms were first given permission to invest part of their assets abroad in the early 1980s and have done so since that time. However, in the years since 1990, they do not appear to have become more heavily engaged in international portfolio investments.

For life insurance companies, foreign securities formed 13.1 percent of total assets in fiscal 1990, and 14.3 percent in fiscal 2010. Looking at 2005 to avoid inclusion of Postal Life, foreign securities were a modestly higher 18.8 percent (LIA 2004, 4; LIA nd).

For the non-life insurance industry, foreign securities were 14.5 percent of total assets in fiscal 1996 (the earliest year of data available to the author) and a slightly higher 15.8 percent in fiscal 2010 (GIA 1998, 8; GIA 2010, 7).

Japanese insurance firms do most of their insurance business at home, and their assets are mostly domestic investments.

Securities Firms

The securities industry has been dominated by four large firms, but it includes many smaller ones, with considerable entry and exit. As of March 2010 the Japan Securities Dealers Association had 305 members, up from 265 in 1992. In fiscal 2009 the association gained 10 new members and lost 26, a pattern similar to the earlier years of the decade. (Japan Securities Dealers Association [JSDA] 2002, 12; JSDA 2009, 24).

Industry structure at the top has undergone considerable change since 1990. Until 1997 the four dominant firms were (listed by revenue) Nomura Securities, Daiwa Securities, Nikko Securities, and Yamaichi Securities.

Nomura remains the largest domestic firm and remains unattached to any broader financial group. Nikko began a joint venture with Salomon Smith Barney; became Nikko Cordial; was purchased in 2008 by Citigroup; and was sold the next year to a subsidiary of Sumitomo Mitsui Financial Group when Citi needed to liquidate assets as a result of the global financial crisis. Daiwa entered into an agreement to become part of the Sumitomo-Mitsui Banking Corporation (using the name Daiwa SMBC Securities), but this alliance was dissolved in 2009 when SMBC chose to purchase Nikko Cordial, so Daiwa is once again a stand-alone securities company.

Yamaichi Securities went bankrupt in 1997 and had its retail operations purchased by Merrill Lynch, but Merrill abandoned the effort in 2002. (For a short analysis of why Merrill Lynch failed, see Bremner 2001.)

The new member of the big four is Mizuho Securities, part of the Mizuho Financial Group. It was created in 2000 through the merger of the securities subsidiaries of the three banks that formed Mizuho (Fuji Securities, IBJ Securities, and DKB Securities) (Mizuho Securities 2010).

As of 2010 these four firms represented 72 percent of total assets of the members of the Japan Securities Dealers Association and 76 percent of operating revenue. But even though the industry remains dominated by four firms, the change in composition (losing Yamaichi, gaining Mizuho) and shifts in ownership indicate at least some structural transformation.

The other major change in the industry has been the arrival of foreign investment banks. These had tiny offices in Tokyo until the mid-1980s and then rapidly expanded as deregulation made it easier for foreign institutions to participate in capital markets. Typically, foreign firms expanded from just a few people to offices of one to two thousand by the 1990s.

Capital Markets: Equity

The Tokyo Stock Exchange (TSE) is by far the largest of Japan's exchanges, with the Osaka Stock Exchange a distant second. Once owned by the brokers who used them, both demutualized in 2001 and are now listed companies. Three small regional exchanges merged into TSE in March 2000: Hiroshima, Fukuoka, and Niigata. The Kyoto exchange merged with Osaka in March 2001.

Equity markets provide a means for firms to raise new funds by issuing new equity shares, and a venue for buying or selling shares (including efforts to gain or sell control over corporations). In the case of Japan, equity markets have played only a moderate role in raising corporate funds and have not been a center for contesting corporate control.

RAISING FUNDS Despite the historical reliance of Japanese firms on bank loans as a means of raising funds, corporations have raised some new capital through the stock market. At one time the cost of doing so was high due to the practice of selling new shares to existing shareholders at par value, but that practice had declined significantly by 1990 and is now gone. The amount of new funds raised annually by listed Japanese corporations through the stock market is shown in figure 3.6.

Since the annual amount issued has varied widely, it makes some sense to simply compare the two decades. Firms raised an annual ¥2.2 trillion in the 1990–1999 period and ¥2.9 trillion in the 2000–2010 period, only a modest increase (although the 1990s are skewed upward by the abnormal jump in funds raised in 1999 during the dot.com frenzy). For the 2000s equity funds raised in Japan were 17 percent the size of those raised in the United States, a ratio lower than the relative

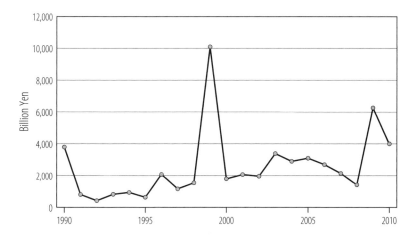

Figure 3.6 New Funds Raised in the Stock Market (billion yen). *Source*: Tokyo Stock Exchange, *Fact Book 2010*, p 78.

size of the two economies. (Japan's GDP was roughly one-third that of the United States.)

Comparisons of fund raising in various world markets justify at least a rough conclusion that equity markets continue to be of less importance in Japan than in the United States, and even Australia. (See, for example, data in World Federation of Exchanges [WFE] 2009, 68). Start-ups are treated more fully later.

TRADING   The stock market is also a venue in which existing shares are bought and sold. The big development was the decline in share prices since 1990, discussed earlier. The collapse of the bubble has meant the Tokyo Stock Exchange (TSE) has diminished in size (measured by total market capitalization) relative to other foreign exchanges, and the New York Stock Exchange (NYSE) in particular. In 1990 market capitalization of $2.9 trillion was slightly larger than the NYSE's $2.7 trillion, making TSE the largest exchange in the world. By 2005 NYSE's market capitalization had risen to $13.6 trillion, while TSE's had declined to $4.6 trillion (NYSE nd). By 2010, after the major decline and partial recovery of stock prices accompanying the global recession, the TSE market capitalization was $3.8 trillion (just slightly larger than London and just behind NASDAQ), compared to $13.4 trillion for the NYSE (WFE 2010, 74).

TABLE 3.5
Distribution of Outstanding Amounts of Bonds (percentage of total issues outstanding)

	Central Government	Municipal Government	Government Guaranteed	Corporate	Bank Debentures
1990	57.6	6.0	6.1	9.2	21.1
2010	84.0	4.7	3.5	6.1	1.6

Source: Japan Statistical Yearbook 1996, 474 and 475.

Capital Markets: Bonds

The major story of bond markets in Japan has been the rising dominance of government bonds. Data on outstanding bonds are shown in table 3.5.

During the study period (since 1990), corporations have been somewhat disinterested in issuing bonds, and the market has been skewed toward government issues. Already in 1990, government bonds (central government, municipal, and government-guaranteed) were 70 percent of all bonds in the market. By 2010 this share had risen to an overwhelming 92 percent.

In the private sector, long-term credit banks were the largest issuers of bonds. Their shorter-term bonds (one-year debentures) were sold mostly to individuals. This is because they were more like certificates of deposit than bonds and were bearer (not registered), enabling tax evasion. Bank debentures had largely disappeared by 2010 due to the disappearance of their issuers; the long-term credit banks had transformed into regular commercial banks that were not authorized to issue bank debentures.

Start-ups

Since the 1980s the Japanese government has had a goal of encouraging start-up firms. The postwar financial system was biased against the provision of capital for new firms. Collateralized lending by the banking system made it difficult for start-ups with no assets (especially no land) to use as collateral. This situation was exacerbated by the relationship-based nature of bank lending decisions, making it difficult for newcomers to borrow. Listing requirements hindered young firms from using the stock market to raise capital.

The rationale was that existing firms, with strong management and financial connections, could (and would) move into new, innovative businesses. Thus, the American model of extensive financing for start-ups, and a constant churning of new firms replacing old ones, was not considered necessary or desirable. If large firms could move in new directions, that would, for example, lessen the burden on workers, who could be reallocated to new positions with the firm rather than laid off by failing firms and forced to find new jobs on their own.

But by the 1980s, the government attitude began to shift toward a view that venture capital markets should be encouraged, based at least in part from observing the success of American high-tech start-ups.

VENTURE CAPITAL FUNDS Since the 1980s the government has pursued two approaches to assist new firms: promotion of venture capital funds and creation of stock markets where small, young firms could carry out an initial public offering (IPO).

Promotion of venture capital funds has included regulatory change (such as a 1998 guarantee of limited liability for venture capital partnerships), subsidized loans from the government, and even three government-owned venture capital funds. The industry is largely domestic: Japanese funds make only 8 percent of their investments abroad. (For a thorough review of the policy changes from 1963 to 2006 affecting venture capital funds, see Schaede [2008, pp 206–21].)

The venture capital industry remains small. For comparison, US venture capital firms had outstanding investments of about $214 billion by the mid-2000s (¥25 trillion at 2007 exchange rates), as had the rapidly expanding venture capital industry in Europe. In Japan, however, the amount has remained a minuscule $8 billion (¥1 trillion). From the late 1990s the European venture capital industry was growing rapidly and actually exceeded the size of that in the United States by 2007. In contrast, little growth occurred in the small Japanese industry—or in the United States after 2001. Data are in figure 3.7.

JASDAQ AND MOTHERS The second policy development has been the creation and expansion of specialized stock markets with lower requirements for initial listing than the main exchanges. Japan has had three such markets: JASDAQ (founded in 1963 as an over-the-counter

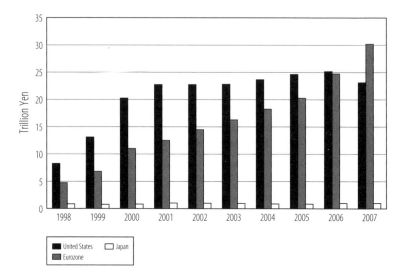

Figure 3.7 Venture Capital Investments (trillion yen). *Source*: Japan Small Business Research Institute, Ministry of Economy Trade and Industry, 2009 White Paper on Medium and Small Enterprises in Japan, p 146.

market and transformed into an exchange in 1999); Mothers (a subsidiary of the Tokyo Stock Exchange founded in 1999); and Hercules (the renamed former joint venture of NASDAQ with the Osaka Stock Exchange). Hercules was formed initially in 2000 but merged into JASDAQ in 2009.

From 2000 to the mid-2000s, the number of initial public offerings, the numbers of new firms added to the exchanges, and share prices were all rising, leading one analyst to conclude in 2008 that these markets were producing a "sea change in new company formation" (Schaede 2008, 224). That conclusion is less certain now given developments during and after the global financial crisis.

Consider first what has happened to the Mothers exchange, where activity has faded over time. Peak activity was in 2004. In 2007 (before the recession) new equity raised was just 43 percent of the peak level. In the post-recession year of 2010 there were 26 new listings, compared to 56 at the 2004 peak. Data are in table 3.6.

An additional discouraging aspect of the Mothers exchange has been a sharp decline in share prices, which might explain the drop in the

TABLE 3.6
Initial Public Offerings on the Mothers Exchange: Number and Amount
Raised

2002	2003	2004	2005	2006	2007	2008	2009	2010	
8	31	56	36	41	23	12	4	6	Number of IPOs
18.3	76.7	126.1	118.0	87.4	54.2	22.2	13.2	16.3	Total raised (billions of yen)
2.2	2.4	2.2	3.2	2.3	2.3	1.8	3.3	2.7	Average raised (billions of yen)

Source: Tokyo Stock Exchange, Mothers Monthly Report, July 2011, 7.

number of IPOs. The Mothers price index peaked in early 2006 and then fell steeply, well before the onset of the global economic recession in 2008. In 2010 the index was 80 percent below its 2006 peak. TOPIX, the price index for all companies listed on the First Section of the Tokyo Stock Exchange, also declined due to the 2008–2009 recession, but the decline began later (the fall of 2007) and, as of the end of 2010, TOPIX was down 46 percent from the 2007 peak, far less than the drop in Mothers.

Trends on the other special exchanges for new companies parallel that of the Mothers Exchange. The JASDAQ price index declined by two-thirds from a peak in 2006 through July 2010, while volume was down about 80 percent, and issues by newly listed companies dropped 75 percent.

Figure 3.8 shows what has happened to all IPOs of new firms on stock exchanges in Japan (including those on the main exchanges). The total peaked in 2006 at 188 and fell to 49 in 2008, and then to only 19 in the recession year of 2009.

OVERVIEW OF CREATING NEW FIRMS Despite the emergence of some venture capital funds and the creation of new exchanges, Japan remains very low in comparison to other countries in terms of creation of new corporations. An Organisation for Economic Co-operation and

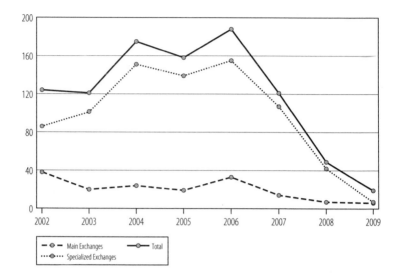

Figure 3.8 Initial Public Offerings. *Source*: Venture Enterprise Center, Venture Business Review in Japan 2008–2009.

Note: The main exchanges are Tokyo, Osaka, Nagoya, Fukuoka, and Sapporo. Specialized exchanges include JASDAQ, Mothers, Hercules, Centrex, Q-Board Ambitious, and NEO (JASDAQ).

Development (OECD) report found that for 2000–2007, Japan ranked lowest among a sample of 39 countries for firm formation (measured as the percentage of newly registered corporations as a share of all corporations). For Japan the percentage was only 4 percent. In contrast, it was 13 percent in the United States and 16 percent for the United Kingdom (the highest percentage) (OECD 2010a, 64). Figure 3.9 shows the trend in birth and death of corporations in Japan over time.

New corporate registrations as a percentage of existing corporations decreased as the bubble collapsed in the early 1990s, and the rate has remained low ever since, at 4 percent or less. Although the rate rose from 2002 to 2006, that increase was only from 3 percent to 4 percent. Thus, throughout the period from the early 1990s through the 2000s, the birth rate of new corporations was consistently far below that in other industrialized countries. Also note that in some years (1997 and 2003) the exit rate was higher than the entry rate.

The general conclusion that follows from these data is that the market for financing new corporations remains limited, despite two or

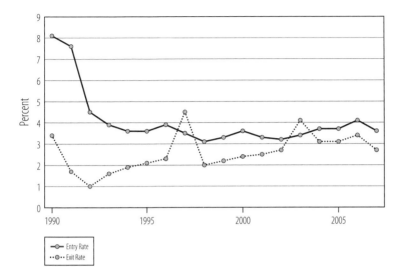

Figure 3.9 Birth and Death of Corporations (percent of all corporations). *Source*: Japan Small Business Research Institute, Ministry of Economy Trade and Industry, 2009 White Paper on Medium and Small Enterprises in Japan, p 326.

Note: The data in this figure are for corporations; other METI data for "companies" include sole proprietorships and show a wider gap between entry and exit (with exit exceeding entry from the second half of the 1980s (see META 2008, p 338.)

more decades of regulatory change and government-subsidized financing. The creation of new corporations remains quite low in international comparison and showed no more than a minor increase in the several years prior to the 2007–2008 recession.

Why have efforts to promote venture capital and new firm creation failed for two decades? In the past, strong long-term supply chain ties among existing firms (vertical keiretsu relationships) inhibited new entry. Despite some change or loosening in these relationships, perhaps this factor remains.

Probably more important is the general risk-averse nature of society. New-firm formation requires risk-taking entrepreneurs, risk-tolerant venture capital funds that are also capable of providing expert management guidance to fledgling firms, and financial institutions plus individuals willing to invest when firms carry out an IPO. None of these characteristics describes contemporary Japanese society very well. University graduates still prefer the security of jobs with large corporations, if they can obtain them, to the uncertainty of working for a start-up, a preference reinforced by the poor job prospects for any individual losing a position at a failed start-up. Venture capital funds are few in number and do not have as much appetite for risk as do their American counterparts. Also, banks prefer government bonds to risky assets, and individuals hold little stock (of all kinds, much less shares of newly listed firms). These characteristics have proven resistant to change.

Household Financial Assets

To put the changes occurring in the individual parts of the financial sector into perspective, it is helpful to look at how households allocate their financial portfolios. Historically, the bulk of household financial assets has been in the form of cash plus demand and savings deposits at banks, rather than in the form of investment in stocks or bonds (either directly or through mutual funds). This pattern has not changed in the years since the beginning of the 1990s, as table 3.7 indicates.

TABLE 3.7
Distribution of Household Financial Assets (as percentage of total assets)

Japan			United States[a]	
1991	2000	2010	2010	Asset
7	12	19	1	Cash and demand deposits[b]
50	45	32	18	Time and savings deposits[c]
57	57	55	19	Cash and bank deposits
21	28	28	35	Insurance and pension reserves
19	15	12	44	Stocks and bonds
1	0	5	2	All else

Sources: Federal Reserve, "Z.1, Flow of Funds Accounts of the United States, Balance Sheet Tables"; Bank of Japan, "Flow of Funds, Releases, Annual Data (Calendar Year); Bank of Japan, *Economic Statistics Annual 1991*, 209 and 210.

[a]US data include a line item for proprietor's equity in noncorporate businesses, but this is excluded for comparability with Japanese flow of funds data.

[b]Cash is not held in banks, but the US data on household financial assets lump together cash and checkable deposits. For Japan in 2010, holdings of cash were 4% (so demand deposits were 15%, and total bank deposits were 51%, of total household financial assets).

[c]For the United States, "Time and savings deposits" includes money market funds (MMF).

From 1991 to 2010 the share of assets held as currency and demand deposits remained virtually steady. However, the share held as currency and demand deposits increased while time and savings deposits declined. This seemingly odd development may be due to the very low interest rates on savings deposits since the mid-1990s (Why put money in a savings deposit when the interest rate is only 0.1 percent?) or other factors, such as a desire to avoid recorded transactions to evade taxes (although why this motive would have increased over this time period is unclear).

As society has aged, the share of assets in the form of insurance and pension fund reserves increased (as it has in the United States), but the share held in the form of stocks and bonds fell. Obviously, a major cause of this decline in relative share was the collapse of stock prices.

The contrast with the United States is startling. Americans hold little of their financial assets in the form of currency or demand deposits, in contrast to the 19 percent held in Japan. Americans also held almost half of their assets in the form of equity and bonds, compared to only 12 percent for Japanese households.

Over the past decade, conversations with people working in the Japanese financial sector indicate a growing market for mutual funds, particularly for funds investing outside Japan. The story goes like this: Mrs Watanabe (as the representative keeper of Japan's household savings is often referred to) is tired of near-zero returns on savings accounts and is putting money into higher-return financial instruments. Since the stock market has performed so poorly and erratically, foreign investments have become more attractive.

The data paint a different picture. Investments in foreign stocks and bonds were only 0.6 percent of total household financial assets in 2010. That amount undoubtedly represents an increase (as no number is even reported for 1990, and was a slightly lower 0.5 percent in 2000), but does not represent substantial change. Anecdotal evidence, at least in this case, stands in stark contrast to the broader reality; households have not shifted the allocation of their financial portfolios away from bank deposits since 1990.

If the behavior of households has not changed, then any shift in financial flows (away from loans and toward bonds, for example) required that commercial banks change their own portfolio behavior. Banks have indeed shifted from loans toward bonds, providing an indirect channel through which household savings have ultimately been mobilized for investment in bonds. However, overwhelmingly these have been government bonds, which pay quite low interest rates.

Corporate Borrowers

Another way to evaluate the overall impact of shifts in the financial sector is to look at how nonfinancial corporations raise funds.

COMPOSITION OF LIABILITIES   Table 3.8 shows the structure of nonfinancial corporate liabilities in the flow of funds accounts. Although some change has occurred, the shifts are insufficient to conclude that the pattern of corporate financing has undergone fundamental alteration over the 1990–2010 period.

This lack of change is, on the surface, different from the story of chapter 5 by Seok and Shin. They tell of firms coming to rely on bond issues rather than loans. However, their emphasis is on large corporations; the table here presents data for all nonfinancial corporations. Further, they focus on the second half of the 1980s, a special time when relaxation of the previously tight MOF rules under which corporations were permitted to issue bonds enabled firms that had previously not issued any bonds to do so. It was also a time when leading corporations were able to take advantage of the rapidly rising prices on the Tokyo Stock Exchange to issue new equity.

Loans (from both commercial and government banks) experienced a drop of 10 percentage points for the entire period. (Loans' share was down 13 points at its low in 2007). Much of the drop came from a decline in loans from domestic commercial banks, while loans from government-owned banks and miscellaneous other sources increased slightly over the entire period, though the share is volatile.

The decline in the share of loans did not imply an increased reliance on bonds and other debt instruments. All forms of debt securities as a share of total liabilities increased only 1.7 percentage points over this time period, ending at 11.7 percent. However, there was an increase in domestic debt securities because overseas bonds declined.

Commercial paper, an important form of short-term debt in the United States, remained minor in Japan and actually declined (from 1.7 percent to 1.2 percent).

Trade credit among nonfinancial corporations remained important throughout the period, accounting for over 20 percent of liabilities.

TABLE 3.8
Distribution of Private Nonfinancial Corporate Liabilities (as percentage of total liabilities)

	Total Liabilities (trillion yen)	Loans				Debt Securities				Trade Credit	All Else[a]
		Total	From Domestic Financial Institutions	From Government Financial Institutions	From Others	Total	Domestic Corporate Bonds	Overseas Securities	Commercial Paper		
1990	790	57.5	49.5	3.8	4.1	10.0	3.9	4.4	1.7	23.1	9.4
1991	852	58.3	49.9	3.8	4.6	9.1	3.7	4.1	1.3	23.2	9.4
1992	890	59.3	48.5	4.4	6.3	9.3	3.9	4.3	1.1	21.7	9.7
1993	879	59.8	50.3	4.7	4.8	9.3	4.6	3.6	1.1	20.7	10.2
1994	884	60.0	50.1	5.4	4.6	8.9	5.0	2.9	1.0	21.0	10.1
1995	882	59.7	49.2	5.7	4.9	8.8	5.5	2.4	1.0	21.8	9.7
1996	910	59.7	46.1	5.4	8.2	8.8	5.7	2.3	0.9	22.8	8.6
1997	891	59.0	45.6	5.0	8.4	9.4	6.6	1.7	1.1	22.5	9.1
1998	839	59.9	47.2	5.5	7.2	10.2	7.3	1.3	1.7	21.6	8.3
1999	808	58.6	45.4	5.7	7.5	10.1	7.5	1.1	1.5	22.7	8.6
2000	787	56.7	44.5	5.7	6.4	9.8	7.7	0.9	1.1	24.7	8.9
2001	742	56.5	44.4	5.6	6.5	10.4	7.9	1.0	1.5	23.6	9.5
2002	746	52.8	40.4	5.3	7.2	10.3	7.7	1.0	1.6	22.7	14.1
2003	736	49.7	37.3	5.1	7.3	10.0	7.5	1.1	1.4	22.9	17.4
2004	714	48.3	35.7	5.1	7.5	10.3	7.8	1.4	1.1	24.2	17.3
2005	710	45.6	34.7	4.8	6.1	10.6	7.8	1.6	1.2	25.7	18.1
2006	721	45.5	34.5	4.4	6.6	10.4	7.7	1.6	1.1	27.7	16.4
2007	737	44.5	34.2	4.6	5.7	11.3	8.1	1.6	1.5	28.1	16.1
2008	714	49.9	38.7	4.6	6.6	11.5	8.4	1.5	1.5	24.4	14.3
2009	700	48.5	35.9	5.3	7.3	11.5	8.9	1.4	1.2	23.8	16.3
2010	686	47.8	34.8	5.3	7.6	11.7	9.2	1.3	1.2	24.9	15.6

Source: Bank of Japan, "Flow of Funds (Fiscal Year), Financial Assets and Liabilities, Private Nonfinancial Corporations."

[a]All else includes accounts payable, financial derivatives, deposits, and other.

Although trade credit is not a net source of funding to the corporate sector as a whole, it has played a larger role in Japan than in the United States for intercorporate finance, especially in the form of large corporations providing financing to their suppliers.

The data show some change in the composition of corporate liabilities; the 10 percentage point decline in reliance on bank loans is significant. But there is scant evidence for that decline leading to a shift toward securities. The biggest offset to the decline in bank loans is "all else," within which the main elements are accounts payable and deposits, two forms of informal financing among firms akin to trade credit.

Total liabilities of corporations declined. From a high of ¥910 trillion in 1996, liabilities fell 25 percent to ¥686 trillion by 2010. The big story, therefore, is the sustained effort by corporations since the mid-1990s to reduce leverage as firms recognized that they faced a slow-growth future in which high debt levels could be risky.

CORPORATE FUNDRAISING   Another way to look at corporate behavior is through data that report funds raised by all corporations (both firms listed on stock exchanges and those that are not) that is available to them for all purposes (including fixed capital expenditures). These data are shown in table 3.9.

The table shows that, for much of the period since 1998, corporations have been more than able to finance their fixed investment needs through internal sources, mainly depreciation. Whether depreciation allowances available to Japanese firms are generous because of deliberate government policy in the earlier postwar period is unclear, though tax policies were generally favorable toward industry at that time. However, that Japanese firms can now finance most of their fixed capital investment from cash available from depreciation allowances is extraordinary. This is not a result of a collapse of fixed corporate investment, as later discussion in this chapter will show that the ratio of private fixed nonresidential investment remains high.

With depreciation so large, firms were in a position to cut their use of other financing sources. New equity issues, for example, are negative in most of these years as firms bought back more existing shares than were newly issued. In addition, overall net annual external borrowing has been negative in most years as firms paid back loans faster than they borrowed new money. Bond issues exemplify this trend, with net bond issues negative in most years.

TABLE 3.9
Corporate Fundraising (in billion yen, percent)

| Year | Corporate Fund-raising | Capital Increases | Internal Sources | | | External Borrowing | | |
			Total	Retained Earnings	Depreciation	Total	Bond Issues	Loans and Other Borrowing
1998	370,740	3.8	95.1	−20.8	112.1	4.9	9.8	−4.9
1999	453,169	6.1	127.7	32.9	88.7	−27.7	−2.5	−25.2
2000	571,927	7.8	126.2	45.5	72.8	−26.2	−5.9	−20.3
2001	331,737	−0.2	120.2	−2.2	122.6	−20.2	−6.8	−13.4
2002	177,127	−24.1	208.8	12.6	220.3	−108.8	−10.3	−98.5
2003	459,989	−17.5	139.1	63.5	93.1	−39.1	0.1	−39.2
2004	476,754	−35.5	131.5	75.6	91.5	−31.5	−3.3	−28.2
2005	745,814	−20.7	114.8	77.9	57.6	−14.8	−1.5	−13.4
2006	632,820	−17.5	104.7	52.8	69.4	−4.7	−0.2	−4.5
2007	540,729	−19.0	87.2	24.0	82.2	12.8	0.1	12.7
2007	540,729	−19.0	87.2	24.0	82.2	12.8	0.1	12.7
2008	375,526	−10.8	55.6	−50.1	116.5	44.4	1.6	42.8
2009	443,284	−8.2	106.6	23.4	91.4	−6.6	3.4	−10.0

Source: Ministry of Finance, "Financial Statements Statistics of Corporations by Industry."

As an internal source of funds (along with retained earnings), depreciation allowances are used at the discretion of management. In theory, management should allocate these funds on the basis of expected return—no different than what markets are supposed to do. However, if management is subject to little oversight by shareholders, then the possibility exists for misallocation of funds without punishment by shareholders. Management may have goals other than profit maximization, such as market share maximization or protection of jobs (especially for managers), that lead to investment in projects that yield little profit. Later sections of this chapter argue that this is the case for Japan. Therefore, the high depreciation allowances are an obstacle to efficient capital allocation.

Government Regulatory Policies

The shifts in financial sector structure detailed in the previous section were enabled in part by important changes in regulatory policy. This section considers three major policy changes that have affected the structure and performance of private-sector financial firms. The first was a broad restructuring of the Ministry of Finance (MOF) that saw its powers reduced by stripping away several of its functions. This included a shift of regulatory power to a newly created Financial Services Agency and a reduction of MOF influence over monetary policy as the Bank of Japan became more independent. The second was a series of deregulatory measures, the most prominent being the "Big Bang" deregulation of financial markets in the late 1990s. The third concerned the government's direct role in financial intermediation, with alteration of the Fiscal Investment and Loan Program (FILP) and the status of the postal savings and insurance plans that fed funds into it.

MOF to FSA and BOJ

Throughout the postwar period, MOF had control over policy on taxation and the budget, as well as regulation and oversight of much of the financial sector (with the exception of agricultural credit cooperatives that were under the jurisdiction of the Ministry of Agriculture, and cooperative institutions for small business that fell under what was then the Ministry for International Trade and Industry and is now the Ministry for Economy, Trade and Industry).

With this collection of responsibilities, MOF had a reputation as the most powerful of all the economic ministries. Its top career officials were almost exclusively graduates from the law program at the University of Tokyo, the most prestigious and difficult to enter program at the most prestigious university in the country. This enhanced respect for the ministry.

To put MOF in an American context, it combined the functions of the Department of the Treasury, Office of Management and Budget, and the Securities and Exchange Commission. In addition, MOF had considerable influence over the monetary policies of the Bank of Japan (BOJ). However, as the events of the 1990s unfolded, MOF's reputation was badly damaged. This led to a number of its functions being placed in new agencies outside the ministry, reducing its overall power within the government bureaucracy.

As real estate prices began falling and borrowers began having difficulty repaying loans to commercial banks, MOF's preferred strategy was to collude with the banks in hiding the extent of the problems from the public. The excuse was threefold.

First, the ministry believed the problems were temporary and would disappear as real estate and stock market prices reversed their decline (something that did not happen). Second, MOF believed that the public would lose confidence in the banking system if too much information was revealed. Finally, MOF was confident that it could quietly handle any problem banks had on an ad hoc basis by pressuring strong banks to absorb failing ones (as it had done on a few earlier occasions).

MOF attitudes were also affected by an incestuous relationship with the financial sector. Senior career officials routinely retired into positions at financial firms in hiring deals arranged officially between the ministry and the firms, creating an obvious conflict of interest.

The first major crack in the reputation of the Ministry of Finance came in 1995 when all seven *Jūsen* (non-bank lending institutions specialized in real estate mortgages) collapsed. The *Jūsen*, owned by large commercial banks, had been created with the encouragement of MOF in the 1970s and 1980s when commercial banks were looking for a way to increase their involvement in real estate lending. Entering this market was seen as a way of offsetting stagnating demand for loans from traditional customers. All seven *Jūsen* had retired MOF officials as CEOs (most of whom quietly resigned shortly before the failures).

The collapse led to a bitter argument among commercial banks, agricultural credit cooperatives, MOF, and the Ministry of Agriculture over which organizations should take primary responsibility for covering the losses involved. This inter-bureaucratic struggle undermined MOF's reputation as a legitimate, fair arbiter of problems involving multiple players (Milhaupt and Miller 2000). At one point in 1995, the ministry shut its gates and had its entrances protected by riot police as a large group of protesters collected outside for two weeks. (For more detail on the *Jūsen* issue, see Hoshi and Kashyap (2001, 269–71).)

MOF was further rocked by a series of revelations of unethical behavior. The media reported officials being wined and dined by the senior executives of banks being audited, the leaking (for bribes) of upcoming "surprise" inspections, and the inclusion of MOF officials among the list of VIP account holders at Nomura Securities who were guaranteed sizable returns on their stock portfolios. As Yamaichi Securities was heading toward bankruptcy in 1997, MOF officials were accused of providing the firm with guidance on how to hide its losses through a variety of imprudent, unethical, and illegal means (Lincoln 2001, 66). (For a longer and more detailed analysis of these scandals and their impact, see Amyx 2004.)

The outcome was a political decision to strip MOF of some of its functions, thereby reducing its dominant bureaucratic role. Oversight of fiscal policy and broad budget guidelines was moved to a new cabinet position in 2001, the Minister of State for Economic and Fiscal Policy. Informal influence over the Bank of Japan was ended in 1998 by a law that clearly enunciated BOJ independence. The key change for oversight of the financial sector was to create a new independent agency, the Financial Services Agency (FSA), which came into existence in mid-1998.

When the FSA was created, many of the employees were simply moved from MOF, and the first several political appointees to run the agency demonstrated tepid enthusiasm for dealing decisively with the nonperforming loan problem. However, that changed when Heizo Takenaka (an academic economist who eventually became a member of the Diet) was appointed to head the agency in 2001 and was given strong backing by Prime Minister Junichiro Koizumi. Starting with his leadership, the FSA played a much stronger role in pressuring banks to deal with nonperforming loans and to comply with new directives concerning prudent behavior.

The BOJ was also affected by the stripping of power from MOF. A law passed in 1997 made BOJ more formally independent from MOF. This paralleled change in some other countries, underwritten by the view among economists that central banks should be as independent as possible from political and bureaucratic interference. As is obvious from the data presented earlier, however, the new independence of the BOJ did not lead to an end of deflation. In fact, the more independent BOJ soon made a major policy mistake by raising interest rates and shrinking the monetary base (causing money supply growth to slow), a move taken despite vocal opposition from MOF and politicians. This helped push the economy back into recession in 2001 and exacerbated deflation.

Regulatory Change

Since the 1970s the government has engaged in a piecemeal process of deregulation of both financial and nonfinancial sectors of the economy. From the mid-1990s to the mid-2000s, however, some acceleration appears to have occurred, driven by both distress in the financial sector and the desire to promote Tokyo as an international financial center. A key driving force in accelerating change was the crisis of 1997–1998, when efforts to contain the nonperforming loan problems in the banking sector by traditional approaches failed and the banking sector neared collapse. Some of the most important changes are listed in table 3.10.

Summarizing the changes is difficult, as the common practice has been to make individual small regulatory changes and then codify and expand their scope through major changes in various laws. But added up over time, significant legal changes have occurred.

In 1990 Japan had no formal procedures for handling failed financial institutions, relying instead on an informal process of government-arranged takeovers of weak institutions by strong ones. Regulation made it difficult for corporations to spin off individual operating divisions (or for other firms to buy those divisions). Half-year financial reports from corporations were widely regarded as inaccurate. And regulation and transaction taxes inhibited Tokyo's role as an international financial center.

By around 2006 Japan had laws to handle failed financial institutions and had experienced two rounds of recapitalization of banks with government funds; new rules made mergers and acquisitions easier;

TABLE 3.10
Important Policy and Legal Changes Affecting Financial Development

Year	Financial Markets	Commercial Law	Accounting Rules
1996	Announcement of the Big Bang reforms		
1997	Ban lifted on holding companies; New Foreign Exchange Law; Financial System Reform Law	Simplification of merger procedures	
1998	Two laws to deal with troubled financial institutions	Stock repurchases allowed	
1999		Industrialization Revitalization Law (to assist failing firms)	Adoption of tax effect accounting and cash flow statements
2000		Civil Rehabilitation Law (new bankruptcy procedures); new simplified corporate spin-off (and spin-on) procedures	Consolidated accounting reform; mark-to-market valuation of financial assets (except for cross-share holdings)
2001	Abolition of par value stock issues; introduction of treasury stocks (repurchase of own shares); "Guidelines for Multiparty Workouts" for bank rescues		New accounting of retirement benefits; mark-to-market for cross-shareholdings; statutory auditor system expanded; revised corporate reorganization tax rules
2002	New stock option system; Program for Financial Revival; Bank Stock Ownership Law		Consolidated tax return system
2003	Treasury stock purchase system for M&A	Revised Corporation Reorganization Law; Liquidation Law; New Business Promotion Law	New accounting rules for impaired assets; quarterly earnings reports for TSE-listed firms
2005		Corporation Law revised; revision of Antimonopoly Law; takeover guidance	
2006	Financial Instruments and Exchange Law		LLP Law; statutory quarterly earnings reports for listed firms; new reporting system for large shareholdings

Source: Adapted from Schaede 2008, 14 and 15.

mandatory quarterly financial reports were required for all listed firms; accounting rules were generally more robust; rules governing international finance were eased; and financial firms were permitted to establish holding companies as a means for expanding into previously separated segments of financial activity.

For the financial sector, the major development was the Big Bang reform, announced in 1996. These reforms had the dual purpose of promoting efficiency and stability in the financial sector (encouraging a shift away from banks toward capital markets) and of making Tokyo a more significant international financial center. The Big Bang involved many small, individual changes, although some were codified in 1997 in the Foreign Exchange Law and the Financial System Reform Law.

The list of individual regulatory changes associated with the Big Bang is quite extensive, occurring over the five years from 1997 to 2001. (For a detailed list of all these reforms, and a careful analysis of their impact, see Shirai 2009, 130–78.)

According to Shirai, the reforms had four motivations. The first was a belief that greater internationalization of Japanese financial markets would enable more efficient allocation of financial resources within Japan. The second was to promote growth and development of the domestic financial sector itself in order to help increase overall economic growth. Third, the government hoped Japan could play a larger role as an Asian financial hub, to the benefit of the whole region. Fourth, with the reforms, the government hoped Japanese financial institutions would be better positioned to play a leading role in promoting Asian regional financial development.

Direct Government Financial Intermediation

The final major policy shift affected the role of the government as a direct participant in financial markets. Since the nineteenth century, Japan, like a number of other countries, has used the post office as both a savings bank and life insurance company. Funds received through the post office, plus some other funds (including social security funds) were funneled to MOF, which lent money to a variety of government-sponsored projects (such as hospitals, toll roads, and national universities) and to government-owned financial institutions (such as the Japan Development Bank and the Japan Bank for International Cooperation).

FISCAL INVESTMENT AND LOAN PROGRAM   The system channeling postal saving and other funds through MOF was the FILP. The program enabled the government to play a role in the allocation of financial resources, both directly by lending to favored private-sector projects and firms through the government-owned banks and indirectly through a demonstration effect on private-sector banks. The annual FILP budget was reported to the Diet but not voted on (in contrast to the general government budget), giving bureaucrats and the ruling party considerable discretion in the allocation of loans.

Efficacy of the FILP for the growth and development of the economy has been hotly debated for decades. The important issue to consider for this chapter is the rising disenchantment with the program and the resulting reforms that occurred in the 2000s. (For more on the FILP, see Cargill and Yoshino 2003.)

The essence of the problem was the nontransparent manner in which funds were allocated, and opportunities for poor decisions or politically motivated ones were legion.

Whereas a new airport in the United States would normally be financed with a municipal bond issue (usually subject to both approval from voters in the city or state plus a market test), in Japan financing required only a private discussion among local officials, Ministry of Transportation officials, and the officials at MOF in charge of disbursing FILP loans. As a result, in 2010 Japan had 98 airports with scheduled air service in an area roughly the size of California. The Ministry of Transportation concluded in 2009 that 72 were not economically viable (*Japan Times* 2010). Therefore, as criticism of excessive public works spending rose in the 1990s, the structure of the FILP came under attack as well.

The first major step, in 2001, was to reorganize how borrowers in the FILP program would raise money. The post office was given authority to invest its funds as it wished, rather than turn them over to MOF. Borrowers, meanwhile, would be financed either through their own individual bond issues (FILP Agency bonds) or out of a pool of funds raised by special MOF bond issues (FILP bonds). In theory, this created a system much more like that of the United States, in which at least some of the organizations formerly receiving funds through negotiation with MOF would be required to issue their own bonds (with the Development Bank of Japan a prime example). In reality, the

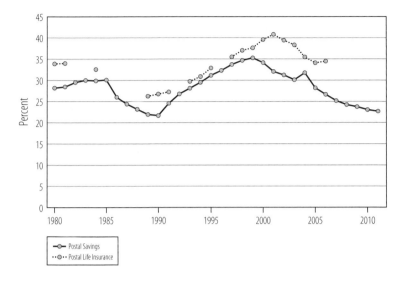

Figure 3.10 Postal Savings as a Share of Total Bank Deposits and Postal Life Insurance as a Share of Total Assets in the Life Insurance Industry (percent). *Sources*: Ministry of Internal Affairs and Communications, *Japan Statistical Yearbook*, various years; Bank of Japan, "Long Term Data Series"; and Japan Post Bank, "Financial Data, Summary of Financial Results for the Fiscal Year Ended March 31, 2011."

post office continued to invest most of its funds in government securities, including both FILP Agency bonds and FILP bonds. Even so, an important institutional change had been made.

POST OFFICE PRIVATIZATION The more dramatic step came in 2006 with passage of a bill to privatize the post office. Under this legislation, the post office would be a holding company under which the savings bank and life insurance operations would be wholly owned financial institutions. By 2017 two-thirds of the shares of the holding company were to be sold to the public. In part, this resulted from decades of protests from commercial banks and life insurance companies that they faced unfair competition from the post office. The grounds for the complaint can be seen in the post office having more branches than all the commercial banks combined.

Figure 3.10 shows that a major development of the 1990s was a sustained rise in postal savings as a share of all bank deposits and of postal life insurance as a share of total assets in the life insurance industry.

Problems in the private sector of the financial industry clearly pushed households to seek the safety of this government institution. At its 2000 peak, postal savings had a 35 percent share of total bank savings deposits. At its 2002 peak, postal life insurance was 40 percent of total assets in the life insurance industry.

After 2000, as talk mounted of privatization, the share of postal savings diminished. By March 2011 it was 23 percent of total deposits, about where it had been in the late 1980s. The market share of postal life insurance, however, has remained high, diminishing only to 35 percent (at least through 2007 when available data end). These high levels explain the angst of the commercial financial industry about having to compete against a government entity.

Officially the post office was privatized in 2007, albeit with the government holding 100 percent of the shares of the new holding company. With this change in status, deposits were now guaranteed only up to ¥10 million (rather than the implicit blanket guarantee that the public had assumed in the past). In addition, the privatized savings bank and life insurance companies would eventually be subject to the same rules and regulations that applied to their private-sector counterparts (including payment of taxes). The timing of these changes has been somewhat controversial, but eventually both the savings bank and life insurance company would be on a more level playing field with their commercial competitors. However, in the interim (or longer, if postal privatization continues to be blocked), the playing field is not level, a cause of much concern to both domestic and foreign insurance firms (Hufbauer and Muir 2010).

Sale to the public of two-thirds of holding company shares was supposed to occur gradually from 2010 to 2017. However, this became uncertain when the Democratic Party of Japan (DPJ) won control of the lower house of the Diet in August 2009. Legislation to halt privatization passed the lower house in early 2010, but had not passed the upper house prior to the upper house election in July 2010 in which the DPJ lost its majority. The legislation remained in limbo in 2011 as the Diet stalemate continued and earthquake relief legislation took priority. The effort to stop privatization of the post office was a blow to those favoring reform.

OTHER CHANGES Some consolidation or privatization of government financial institutions receiving funds from FILP also occurred.

The Development Bank of Japan (DBJ) had been a principal instrument of industrial policy in the earlier postwar period, using FILP funds to make loans to favored industries. DBJ was slated for privatization under the reforms instituted during the government of Prime Minister Junichiro Koizumi (2001–2006). Initial steps occurred (with the bank incorporated and the government as the sole shareholder), but plans to sell shares to the public were halted in the wake of the 2008 global recession, and the bank was used by the government to make loans to firms hurt by the recession.

Some other institutions were abolished or substantively altered. For example, the Japan Housing Loan Corporation (JHLC) was reconstituted as the Japan Housing Finance Administration (JHFA) and switched to securitizing commercial bank mortgage loans rather than making direct loans to the public (JHFA nd). Meanwhile, the Japan Bank for International Cooperation (JBIC, handling trade and FDI financing), National Life Finance Corporation (NLFC), Agriculture, Forestry and Fisheries Finance Corporation (AFC), and Japan Finance Corporation for Small and Medium Enterprise (JASME) were all merged in 2008 into a single organization called the Japan Finance Corporation (JFC), although in 2011 new legislation reestablished JBIC as an independent policy bank separate from JFC. In summary, government policy-based lending institutions underwent considerable changes as FILP was altered, but they did not disappear.

Summary

Important regulatory policy changes occurred over the years after 1990. And changes in FILP and the planned privatization of the post office paved the way for a smaller role of government in mediating financial flows.

The government finally came to grips with the banking crisis in the late 1990s, creating the Financial Services Agency to take over bank supervision from MOF and passing new laws to handle failed banks and to recapitalize viable banks. Other policy changes, such as permission for holding companies, enabled a major restructuring of the financial sector. Changes in accounting rules, procedures for mergers and acquisitions, and other aspects of corporate governance presumably improved the accuracy of information to those making decisions about the allocation of capital and opened the way for shareholders to exercise ownership rights more fully.

With greater accuracy of financial reporting, a potential was created for less reliance on bank loans (characterized by a nontransparent interface between banks and borrowers that relied heavily on information unavailable to the public and on the integrity of bank lending officers) and more on capital markets (bonds and equity).

Potential, however, is the important term. As of 2012 changes in financial flows and corporate behavior were insufficient to declare that Japan has undergone significant structural change in the functioning of financial markets.

Tokyo as an International Financial Center

Part of the deregulation process has been to dismantle the plethora of regulations that impeded all forms of investments into and out of Japan (foreign direct investment, portfolio investment, and loans). Already by the mid-1980s, most formal barriers to these flows had been eliminated. In more recent years the government took steps to make the country a more attractive place for international firms to carry out financial transactions, culminating in the Big Bang of the late 1990s. Nonetheless, and despite inroads of foreign firms in the insurance and securities industries, in 2010 Japan was less of an international financial center than expected in 1990.

There are three questions to ask when thinking about Tokyo as an international financial center. First, has there been an increase of international investment into Japan, based on increased openness of financial markets and the perception of opportunities for foreign investors? Second, has there been an increase in international investment flows out of Japan, based on both local financial expertise (such as skill in arranging IPOs) and the availability of money? Third, are Japanese financial institutions significant players in international financial markets?

Attracting Foreign Capital

In the broadest sense, Japan has attracted increased inward foreign investment since 1990. According to the balance of payments data, total liabilities owed to nonresident investors increased more than 40 percent

TABLE 3.11
Liabilities to Nonresidents in the Balance of Payments (in billion yen and percents)

End of Dec	Total Liabilities	FDI	International Portfolio Investment			Loans and Other	Total Liabilities as a Share of GDP (%)
			Equity	Debt Securities	Derivatives		
1990	221,544	1,426					50
1996	204,344	3,473	36,615	28,226	315	135,716	40
2000	213,052	5,782	64,174	36,358	366	106,738	42
2005	325,492	11,903	132,842	49,117	3,921	127,709	65
2010	312,031	17,502	80,537	71,914	5,267	136,810	65

Sources: 1990 data are from Bank of Japan, *Economic Statistics Annual* 1991, 250. Later data are from Ministry of Finance.

Note: A major reorganization in 1996 of the presentation of assets and liabilities in the balance of payments makes inclusion of detailed data for 1990 impossible.

from 1990 to 2010, at which time the total was ¥312 trillion ($3.5 trillion at then-current exchange rates). Total liabilities as a share of GDP rose from 50 percent to 65 percent. However, the level of liabilities was 4 percent lower than in 2005, as macroeconomic developments such as continued deflation and the strong impact of the global recession caused international investors to remove money from Japan to invest elsewhere. Data are in table 3.11.

The largest change was the influx of foreign investors into the stock market. From 1996 to 2005 portfolio ownership of corporate equity by foreign investors increased by more than 263 percent (¥96 trillion), accounting for much of the increase in total liabilities over that period. From 2005 to 2010, though, the value of equity owned by foreigners declined almost 10 percent (¥52 billion). The role of foreigners in Japanese equity is considered further later.

Other forms of investment have held up better than investment in the stock market. The stock of foreign direct investment was very low in 1990, but then rose, even in the 2005–2010 period despite the 2008–2009 recession. Part of the increase in the stock of inward direct investment may have resulted from increased availability of Japanese firms for

TABLE 3.12
US Liabilities to Nonresidents in the Balance of Payments ($ billions)

	Total	FDI	Equity	Bonds	Derivatives	Loans and Other	Total Liabilities as a Share of GDP (%)
1990	2,409	505	222	619	0	911	42
1995	3,916	680	511	1,149	0	1,249	53
2000	7,576	1,421	1,554	2,106	0	2,113	76
2005	13,894	1,906	2,110	4,556	1,132	3,546	110
2010	22,786	2,659	2,992	7,890	3,542	4,455	157

Sources: Bureau of Economic Analysis, US Department of Commerce, "International Investment Position: Yearend Positions, 1976–2010," and "Gross Domestic Product (GDP): Current Dollar and 'real' GDP."

sale, including those for sale to private equity groups. Also note that the stock of derivatives held by foreigners has increased substantially, particularly after 2000.

Overall, the table suggests that Japan has become a more attractive destination for foreign capital and that innovations such as derivatives (relatively unavailable in Japanese financial markets prior to the 1990s) may have helped that trend.

How does Japan compare to the United States? Since the United States is a net debtor, and Japan is a net creditor, it is reasonable to expect that the stock of liabilities owed to foreigners is larger in the US case. Nonetheless, net positions can be the result of very large gross amounts of liabilities and assets, so the difference among countries for gross liabilities need not necessarily be large. Table 3.12 provides comparable data for the United States over the years since 1990.

Between 1990 and 2010 the ratio of liabilities owed to foreigners to GDP more than tripled from 42 percent to 157 percent. Thus, although foreigners became moderately more important holders of Japanese assets, the change over time hardly compares to the United States.

The stark difference in financial sector structure between the two countries is evident in the example of derivatives. Even though the stock of derivatives in Japan owned by nonresidents rose sharply to ¥5.3 trillion in 2010 ($64 billion at December 2010 exchange rates), that was only 1.9 percent of the $3.4 trillion in derivatives owned by nonresidents in the United States. (This is an even smaller percentage than in 2005. There are simply not a lot of derivative products in Japan for foreigners to purchase.)

Foreign direct investment remains low in comparison to other advanced economies. In 2010 the ¥17.5 trillion of foreign direct investment assets ($200 billion) owned in Japan by foreigners amounted to 3.7 percent of GDP (enhanced somewhat by the drop in nominal GDP during the global recession). In the United States, the $2.7 trillion stock of foreign direct investment by foreigners was 18.3 percent of GDP, a share almost five times higher.

A broader international comparison for the prerecession year of 2007 shows Japan at the bottom (OECD 2010b). The next lowest country was India, at 9.1 percent. Even the other two countries considered in this volume are well ahead of Japan, with the stock of foreign direct investment in Korea at 9.4 percent relative to GDP, and the ratio in China at 20.0 percent in 2007, compared to Japan's 3.1 percent.

The one area in which foreigners have established a major presence is the stock market. Foreigners have become major owners of Japanese equity since 1990. From only 4 percent in 1990, foreigners owned 26 percent of outstanding Japanese corporate equity by 2010, a major increase. In addition, foreigners brought a different pattern of behavior as shareholders. Data on trading by foreigners only begins with 1995, at which point they were already 15 percent of daily selling on the stock markets and 20 percent of daily buying. In 2010 these ratios were 47 percent for buying and 48 percent for selling, an extraordinarily high level. Further data are in figure 3.11.

Foreigners are more active traders than Japanese. That foreign shareholders behave differently from Japanese shareholders is interesting. Presumably most of the foreign holdings are by foreign mutual funds, and perhaps foreign fund managers possess more specialized expertise in stock market investing based on short-term price movements than their Japanese counterparts. Whatever the explanation, the fact that foreigners represent close to half the daily trading on the Tokyo Stock Exchange is an extraordinary development given the relatively closed nature of Japan's stock market prior to 1990.

The shares of foreigners in total equity ownership in 2005 were 27 percent for Japan, 13 percent for the United States, 33 percent for the United Kingdom, and 20 percent for Germany (Shirai 2009, 147).

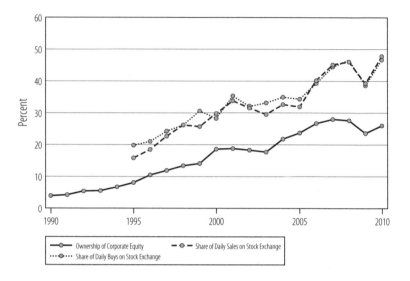

Figure 3.11 The Role of Foreigners in Equity Ownership and Daily Trading on the Stock Exchanges. *Source*: Tokyo Stock Exchange, *Fact Book 1998*, p 15, 79, 115; *Fact Book 1999*, p 3; *Fact Book 2002*, p 4; *Fact Book 2006*, p 4; *Fact Book 2011*, p 4, 84.

Japan is thus comparable to other countries and higher than the ratio in the United States.

Japan as a Supplier of Capital to the World

The emergence of a chronic current account surplus after 1980 meant that Japan became a major gross and net supplier of capital to the rest of the world over the course of the 1980s. By the end of the 1980s, Japan had become the largest net creditor in terms of the stock of net assets held abroad, a position it maintained in 2010 (Reuters 2008). However, in some respects, this role has not blossomed. For example, Tokyo has not become a global or even regional center where many foreign companies come to raise equity money.

Table 3.13 shows what has happened to ownership of foreign assets. As of 2010 Japan's net foreign assets were $3.1 trillion, comparable in scale to those of the United States and more than three times those of either China or Germany. Japan's total assets expanded from 1990 to 2010, as did net assets. As a share of GDP, gross assets almost doubled, from 61 percent to 118 percent. For the United States, total assets

TABLE 3.13

Assets Abroad Held by Japanese Residents in the Balance of Payments (trillion yen and percent)

End of December	Total Assets	Net Assets	FDI	Equity	Debt Securities	Derivatives	Loans and Other	Total Assets as a Share of GDP (%)
1990	269.0	47.5	29.2					61
1996	307.7	103.4	30.0	18.0	90.7	0.461	143.8	61
2000	346.1	133.0	32.0	30.1	113.3	0.381	129.2	69
2005	506.2	180.7	45.6	48.2	201.3	3.1	108.5	101
2010	563.5	251.5	67.7	55.3	217.3	4.3	129.7	118

Note: columns FDI, Equity, Debt Securities, Derivatives are grouped under "Portfolio".

Sources: 1990 data are from Bank of Japan, *Economic Statistics Annual* 1991, 250. Later data are from Ministry of Finance.

owned abroad were 38 percent of GDP in 1990 and 140 percent in 2010. The big difference, therefore, is in net assets. Japan is a large net supplier of capital to the world, whereas the United States was the world's largest net debtor in 2010 ($20.3 trillion in assets and close to $22.8 trillion in liabilities) with net foreign liabilities of $2.5 trillion (Cuadra 2011).

However, US investors had different preferences. The contrast is striking. Despite the common perception of Japanese firms engaging in large amounts of direct investment abroad, foreign direct investment accounted for only 9 percent of Japanese assets abroad in 2010, compared to 22 percent for American assets abroad. Further data are in table 3.14.

Japanese investors show a strong preference for loans (23 percent in 2010, though down from 47 percent in 1996) and debt securities (39 percent in 2010). The high percentage for debt is partly the result of the government's huge foreign exchange reserves, held mainly in US Treasuries. Roughly half of all the debt securities are represented by foreign exchange reserves. Americans, on the other hand, have much larger shares in portfolio equity (22 percent, compared to 9 percent for the Japanese) and derivatives (19 percent in 2009, compared to only 0.1 percent for the Japanese). One obvious conclusion from these data is that Japanese investors are relatively risk averse, preferring bonds and

TABLE 3.14

Distribution of Assets Held Abroad by Japanese and US Investors (percent)

| End of December | | FDI | Portfolio | | | Loans and Other |
			Equity	Debt Securities	Derivatives	
Japan	1996	9.7	5.8	29.5	0.1	46.7
	2010	12.0	9.8	38.6	0.8	23.0
United States	1996	24.5	25.0	11.9	—	32.4
	2010	22.0	21.8	8.6	18.0	26.4

Sources: Japan: based on Table 3.13; United States: US Department of Commerce, Bureau of Economic Analysis.

loans over equity and derivatives. This should not be surprising since it reflects the structure of domestic financial markets as well.

One way to mediate the flow of funds overseas that enhances the role of Tokyo as a financial center is through bond issues. Since the 1970s foreigners have been permitted to issue bonds in Japan, first in yen, and then (1985) in other currencies. The yen-denominated bonds are popularly known as *samurai bonds* and the foreign currency–denominated ones as *shogun bonds*.

In the years that have followed, the government has carried out a lengthy series of regulatory changes designed to make such issuances more attractive. A sampling of the changes include allowing, in 1979, corporate issuers (rather than only sovereign governments); a gradual lowering of the permissible credit rating by issuers (so that by 1994 both sovereign and corporate issuers with BBB ratings could issue bonds); and, by 1997, allowing both bank and non-bank financial institutions to issue bonds. Nonetheless, a variety of rules and regulations inhibited the market into the 2000s, mainly through requirements that raised the cost of filings (such as need to submit documents in Japanese) (Nishi and Vergus 2006, 147–51; Shirai 2009, 159–61).

Figure 3.12 shows how volatile the issuance of new bonds by foreigners in Japan has been. Samurai (yen-denominated) bonds peaked in 2000 and have not regained that level. Shogun (foreign currency) bonds spiked in 1996 and, after dropping to near-zero levels, reached a new high in 2010. The choice of yen- or foreign currency–denominated bonds depends on exchange rate expectations, explaining some of the

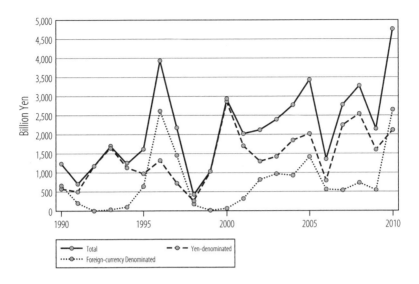

Figure 3.12 Bond Issues in Japan by Foreign Issuers (billion yen). *Source*: MOF, "Securities Issuance: Historical Data."

fluctuation. Issues in 2009 amounted to roughly 1 percent of the global market for international bond issues (some $2.4 trillion) (TheCityUK 2010, 1).

Successive rounds of deregulation in the 1990s and early 2000s did not bring about a continued expansion of the market or turn Japan into a major center for international bond issues. This outcome is somewhat surprising: low interest rates on yen-denominated bonds after the mid-1990s should have made Japan a preferred location for international bond issues. Clearly some formal or informal obstacles have impeded the market.

A larger market has been the euro-yen bond market. MOF has managed to exercise authority over rules and regulations for such bonds issued by Japanese firms even though they are issued outside Japan—in the United States as well as Europe. Issues began in 1977, and a series of liberalization measures occurred earlier than in the domestic market. Figure 3.13 tracks the amount of new issues in this market.

Volume peaked in 2001 and has mostly fallen since. The 2010 total is less than half the peak and, at about $85 billion, less than 4 percent of the total global market for international bond issues. Most euro-yen bonds have been issued by foreigners. However, it is unclear whether

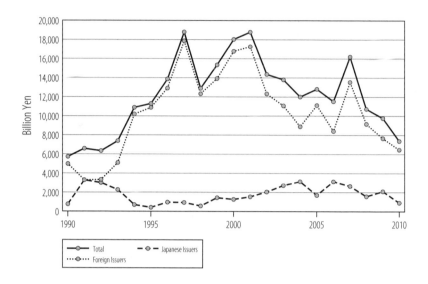

Figure 3.13 Annual Euroyen Issues (billion yen). *Source*: MOF, "Securities Issuance: Historical Data."

"foreign" issuers are truly foreign or include the foreign subsidiaries of Japanese firms. In general, Japanese firms were motivated to issue such bonds during the 1980s by looser restrictions imposed by MOF on who could issue such bonds, and the purchasers were primarily Japanese financial institutions. Many of the issuing firms returned to the domestic bond market as further deregulation in Japan lessened the advantage of issuing abroad.

TOKYO AS AN INTERNATIONAL EQUITY MARKET One way to make it easier for Japanese investors to buy stock in foreign companies is to let foreign firms list on stock exchanges in Japan. In the 1980s, as Tokyo began to be recognized as a large financial center, the Tokyo Stock Exchange (TSE) encouraged foreign firms to list, and an increasing number did so. Listings peaked in 1990 at 125. However, since then the number has fallen almost continuously, to only 12 in 2010, which is fewer than in 1980. There was one foreign listing in Osaka, for a total in Japan of 13.

In the 1980s getting foreign firms to list was considered a matter of national prestige, with the rising number of listings serving as an emblem of the importance of Tokyo as a global financial center. The decline implies that the Tokyo Stock Exchange has reverted to being almost entirely devoted to domestic finance. Behind the decline lie a number of causes, including high listing fees and low turnover (with Japanese investors disinterested in buying foreign shares at home).

The collapse of listings of foreign firms on the TSE stands in considerable contrast to some other major exchanges. The New York Stock Exchange had 90 non-US firms listed in 1990, and 451 in 2010, while an additional 298 were listed on NASDAQ. Note, however, that even Hong Kong exchanges had only 17 foreign firms listed (Chinese H shares are considered local), as did Korea. And exchanges in China and India have none at all.

EVALUATION The conclusion concerning the role of Japanese financial markets as a source of capital for the rest of the world is somewhat mixed. Japan is a large gross and net supplier of capital to the world. However, the evidence concerning the experience of the samurai, shogun, and euro-yen bond markets suggests that some aspects of international financial intermediation are not well developed.

Risk aversion explains some of this. The large role for bonds in assets held abroad, for example, is due to both the government's large foreign exchange reserves and private-sector Japanese investor preferences. The balance of payments data suggest that private-sector investors (mainly banks and investment banks) have a strong preference for debt securities (particularly sovereign debt) rather than corporate equity.

A preference for low-risk investments abroad is also consistent with the limited number of foreign firms listed on the Tokyo Stock Exchange. The relative preference for loans and bonds both at home and abroad is consistent with a limited demand for foreign equity even when it is easily available on the domestic exchange.

Japanese Financial Institutions as Global Players

Given Japan's role as a major supplier of global capital, to what extent are Japanese financial institutions among the leading players? The short answer is that they play a rather modest role, and less of a role than in 1990.

One indicator of global presence is size. Of course, sheer size does not necessarily indicate a global presence. A large domestic bank, for example, might have a huge domestic deposit base but, for reasons of regulation or preference, maintains a purely domestic loan portfolio. Nonetheless, size is at least a first step in assessing the role of Japanese financial institutions.

Japanese banks in the 1980s appeared large due to their huge deposit bases (one measure of size), attracting international attention and causing some trepidation among foreign competitors as the Japanese moved aggressively into international lending markets. In 1990 the top-five commercial banks in the world measured by deposits were Japanese. Over the next 20 years, however, Japanese financial institutions fell behind in the pantheon of large institutions.

The Fortune Global 500 list for 2010 has one Japanese firm among the top 15 financial institutions ranked by revenue: Japan Post, a state-run enterprise with a huge deposit base but virtually no international presence. Nippon Life is the only other Japanese firm in the top 30 (Fortune 2011). The 2005 Businessweek Global 1200 had Mitsubishi UFJ Group, Mizuho, and Sumitomo Mitsui Financial Group among the top 15 banks ranked by market value (*Businessweek* 2005).

Consider the top private-sector Japanese financial institution in international rankings: Mitsubishi UFJ Group. How global is it? The group operates in over 40 countries, with 463 offices overseas (Mitsubishi UFJ Financial Group [MUFJ FG] 2010a, p 29). But its loan business is predominantly domestic; as of March 31, 2010, only 15 percent (¥11.7 trillion = $124 billion) of outstanding loans had been extended through overseas offices (MUFJ FG 2010b, 29).

Now consider Citigroup, generally the leading US financial institution on international lists. In 2009 43 percent ($253 billion) of Citi's loan portfolio was outside the United States, including 35 percent of consumer loans and 63 percent of corporate loans (Citigroup 2009).

Although a one-to-one comparison of these two firms is not definitive, it is at least illustrative of the more domestically rooted business orientation of large Japanese commercial banks. Further, the reputation of Japanese banks is that their foreign loan business has been mainly to overseas operations of Japanese firms based on existing ties in Japan.

The same picture is true for investment banks. A list of the top investment banks in the world in 2009 does not list a single Japanese firm in the top 10 (Maps 2010). In a Bloomberg ranking for 2008 (based on fee income), two Japanese firms were in the top 20 (Nomura, 10th, Daiwa 19th).

Turning to other ranking methods, Dealogic's merger and acquisitions rankings for 2010 has one Japanese firm among the top 20: Nomura at 13th with a 4.3 percent market share (*Wall Street Journal* [WSJ] 2011). Most deals have multiple advisers, and each adviser gets full credit, but even when Japanese firms are participants, they have not gained much of a reputation as global players in international mergers and acquisitions.

Among Japanese firms, Nomura has had the most aggressive strategy to move into global markets, boosted by its purchase of the Asian and European operations of Lehman Brothers after that firm collapsed in September 2008. Partly as a consequence, 74 percent of Nomura's employees were in Japan in March 2003, but only 57 percent in June 2010; for the first quarter of 2010, 38 percent of net revenue was reported to be from outside Japan (Nomura 2011, 7, 34). However, that strategy did not catapult Nomura into the ranks of major global investment banks. By 2012 the top two executives who had engineered the Lehman purchase were gone (albeit forced out by a domestic insider trading scandal), most of the senior executives from Lehman had left or been forced out, international operations were losing money, and the firm's bond rating was just above junk status. Even for Nomura, therefore, transforming itself into a more global player proved to be difficult.

For Daiwa Securities, 26 percent of net revenue in 1999 was from overseas, but by 2009 that was down to 10 percent. However, Daiwa was planning on doubling its personnel in other Asian countries by March 2012 as part of an "aim to make Asia our 'home market.'" (Daiwa 1999; Daiwa 2010, 18, 114). Neither Nikko Cordial nor Mizuho Securities provides a breakdown of revenue by geographic area. For MUFJ Securities (the fifth largest investment bank), 14.5 percent of net revenues in 2008 came from abroad (MUFJ 2008, 104).

With the partial exception of Nomura, securities firms remain strongly rooted in the domestic market. Even Daiwa's regional expansion plan involves bringing regional stocks to its domestic client base. And the tale of Nomura's inability to successfully use the acquisition of part of Lehman to become a stronger global player is indicative of the competitive disadvantage of Japanese investment banks in global markets.

In short, although Japanese institutions are not entirely absent, their global presence is limited considering the size of the economy.

Access to low-cost funds at home has not translated into a prominent role in global financial markets for Japanese financial firms, for
reasons that follow.

Whether Nomura Securities will successfully break this pattern, with
its large staff of foreigners acquired in the takeover of Lehman's Asian
and European operations, remains to be seen. The corporate cultures
and compensation patterns are so different (with Lehman employees
better paid and more dependent on performance-based bonuses) that
there could be some difficulty in blending the two firms. (See, for
example, Slater 2008; Levin 2009; Foley and Cox 2011.)

Summary

The picture of Tokyo or Japan as an international financial center is
decidedly mixed. There is no doubt Tokyo is one of the large financial
centers in the world—the size of the economy, the progress in deregulation of international capital flows in the 1970s through 1990s, and the
size and relative sophistication of financial institutions have guaranteed
that. But Tokyo has never lived up to the expectations of government
officials, academics, or the media in the late 1980s.

Foreign investors are major players on the Tokyo Stock Exchange, but
are not deeply involved in other financial markets. Outward capital flows
are large, but appear quite traditional and risk averse. Some Japanese
financial firms are active internationally, but they have played a more
modest role in global financial competition than many expected in 1990.

Tokyo has certainly become an international market, mediating
inward investments and handling outward investments, but the rest
of the world has evolved in a more internationally connected direction
too. As a result, the scale of Japan's importance in global financial markets remains moderate.

What explains these developments? Four factors stand out: language, the cost of stationing expatriates in Tokyo, risk aversion, and
the culture of corporate management. Technical issues (such as fees
and taxes on transactions) attract attention in studies of how to make
Tokyo a larger international financial center, and these matter. But the
broader factors are critical in explaining why two decades of deregulation and reduction of fees have not produced a larger result.

Language is particularly important. International financial markets operate in English. The poor level of English language skill

characterizing Japanese society hampers Japanese financial institutions operating in an international context. This author has been rather surprised, for example, at the relatively limited English language abilities of many senior managers at Japanese financial institutions in New York City.

Japanese is a language spoken by relatively few non-Japanese, presenting a barrier for non-Japanese employees of Japanese financial firms where upper management operates in the Japanese language. These firms do not generally place foreigners in significant senior positions. Lack of promotion beyond a mid-ranking discourages the very best talent from seeking employment at Japanese firms in general, and financial firms in particular.

The language problem also disadvantages foreign financial firms attempting to operate in Japan, though they do offer management opportunities for bright, English-competent Japanese employees.

Second, the cost of stationing expatriates in Tokyo has been high. In 2010 (and 2011), Tokyo was more expensive than any other international financial center in the world according to the three most cited surveys: Mercer, Economist Intelligence Unit (EIU), and ECA International. For 2010, EIU estimates put costs in Tokyo almost 50 percent higher than New York, 20 percent above London, and 45 percent above Shanghai (*Economist* 2010).

For Tokyo to play a major role as a global financial center, both foreign financial institutions and some non-Japanese employees must be present. Foreign firms can operate in Tokyo with a largely local staff, but firms want to place the best people in each position, and in some cases that means bringing in employees from elsewhere.

New York, London, Hong Kong, and Singapore have many international financial firms and employees from many parts of the world. Tokyo also has expatriates in the financial sector, but their presence has been hampered by the high cost and for some a difficult cultural adjustment. As consulting firm ECA International put it in 2010, companies "will still bring staff into Japan, but only when there is an absolute need to do so" (Baylis 2010).

Throughout the 1990s, prices at market exchange rates were high in Japan relative to the rest of the world for most goods and services. Housing suitable for foreigners (larger than typical housing, without tatami rooms, and with amenities such as central heating and air conditioning) was in short supply until at least the mid-1990s. Food prices were high, especially for items such as beef, consumed in higher amounts by foreigners than Japanese. Private schools offering education in English or other foreign languages to expatriate children were very expensive. Much of this cost is borne by the firms.

Some of the burden is borne directly by the employees. For example, the supply of maids and nannies from developing countries (a common source of household labor in many parts of the world) is severely restricted by immigration rules. Only employment with foreign diplomats or top employees, such as CEOs, at foreign firms is accepted in granting work visas to nannies and maids. Lower- and mid-level managers, therefore, do not have access to Filipina or other developing-country maids and nannies, except perhaps on the black market.

Some of the disadvantages for posting expatriates to Tokyo have faded over the period of this study. Housing costs fell with the general collapse of real estate prices and an expansion of modern, Western-style apartments and houses in Tokyo. Other prices, such as food, declined in international comparison, exemplified by the downward drift of the real effective exchange rate of the yen after 1995. But some other obstacles, such as the lack of visas for nannies and maids, continue to be a liability for Tokyo relative to other cities.

Third, risk aversion remains an obstacle. Japanese financial institutions rushed into international markets once they had been unleashed by deregulation in the early 1980s. They had access to low-cost funds but little technical expertise in risk management. Badly burned by their mistakes in the 1980s and 1990s, they appear to be more cautious now.

Perhaps that caution was good, as Japanese institutions avoided investments in the many exotic asset-backed securities created and sold on the US market. Even in the wake of the financial crisis in the United States in 2008–2009, however, sophisticated financial instruments remain in use, and technical skill in risk management is still a key to success in US and European financial markets.

The financial crisis should not be viewed as bringing the collapse of an "American" model, just as the collapse of the newly created junk bond market in the 1980s did not signify the end of junk bonds. Innovation in financial instruments and technical models for risk management will remain hallmarks of the US (and to some extent, European) financial sector. If Japanese firms continue to behave in a risk-averse manner and fail to develop skills in assessing and managing risk, they will remain modest players in international markets compared to US and European competitors.

The same is true of some other aspects of the financial industry, such as international deal making in mergers and acquisitions, and private equity funds. Bold vision and aggressive action, coupled with unsentimental analysis, will remain a key for success in these markets. If Japanese firms behave in a cautious manner, or are confined by historical relationships, they will not be major players in these fields.

Fourth, Japanese firms have management decision-making processes ill suited to the financial sector. Thorough and often lengthy discussion (much of it behind the scenes and informal) before reaching decisions is the norm. The process can have some advantages, such as causing most or all of the group members to endorse the eventual decision, making implementation rapid and thorough. However, the disadvantage is time. Opportunities in financial markets come and go quickly. Japanese financial institutions have had some difficulty operating in an international environment where an opportunity to participate in a deal may close before they have made a decision on participation.

Other aspects of Japanese management style also hinder financial firms in international competition, including less emphasis on individual responsibility (with more limited bonus rewards for individual performance), limited opportunities for non-Japanese managers to rise to significant positions, and a continued bias against women managers.

Adding these four factors together, the result is an uncomfortable fit between Japanese financial institutions and the rest of the world. Hampered by relatively poor English language skills, uneasy with the nature of risk in global markets, and unable to respond to opportunities with decisive rapidity, Japanese financial institutions on average are uncomfortable in global markets. The presence of aggressive foreign managers located in Tokyo who tend to press the government for further regulatory changes, or who want to introduce new financial products, or pursue deals can make government officials and their Japanese competitors nervous and uncomfortable.

To be sure, some Japanese firms have become more international, Nomura being the most prominent among them, although the success of its bold absorption of a large part of the former Lehman Brothers is yet to be proven. But other firms have not changed much. These language and social factors are consistent with the evidence in this chapter concerning an international engagement in the financial sector that remains less than might be predicted simply by the size of the Japanese economy.

Impact

The purpose of a financial sector is to mediate the flow of funds, mobilizing an economy's savings and deploying them to those projects that yield the highest return relative to risk. That function was temporarily in serious jeopardy in Japan due to the possibility of wide-scale collapse of the banking industry in 1997–1998, a collapse that would have disrupted the flow of funds. Japanese authorities, for all their failings, deserve credit for avoiding what could have been a catastrophic collapse of the banking industry. For a brief time during the crisis years, there were allegations of a credit crunch. But, in general, money in Japan has continued to flow from those involved in saving to those who need funds.

The big problem once the crisis passed was a failure on the part of the government to stimulate domestic demand, to restore the economy to close to its potential growth, or to halt the low but persistent deflation. Aside from lost potential output, two decades of subpar growth and deflation have had a corrosive effect on expectations. Although real economic growth has occurred, deflation means that individuals were living in an economy in 2010 with the same level of nominal GDP as in 1991.

Although the 1997–1998 crisis was the clearest threat to financial mediation in Japan, the system has had some longer-term problems with allocating funds efficiently. Economic performance depends on an efficient allocation of investment resources, putting money to work building the most productive or efficient projects on a risk-adjusted basis. By the 1980s there was evidence of misallocation of resources in the economy, for which the financial sector must bear some of the blame.

The problems became evident during the lost decade as banks tried to prop up failing borrowers, throwing good money after bad. Keeping zombie firms on life support delayed necessary restructuring of industries by protecting inefficient firms, and undermining the ability of the best firms to compete (Hoshi, Caballero, and Kashyap 2008). Eventually, banks did deal with nonperforming loans, and changing laws and regulations made it easier to restructure or close troubled firms.

However, as the following sections indicate, Japanese firms generally retain the ability to misallocate resources or overinvest, helping to explain a low level of profitability.

Continued Misallocation

The question now is whether the restructuring of the financial industry and continued regulatory change affected the allocation of resources in a positive way. Banks perform their own internal evaluation of potential borrowers; investment banks perform a sorting function in underwriting bond issues; and millions of buyers of bonds and equity provide a market for discriminating among firms needing funds.

A well-functioning financial sector supplies funds through all these channels to those that deserve them the most and withdraws funds from those that do not perform well. Does this description characterize Japan? The evidence is not definitive and is somewhat mixed, but the basic answer appears to be that misallocation continues.

Since the financial system remains skewed toward loans rather than equity or bonds, banks continue to play a major role in allocating funds among competing uses. To be sure, earlier discussion in this chapter pointed out that corporations have reduced their loans from banks in most years since 1998. Nonetheless, to the extent that corporations need external sources of funding, banks remain an important supplier. The fact that banks managed to reduce their nonperforming loans over the course of the 2000s is a good sign, as is the fact that bad loans did not rise much during the global recession of 2008–2009. These numbers suggest that banks are doing a more careful job in evaluating borrowers.

On the other hand, the failure of venture capital markets to expand suggests a misallocation of funds. The earlier model of depending on existing large firms rather than upstart new firms was outmoded by the 1990s. Japan would have benefited over the past 20 years if a larger number of high-tech start-ups had occurred. Therefore, the failure of this market to expand—with more venture capital financing and more IPOs on the special exchanges for new firms—represents a misallocation of financial resources.

Capital Output Ratios

A broader way to see if resources are being misallocated is to consider the ratio of fixed nonresidential investment to GDP. To grow, economies must allocate some portion of GDP to fixed investment, both to replace depreciated capital stock and to add new capital stock. The faster an economy grows, the higher this ratio needs to be. In the years since 1990, the US economy has grown more rapidly than the Japanese economy, so a logical result would be for the ratio of private gross fixed nonresidential investment to GDP in the United States to be higher than the ratio in Japan. As shown in figure 3.14, however, this has not been the case.

In the United States, the ratio has varied between 10 percent and 13 percent of GDP in the 30-year period since 1980. In Japan, the ratio has varied from 13 percent to 20 percent (with the high point coming during the bubble). In no year was the ratio in Japan as low as that in the United States. From 1981 through 1989, Japan's GDP grew at an annual average real rate of 4.5 percent, while that of the United States

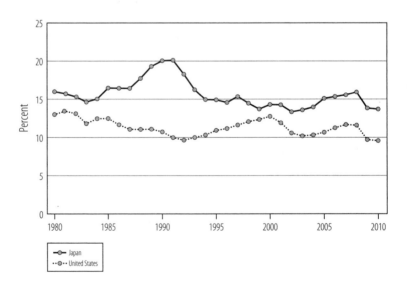

Figure 3.14 Gross Private Nonresidential Fixed Investment as a Share of GDP (percent). *Sources*: ESRI, "Annual Nominal GDP"; and Bureau of Economic Research, Department of Commerce, "National Income and Product Accounts Table."

grew at 3.4 percent, so in the 1980s a higher ratio of investment to GDP for Japan is understandable. Even in that decade, however, it is puzzling that Japan needed a ratio as high as 20 percent to produce the 4.9 percent growth that characterized the second half of the decade.

In both the 1990s and 2000s, US growth outpaced Japan's. In the 1990–1999 period, the US economy grew at an annual average real rate of 3.2 percent, while Japan grew at 1.5 percent. And in the 2000–2010 decade, the United States grew at 1.8 percent and Japan at 0.9 percent. Even if the comparison period is 2000–2007, prior to the onset of the recession, the United States grew at an average rate of 2.6 percent, while Japan grew at 1.7 percent. Thus, for two full decades, growth in the United States has been higher than in Japan by a wide margin, and yet the ratio of fixed nonresidential investment to GDP has been consistently higher in Japan.

The high ratio of gross fixed investment to GDP is strongly suggestive of excess investment, but could be the result of a large fixed capital stock relative to the United States, so that depreciation would be larger. Comparable data on capital stock and depreciation are not easily constructed because Japanese depreciation is reported only in nominal terms and capital stock only in real terms and US data are reported in nominal terms. With that caveat, the ratio of annual depreciation (consumption of fixed capital) as a percentage share of total private-sector fixed capital is shown in figure 3.15.

Annual depreciation of total fixed capital in Japan was 4.5 percent in 1980 and rose to close to 10 percent in the 2000s. In contrast, it has been a relatively constant 4 percent in the United States. This rise to a level more than double that of the United States is puzzling, but leads to a tentative conclusion that Japanese firms are writing off a larger share of their gross fixed investment as a replacement of depreciated capital than is economically justified.

In the past, one could make the argument that fixed capital assets in Japan depreciated more rapidly than those in the United States (more rapid technical obsolescence while Japan was catching up with the developed economies, less sturdy manufacturing equipment). But such an argument is difficult to justify after 1990. The data suggest, therefore, that depreciation is overly generous in Japan—equipment and structures are replaced more rapidly than necessary, and what is called depreciation is often a net expansion of capital stock. High official depreciation, therefore, contributes to overinvestment in the economy.

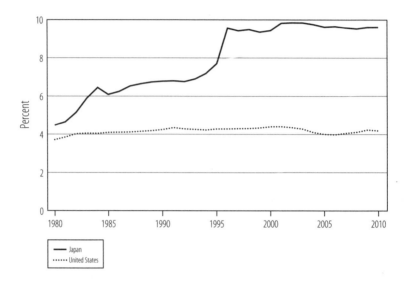

Figure 3.15 Private Sector Depreciation as a Share of Total Private Sector Fixed Capital (percent). *Sources*: Bureau of Economic Analysis, US Department of Commerce; and ESRI.

Note: US data are nominal. Japanese data for private-sector fixed capital are reported in real terms, while depreciation is reported in nominal terms. For consistency, depreciation data are converted to real terms using the price index for fixed capital investment.

INCREMENTAL CAPITAL-OUTPUT RATIO A more formal way to look at the relation between investment and growth is to calculate the incremental capital-output ratio (ICOR). This measures how much additional output results from an additional unit of capital stock. A crude calculation of the ICOR for Japan and the United States is presented in table 3.15.

Decade averages help to overcome the problem of short-term variation in the ratio caused by demand fluctuations. Investment in both countries is measured as net (of depreciation) private-sector nonresidential investment—in other words, how much extra plant and equipment in the private sector is required to produce an additional unit of GDP.

Japan had an ICOR ratio somewhat lower than that of the United States in the 1980s, but then experienced a spike in the 1990s, perhaps as corporations were slow to respond to slower economic growth by cutting investment in new plant and equipment. However, these data

TABLE 3.15

Incremental Capital-Output Ratio (ICOR), Based on Net Fixed Nonresidential Investment

Average during	I/GDP	GDP growth	ICOR
	Japan		
	Using Reported Data		
1981–1990	5.0	4.7	1.1
1991–2000	2.6	1.2	2.1
2001–2010	1.0	0.7	1.4
	Japan		
	Assuming 4.5% Depreciation of Capital Stock		
1981–1990	7.4	4.7	1.6
1991–2000	8.1	1.2	6.7
2001–2010	8.3	0.7	11.2
	United States		
1981–1990	5.7	3.3	1.8
1991–2000	3.4	3.4	1.0
2001–2010	2.2	1.6	1.4

Sources: Department of Commerce, Bureau of Economic Analysis, "National Economic Accounts," "Tables of GDP and Its Components."

Note: ICOR can be approximated as the ratio of net fixed investment to GDP (I/GDP) divided by the real GDP growth rate.

further suggest that the spike ended in the 2000s, with the ICOR back to a level comparable to that of the United States.

However, if there is excessive accounting for depreciation, then net nonresidential fixed investment is actually larger than that indicated by the official net investment numbers. For example, if one assumes that a more realistic depreciation rate for fixed capital stock is 4.5 percent (the level in Japan in the early 1980s, and slightly higher than the average in the United States), then the results are quite different. Under this assumption, ICOR begins at a level somewhat lower than that of the United States in the 1980s, but explodes in the 1990s and 2000s, rising to more than 10 times the US level.

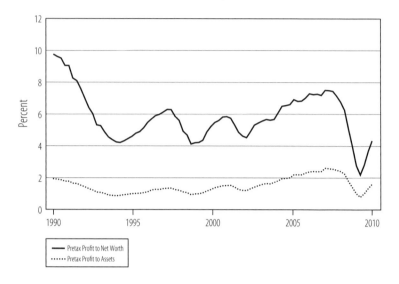

Figure 3.16 Ratio of Net Profits ("Ordinary Profits") to Total Assets and to Net Worth (percent). *Source*: Policy Research Institute, Ministry of Finance.

Note: These ratios represent profits earned in the four quarters ending with the quarter in which assets and net worth are measured.

Is this adjustment of the data fair? Conceivably Japanese corporations really do have unusually high depreciation, perhaps in the form of discarding capital assets well before their useful economic life has expired. But even if this is the case, the conclusion remains that Japanese firms invested excessively (excess depreciation plus real net additions to capital stock) over the course of the 1990s and 2000s.

Return on Assets and Equity

Figure 3.16 shows the ratio of pretax profits to total corporate assets, and the ratio to net worth (return on equity).

Return on assets (ROA) has varied from 1 percent to 2 percent over the period 1980–2010. There is no evidence of any sustained increase, although the recovery of the 2000s did bring the ratio back to just over 2 percent.

Return on net worth (return on equity, ROE) declined sharply from the 1980s to the late 1990s, reflecting the fact that corporations were responding to slow growth by reducing leverage, so the ratio of net worth to total assets was rising. ROE, like ROA, staged a rally in the 2000s prior to the recession, but remained well below earlier levels. Since both ROA and ROE fluctuate over the course of the business cycle, it is not possible to attribute the rise in these ratios over the 2002–2007 period to reform of corporate governance rather than simply the normal increase during a period of economic recovery.

Return on assets and return on equity also remain considerably lower than in the United States. The US government does not publish these data for the corporate sector as a whole. One calculation for a set of large US firms for the 40 years from 1955 to 1995 shows an average ROA of 6.0 percent (fluctuating between 3 percent and 8 percent) and ROE of 12.6 percent (fluctuating between 10 percent and 18 percent) (Reilly 1997).

Other sources for different large samples of firms indicate an average return on equity in excess of 10 percent in more recent years. For example, *Equity Clock* (2010) put the early 2010 ROE for the S&P 500 at 14.5 percent. *Maxi-Pedia* (2010) claims that the ROE for the S&P 500 averaged between 10 percent and 20 percent for "most of the 20th century" and 20 percent in the 1990s. Thus, returns on equity and total assets continued to be higher in the United States than Japan throughout the 20-year period 1990 to 2010.

The Role of Shareholders

Japanese corporations have long been known for managerial discretion with little or no pressure from shareholders, or even from the banks from which they borrow. However, shareholders can play an important role in the financial system in two important ways. First, if investors sell shares, causing the share price for a firm to fall, that decline can trigger takeover attempts. Second, if large shareholders are dissatisfied with management, they can exercise their role as owners of the firm to attempt to force changes through informal pressure, proxy fights, or lawsuits.

Until the 1990s shareholder meetings in Japan were short and highly scripted. In the 1950s firms hired thugs (*sokaiya*) to intimidate any shareholder bold enough to ask challenging questions. Eventually the *sokaiya* learned that discovering damaging information and threatening management with embarrassing questions at the meeting was more lucrative than threatening other shareholders. A law passed in 1997 increased fines for such activities (and on the firms acquiescing to such threats) and an increase in prosecutions has supposedly caused the number and activism of *sokaiya* to decline (*Mainichi Daily* 1999). As the *sokaiya* faded, perhaps legitimate shareholder concerns could get more voice, including at somewhat longer annual shareholder meetings.

Japanese firms have had extensive cross-shareholding particularly among firms belonging to horizontal *keiretsu* groups. The practice dates from the early 1950s when firms were allowed to legally own stock in each other, and expanded in the late 1960s (when capital controls were being loosened) as a means to deter takeovers by foreign firms. One question, therefore, is whether the pattern of share ownership has changed.

In the 1990s banks (which could hold up to 5 percent of the outstanding shares of other corporations) faced a need to reduce their equity holdings over the course of the prolonged financial crisis. What has happened to the ownership of equity by various categories of owners is shown in table 3.16.

Financial institutions reduced their holdings of equity. As a group, their share has declined 10 percentage points, from 42 percent to 32 percent. All of this change is due to the substantial drop in ownership by large commercial banks (city banks and regional banks), from 15 percent to 5 percent during the shorter 1997 to 2009 period for which detailed data are available. In contrast, trust banks actually increased holdings. However, ownership of shares by nonfinancial Japanese corporations has not changed much (22 percent of total shares in 2009, down only slightly from the 24 percent level of 1990), suggesting cross-shareholding among nonfinancial firms with a business relationship has not disappeared as an objective of corporate managers in nonfinancial firms. But the big story is the increase in the role of foreign investors, rising from 4 percent to almost 24 percent.

FOREIGN AND ACTIVIST SHAREHOLDERS   If foreign shareholders tend to be more activist than domestic ones, then this change could have had an impact on corporate governance, both through their own activism and through a demonstration effect on Japanese individual shareholders to speak up.

Hamao, Kutsuna, and Matos (2010) looked at a large data set of activist actions by shareholders in the period 1998–2009. On the surface,

TABLE 3.16
Distribution of Ownership of Corporate Equity (percent)

Year (as of March 31)	Government	Financial Institutions				Nonfinancial Corporations	Foreigners	Individuals
		Total	City and Regional Banks	Trust Banks	Securities Companies			
1990	0.7	42.3			2.0	24.8	3.9	22.6
1991	0.6	41.6			1.7	25.2	4.2	23.1
1992	0.6	41.5			1.5	24.5	5.4	23.2
1993	0.6	41.3			1.2	24.4	5.5	23.9
1994	0.6	40.8			1.3	23.9	6.7	23.7
1995	0.3	42.8			1.2	27.7	8.1	19.9
1996	0.3	41.1			1.4	27.2	10.5	19.5
1997	0.2	41.9	15.1	11.2	1.0	25.6	11.9	19.4
1998	0.2	42.1	14.8	12.4	0.7	24.6	13.4	19.0
1999	0.2	41.0	13.7	13.5	0.6	25.2	14.1	18.9
2000	0.1	36.5	11.3	13.6	0.8	26.0	18.6	18.0
2001	0.2	39.1	10.1	17.4	0.7	21.8	18.8	19.4
2002	0.2	39.4	8.7	19.9	0.7	21.8	18.3	19.7
2003	0.2	39.1	7.7	21.4	0.9	21.5	17.7	20.6
2004	0.2	34.5	5.9	19.6	1.2	21.8	21.8	20.5
2005	0.2	32.7	5.3	18.8	1.2	21.9	23.7	20.3
2006	0.2	31.6	4.7	18.4	1.4	21.1	26.7	19.1
2007	0.3	31.1	4.6	17.9	1.8	20.7	28.0	18.1
2008	0.4	30.9	4.7	17.5	1.6	21.3	27.6	18.2
2009	0.4	32.4	4.9	19.0	1.0	22.4	23.6	20.1

Sources: Tokyo Stock Exchange, *Fact Book 1998*, 79 and 115; *Fact Book 2010*, 64.

Note: There is a slight discontinuity in the numbers: 1990–1994 are based on the number of shares owned; 1995–2009 are based on the market value of shares owned. In most cases, this makes a difference of only a few tenths of a percent.

change appears substantial. They identify 34 activist funds (Japanese and foreign) that carried out 916 acquisitions of large blocks of stock over this period. Although they do not have earlier data, such actions up to the 1990s can be presumed to have been virtually nonexistent (other than the invisible bribery of the *sokaiya*).

Their conclusions are decidedly cautious. They find a small positive impact on the stock price of target firms when an activist fund acquires blocks of stock. They also find a modest impact in the longer run in increasing dividend payouts by target firms. However, activist investors appear to have no impact on other aspects of corporate behavior, such as the firm's growth rate or profitability in the longer run. They conclude that investor activism has had only limited success in Japan relative to what studies have shown for the United States.

So, although dividend payouts appear to have increased, the overall role of shareholders in forcing changes in corporate behavior that yield higher profits from which dividends can be paid remains limited.

This is consistent with the media coverage of activist foreign funds. The frequent experience of such funds has been extreme frustration when they try to use ownership of a large block of stock to force changes on management (such as the sale of unused land or higher dividend payouts).

Steel Partners, for example, purchased an 18 percent stake in Sapporo Beer in 2004, sought to force changes on management to improve poor performance, and attempted to obtain a controlling ownership share. Sapporo successfully resisted the pressure for change and the takeover attempt, causing Steel to sell its stake in 2010. Steel also purchased 10 percent of Bull-Dog Sauce Company (a manufacturer of *tonkatsu* sauce) in 2007 and then made a takeover offer. Bull-Dog resisted by beefing up its cross-shareholding with friendly companies (a maneuver upheld by Japanese courts). After a year, Steel sold its stake. The media have tended to portray Steel Partners and other foreign funds in a negative way (for example, using the term *vulture funds* to describe them). Discouraged by these and other thwarted efforts, Steel Partners dissolved its Japan fund in 2011 (Worsley 2008; Kurdas 2011).

As foreign funds began seeking to take over or influence Japanese firms in the 2000s, many Japanese firms strengthened cross-shareholdings and other anti-takeover defenses (Fujita and Tudor 2008).

In general, efforts of outside investors (including some Japanese funds) have been unsuccessful in conducting hostile takeovers or using a minority ownership stake to get management to change policies. To be sure, takeovers (mostly, but not entirely, friendly) by some private equity groups (both Japanese and foreign) have occurred, but the number is not large, and whether they represent a trend that will strengthen remains unclear (Milhaupt 2005; Schaede 2008, 114–26).

Conclusion

This chapter has examined a broad array of aspects of Japanese financial markets and how they have evolved in the years since 1990. Compared to Korea and China, Japan had already experienced considerable reform prior to the 1990s. Financial repression had been substantial from the 1950s to the 1980s, but was gone by 1990. Financial markets were already large, and had been opened to international capital flows. Nonetheless, the years since 1990 were fraught with problems and a multitude of further reforms were set in motion.

As of 2010 Japanese financial markets were more robust than in 1990 due to the resolution of the nonperforming loan crisis of the 1990s and the active role of the Financial Services Agency in enforcing rules on prudential behavior. Meanwhile, deregulation and the effort to promote both new forms of finance (such as the Mothers Market for listing young firms) opened the way for reducing the heavy reliance on banks and for improving the efficiency of capital allocation. Deregulation through this period also increased the possibility that Tokyo could become a larger and more vibrant international center for finance than it already was in 1990.

This chapter, however, has indicated that the picture is quite mixed. Some changes have been quite significant. Banks hold less corporate equity, causing the cross-shareholding system to decline (but not disappear), while foreign investors have become large players in portfolio ownership of equity and in trading on the Tokyo Stock Exchange. A wave of consolidations dramatically changed the banking industry and led to the formation of four large financial holding companies that include banking, securities, and insurance.

Nonetheless, in a variety of ways the Japanese financial system has undergone relatively little transformation. The predominant flow of money from savers to borrowers continues to be through the banking system. More importantly, some evidence suggests that continued misallocation of resources, particularly in the form of excessive fixed investment in the corporate sector, yielding low returns on both equity and assets. Foreign, and some domestic, shareholders may be playing a more activist role but have not made much of a dent in corporate behavior.

Overall financial markets in Japan and Japanese-owned financial institutions remain less internationalized than one might expect. Capital flows into and out of Japan have increased, but so have those of the United States and other countries. Meanwhile, Japanese financial institutions do not appear to be as engaged in international markets as their peers in other major industrial countries.

In 1990 Tokyo and Japanese financial institutions appeared to be on the cusp of becoming major international players. Two decades later the same question remains: Will Japan emerge as a more important international financial center? Probably not.

The one real factor that drove the concept of Tokyo as a center in the 1980s was the availability of a vast pool of savings that could be invested abroad. But over the next 20 years this factor will diminish because of demographic shifts (a decreasing and aging population) and their implications for savings and government spending. Household savings as a ratio to after-tax income are now as low as in the United States. In 2010 those age 65 and older comprised 23 percent of the population, and that number will rise during the next 20 years to over 30 percent. An absolute decline in the stock of household savings as the savings rate turns negative in the next two decades is possible. Individual Japanese investors might seek higher returns abroad, but, for some time, forecasters have been anticipating this in vain.

As recently as 1996, when the Big Bang reforms were announced, the government appeared committed to the concept of making Japan a more significant international financial center, motivated in part by envy of the rapid growth of London as an international center after the major financial reforms there in the early 1980s. Today it is less clear that government officials care about Japan's role in global finance. So long as the financial system fulfills its primary domestic function of mediating the flow of funds at home, officials appear relatively content—though they should be concerned about the misallocation of domestic funds.

Despite the official enthusiasm in the past for reform and internationalization, the problem was that foreign financial institutions have been troublesome—pressing for changes that the government was often reluctant to grant. Or foreigners pursued actions viewed with abhorrence by both government and the media. As a consequence, in a competitive global financial market, international firms may gradually shift activities away from Tokyo.

To explain these developments, this chapter has relied primarily on social explanations: language, high expat living costs in Tokyo, risk aversion, and group decision-making dynamics. Poor English language ability hampers Japanese financial firms in global markets. Expensive expat living packages make Tokyo a less desirable international center than some other cities. Risk aversion militates against major change in the bank-centered nature of domestic finance, and has left Japanese financial firms behind foreign competitors in global markets. Group dynamics yielding slow decisions hurt the ability of Japanese financial firms to participate in fast-moving international deals. Altogether, one can describe these factors as contributing to a generally uncomfortable fit between the Japanese domestic financial sector and the rest of the world.

In principle, there is nothing wrong with an inward-looking financial sector and a continued reliance on banks as the primary source of financing for the corporate sector, so long as the system operates efficiently. Indeed, the 2008–2009 financial crisis in the United States and Europe cast considerable doubt on the need for Japan to change.

In theory, banks can serve well as the primary allocator of funds in the economy if they make loan decisions on the basis of careful financial analysis. If that is the case, then there would be no need for Japan to change. However, the evidence concerning overinvestment and low returns on assets suggests that the Japanese bank-centered financial system does not conform to this ideal.

Further, if a better market for high-tech start-up firms continues to languish, then the consequence is likely to be a relative loss of global competiveness in emerging industries (since commercial banks are not well suited as backers of risky start-up firms). Firms flush with generous depreciation funds and loans from uncritical bank lenders will continue to misallocate their resources and overinvest in plant and equipment. Rather than investing in fixed capital at home, more funds should flow to higher-return, but inherently riskier, investments abroad.

One solution to these problems would be to retain the reliance on banks but make them more congruent with globally efficient credit allocation. This would require banks to reduce their appetite for domestic bonds, to quickly abandon zombie firms, to make loans on hard-nosed financial analysis, and to increase lending abroad. To date, however, there is little evidence that these outcomes are occurring. Nor are they likely to in the near future.

Another solution is for the economic system to become less reliant on banking and more reliant on bonds and equity markets. The key is to bring about an alteration in the behavior of recipients of credit to raise returns on capital, by allowing successful firms to expand, and to force out the failures. That outcome is more likely to occur by reducing the relative role of banks and increasing that of capital markets, and by encouraging greater participation by non-Japanese financial firms in all aspects of the domestic market. The evidence presented, however, suggests that this solution is not occurring either.

The highest probability outcome for the next decade is a lack of decisive change. The financial system is sufficiently robust that a repeat of the near disaster of the 1990s is unlikely. But the pressure for changes—either to make a bank-centered system behave more efficiently or to cause a shift to a less bank-centered system—seems rather limited.

Should the system remain resistant to further change, the disappointing outcome will be continued below-potential economic growth and a continued modest role of Japanese financial firms in global markets.

References

Much of the data were collected from Internet sources that are now dead links, or have had the data replaced by more recent numbers. Full information on links used is available from the author.

Amyx, Jennifer. 2004. *Japan's Financial Crisis: Institutional Rigidity and Reluctant Change.* Princeton University Press.

Aoki, Masahiko, and Hugh Patrick, eds. 1994. *The Japanese Main Bank System: Its Relevance for Developing and Transforming Economies.* Clarendon Press Oxford.

Baylis, Paul. 2010. Japan Real Time. http://blogs.wsj.com/japanrealtime/2010/06/30/japan-gets-cheaper-and-more-expensive/ (accessed December 5, 2011).

BOJ = Bank of Japan. 1991. *Economic Statistics Annual.*

Bremner, Brian. 2001. "How Merrill Lost Its Way in Japan." *Businessweek,* November 12.

Businessweek. 2005. "The Businessweek Global 1200." *Businessweek*, December 26.

Cargill, Thomas F., and Yoshino Yoshino. 2003. *Postal Savings and Fiscal Investment in Japan: The PSS and the FILP*. Oxford University Press.

Citigroup. 2009. 2009 Annual Report.

Cuadra, Leslie. 2011. "List of World's Largest Creditor and Debtor Nations." www.financialsense.com/ (accessed August 31, 2012).

Daiwa Securities. 1999. 1999 Annual Report: Daiwa Securities Faces the 21st Century with Confidence.

Daiwa Securities. 2010. Annual Report 2010: New Endeavor with Originality.

Economist. 2010. "The Cost of Living in Cities." March 10.

Equity Clock. 2010. "Stocks with the Best Return on Equity (ROE)." http://www.equityclock.com/2010/03/08/stocks-with-the-best-return-on-equity-roe/ (accessed August 15, 2012).

Foley, John, and Rob Cox. 2011. "Nomura Evolves, Just Not So Fast." *New York Times*, February 2.

Fortune. 2011. "Global 500." http://money.cnn.com/magazines/fortune/global500/2011/full_list/ for previous 7 years (accessed August 2, 2011).

FSA = Financial Services Agency, Japan. 2005. "Financial Statements of Major Banks: March 2005 (Non-consolidated)." http://www.fsa.go.jp/news/newse/e20050525–1.pdf (accessed August 1, 2011).

FSA = Financial Services Agency. 2010. "Table 1: Transition of Loans Based on the Financial Reconstruction Act." http://www.fsa.go.jp/en/regulated/npl/20100205/01.pdf (accessed September 23, 2012).

FSA = Financial Services Agency, Japan. 2011a. "Overview of Major Banks' Financial Results as of March 31, 2011." http://www.fsa.go.jp/en/news/2011/20110630–3/01.pdf (accessed August 1, 2011).

FSA = Financial Services Agency. 2011b. "Table 5: Transition of Total Losses on Disposal of Non-Performing Loans of All Banks." http://www.fsa.go.jp/en/regulated/npl/20110210/05.pdf (accessed September 23, 2012).

Fujita, Junko, and Alison Tudor. 2008. "Japanese Companies Start to Question 'Poison Pill' Strategy." *New York Times*, May 8.

GIA = General Insurance Association of Japan. 1998. Factbook: Non-life Insurance in Japan 1997–1998. http://www.sonpo.or.jp/en/publication/pdf/fb1998e.pdf (accessed August 1, 2011).

GIA = General Insurance Association of Japan. 2003. Factbook: Non-life Insurance in Japan 2002–2003. http://www.sonpo.or.jp/en/publication/pdf/fb2003e.pdf (accessed August 1, 2011).

GIA = General Insurance Association of Japan. 2010. Factbook 2009–2010: General Insurance in Japan. http://www.sonpo.or.jp/en/publication/pdf/fb2010e.pdf (accessed September 1, 2010; August 1, 2011).

Hamada, Koichi, Anil Kashyap, and David E. Weinstein, eds. 2011. *Japan's Bubble, Deflation, and Long-term Stagnation*. The MIT Press.

Hamao, Yasushi, Kenji Kutsuna, and Pedro Matos. 2010 May. "Investor Activism in Japan: The First 10 Years." Working Paper 289, Center for Japanese Economy and Business, Columbia University.

Hoshi, Takeo, Ricardo Caballero, and Anil K. Kashyap. 2008. "Zombie Lending and Depressed Restructuring in Japan." *American Economic Review* 98 (5) (December): 1943–77.

Hoshi, Takeo, and Anil K. Kashyap. 2001. *Corporate Financing and Governance in Japan: The Road to the Future*. The MIT Press.

Hoshi, Takeo, and Hugh T. Patrick, eds. 2000. *Crisis and Change in the Japanese Financial System*. Kluwer Academic Publishers.

Hosono, Kaoru, Koji Sakai, and Kotaro Tsuru. 2009. "Consolidation of Banks in Japan: Causes and Consequences." *National Bureau of Economic Research, Financial Sector Development in the Pacific Rim, East Asia Seminar on Economics* 18: 265–309.

Hufbauer, Gary, and Julia Muir. 2010 October. "Turning Back the Clock: Japan's Misguided Postal Law Is Back on the Table." Policy Brief PB10–17. Peterson Institute for International Economics.

Ito, Takatoshi. 2000. "The Stagnant Japanese Economy in the 1990s: The Need for Financial Supervision to Restore Sustained Growth." In Takeo Hoshi and Hugh Patrick, eds., *Crisis and Change in the Japanese Financial System*, 85–107. Kluwer Academic Publishers.

Japan Times. 2010. "Editorial: When Airports Eat Each Other." March 23.

JCER = Japan Center for Economic Research. 2003. "The Profitability of Japanese Industries: Non-financial Sectors, Banks and Life-Insurance Companies." *Japan Financial Report* 9 (October): 19–23.

JHFA = Japan Housing Finance Agency. nd (c 2007). [An overview of JHFA] http://www.jhf.go.jp/files/100012580.pdf (accessed December 15, 2011).

Johnson, Chalmers. 1982. *MITI and the Japanese Miracle*. Stanford University Press.

JSDA = Japan Securities Dealers Association. Fact Book 2002 and 2009. http://www.jsda.or.jp/en/newsroom/fact-book/.

Kashyap, Anil K., and Takeo Hoshi. 2009. "Will the US Bank Recapitalization Succeed? Eight Lessons from Japan." Chicago Booth Research Paper 09–28.

Katz, Richard. 1998. *The System That Soured: The Rise and Fall of the Japanese Economic Miracle*. ME Sharp, Inc.

Kurdas, Chidem. 2011, May 30. "Steel Partners Liquidates Japan Fund." http://hedgefundsmarts.wordpress.com/ (accessed August 04, 2011).

Levin, Bess. 2009, July 9. "Nomura Finding Lehman Employees to Be Extremely Difficult." http://dealbreaker.com (accessed August 2, 2011).

LIA = Life Insurance Association of Japan. 2004. Life Insurance Business in Japan 2003/2004. [Specific link dead 120815.]

LIA = Life Insurance Industry Association of Japan. 2009. "Overview of the Life Insurance Business in Japan in Fiscal 2008." [Specific link dead 120815.]

LIA = Life Insurance Association of Japan. nd. "Monthly Statistics." [Specific link dead 120815.]

Lincoln, Edward J. 1998. "Japan's Financial Problems." *Brookings Papers on Economic Activity* 2: 347–85.

Lincoln, Edward J. 1998. *Japan Facing Economic Maturity*. Brookings Institution.

Lincoln, Edward J. 2001. *Arthritic Japan: The Slow Pace of Economic Reform*. Brookings Institution.

Mainichi Daily. 1999. "Sokaiya Scandal." September 12.

Maps = Finance.mapsofword.com. 2010. "Top 10 Investment Banks."

Maxi-Pedia. 2010. http://www.maxi-pedia.com/Return + on + Equity + ROE (September 12, 2010).

Milhaupt, Curtis J., and Geoffrey P. Miller. 2000. "Regulatory Failure and the Collapse of Japan's Home Mortgage Lending Industry: A Legal and Economic Analysis." *Law and Policy* 22 (3 and 4): 245–90.

Milhaupt, Curtis J. 2005. "In the Shadow of Delaware? The Rise of Hostile Takeovers in Japan." *Columbia Law Review* 105 (7) (November): 2171–2216.

Mizuho Securities. 2010. "Corporate History." http://www.mizuho-sc.com/english/info/history/index.html (accessed September 2, 2010).

MUFJ = Mitsubishi UFJ Securities. 2008. Annual Review.

MUFJ FG = Mitsubishi UFJ Financial Group. 2010a. Corporate Review 2010.

MUFJ FG = Mitsubishi UFJ Financial Group. 2010b. MUFJ Fact Book.

Nishi, Fumiaki, and Alexander Vergus. 2006, November. "Asian Bond Issues in Tokyo: History, Structure and Prospects." BIS Papers 30.

Nomura Securities. 2011. "Consolidated Results of Operations (US GAAP), First Quarter, year ending March 2011." http://www.nomuraholdings.com/investor/summary/financial/index.html (accessed September 14, 2012).

NYSE = New York Stock Exchange. nd. "Facts and Figures."

OECD = Organization for Economic Co-operation and Development. 2010a. Measuring Innovation: A New Perspective. http://www.oecd.org/sti/measuringinnovationanewperspective.htm.

OECD = Organisation for Economic Co-operation and Development. 2010b. OECD Fact Book 2010. http://www.oecd-ilibrary.org/economics/oecd-factbook-2010_factbook-2010-en.

Okimoto, Daniel I. 1989. *Between MITI and the Market: Japanese Industrial Policy for High Technology*. Stanford University Press.

Patrick, Hugh T., and Yung Chul Park, eds. 1994. *The Financial Development of Japan, Korea, and Taiwan: Growth, Repression, and Liberalization*. Oxford University Press.

Posen, Adam. 1998. *Restoring Japan's Economic Growth*. Peterson Institute for International Economics.

Reilly, Frank K. 1997. "The Impact of Inflation on ROE, Growth and Stock Prices." *Financial Services Review* 6 (1): 5–6.

Reuters. 2008. "Japan Holds Top Creditor-Nation Spot for 17th Year." May 23.

Schaede, Ulrike. 2008. Choose and Focus: *Japanese Business Strategies for the 21st Century*. Cornell University Press.

Shirai, Sayuri. 2009. "Promoting Tokyo as an International Financial Centre." In Soongil Young, Dosoung Choi, Jesus Seade, and Sayuri Shirai, eds., *Competition Among Financial Centres in Asia Pacific*. Utopia Press.

Slater, Dan. 2008. "Questions Linger over Nomura's Lehman Acquisition." *Bloomberg Businessweek*, November 21.

Tett, Gillian. 2003. Saving the Sun: *A Wall Street Gamble to Rescue Japan from Its Trillion-Dollar Meltdown*. HarperBusiness.

TheCityUK. 2010, June. "Bond Markets 2010." Home: http://www.thecityuk.com/ (accessed August 31, 2010).

Trezise, Philip H. 1976. "Politics, Government, and Economic Growth in Japan." In Hugh Patrick and Henry Rosovosky, eds., *Asia's New Giant: How the Japanese Economy Works*. Brookings Institution.

WFE = World Federation of Exchanges. 2009. Annual Report and Statistics. http://www.world-exchanges.org/files/statistics/pdf/WFE09%20final.pdf.

WFE = World Federation of Exchanges. 2010. Annual Report and Statistics. http://www.world-exchanges.org/files/statistics/pdf/WFE2010AR%20final.pdf.

Worsley, Ken. 2008. "Steel Partners Sell off Stakes." April 18. www.japaneconomynews.com/ (accessed August 15, 2012).

WSJ = *Wall Street Journal*. 2011. "Morgan Stanley Takes the 2010 MA Crown." January 3.

CHAPTER FOUR

Financial Development and Liberalization in Korea: 1980–2011

YUNG CHUL PARK

ONE OF the more salient features of financial development in Korea over the three decades since 1980 has been financial market liberalization and opening. It has attracted a great deal of interest, largely because Korea has been successful in building a market-oriented financial system in the wake of the 1997–1998 financial crisis. This is notwithstanding a series of financial turbulences that includes the bursting of a credit card lending boom in 2003, a real estate boom-bust in 2003–2007, a liquidity crisis in 2008, and a run on savings banks in 2011.

Clearly, financial liberalization does not provide a guarantee of immunity to financial crisis. Indeed, there is some evidence that deregulation of the capital account should in part be held responsible for precipitating Korea's two major crises of 1997–1998 and 2008. Still, it should be noted that the two crises do not negate the overall benefits of financial liberalization, although they do underscore the need to rethink the speed and conditions under which liberalization can proceed with a minimum of adverse consequences. This is because—in theory and from experience—the risks to financial stability could overwhelm the favorable effects of transition to a liberalized financial system.

The linkages between financial liberalization and real-sector variables are not clear, and there is also ambiguity on causal relations between financial liberalization and financial stability.

Theories predict that transition to a liberalized financial system could spur growth by increasing saving and investment and by improving the efficiency of investment through various channels. A number of country studies suggest that this is not consistently supported by empirical evidence. For example, an empirical examination using Korean data does not provide any concrete evidence of an efficiency improvement associated with financial deregulation. Financial reform may or may not improve distributive equity, depending on the level of development of the financial system. In general, the effects of financial liberalization on real sector variables remain largely empirical issues.

This chapter analyzes the background and consequences of financial market deregulation and opening since the early 1980s with a view to assessing its effects on the growth, efficiency, equity, and stability in the Korean economy.

The chapter begins with an overview of the financial system's evolution, with particular attention to growth and structural change since 2000. Next, the 1997–1998 and 2008 crises are examined in depth to gain insight into the causal relationships between financial liberalization and stability. Two locally generated crises are also examined. The analysis seeks to throw light on whether even a well-functioning financial system needs to be complemented by an efficient system of regulations to safeguard against financial instability. In particular, the importance of mismatches in currency and maturity are examined, as they were the key elements in both of Korea's two major financial crises during the period covered here.

The consequences of liberalization are then evaluated. A financial liberalization index and three models are created to analyze effects of liberalization on access to capital and on efficiency at both the firm and industry levels. This is followed by an investigation of the causal nexus between financial liberalization and distribution of income and wealth. The chapter concludes with an evaluation of liberalization.

Evolution of Korea's Financial System

During the three decades of this study, Korea has shifted from a highly regulated, bank-based financial system to a more market-oriented system with a much larger role for direct finance. The deregulation of financial markets and institutions that has facilitated this shift has been an intermittent process marked by relapses and regressions. There was no clear direction for reform until 1997 when the country succumbed to a major financial crisis. The rescue financing Korea sought from the IMF set in motion an extensive reform that has constructed a deregulated and open financial system. (See, for example, Ghosh 2006.)

Four Waves of Reform, 1980–2007

During much of the postwar period to the late 1970s, Korea's financial system was classified as one of the most repressive. Asset-liability management at banks and non-bank financial intermediaries, market interest rates, the foreign exchange rate, and capital account transactions were all under tight government control and were used as instruments of industrial policy.

By the early 1980s the collusive arrangement among the government, the *chaebol* (conglomerates), and banks—the main players of a Chalmers Johnson developmental state (1982)—was coming apart at the seams, with mounting inefficiencies in resource allocation, internal and external imbalances, and corruption bred by mismanagement of industrial policy.

Realizing the limitations of the developmental state, in the early 1980s Korea's policy makers began an extensive array of economic reforms that included an overall financial liberalization. However, the government could not forsake its interventionist fixation and so stayed with its dirigiste policy regime until 1997. This meant it dithered over reform plans.

The first wave of reform was domestic market deregulation undertaken in the early 1980s under Chun Doo Hwan, who served as president from 1980 to 1988. It did not make much progress in removing many of the repressive features of the financial system. Instead, what was achieved was no more than cosmetic liberalization.

The Kim Yong Sam government, inaugurated early in 1993, launched a second wave by placing economic globalization at the top of the list of its policy priorities. In moving forward with its globalization strategy, the government combined domestic financial deregulation with market opening to loosen and gradually phase out the regulatory system controlling capital account transactions.

Given the huge interest rate differentials between foreign and domestic financial markets in a managed floating exchange rate regime, the lifting of many of the restrictions on capital flows—in particular, inflows—induced a massive increase in foreign borrowing, much of which was secured from the international wholesale funding market and re-lent to *chaebol* and large corporations for financing their long-term investment.

The rate at which short-term foreign liabilities were piling up was excessive compared to debt servicing capacity and holdings of foreign exchange reserves. This rendered the economy highly vulnerable to a sudden reversal of capital flows. In 1997 such a reversal threw the economy into a severe crisis that brought the entire financial system to the edge of insolvency. There were huge losses of output and employment. In retrospect, continuation of financial repression was not itself a direct cause of the crisis, although it deepened and made it more difficult to manage the meltdown.

The 1997 crisis marked a watershed in financial reform, launching the third wave of liberalization with implementation of the International Monetary Fund (IMF) conditions that Korea was subjected to in return for rescue financing. The reform was designed to transform Korea's financial system into one that was as free and open as in advanced economies. During the three years following the crisis, the controls over market interest rates and the foreign exchange rate were removed. Most of the regulatory restrictions on asset and liability management at banks and other financial institutions, as well as on account transactions, were lifted or scheduled to be phased out.

The financial reform also included the creation of a new regulatory system. In December 1997 the Bank of Korea Act was revised and the Act on the Establishment of Financial Supervisory Organizations (EFSO) was passed. This legislation established the Financial Supervisory Commission (FSC) and its executive arm, the Financial Supervisory Service (FSS), by consolidating the four financial supervisory authorities: the Office of Bank Supervision, the Securities Supervisory Board, the Insurance Supervisory Board, and the Non-bank Supervisory Authority (which had overseen non-bank financial institutions). The FSC serves as a consolidated policy-making body for all matters pertaining to supervision of the financial industry as a whole. The FSC reports directly to the Prime Minister's Office.

In 2008 the new Lee Myung Bak government revamped the financial regulatory system by integrating the supervisory policy functions of the Financial Supervisory Commission and the financial policy functions of the Ministry of Finance and Economy and separating policy-setting and execution functions through the division of the posts of the FSC Chairman and the FSS Governor. As a result, the FSC was renamed the Financial Services Commission.

The third wave of reform touched off a number of fundamental changes in financial structure. One change has been the elevation of the role and the importance of capital markets (direct finance)—in particular the equity market—as a source of funding for corporations relative to financial intermediaries (indirect finance). Another has seen the demise of non-bank financial institutions, especially merchant banks. A third has brought about a rapid growth of consumer loans (including mortgage loans). Finally, there has been a dramatic increase in foreign investments in financial industries, including ownership of banks and other financial institutions. These are analyzed at length later.

Following the 1997 crisis, Korea began running large and persistent surpluses on its current account, a result of a domestic recession and soaring exports powered by a massive depreciation of the won. By the end of 2004 the volume of foreign exchange reserves had risen to more than 25 percent of GDP. The continuing sterilization of current and capital account surpluses built up pressure on the won to appreciate vis-à-vis major international currencies.

These developments on the external side were taken as indications that Korea was ready for a more extensive financial market opening. During the early years of the Roh Moo Hyun administration (2003–2008), the fourth wave of financial liberalization took off with the lofty goal of hosting an international finance center in Seoul.

Soon after the plan was announced, however, Korea's policy makers were overwhelmed by the daunting tasks implied by this goal: fully liberalizing capital account transactions, making the won fully convertible and internationalized, and allowing offshore trading in won. Korea simply did not meet many of the threshold conditions for a country capable of exporting financial services. (See Kose et al. 2009 for the conditions.) Not surprisingly, the fourth wave died before hitting the shore.

However, something had to be done to dissipate the mounting pressure for currency appreciation, and Korea's policy makers stepped up deregulation of capital outflows. A series of measures for the relaxation of outflows of portfolio capital induced a large increase in short-term foreign liabilities, ultimately to an unsustainable level in the eyes of foreign lenders, as had happened in the run-up to the 1997–1998 crisis.

The increase sowed the seeds of the liquidity crisis Korea was exposed to during the fourth quarter of 2008 after the collapse of Lehman Brothers. As it did 10 years earlier, Korea needed external financial assistance to bring the crisis to an end. This time the help came from the US Federal Reserve. The 2008 crisis is the second major financial event explored at length in the following discussion.

Reform Since 2007

Although the financial reform in the aftermath of the 1997 crisis intended to cover all financial markets and intermediation industries, financial investment service providers—brokerages, asset management firms, futures companies, and trust companies—had been left to be regulated by fourteen separate acts limiting them to provide services and products in various segmented markets. This market restriction had long been criticized as impeding competition across the entire spectrum of financial markets and hindering the development of investment banking.

In 2007 the Korean government set out to deregulate these industries, and in 2009 the Capital Market Consolidation Act, which amalgamates six existing laws, including the securities and exchange act, the indirect investment asset management business act, and the trust business act, went into effect.

The 2009 act stipulates a set of rules governing the activities of financial investment companies other than banks and insurance companies. It does this by dividing investment products into categories and listing types of securities and categories of financial products and services. The act then requires individual firms either to receive selective approvals or to be registered for providing one or several of these products and services. There are six categories of financial products and services: investment trading, investment brokerage, collective investment, trust, discretionary investment, and investment advisory.

The act is designed to achieve two main purposes: first, to deregulate financial markets to allow financial companies to grow larger and benefit from economies of scale and scope by taking part in a wider range of financial activities; and, second, to impose tighter controls to safeguard the interests of financial consumers. Under the act, financial investment service providers are allowed to compete with each other to sell a varied range of financial products. The consumer protection measures include grading financial products for risk, selling only products with a risk level appropriate to the individual customer, and not recommending a product unless the customer asked about it first.

Growth and Structural Change Since 2000

The 1997 financial crisis and the subsequent reforms have reconfigured Korea's financial system into one of the most liberalized, open regimes in the emerging world. This section highlights some of the most significant changes that have taken place since 2000.

Financial Growth

For almost seven years after the 1997 crisis broke out, the ratio of total financial assets to GDP was stagnant. Then, in 2005 it started climbing again. Data are in figure 4.1.

Much of the setback during the 1998–2005 period had its causes in a significant financial restructuring. This involved the exit of 1,561 financial institutions, including 11 commercial banks; resolution of nonperforming loans that reduced capacity for credit creation; a slowdown in investment demand caused by the dot-com bubble bursting in 2001;

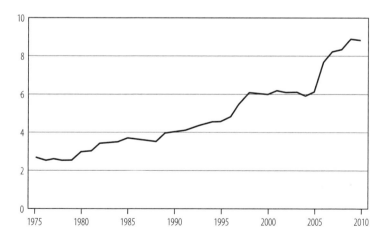

Figure 4.1 Ratio of Financial Assets to GDP. *Source*: The Bank of Korea.

Note: Ratio of total financial assets, including those of financial institutions, to GDP.

and risk aversion by household savers. Once the crisis was over, however, financial growth has accelerated despite a series of small and large financial crises.

Expansion of Direct Finance

Before the 1997 crisis, Korea's financial system can be characterized as a bank-based system. The post-1997 financial deregulation has powered a marked increase in the share of direct finance—funding through money and capital markets—that has transformed the financial system into a more market-oriented one.

Much of the expansion of direct finance has been spurred on the demand side by the migration of household savers to money and capital markets in search of greater returns and by the influx of foreign portfolio investment. On the supply side, corporate restructuring after the 1997 crisis obligated large firms and the *chaebol* to lower their debt-to-equity levels.

From the early 1960s onward to the late 1990s, banks—both commercial and specialized—dominated Korea's financial system as the major source of external financing to firms and households. Even in the early 1990s, nonfinancial firms relied heavily on bank loans for working capital, as well as fixed investment. Bank of Korea data show that bank loans accounted for more than 50 percent of their total financing, whereas equity was less than 23 percent, and bond financing about 10 percent.

This dominance fell off substantially with the growth of money and capital markets in the wake of the 1997 crisis, thereby fostering a market orientation of the financial system. For example, the share of financing through financial markets—direct finance—rose to 67 percent of total finance, including financing through financial intermediaries in 2010 from about 45 percent in the middle of the 1980s, as shown in table 4.1.

In this transformation process, the most conspicuous aspect was the rise in equity financing: its share shot up to 45 percent in 2010 from about 20 percent throughout the 1990s.

Much of the expansion of direct finance has been spurred by the migration of household savers to money and capital markets in search for higher returns. The corporate restructuring after the 1997 crisis that targeted redressing the excessive leverage of large corporations, including the *chaebol*, obligated firms to lower their debt-equity ratios

TABLE 4.1
Total Finance and the Relative Size of Financial Markets (in trillion won and percents)

	1980[a]	1990	2000	2005	2010	2011[b]	b/a	
A	30.9	340.5	1,430	2,729	4,393	4,538	–	Total finance (B + C)
B	24.3	182.2	677	1,099	1,827	1,978	81	Indirect finance[a]
C	6.6	158.3	753	1,630	2,566	2,559	388	Direct finance (D + E)
D	1.5	44.3	138	213	267	271	181	Money markets[b]
E	5.1	114.0	614	1,417	2,299	2,288	449	Capital markets
	2.5	35.0	397	691	1,059	1,140	456	Bonds[c]
	2.5	79.0	217	726	1,240	1,148	459	Equities[d]
	79	178	237	315	374	367	–	Total finance as % of GDP
	79	54	47	40	42	44	–	Indirect as % of total finance (B/A)

Source: Korea's Financial Markets (2009), The Bank of Korea.

[a]Total loans (excluding Bank of Korea loans) from "financial assets and liabilities."

[b]The sum of call loans, RPs, commercial paper, financial debentures, CDs, covered bills, and monetary stabilization bonds (maturity less than one year).

[c]Par value of listed bonds.

[d]Stock market capitalization.

to below 250 percent from more than 500 percent before the crisis. This restructuring has driven them to rely on equity financing more than before. At the same time, the influx of foreign investment in local bonds and stocks, and the sustained increase in stock prices, as shown by the doubling of the KOSPI (the major stock price index) between 1997 and 2010, has powered the expansion of direct finance.

Between 2000 and 2011, the capital market (long-term bonds and stocks) measured by market capitalization saw more than a three-fold increase. There was a more than two-fold increase in the size of the money market.

The total amount of funds raised on the money and capital markets amounted to less than 80 percent of the total volume of intermediated credits before the 1997 crisis. The level surged to 150 percent in 2005 before falling to about 122 percent during the 2008 liquidity crisis. By the end of 2011 it had returned to the pre-2008 crisis level.

MONEY MARKETS Money market instruments include call loans, repurchase agreements (RPs), commercial paper (CP), financial debentures, certificates of deposit (CDs), cover bills, monetary stabilization bonds, and treasury bills. The growth of the money market has been phenomenal. In 1980 the total amount of funds raised was 1.5 trillion won. Ten years later it had shot up to more than 44 trillion won. Growth did not slow in the 1990s. Between 1990 and 2000, there was a more than threefold increase in market size. Since then, growth has been moderate, yet the market was twice as large in 2011 as it had been a decade earlier.

Much of the growth reflects a shift to a more balanced portfolio in terms of risk and return by household and corporate investors who have become more sensitive to changes in market interest rates. Throughout the 1990s, CP, monetary stabilization bonds, and CDs were the most widely used means of short-term financing. They had a combined market share close to 80 percent of the total money market (wholesale funding). Since the 1997 crisis CDs and RPs have emerged as the dominant instruments of short-term funding. This share increase has come at the expense of monetary stabilization bonds, as their maturity has become longer over the years.

STOCK MARKET Resolution of the 1997 crisis and attendant reforms freed the market, bringing about a massive increase in equity financing. In 1996 stock market capitalization amounted to a mere 117.4 trillion won, a fraction of indirect financing. The market collapsed in 1997. But, two years later, market size had almost tripled to 349.5 trillion won. Then, with the bursting of the global IT bubble in 2000, for two years the market suffered again.

Beginning in 1981 the government began gradually opening the stock market to foreign investors. As a first step, foreign investors were given opportunities to indirectly invest in Korean stocks in the form of beneficiary certificates and through Korea country funds established exclusively for them. In 1992, for the first time, foreign investors were allowed a limited investment in listed stocks. The government imposed an overall limit on foreign ownership of 10 percent of total outstanding shares for each individual issue and a ceiling of 3 percent per issue for a single foreign investor. Thereafter, the government expanded the ceilings several times before lifting them in 1998, except for public corporations.

From 2000 to 2011 the stock market capitalization of the main (KOSPI) exchange grew 454 percent, from 188 trillion to 1,042 trillion won. This reflects both price appreciation and especially new and secondary issues (generally done as rights offerings). Thus, the number of listed firms rose from 704 to 791 companies. The KOSDAQ market for smaller companies went from 604 to 1,031 listed companies.

With the complete opening of the market, the share of foreign investments in Korean stocks jumped to a record high of 45 percent in March 2004. Then it declined below 30 percent in both 2008 and 2009 on a monthly average before rising to 34 percent in April 2012.

BOND MARKETS In the early 1990s corporate bonds with a three-year maturity had a commanding share of Korea's bond market at 60 percent. This share had plunged to less than 17 percent in 2009, largely because of the massive increase in government bonds issued for financial restructuring following the 1997 crisis, as well as for covering the fiscal deficit and for foreign exchange sterilization.

In the wake of the 1997 crisis the government had to borrow heavily to finance the restructuring of banks and indebted corporations. The collapse of the banking industry resulted in a severe contraction of the lending capacity of banks. In an effort to supplement bank financing, the government eased the restrictions on bond financing, allowing corporations to issue bonds up to four times their equity capital and also to issue asset-backed securities (ABS).

The post-crisis reform also placed emphasis on expanding and bolstering market infrastructure as part of the plan for building a stable and efficient bond market. In 1999 the primary dealer system, an inter-dealer market for government bonds, and high-yield and collateralized bond obligation (CBO) funds were established. These changes were followed by additional reforms in 2000 with the creation of private bond evaluation companies, fungible issues, and the Dutch system for auctioning government bonds, in addition to introducing the mark-to-market fair value accounting system.

These institutional reforms were succeeded by the launching of a plan for fostering a market for bonds with maturities greater than 5 years. This paved the way for the issuance of 20-year government bonds in 2006 and 10-year TIPs (Treasury Inflation-Protected securities) in 2007. However, since then their outstanding amounts and trading volumes have been relatively small.

The various reforms appear to have spurred rapid growth of the market. Between 1990 and 2000 the outstanding amount of listed bonds grew more than 11-fold in terms of par value. In 2011 the size of the market was three times as great as a decade earlier. At the end of 2011, government bonds and public bonds (which include monetary stabilization bonds), special bonds (those issued by funds for deposit insurance and nonperforming loan management), and KEPCO (the largest electric company) accounted for almost 65 percent of the outstanding amount, whereas the share of corporate bonds other than KEPCO was only 15 percent.

The large interest rate differential between domestic and international financial markets prior to market liberalization held back opening of the bond market until 1997 when the ceiling on foreign investment in listed bonds was abolished. Despite the extensive opening, foreign demand had remained weak, with a market share around 0.5 percent until 2005.

However, beginning in the second half of 2007, when the US subprime crisis broke out, the yields on short-term government bonds rose above the dollar-won swap (CRS) rate. This differential created opportunities for arbitrage, causing a sharp increase in the foreign demand for short-term government and monetary stabilization bonds (discussed later). The liquidity crisis of 2008 slashed foreign demand, but since then the positive differential between short-term government and CRS interest rates, together with economic recovery, increased foreign demand again. Foreign holdings had reached 7.3 percent at the end of 2011. Foreign investors held mostly short-term treasury bonds (13.3 percent share) and monetary stabilization bonds (15.4 percent), as they were engaged in arbitrage transaction. In fact, these two instruments accounted for more than 98 percent of foreign-owned Korean bonds outstanding at the end of 2011.

ASSET-BACKED SECURITIES   Financial reform has also stimulated financial innovation to bring into the markets a large number of new financial instruments designed to facilitate diversification of funding. Among these are asset-backed securities (ABS). These include collateralized bond obligations, collateralized loan obligations, mortgage-backed securities, and asset-backed commercial paper.

ABS were first issued in 1999, following enactment of the law on asset securitization in 1998. The market saw explosive growth in 1999 and 2000 as financial institutions and corporations used them to resolve nonperforming loans, recapitalize, secure liquidity, and deleverage. In 2001 credit card companies began securitizing their card loans and other receivables as a new means of financing.

The first phase of financial and corporate restructuring ended in 2003. Since then, the credit card crisis, the 2008 liquidity crisis, and stagnation of housing markets have led to a substantial contraction of ABS markets.

Completion of financial and corporate restructuring changed the type of ABS issued to issuance of mortgage-backed securities and ABS for the financing of large long-term infrastructure projects. Beginning in 2007, stagnation in the housing and other real estate markets slashed the demand for ABS so much that, in 2011, the amount of new ABS fell to one-third of the level of a decade before.

FINANCIAL DERIVATIVES   Market deregulations have made interest rates, stock prices, and the foreign exchange rate more volatile. Financial institutions thus needed to improve their market risk management, and this need led to a growing demand for a broad range of financial derivatives as risk-hedging instruments.

A market for financial derivatives was first established with the issuance of stock price index futures in 1996 and options in 1997. After the establishment of a Korea futures exchange in 1999, a plethora of new derivatives products began to be traded. These ranged from stock index futures and options to CD interest rate futures to currency futures, swaps, and options.

As a result, between 2001 and 2011, the market for derivative instruments saw a massive increase in trading volume. The total volume of trading in derivatives for underlying assets such as foreign exchange, bonds, equities, and money market instruments amounted to 1,023 trillion won in 2011, more than 13 times the level of 2001.

Between 2001 and 2011, the amounts of currency-related derivatives transactions grew more than ten fold. For interest-rate derivative products, the transaction volume in 2008 was almost 35 times the figure in 2001; for stock derivatives, it was 12 times higher.

Financial Conglomeration and Market Concentration

The global trend toward consolidation and conglomeration of financial industries has also taken hold in Korea. This trend has been most conspicuous in banking. Following the 1997 crisis, Korea's policy makers have made concerted efforts to enhance the competitiveness of the financial sector by exploiting economies of scale and scope through consolidation and conglomeration of financial institutions vis-à-vis the large global financial firms that offer a wide range of financial services.

Due largely to the closing of 11 banks following the 1997 crisis and subsequent mergers and acquisitions, the number of banks was reduced to 7 nationwide commercial banks and 5 regional banks at the end of 2007. The share of the three largest banks in total bank assets rose from less than 40 percent in 1999 to almost 55 percent in 2002. After a setback in 2003–2005, it had risen to 60 percent in 2008. At the end of 2010 the four largest banks accounted for more than 70 percent of total bank assets. The four banks are, in order of asset size, Kookmin, Shinhan, Woori, and Hana.

The financial reform has also broken up much of the wall separating banking from the securities and insurance industries. This, together with enactment of the Financial Holding Company Act (FHCA) in 2000, has led to conglomeration in which a growing number of financial groups are allowed to engage in a range of activities including banking, securities, and leasing.

Financial Holding Company Act

As defined by the Financial Holding Company Act (FHCA), a financial holding company is a company with the primary business of controlling companies engaged directly in finance or in activities related closely to finance. A financial holding company is able to offer an extensive menu of financial services through subsidiaries engaged in different financial activities. In 2007 the act was amended to permit foreign financial institutions to establish financial holding companies.

From 2003 to 2007 there were only four holding companies. They remain the four largest. By the end of August 2012, eight others had been established, as shown in table 4.2.

Kookmin has long been the largest bank, but Shinhan and Woori are larger holding companies. Together the 10 owned 248 financial subsidiaries at the end of 2010.

Return on assets for the group had risen to 1.16 percent in 2005 but fell to 0.32 percent in 2009 after the 2008 liquidity crisis. For the same years, return on equity went from 19 percent to 4.8 percent.

TABLE 4.2

Financial Holding Companies Ranked by 2011 Assets (in million won)

Assets at the End of 2011	Name
312,804,000	Woori Finance Holdings Co[*][a]
288,117,500	Shinhan Financial Group[*]
277,600,800	KB Financial Group Inc[*][b]
178,228,900	Hana Financial Group Inc[*]
172,022,800	Korea Development Bank (KDB)[c]
73,687,800	Standard Chartered Bank Korea Ltd[d]
58,460,700	Citibank Korea[e]
39,358,673	BS Financial Group Inc[*][f]
31,294,000	DGB Financial Group[*][g]
29,427,000	Korea Investment Holdings Co
1,457,000	Golden Bridge
3,277,000	Meritz Financial Group

Source: Asset data are from the FSC. Notes compiled by the author from company sources.

[*]Shares trade on the Korea Stock Exchange. The three largest also have ADRs that trade in New York.

[a]The government owns 57% of Woori, which it has been seeking to sell. The holding company owns Woori Bank, Kwangju Bank, and Kyongnam Bank.

[b]KB Financial Group is the parent of Kookmin Bank.

[c]KDB is government owned.

[d]Foreign owned. Called SC First Bank from the time Standard Chartered plc acquired First Bank of Korea in 2005 until January 2012.

[e]Owned by Citigroup Inc.

[f]BS is the parent of Busan Bank, a regional bank based in Busan, Korea's second largest city.

[g]DGB is the parent of Daegu Bank, a regional bank based in Daegu, in the southeast, inland from Busan, and Korea's fourth largest city.

An empirical study (Park 2011) shows that the mergers, acquisitions, and consolidation of banks have not contributed to any gains in scale and scope economies. Instead, the increase in financial market concentration has resulted in a decrease in efficiency measured by X-inefficiency, labor inefficiency, and asset inefficiency. The author finds that the financial sector has an oligopolistic structure, which may explain the rise in the interest margin between loans and deposits, as well as inefficiency, during the sample period.

Portfolio Balance of the Household Sector

Financial liberalization has changed the asset preferences of households to increase their holdings of bonds and equities at the expense of bank deposits and real property. Before the crisis the shares of bonds in household asset portfolios was less than 10 percent and of equities 5 percent. Since 2005 they have on average been almost twice the levels of before.

On the liability side, following the relaxation of restrictions on consumer loans, household lending took off as banks and non-bank financial institutions (NBFIs) set out to attract household borrowers to fill the room vacated by their traditional business borrowers. Households have been borrowing rather heavily from banks and other NBFIs to finance investments in housing and other real estate. From 1999 onward, household credits—consumer and mortgage loans—have comprised a little over 50 percent of total loans extended by banks and NBFIs.

As shown in table 4.3, total consumer credit grew over 28 percent in both 2001 and 2002. The annual rate of growth of mortgage loans was even higher, at 56 percent on average. Despite the imposition of a loan-to-value (LTV) regulation in September 2002, mortgage loans continued to grow by 10 percent to 16 percent annually until 2006. Only when the debt-to-income ratio (DTI) was raised in 2006, busting the housing bubble, did mortgage growth drop, falling to 2.1 percent. (DTI measures principle and interest payments on total loans against income.)

A Granger causality test shows that causality runs from household credit to housing prices. This causal relationship indicates the significance of pro-cyclicality in household lending in which an expansion of household loans for housing finance inflates housing prices, which in turn feed into housing loans. The housing market that burst in 2005 was caused by the cutback in housing loans.

Financial Imbalances and Systemic Risk

At the time of implementation of the IMF-led crisis resolution in 1998, there was general consensus that a market-oriented financial reform would help better prevent the buildup of financial imbalances over time and across financial markets and institutions to stabilize the financial system as a whole and strengthen its resilience to cope better with

TABLE 4.3

Household Credit, by Creditor (outstanding volume at the end of year in trillion won and percents)

	Commercial and Specialized Banks (CSBs)		Non-bank Depository Corporations[a] (NDCs)				
		Percent Housing Related		Percent Housing Related	Other Financial Corporations[b]	Merchandise Credit	Total Household Credit[c]
2000	107.3	–	50.4		83.4	25.8	266.9
2001	156.7	–	49.3		97.5	38.2	341.7
2002	222.2	–	55.0		114.1	47.9	439.1
2003	253.8	–	68.3		98.9	26.6	447.6
2004	276.4	–	79.2		93.9	25.3	474.7
2005	305.6	68.2	87.3		100.2	28.0	521.5
2006	346.2	69.6	97.1		107.1	31.5	582.0
2007	363.7	67.6	110.4	42.6	155.9	35.3	665.3
2008	388.6	65.6	127.4	44.3	168.9	39.9	724.8
2009	409.5	66.8	141.2	45.9	187.1	41.7	779.6
2010	431.5	67.1	164.4	44.5	201.6	49.4	846.9
2011	455.9	67.8	186.8	44.5	215.4	54.7	912.9

Source: Bank of Korea, ECOS database.

[a]Include merchant banking corporations, asset management companies, and mutual savings banks.

[b]Include insurance firms, pension funds, specialized credit financial companies, public financial institutions, and others.

[c]In 2000 total household credit was 44% of GDP; in 2005, 60%; and in 2011, 74%.

exogenous shocks disruptive to the economy. The reality has been contrary to the expectation.

Financial stability defies precise definition or measurement, although it is a term of common usage. According to the European Central Bank: it is "a condition whereby the financial system is able to withstand shocks without giving way to cumulative processes, which impair the allocation of savings to investment opportunities and the processing of payments in the economy" (Padoa-Schioppa 2003).

The Bank of Korea has been devising a financial stability index. A prototype, which is a composite of eight variables, is shown in figure 4.2.

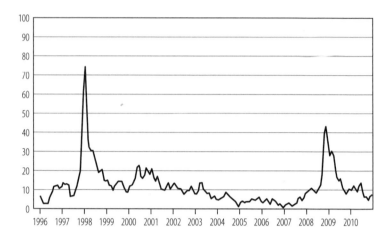

Figure 4.2 Financial Stability Index. *Source*: The Bank of Korea.

Note: The eight variables are: covered interest rate differentials between corporate (3 years) and government (3 years) bonds; covered interest rate differentials between government bonds (3 years) and monetary stabilization bonds; volatility of the nominal exchange rate; a stress index for the foreign exchange market (changes in the exchange rate adjusted for changes in foreign exchange reserves); volatility of KOSPI (the principal stock price index); the rate of decline in KOSPI; CDS spreads for major commercial banks; and volatility of stock prices of financial firms adjusted for changes in KOSPI.

The index displays greater financial stability from 1998 onward to 2007, a period that witnessed a considerable advance in financial liberalization. However, this does not prove that a market-oriented and open financial system is better in adjusting to internal and external shocks, as the same period is also marked by a home-grown crisis and the emerging major liquidity crisis that hit in 2008, as well as a massive increase in household debt that threatens systemic risk.

Korea's financial system went into a tailspin in 2008 and 2009, as it was not able to absorb or deflect the exogenous shocks emanating from the US subprime crisis.

Would Korea have been able to mitigate the impact of the adverse shock better had it persisted with a closed financial system? The answer is unclear. However, as this chapter shows, a liberal system where the exchange rate and interest rates are market determined does not necessarily provide a buffer against the onslaught of capital inflow and outflows caused by market overreactions.

A small emerging economy with an open financial regime is severely constrained in safeguarding its financial markets largely because capital flows are dictated not only by changes in domestic economic conditions but also by events in international financial markets over which it has no control. Large international banks and other non-bank institutions are literally like big fish in a small pond when they move into the markets of emerging economies.

The lack of proof is further substantiated by the increase in procyclicality in bank lending and the buildup of household loans. Jeong (2009) examined an unbalanced panel of data of Korean banks from 1993:1 to 2008:3. It shows that banks became more pro-cyclical in their business lending after the 1997 crisis, and this increase is in part explained by the banks' heavier reliance on domestic and international wholesale market funding.

At the end of 2011, the total volume of household credit crept up to 913 trillion won, equal to 74 percent of the nominal GDP. More than 40 percent of total loans by commercial and specialized banks was extended to households; almost 70 percent of this was financing housing and other real estate investment. The bursting of the real estate bubble has led to negative equity in housing for many borrowers. Many households are finding themselves unable to repay debts or even stay current on interest payments. The economic downturn will add to the debt burden of households. A substantial increase in nonperforming household loans could destabilize the banking system as it cuts into bank profits. This threatens the solvency of many weaker banks.

Foreign Investors

In December 1997 all restrictions on foreign investments in listed bonds were abolished. This was followed in May 1998 by the lifting of the ceiling on foreign investment in equities, except for investment in public corporations.

Foreign investments in Korean bonds compared to equities have been relatively small. Between 2000 and 2008, the foreign share was on average less than 8 percent of listed bonds. The limited menu in terms of maturity, paucity of investment-grade bonds, and withholding taxes has discouraged foreign bond buying. In contrast, foreign ownership of stocks climbed from a little over 10 percent of total market capitalization in 1996 to more than 40 percent in 2004, but then fell to about 30 percent after the 2008 liquidity crisis.

Reflecting the high degree of openness and liquidity of the market, trading in Korean stocks has been sensitive to changes in stock markets in the United States and elsewhere. In fact, there has been a significant increase in the positive correlation between changes in the S&P 500 and the KOSPI (the primary broad stock index for Korea), and a substantial increase in the negative correlation between changes in the KOSPI and the won-US dollar exchange rate since the outbreak of the US subprime crisis in August 2007. The stock index correlation was less tight, but also positive and high, before the crisis. Thus, whenever the S&P 500 falls, so does the KOSPI because foreign investors withdraw investments from Korea and many local investors follow, independently of any changes in Korean stock market conditions or economic fundamentals.

Foreign Involvement in Banking

Perhaps one of the most significant financial reforms has been the liberalization of foreign entry into the financial intermediation industries. The 1997 crisis set the stage for a large increase in foreign acquisitions of domestic banks, as Korea's policy makers were actively seeking foreign buyers of ailing banks and non-bank financial institutions. The Foreign Investment Promotion Act of 1998 provided the legal framework for this. At the retail level, for many foreign investors, at a time when the stock market was breaking out of the 1998 crash, restructured banks were attractive choices for portfolio investments. Foreign ownership surged to 47 percent in 2011 from 26 percent of the total outstanding stock of 10 commercial banks, excluding the three foreign-owned ones.

Among the four largest nationwide commercial banks—Kookmin, Shinhan, Woori, and Hana—foreign ownership ranged from 67 percent in Hana to 22 percent in Woori at the end of 2011. (Woori is just over half government owned.) Foreign ownership was also very high for the two largest holding companies based on regional banks—Daegu at 74 percent and Busan at 59 percent. Among non-bank financial institutions, foreign holders held more than 10 percent of shares in 10 of 16 insurance firms and more than 20 percent in 9 of 30 securities firms at the end of 2009.

Foreign investors do not control the management of the largest domestic banks even though, as a group, they hold a majority of outstanding shares. There are several reasons for this, including that foreign holders are a large and a diverse group with no interest in exercising control.

For example, index funds are large holders. But foreign owners may exercise influence more than Korean stock holders by monitoring performance and putting pressure on bank mangers to maximize value. And they may have helped government policy makers resist the temptation to resurrect industrial policy through the management of bank assets.

The three second-tier banks in terms of assets are owned and managed by foreign financial institutions. These are, in order of asset size, Korea Exchange Bank (KEB; owned by Lone Star Funds), Standard Chartered Bank Korea Ltd (called SC First Bank from the time Standard Chartered plc acquired First Bank of Korea in 2005 until January 2012), and Citibank Korea (Citigroup Inc). The staff at the foreign-owned banks is almost entirely Korean. Together the three accounted for about 18.5 percent of total commercial banks assets, but only about 15 percent of the total bank loan market.

As far as asset-liability management, efficiency, and soundness are concerned, there is little difference between the foreign-owned and the other banks. The three foreign-managed banks have not done well in enlarging market shares in terms of bank deposits and loans. In fact, over the seven-year period 2005–2011, their combined share of deposits dove from 26 percent to 14 percent. During the same period, their loan market share dropped from 19 percent to about 15 percent. One possible explanation for this is that, unlike other Korean-managed banks' predatory behavior, these banks have placed a higher value on earnings and profits than on enlarging the client base. However, the data to test this are not available.

Since building a large customer base is costly and time consuming in a banking system characterized by relationship banking, the three foreign-controlled banks have chosen an asset management strategy drawing the bulk of income and profits from investments in bonds, equities, and other marketable instruments in preference to commercial lending. They accounted for 26 percent of the total holdings of securities of the entire banking sector.

Foreign Bank Branches

Without a retail banking network, foreign bank branches specialize in wholesale banking, foreign exchange trading, and trading in derivatives. Like the foreign-controlled banks, foreign bank branches have added a variety of local securities to their asset portfolios. In 2001 their combined share of total securities held by the entire banking sector was 7 percent; it soared to more than 30 percent on average during the 2007–2009 crisis period.

On the liability side, deposits in both local and foreign currencies have been less than 4 percent of the banking sector total since 2000; the bulk of their funding has come from borrowing from wholesale funding markets abroad and their headquarters. As most of their liabilities are short term, their assets consist mostly of short-term foreign currency loans and securities such as Bank of Korea monetary stabilization bonds.

Reflecting their specialization in wholesale banking and trading in financial derivative products, the branches obtain a large share of their income and profits from trading in derivative products and fee-based services such as foreign exchange trades on behalf of customers, providing backup lines of credit, and guaranteeing debt securities. Between 2000 and 2004, non-interest income comprised about 30 percent of their earnings. During the crisis period 2006–2008, almost 60 percent of their income came from non-interest earnings.

Most of the foreign banks with branches in Korea are large global banks active in international finance. For this reason, their Korean branches have served as channels through which the bulk of foreign capital flows in and out of Korea. During the two crisis periods (1997–1998 and 2008), they withdrew large amounts of their foreign currency lending and unloaded their investments in local securities, aggravating the liquidity crisis. It is estimated that much of the loss of $60 billion in foreign exchange reserves in 2008 was the result of withdrawal of foreign currency funds by foreign bank branches.

Because they account for anywhere from 30 percent to 40 percent of the volume of daily foreign currency transactions in Korea, they have been singled out as being mostly responsible for the high degree of volatility of capital flows. This assessment prompted regulations limiting foreign currency forward exposure to 250 percent of their capital.

The Financial Crisis of 1997–1998

This section examines the causes and consequences of the 1997–1998 crisis. The crisis of 1997 was as dramatic as it was unexpected. In two months beginning in October, Korea, the world's eleventh largest economy, was reduced to surviving on overnight loans from the international money markets.

What was so surprising about the crisis was that, even as it was building, no one, including the international credit rating agencies, predicted that Korea would be pushed to the brink of financial collapse. But with the spread of the Thai crisis that broke out in June 1997, a painful crisis was indeed already looming large because Korea was borrowing from abroad beyond its debt-servicing capacity.

Borrowing Short and Lending Long

Economic growth from 1994 to the beginning of 1997 was mostly fueled by a large amount of investment, which rose from 26 percent of GDP in the fourth quarter of 1994 to 31 percent two years later. Another cause was the strengthening of the yen, which brought about a sharp increase in export earnings, which stimulated a great deal of the capital investment in 1994–1996. This increase resulted in a current account deficit of a little over 4 percent of GDP in 1996.

Partial deregulation of capital inflows allowed banks, other financial institutions, and large corporations greater access to low-cost foreign credit. This induced a surge in foreign capital inflows—from less than 30 percent of GDP on average during the three-year period ending with 1994 to 47 percent in 1996. Short-term external liabilities climbed to over 300 percent of foreign exchange reserves at the end of the third quarter of 1997, as shown in figure 4.3.

A large fraction of these inflows was channeled to financing the long-term investments of Korea's industrial groups. Banks and other financial institutions were borrowing short and lending long in foreign currency, thereby creating currency and maturity mismatches (see the box "Mismatching").

Mismatching

Mismatching is inherent in the role of banks as asset transformers. Banks are essentially engaged in maturity transformation: they borrow short and lend long. To Allen and Gale (2007, 59), this maturity mismatch "reflects the underlying structure of the economy in which individuals have a preference for liquidity, but the most profitable investment opportunities take a long time to pay off." When banks are engaged in international financial intermediation, they are therefore also bound to commit a currency mismatch (borrowing in one currency to lend in another).

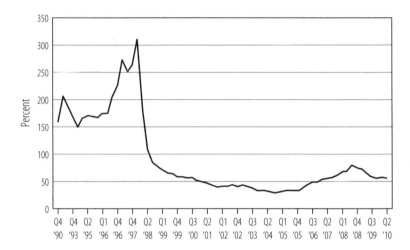

Figure 4.3 Short-term Foreign Liabilities as a Percentage of Foreign Exchange Reserves, 1990–2010. *Source*: The Bank of Korea.

Worse, the dual mismatches created risk for the entire financial system. Compared to the other crisis countries in East Asia, Korea was second only to Indonesia in terms of currency mismatching (fig. 4.4).

An investment boom supported by foreign credit can last only so long. When the slowdown in export growth, together with deterioration in the terms of trade, burst the investment bubble in 1996, the number of corporate bankruptcies began to soar, as did the volume of nonperforming loans at financial institutions.

Korea's exports suffered in part as a result of greater Japanese competition brought on by the depreciation of the yen beginning in the third quarter of 1995. The terms of trade then moved against Korea for the next two years. In the first half of 1997, nonperforming loans as a proportion of total bank loans almost doubled (see Park 1998).

By the first week of September 1997, the slowdown had already dragged on for nearly two years, and both foreign banks' rollover rates of short-term loans to Korean financial institutions and foreign exchange reserves were falling. Despite mounting pressure for depreciation since the early months of 1997, the government made a goalline stand at 1,000 won per dollar, intervening heavily in the market. Between July and November, the Bank of Korea (BOK) sold $12.2 billion in the spot market and made forward sales amounting to $7 billion

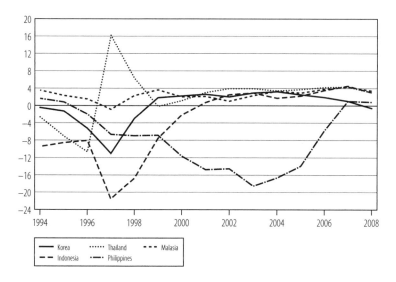

Figure 4.4 Currency Mismatches. *Source*: Goldstein and Turner (2004 and 2008).

Note: This figure tracks "aggregate effective currency mismatch (AECM)" as defined by Goldstein and Turner (2004).

AECM = (NFCA/XGS) (FC/TD), where

NFCA = net foreign currency assets (+) or liabilities (–);

XGS = exports of goods and services (national income account), when NFCA is negative;

MGS = imports of goods and services (national income account), when NFCA is positive; and

FC/TD = foreign currency share of total debt.

to defend the won. As a result, during the same period, the central bank's reserve holdings fell by $10 billion (table 4.4).

The government strained investor credulity by failing to divulge BOK's actual level of foreign reserves or its forward market commitments. It asserted that BOK held about $30 billion in reserves, a figure investors found implausible. The actual level of usable reserves had already dropped below $22 billion at the end of March. By the end of November, it fell to $7 billion.

The dire financial situation was further compounded by downgrading of Korea's sovereign credit ratings. In January 1997 S&P ranked Korea AA–, at the low end of its second tier. Moody's A1 put Korea at the high end of its third tier. On October 24 S&P lowered its rating one notch to a third-tier A+, and on November 28, Moody's cut its rating two notches to A3. On December 11 both rating agencies reduced their ratings again.

TABLE 4.4

Foreign Reserves of the Bank of Korea (billion US dollars)

1996	1997						1998	
	Mar.	Jun.	Sep.	Oct.	Nov.	Dec.	Jan.	
33.2	29.2	33.3	30.4	30.5	24.4	20.4	23.5	Official foreign reserves (A)
3.8	8.0	8.0	8.0	8.0	16.9	11.3	11.0	Deposits at overseas branches (B)
				0.2	0.2	0.2	0.2	Other (C)
29.4	21.1	25.3	22.4	22.3	7.3	8.9	12.4	Usable reserves (A-B-C)

Source: The Bank of Korea.

Note: Official foreign reserve holdings are based on the IMF definition. Deposits at overseas branches are those deposits made by the Bank of Korea at overseas branches of domestic commercial banks. In November 1997, when the domestic commercial banks were unable to repay their loans from the foreign banks, the Bank of Korea supported them by making foreign currency deposits at their overseas branches.

Each time the sovereign rating was downgraded, the premium on Korean securities denominated in dollars rose, worsening market sentiment. In response to the deterioration in confidence, the rating agencies adjusted their sovereign ratings downward again, thereby generating a vicious cycle of declining ratings and market sentiment. By the end of 1997, Moody's had adjusted its rating downward twice, and S&P three times.

When the crisis that broke out in Thailand spread to Korea, neither Korea nor the IMF was prepared to deal with what was essentially a capital account crisis. When Korea's reserves were depleted toward the end of the second quarter of 1997, in the absence of any regional arrangement or foreign central banks ready to provide short-term US dollar liquidity, Korea had no choice but to ask for IMF rescue financing. But for some time Korean officials were unwilling to do so because of domestic political opposition and the harsh policy conditionality that came with it.

Toward the end of October, it became clear to policy makers, as well as market participants, that the situation was getting out of control. Foreign investors moved out of the stock market in droves, and Korean banks were increasingly unable to roll over their short-term foreign loans. With the sense of panic rising by the day, the government made public its decision to approach the IMF for assistance on November 19.

Consequences

In the run-up to the 1997 crisis, many of Korea's commercial banks were struggling with massive increases in nonperforming loans (NPLs) as a large number of corporate loans fell into arrears. As a result, they lost much of their capital, pushing them to the edge of insolvency. After accepting IMF rescue financing, the government embarked on a drastic restructuring of the financial sector, the first phase of which lasted until June 2001. The legal basis for this was a January 1998 amendment of the January 1997 Act on the Structural Improvement of the Financial Industry (ASIFI). Table 4.5 provides data on consolidation.

A new financial regulatory authority, the Financial Supervisory Commission (FSC), found 12 commercial banks (out of a total of 33) had capital adequacy ratios below 8 percent at the end of 1997. These banks were ordered to submit rehabilitation plans by April 1998. In June 1998 five banks that were assessed as insolvent were merged with healthier banks through the purchases of assets and assumptions of liabilities. Over the next two years, six other banks were acquired by, or merged with, stronger banks, reducing the number of banks to 22 at the end of June 2001. Subsequently, there have been four more bank mergers and acquisitions.

For non-bank financial institutions the restructuring was even more brutal. Among merchant banks, only 4 of 30 remained in June 2001. More than half of mutual savings banks and finance companies, and 10 of 25 leasing firms, disappeared.

In restructuring the financial system, the government created two state-owned corporations, the Korea Asset Management Corporation (KAMCO) and the Korea Deposit Insurance Corporation (KDIC), to buy nonperforming loans from troubled financial institutions that failed or were likely to fail, and to collect those loans. KDIC insured all deposits, including those at non-bank financial institutions, and paid off depositors at liquidated institutions. It also assisted healthy banks to acquire failed financial institutions and served as the conduit for recapitalization of banks using public funds.

As shown in table 4.6, all this was costly. By the end of June 2001, when the critical phase of the restructuring was completed, the

TABLE 4.5
Restructuring of Financial Institutions, 1997–2001 (number of institutions)

	Total at the End of 1997 (a)	Restructuring (November 1997–June 2001)					New Entries	Total at the End of June 2001
		License Revoked	Merged or Acquired	Dissolved, Bankrupt, and Suspended	Sub-total (b)	Ratio (%) (b/a)		
Total (A) + (B)	2,101	121 (174)	148 (207)	321 (564)	590 (945)	28.1 (45.0)	50 (148)	1,561 (1,305)
Banks (A)	33	5	6 (11)	–	11 (16)	33.3 (44.9)	– (1)	22 (18)
Non-bank financial institutions (B)	2,068	116 (169)	142 (196)	321 (564)	579 (929)	28.0 (42.4)	50 (147)	1,539 (1,287)
Merchant banks	30	22	5 (7)	–	27 (29)	90.0 (96.7)	1	4 (2)
Securities firms	36	5	1 (8)	1 (3)	7 (16)	19.4 (44.4)	16 (27)	45 (47)
Insurance	50	5 (10)	6	4 (6)	15 (22)	30.0 (44.0)	3 (25)	38 (53)
Investment trust funds	30	6	1 (8)	–	7 (14)	23.3 (45.3)	6 (50)	29 (67)
Mutual savings and finance companies	231	67 (113)	26 (28)	25 (1)	118 (142)	51.1 (61.5)	12 (17)	125 (106)
Credit unions	1,666	2	102 (137)	291 (553)	395 (692)	23.7 (41.5)	9 (14)	1,280 (988)
Leasing firms	25	9 (11)	1 (2)	– (1)	10 (14)	40.0 (56.0)	3 (13)	18 (24)

Source: White Paper on Public Fund Management, Public Fund Management Committee (2004 and 2009); 2011 data from Bank of Korea.

Note: Figures in parentheses are the number of institutions when the end date is 2011.

TABLE 4.6
Public Funds Injected (November 1997–June 2001) (trillion won)

Recapitalization	Capital Contributions	Deposit Repayment	Asset Acquisitions	Acquisitions of Nonperforming Loans[a]	Total	Mode of Financing
35.5	11.2	15.3	4.2	20.5	86.7	Bonds issued
14.2	–	0.5	6.3	2.0	23.0	Other
3.3	1.0	4.2	3.6	15.7	27.8	Funds recovered[b]
53.0	12.2	20.0	14.1	38.2	137.5	Total at end of June 2001
63.5	18.6	30.3	17.7	38.5	168.6	Total at end of 2009

Source: Public Fund Management Committee (PFMC), *White Paper on Public Funds* (various annual issues). The PFMC was created to oversee public funds injected into the financial sector. Under the Ministry of Finance and Economics, it includes academic and private-sector participants, as well as government officials.

Note: Most of the funds were provided through the Korea Deposit Insurance Corp (KDIC).

[a]Nonperforming loans were purchased by KAMCO, primarily using funds raised by issuing bonds.

[b]The table is the gross amount injected. Some of the funds were later recovered.

government had spent 137.5 trillion won. This amounted to 25 percent of Korea's 2002 GDP. Subsequently, an additional 31 trillion won was needed. About 56 percent of the total cost had been recovered by the end of 2009.

Prices leapt by 7.5 percent in 1998, mostly due to a marked depreciation of the won, which fell in value by 27 percent vis-à-vis the dollar. Unemployment reached 8 percent, the highest since Korea embarked on an outward-looking strategy in the early 1960s. However, to the surprise of many, the crisis was short lived.

Six months after accepting IMF help, market sentiment began to turn in Korea's favor, restoring a measure of financial stability. The return of foreign investors and a large increase in exports, supported by the massive depreciation of the won, paved the way for a V-shaped recovery with a burgeoning current account surplus. Quarterly data suggest Korea reached the trough as early as the second quarter of 1998. From a positive 4.7 percent in 1997, the growth rate plunged to –6.9 percent in 1998, and then rebounded dramatically to 9.5 percent in 1999 and 8.5 percent in 2000 (figure 4.5).

The initial GDP contraction in 1998 was largely caused by the collapse of investment; private consumption fell to a lesser degree. The consumption-GDP ratio remained mostly stable in the crisis period,

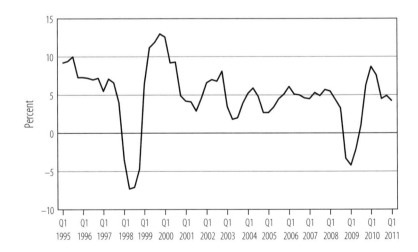

Figure 4.5 Quarterly Annual Real GDP Growth (in percent per annum). *Source*: The Bank of Korea.

whereas the investment-GDP ratio dropped sharply. It fell from 36 percent in 1997 to 25 percent in 1998.

While overall domestic demand was sluggish, a large increase in net exports paved the way for the initial recovery. Import demand declined by 22 percent in 1998, while exports fell by less than 3 percent. It was therefore clear that net exports were speeding the recovery. A real depreciation of the won, amounting to more than 27 percent, supported the quick surge in net exports. There was a huge current account surplus, almost 12 percent of GDP. Despite the large surplus on the current account, foreign debt climbed to 47 percent of GDP largely because of the need for replenishing foreign reserves that were depleted in 1997.

The 2008 Liquidity Crisis

In the second half of 2008, barely a decade after recovering from the 1997 crisis, Korea succumbed to another crippling economic downturn and liquidity crisis. This time Korea was not the epicenter of the crisis. In contrast to the 1997 crisis, before the 2008–2009 global crisis unfolded, Korea held 7.7 times more foreign exchange reserves than in 1997. It was running a current account surplus, the exchange rate was flexible, and its banks were holding an insignificant amount of US toxic assets. In general, Korea's economic fundamentals were much stronger than they had been 10 years earlier, yet it was not spared from the damage inflicted by the global economic crisis touched off by the US subprime crisis in August 2007.

The liquidity crunch was set off by a confluence of factors including panic and herding among international financial market participants. The causes appear to have been exacerbated by structural weaknesses in the financial sector, as well as the reemergence of a current account deficit in the first half of 2008.

Although Korea held $260 billion in reserves at the end of 2007, it had to secure rescue financing from external sources to stop the run on its central bank reserves. It was unthinkable for the Korean authorities to again approach the IMF for assistance. Instead it asked for, and received, a dollar-won currency swap line from the US Federal Reserve, which helped turn around market sentiment regarding the prospect of the Korean economy.

The contagious effects of the US subprime crisis rippled through to Korea in the second half of 2008. With the rising specter of another crash of Korea's financial markets, foreign investors and lenders began selling out of Korea much more than they did elsewhere in East Asia. Apparently, they were led to believe that Korea was more vulnerable to the contagion, and its relatively larger and liquid financial markets made it easier for them to leave.

After the collapse of Lehman Brothers in September 2008, Korean banks became increasingly hard pressed to roll over their short-term foreign currency loans. At the lowest point in November 2009, the renewal rate fell to below 40 percent, causing a large drop in capital inflows and a 20 percent ($60 billion) loss of foreign exchange reserves.

As dollar liquidity evaporated, the nominal exchange rate began a sharp depreciation from about 1,000 won per US dollar in April 2008 to 1,509 won on November 24. The won fell almost 18 percent in October alone. On October 27, at the height of the crisis, the sovereign spread jumped to 751 basis points. (This is the difference between yields on Korean government bonds and yields on government bonds with AAA ratings.) At the same time, the premium for a credit default swap reached 700 basis points.

During the crisis period, the foreign exchange market was marked with a high degree of instability. The won-dollar market in Korea is considered small and shallow, as the number of participants is limited. This contributed to the volatile movements of the exchange rate after the collapse of Lehman Brothers.

Buildup and Causes

At the end of 2008 Korea's short-term foreign liabilities as a proportion of its foreign exchange reserve rose to 97 percent, close to the 100 percent level of reserve adequacy prescribed by the Greenspan-Guidotti-Fischer (GGF) rule. (The rule says reserves should at least equal short-term debt.) At the same time, the loan-deposit ratio at banking institutions had risen steadily since 2001 to over 125 percent when the crisis erupted. Together with the emerging current account deficit, these changes indicated significant mismatching in maturity and currency on bank balance sheets, making the banks vulnerable to a sudden reversal of capital flows.

DISORDERLY LIBERALIZATION OF CAPITAL OUTFLOWS   The won, which had started strengthening against the dollar in late 2005, continued to appreciate to below 920 won per dollar toward the end of 2006. Faced with the erosion of export competitiveness and increasing costs of sterilization, Korea's policy makers took steps to induce capital outflows by liberalizing the rules under which Korean institutional and private investors could make portfolio investments in foreign securities of emerging, as well as developed, economies. This touched off massive outflows in 2006.

In 2005 Korea's total portfolio investments abroad had risen to $16.7 billion. The amount almost doubled in 2006 and soared again to $56.4 billion in the following year. As a result, the market value of stocks, bonds, and Korean paper denominated in foreign currencies held by Korea's institutional investors (banks, insurance companies, asset management companies, and securities firms) more than doubled to $116.6 billion between end 2006 and 2007. Data are in figure 4.6.

In 2007 banks invested $60 billion buying long-term forward dollar contracts from domestic shipbuilders. Since it takes several years to construct a ship, for a typical order the price is paid in installments over the building period. To avoid exchange rate risk, shipbuilders usually

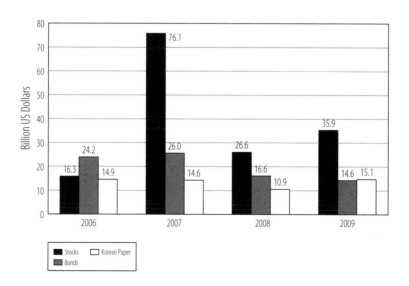

Figure 4.6 Portfolio Investments in Foreign Securities (in billion US dollars). *Source*: Bank of Korea.

take a short position matched by a long position held by banks as counterparties in the forward market.

Because banks hold relatively small amounts of foreign currencies, mostly for day-to-day retail transactions, they borrow the amount of their long position in US dollars of the same maturity. At the end of 2005, the banking sector held $83,429 million in foreign currency liabilities, which was 44 percent of Korea's total foreign debt. Two years later the amount had more than doubled to $194,045 million and reached 50 percent of total foreign debt. Non-bank financial institutions and private and public enterprises were equally active in borrowing from abroad. Their external debt jumped from $88,920 million at the end of 2005 to $134,808 million two years later.

These developments added to the demand for US dollars at a time when the domestic supply was shrinking. The surplus on the current account was falling, but Korea's policy makers continued sterilizing it, adding more than $50 billion to increase central bank reserves to $260 billion at the end of 2007. This squeeze on the availability of US dollar liquidity in the local foreign exchange market was met by a large increase in capital inflows as banks and other financial institutions were forced to finance from abroad a large share of their portfolio investments in foreign securities.

The total amount of external funds raised by banks by borrowing from foreign banks and issuing securities ran to $76 billion at the end of 2006. In the following year, it shot up by 37 percent to $104 billion and by another 28 percent in 2008. Banks and other financial institutions borrowed so much that, despite a substantial increase in capital outflows, the financial account registered a surplus of $6.2 billion in 2007. The bulk of foreign borrowing was from the short end of international financial markets, and so pushed the GGF ratio close to its 100 percent limit.

The growth of short-term foreign liabilities was also bound to exacerbate balance sheet mismatch at banks and other financial institutions. For three consecutive years, a little over 60 percent of foreign currency assets held by banks consisted of foreign currency loans to domestic borrowers. They blundered on making themselves highly vulnerable to a dollar liquidity crunch.

The risks associated with the large increase in short-term foreign liabilities were further compounded by heavy losses sustained by Korean investors who bought large amounts of foreign securities when the global financial system was in turmoil. Of $117 billion invested at the end of 2007, more than half evaporated during 2008 due mostly to the collapse of the financial markets they had entered. Worse yet, more than 80 percent of these investments were hedged against currency risk. Since they had bet against depreciation of the won, most private investors ran up large foreign exchange losses when the won weakened.

Under normal circumstances, these book losses would not provoke any liquidity crunch because short-term foreign loans normally are renewed continuously. But once the crisis erupted, they could not be readily rolled over. When they could not, it was obvious that some of these assets had to be sold at heavily discounted prices. This prospect of capital losses implied a large potential increase in Korea's foreign debt burden and a drain on foreign exchange reserves.

The situation was exacerbated by many ship buyers not honoring their contracts. As a result, on the delivery date, shipbuilding companies were forced to purchase dollars in the spot market to clear their short positions. This additional demand for dollars, together with the capital losses and the emergence of balance sheet mismatches, led to a large requirement for external borrowing even as foreign investors were leaving the Korean market. Evaporation of short- and long-term loans pushed Korea deeper into a liquidity crisis.

INEFFECTIVE REGULATION Having endured the devastating consequences of mismatches in the 1997 crisis, prevention of the same mismatches was at the top of the list of regulatory reform. Korea's regulatory authorities had been on close watch for—and introduced precautionary measures designed to fend off—their reemergence. However, enforcement did little in the way of making banks guard against the potential risks they were assuming in managing assets and liabilities denominated in foreign currencies.

To alleviate the mismatch problems, supervisory authorities instituted a regulation under which banks were allowed to relend in domestic currency to local borrowers a maximum of 15 percent of their foreign currency funds maturing within three months. The other 85 percent could be used for foreign currency loans. The maturity of the local foreign currency loans also had to be less than three months. In reality, however, these measures were not effective in preventing or even moderating the pervasiveness of the mismatches.

Crisis Resolution

Korea was hit harder than any other Asian country by the turmoil surrounding the collapse of Lehman Brothers. The stock market, as measured by KOSPI, fell more than 45 percent from May 2008 (when the index was 1850) to November (when it was barely 1000). In the four months ending in November, the won-dollar exchange rate fell from 1,000 to nearly 1,600. At that point there were fears the exchange rate might spiral out of control, leading to a self-fulfilling loss of confidence as first foreign, and then domestic, investors liquidated positions. To support the currency, the Bank of Korea exhausted more than a fifth of its foreign exchange reserves in a matter of months, but intervention did not work. Clearly, reforms that were supposed to deliver a more resilient financial system did not perform as expected.

Faced with the implosion of the exchange rate and the prospect for a rapid depletion of reserves, on October 12 the government issued sovereign guarantees on new foreign loans maturing before the end of June 2009, up to $100 billion. This was intended to shore up foreign investor confidence in the economy, and had been done during the Asian financial crisis. However, such guarantees had failed to allay fears of financial meltdown in 1997, and they failed again.

Only when Korea secured a swap line of $30 billion from the US Federal Reserve on October 30 did the foreign exchange market settle down somewhat, but not for very long; the exchange rate shot to 1,509 won per dollar three weeks after the swap was announced. In view of the large amount of maturing bonds held by foreign investors and foreign loans coming due in the first quarter of 2009, the swap was apparently not enough to remove the uncertainties surrounding Korea's ability to service its foreign debt.

Korea on December 13 succeeded in arranging swaps with the central banks of China and Japan, each amounting to an equivalent of $30 billion. Japan was reported to have been reluctant at first to offer a yen-won swap line. It asked Korea to approach the IMF first. If more liquidity was needed afterward, it would consider a swap.

These two swaps, together with the renewal of the Fed swap and a stronger current account, calmed the market for a while. But the exchange rate was on a roller coaster, shooting to 1,573 won per dollar on March 3, 2009, before subsiding below 1,300 won at the end of June. The exchange rate is tracked in figure 4.7.

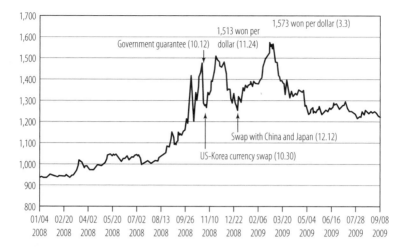

Figure 4.7 Korean Won–US Dollar Nominal Exchange Rate. *Source*: Bank of Korea.

Fortunately, the liquidity crisis did not last long. By the end of March 2009, it was over. Thereafter Korea has engineered an impressive recovery from the global economic crisis ahead of many advanced and emerging economies. Against all odds, the economy posted 0.2 percent growth for 2009 as a whole. Adding to the positive rate of growth, the current account balance returned to a surplus, the stock market managed a sustained rally, and the exchange rate gained vis-à-vis the major currencies.

Consequences

Although the crisis was short lived, economic activity suffered significantly while it lasted. Growth decelerated from its customary 5 percent to 6 percent, still successfully maintained through 2007, to a 3 percent annual rate in the third quarter of 2008, and was –3.4 percent in the fourth quarter of 2008. The bottom came with a –4.3 percent rate in the first quarter of 2009.

Industrial production fell at an astonishing 12 percent year on year in the fourth quarter of 2008 and 16 percent year on year in the first quarter of 2009. The cumulative decline in manufacturing production from its April 2008 peak was a staggering 25 percent. Real GDP fell by more than 4 percent in 2009, but recovered fast, growing 6.3 percent in 2010.

This disastrous performance reflected the veritable collapse of merchandise exports. For a country that prioritized economic growth and a presidential administration that had promised a 7 percent growth rate, this slump was unacceptable. It was an indication that the economic and financial reforms of preceding years were not adequate, and that they were not delivering the expected results.

Or so goes one interpretation. Another perspective is that Korea suffered such a serious economic shock not because of fundamental weaknesses in its own economic and financial system but because, for structural as well as policy reasons, it was increasingly integrated into a global economic and financial system that malfunctioned disastrously in 2008.

Given Korea's limited natural resources and energy reserves, it is natural that it should rely heavily on imports of these essential items and that it should therefore specialize in exports of manufactures. In turn, this meant that Korea was disproportionately affected by the unprecedented collapse of global export markets in 2008–2009. Similarly, given its relatively well-developed financial markets, it was natural that Korea had access to short-term external debt.

When short-term external funding dried up, it followed that the Korean financial system was placed at risk. Given that its financial markets were open to the rest of the world, in conformance with the country's obligations as a member of the OECD, it was natural that foreigners should have owned an unusually large share of the securities traded on domestic equity markets and that those markets should have been hit when foreign investors, with liquidity problems of their own, desperately repatriated their funds.

Rodrik and Velasco (2001), among others, have shown that countries with relatively well-developed financial sectors can and do access relatively large amounts of short-term external debt. However, even during the most difficult period following the collapse of Lehman Brothers, the volume of short-term foreign liabilities was less than the Bank of Korea's foreign exchange reserves. We will return to this point.

Moral Hazard, Regulatory Forbearance, and Corruption

During the period covered by this chapter, Korea had two purely domestic financial crises: the 2003 credit card loan crisis and the 2011 savings bank crisis. The causes and consequences of these episodes are analyzed in this section.

2003 Credit Card Loan Crisis

It may seem incredible, but immediately after recovering from the 1997 crisis, Korea was thrown into another period of financial turmoil during the 2000–2003 period. This was precipitated by a credit card lending boom that ended in a painful bust. The crisis had a significant impact on Korea's financial system, but, unlike in 1997–1998, it did not pose any serious systemic risk largely because credit card firms accounted for a small share of the consumer credit market and were not allowed to borrow from abroad. For these reasons, the crisis was brought under control relatively quickly by an injection of central bank liquidity into the banking system and other regulatory interventions.

At the height of the boom in 2002, the number of credit cards per economically active person was 4.6, having jumped from less than two in 1999, as shown in table 4.7. Between 1999 and 2002 the volume of credit card loans plus cash services grew more than fourfold. A number of developments added fuel to the boom. These included a change in government development strategy that placed more emphasis on domestic demand for growth.

The 2001 bursting of the dot-com bubble in the developed world brought on a mild recession in Korea, slashing further the investment demand that had been battered by the 1997–1998 crisis. To revive the sagging economy, Korea's policy makers injected ample liquidity into financial markets. In 1999 they also gave a tax deduction for purchases made using credit cards and lifted restrictions on the maximum monthly cash advances on a credit card. The main objective was to curtail transactions in cash for tax evasion and other illegal purposes, but the new policy was also in part designed to stimulate consumption (Yun 2004).

Expansionary monetary policy, together with the government promotion of credit card usage, brought a surge in credit card purchases: between 1999 and 2002 the amount of credit card billings almost tripled to 46 percent of private consumption.

At the same time, the slowdown in investment dampened the business demand for bank loans when banks were inundated with liquidity. To make up for the decline in the demand for corporate loans, banks began diversifying into lending to households that were investing in

TABLE 4.7
Credit Card Market

	1999	2000	2001	2002	2003	2004	2005	2006	2007	2008	2009	2010	
	39.0	57.7	89.3	104.8	95.5	83.5	82.9	91.1	88.8	96.2	107.0	116.6	Cards issued, total in millions
	1.8	2.5	4.0	4.6	4.1	3.6	3.5	3.8	3.7	4.0	4.4	4.7	Cards issued per person
	13.8	29.5	36.9	50.9	27.3	15.4	15.7	17.5	18.4	24.0	29.9	37.6	A
	55	69	51	44	18	18	26	35	39	33	36	35	A as % of total assets
	15.5	24.9	39.1	45.7	43.9	41.7	44.8	47.3					Card purchases as % private consumption
	6.4	11.1	10.8	11.6	6.1	3.2	3.0	3.0	2.9	3.5	4.1	4.7	B
	79.9	62.5	53.8	44.3	57.5	32.1	28.0	18.2	19.9	18.7	17.6	18.9	C

Source: Financial Supervisory Service and (for purchases as a percentage of private consumption); Kang and Ma (2007).

A Credit card loans and cash services in trillion won.

B Total credit card assets as a % of household credit

C Cash payment fees and revenues on credit card loans as a percentage of credit card revenues housing and other types of real estate, and for working capital to self-owned and other small firms.

Although the demand for consumer loans was growing, commercial banks were inclined to cater to the credit needs of only those households with collateral and proper credit records. Therefore, a sizable segment of the population had to turn to a large and growing number of semi-regulated moneylenders, which were charging exorbitant interest rates on unsecured short-term loans.

Finding new sources of growth and profits in unsecured retail finance, Korea's commercial banks and industrial groups (*chaebol*) chose the credit card business as an entrance to the retail credit market. They were attracted because credit card issuers were subject to relatively loose regulations and were reaping high returns on their assets—they were allowed to charge interest rates over 20 percent on cash advances and loans. Also, initially, the delinquency rate was relatively low, so provisions for losses were small.

By 2000 there were 25 credit card issuers. Practically all commercial banks offered card services directly or indirectly as part of a group of banks. By then, Korea's *chaebol* had also moved into the business by establishing monoline credit card companies. Among the 25 issuers, only the largest 4—Samsung, LG, KB, and BC—mattered, as together they held a 90 percent market share. The first Samsung and LG are *chaebol* that had limited banking experience: KB is Kookmin Bank, and BC (Bank and Credit) is made up of 11 banking and other financial institutions. Cards issued by *chaebol* handled 76 percent of domestic credit card transactions by value by 2002.

The credit card business is subject to large-scale economies. Constructing the infrastructure for data processing, credit analyses, and account payment and settlements requires a large initial investment (Yun 2004). More importantly, the card issuers need to build a sufficient holder base to attract retailers willing to accept their cards for payments. As a consequence, issuers engaged from the beginning in intense competition for a large market share. In fact, they were so eager to expand the customer base that they were paying $10 for anyone signing up for a new card without scrutinizing the credit records of new customers. This contributed to lowering overall screening and underwriting standards (Kang and Ma 2007). More importantly, the competition led issuers to lend a disproportionately large share of their loanable funds to the least creditworthy, thereby assuming large credit risk in their loan portfolios.

Inevitably, credit quality began to suffer. Since the card issuers did not know, or did not pay much attention to, the creditworthiness of their cardholders, they also had to charge higher interest rates on their loans and higher fees for cash services than otherwise. The high lending rates came back to haunt the card companies as they sowed the seeds of busting the bubble.

On the funding side, credit card firms borrowed from banks and issued debentures, commercial paper, and asset-backed securities. Compared to other types of financial products, including corporate bonds, the paper carried higher interest rates, reflecting the higher default risk card firms were exposed to. But the institutional investors—including investment trust companies, pension funds, and insurance companies, which together were the largest investors in these assets—ignored the real riskiness of their investments. They acted as if their holdings were guaranteed by the commercial banks and industrial groups that owned the card issuers.

This reduced further the incentives for card issuers to be more thorough in screening their borrowers, causing the transfer of much of their credit risk to the institutional investors. This implicit transfer of risk allowed card issuers to borrow and lend much more than they would have otherwise, aggravating the boom and making the bust more costly. (In some respects the unfolding of the boom-bust cycle in Korea reveals problems, including moral hazard, similar to those of "the originate-to-distribute" model of mortgage lending that triggered the subprime crisis in the United States.)

From 2000 to 2002 the share of cash services and loans in total credit card assets rose to more than 55 percent on average. In 2001 the estimated return on credit card company assets was six times more than the average returns of Korean commercial banks (Yun 2004).

The credit card loan boom could last only so long. Given the high cost of loans and cash services, many borrowers could not service their debts at a time when the economy was slowing. Credit card debt snowballed, as many borrowers had several credit cards, using loans from one to repay loans to another. The number of delinquent accounts started to soar, and so did the volume of bad loans.

The massive increase in the volume of credit card loans and delinquent accounts was enough to send a warning signal for an imminent end to the boom. In response to the growing default risk, card firms began imposing tighter screening standards for new cards and loan applicants, as well as for those renewing existing loans. This tightening created a liquidity crunch, sending more accounts into arrears. Concerned about these financial difficulties, institutional investors looked for ways to unload their investments.

An accounting scandal at a subsidiary of SK group, the fourth largest *chaebol*, together with Moody's downgrading of Korea's sovereign rating, coupled with the growing concern about North Korea's nuclear weapons program, disrupted money and capital markets. Fearing losses, investors began cashing in their shares of investment-trust companies (ITCs). Because of restrictions on borrowing, ITCs had to liquidate assets to meet redemptions. Since ITCs could not invest in debentures and asset-backed securities issued by credit card companies as much as they had before, their withdrawal from the market created a severe liquidity crunch for the card industry. This, in turn, pushed up funding costs and, subsequently, delinquency rates. By the early months of 2003, many of the credit card companies were pushed to the edge of insolvency.

To avert the impending crisis, in mid-March the Bank of Korea injected 4 trillion won ($4 billion) into the banking system. In addition, the state-owned Korea Development Bank (KDB) led a bailout of LG Card, the major issuer of cards and a part of the second-largest *chaebol*, by lending it almost 1.5 trillion won. The government also pressed *chaebol* to recapitalize their credit card subsidiaries and leaned hard on banks with card units to inject funds into their credit card arms.

Under the emergency package announced on April 3, 2003, banks and *chaebol* with card businesses were required to put up an additional 4.4 trillion won (about $3.8 billion at then-current exchange rates) to boost the capital of their credit card affiliates. The plan also mandated that banks, brokerage firms, and insurance companies arrange bridge loans amounting to 4.9 trillion won (about $4.2 billion) to rescue the troubled investment-trust companies. At the same time, institutional investors holding credit card debt were required to roll it over indefinitely to give the debt issuers more time to pay.

Debt-equity swaps gave control of LG Card to its creditors, wiping out the equity of LG Card's majority shareholders. Although their stakes were written down substantially, small shareholders retained an interest. In March 2007 Shinhan Bank acquired LG Card in a tender offer that effectively repaid the government. (For more on this, see Kang and Ma 2007.)

In no small measure, the regulatory failure to detect the signs of the credit card lending boom and take corrective actions aggravated the crisis. There was no explicit capital requirement to provide credit card firms with a cushion against the contingent liability arising from securitization of their loans. As Kang and Ma argue, there is little doubt that the failure in upgrading the regulatory system governing rules, as well as the lack of guidelines on the operations of the credit card business during the liberalization process, amplified the boom-bust cycle.

2011 Mutual Savings Bank Crisis

Korean savings banks are community banks catering to low-income households, self-employed people, and small firms with limited access to commercial banks. In 1997 there were 237 savings banks. In the aftermath of the 1997–1998 financial crisis, many were closed, acquired, or merged, reducing the number to 116 at the end of 2002. In the next seven years, 18 more were merged with others or shut down, and 7 new ones were formed.

The country's 105 savings banks, which had combined assets of 87 trillion won ($85 billion) at the end of 2009, swung to a loss of 473 billion won in the fiscal year ended June 30, 2010. Financial difficulties at many of the relatively small banks had been known for some time but did not surface until January 2011 when the Financial Supervisory Commission (FSC) suspended the operation of Samhwa Mutual Savings Bank, the fourth largest in terms of assets, because the bank's BIS ratio fell below zero.

This regulatory move started a run on other ailing banks, forcing the suspension of seven more banks including Busan Savings Bank and its affiliates, the largest group of savings banks in Korea. It appears that regulators knew that the scale of nonperforming loans had reached alarming proportions. However, they failed to act because they were more concerned about the possible bank runs that might be caused by closing or restructuring an insolvent savings bank.

Like the credit card crisis in 2003, the savings bank crisis was homegrown and did not pose a significant threat to the stability of the financial system because the savings bank industry was small, accounting for about 5 percent of total assets and capital of the entire banking system, and they are not allowed to do foreign currency borrowing or lending.

Yet it is of particular interest because it lays bare the pitfalls of regulatory forbearance and the agency problems involving regulators and politicians. Incentives for corruption by regulators escalated a relatively minor issue of insolvency at a limited number of savings banks into a crisis. The pervasiveness of the corruption among regulators took the public by surprise.

The savings and loan crisis in the 1980s in the United States must have been known by Korean policy makers and regulators. Yet Korea, a country hailed for its construction of an elaborate regulatory apparatus, could not forestall a similar crisis.

Mounting losses and nonperforming loans at Busan Savings Bank first erupted as an insolvency problem and has turned into a criminal case. The bank's senior managers engaged in illegal lending to the bank's owners and to building projects, as well as bribing regulators and powerful politicians. The matter has expanded into a corruption scandal and a political crisis, forcing the national assembly to initiate its own investigation of the crisis.

Savings banks acquire more than 80 percent of their loanable funds from savings deposits. In order to compensate for their weaknesses vis-à-vis commercial banks and other depository institutions in competition for funds, they pay higher interest rates on deposits. They also charge higher interest rates on their loans. Deposits are guaranteed by the government for up to 50 million won per account, and a depositor could have multiple accounts at many different banks.

The high interest rates, coupled with the guarantee, attracted a large number of depositors seeking safety and yield. During the 2000–2010 period, deposits at savings banks grew on an annual average twice as fast as those of commercial banks.

In the wake of the 1997–1998 financial crisis, commercial banks began moving into the consumer loan business on a large scale. The proportion of total loans by commercial banks and non-bank financial institutions extended to the household sector increased from less than 25 percent in 1998 to about 50 percent by 2005. As a result, savings banks were losing business to commercial banks, as well as to a growing number of credit card companies and moneylenders. With the loss of their traditional business, savings banks were forced to seek new, riskier business by placing a large share of their loans in real estate investments. By the early 2000s, loans to household borrowers had already fallen to less than 40 percent of total loans by savings banks.

After the 1997–1998 crisis, savings banks also had to adjust to an emerging trend of bank consolidation. Individually they were too small in terms of the volume of assets and were confined to too small an area of operations to realize scale economies in an increasingly competitive environment. To overcome these disadvantages, some of the large savings banks set out to consolidate activities by forming, through stock purchases, horizontally integrated alliances with other banks operating in different localities.

The formation of a group or alliance offered the benefits of scale economies by jointly developing new services and products and by consolidating the data processing systems and back office functions of the participating banks. From the point of view of individual savings banks, it was also an arrangement for more efficient risk diversification, participating in project financing, and enlarging service areas. By the end of June 2010, 11 groups comprising 31 savings banks had been established. It appeared that Korea's policy makers were supportive of such horizontal integration, as it was expected to improve the soundness and safety of savings banks.

Riding on the back of the booming real estate market, the banks belonging to alliances were growing rapidly and generating hefty profits. However, the groupings had a critical weakness: the credit and market risks of all participating savings banks were consolidated into one entity.

The savings banks belonging to the group or alliance were engaged in cross-lending among themselves, and pooled funds to make large loans to special-purpose companies through which they financed housing and other real estate projects requiring large and long-term investment. In so doing, they were transforming themselves into mortgage lenders and property developers, thereby running the risk of exposure to the vagaries of real estate markets. The cooperative arrangements on joint lending therefore meant that the failure of a group-wide project financing or insolvency of a participating bank could endanger the solvency of other banks in the group.

The group formation did not impinge on either profits or asset quality as long as prices of real estate were rising. But once the real estate boom burst following the 2008 liquidity crisis, many savings banks, in particular those belonging to a group, were piling up losses. This put at risk not only their own but the entire group's safety and soundness. (On stagnation in the real estate market, see Kang and Ma 2007.)

In retrospect, the crisis could have been avoided had the regulatory authorities refused to relax a lending constraint in 2006. Through their alliances, savings banks were able to achieve a measure of banking consolidation, but by itself that did not help them to finance large-scale property developments because they were bound by a lending limit of 8 billion won ($8 million) to a single borrower. It was not surprising, therefore, that savings banks mounted lobbying efforts to revoke this regulation, and, they succeeded.

In 2006 the FSC relaxed the rule so that savings banks with a BIS ratio above 8 percent, and a level of substandard loans below 8 percent, were exempted from the 8 billion won limit for up to 20 percent of their capital. But the 20 percent limit proved too difficult to enforce because of the unreliability of balance sheets and income statements. Many were simply falsified.

Freed from the 8 billion won limit, savings banks began making large loans to the special purpose companies (SPCs) they had set up to engage in project financing. Since their main funding source was savings deposits, they were borrowing short and lending long, creating maturity mismatch. By 2010 corporate loans accounted for almost 90 percent of saving bank lending, and more than 50 percent of total loans were extended to construction firms, real estate, project financing, and real estate rental firms. Figure 4.8 illustrates the changes in the price of Korean real estate.

The 2008 liquidity crisis dealt a severe blow to, and hastened the downfall of, the savings bank industry. As property prices plummeted, the proportion of unpaid mortgage loans soared and the expected cash flows from project financing did not materialize.

At the end of 2010, 11 percent of total loans were nonperforming. In particular, loans extended to property developers in arrears for more than a month rose to more than 24 percent of total loans. By the end of June 2010, two savings banks—Samwha and Daejeon—became insolvent with negative BIS ratios. Daejeon was acquired by Busan Savings Bank and Samwha was suspended in January 2011.

At this point, a logical step might have been to close the insolvent banks. Instead, regulators adopted a stance of regulatory forbearance, because the insurance fund was insufficient to pay off depositors, and they did not want to admit that they had failed in proper supervision. It was also found that many regulators were very close to the people they were supposed to be regulating. Given the industry's need for

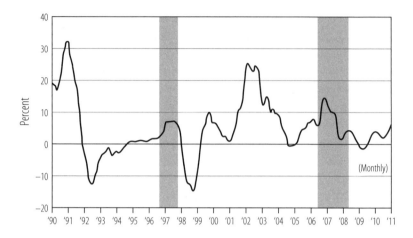

Figure 4.8 Real Estate Price Proxy, Year-on-Year Percentage Change, 1990–2010. *Source*: Bank of Korea.

Note: The Bank of Korea uses the Apartment Purchase Price Index graphed above as a proxy for the price of real estate in Korea. Shaded areas represent the first quarter of 1997 to the first quarter of 2008, and the first quarter of 2007 to the fourth quarter of 2008.

regulatory forbearance, it was not surprising that savings banks spent an enormous amount of money capturing the regulators in return for lenient inspections. Savings banks were in fact conspiring with regulators to sweep their problems under the rug in the hope that they would go away.

During 2011, investigations conducted by the prosecutor's office exposed many lending irregularities and corruption scandals involving Busan Savings Bank Group and Samhwa Mutual Savings Bank. A host of shareholders and senior managers of Busan were indicted for financial crimes involving nearly 7.7 trillion won ($7.1 billion). Samhwa senior executive officers were prosecuted for lending 200 billion won illegally.

It was also uncovered that these banks lobbied top government officials and politicians to prevent their businesses from being forcibly shut down. Incredible as it seems, regulators claimed they did not know that Samhwa tipped off its employees' relatives and important customers about its impending suspension to help them withdraw their deposits in advance. This made the Financial Supervisory Services (FSS) the subject of mounting public criticism and mistrust. Five FSS employees were held by prosecutors for suspected collusion with savings banks.

The prosecution arrested a commissioner of the Board of Audit and Inspection (BAI) on suspicion that he exercised influence to help a troubled savings bank avoid forced exit from the market. He is alleged to have received hundreds of millions of won in exchange for overlooking the bank's illegal lending and other wrongdoings early in 2010 when the BAI was conducting an investigation into the Busan Savings group. A commissioner of the Financial Intelligence Unit (FIU) attached to FSC was arrested for allegedly taking tens of millions of won in bribes from a troubled savings bank in 2003 in return for a promise to use his influence to help the bank escape punishment for its illegal loans.

In retrospect, there is little doubt that regulatory forbearance deepened the crisis. Regulators refrained from enforcing proper regulations on the savings bank industry and from closing down insolvent banks. Instead, they turned a blind eye to accounting irregularities and increases in nonperforming loans. The stance of regulatory forbearance increased moral hazard for savings banks. Knowing that the regulators were unwilling to put them out of business, the banks did not have any incentive for restructuring. Instead, they became more reckless in their lending, and lobbied the regulators and politicians, to whom they donated large amounts of campaign funds, to conceal their problems.

The Effects of Liberalization on Economic Growth and Efficiency

Financial liberalization could affect economic growth through its positive effects on the quantity of saving and investment and the efficiency of investment. However, the effects of financial reform on saving are shown to be rather ambiguous (Bandiera et al. 2000). This is because, at an early stage of liberalization, consumption smoothing through borrowing may reduce saving as a proportion of GDP. However, even in a positive case, an increase in domestic savings may not lead to a corresponding increase in investment if some of the savings are exported, as was the case in Korea since 1999. Further, the level of savings as a proportion of GDP actually may fall as a result of financial liberalization, but investment remains unaffected or even increases, if the country has access to international financial markets to finance its current account deficit.

Deregulation and opening the financial system would increase the availability of funding at lower costs. These changes would, other things being equal, help stimulate investment in the domestic economy. But Galindo et al. (2007) show that in cross-country growth regression analysis, measures of financial development do not have a significant impact on the quantity of investment but do have positive effects on the growth of measures of total factor productivity. The most important growth channel is therefore likely to be the effect of financial reform on the efficiency with which investment is allocated across firms and sectors. This is discussed in the next section.

Taking the Korean case, as shown in figure 4.9, following the 1997 crisis, the ratio of gross investment to GDP fell below 25 percent before recovering around 2000, while the progress in financial liberalization in terms of the index was on an upward trend. At the same time, there had been a dramatic fall in the household net saving rate from around

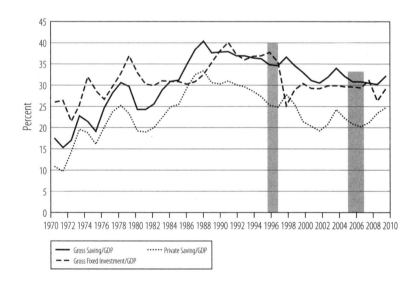

Figure 4.9 Saving and Investment as a Percentage of GDP. *Source*: The Bank of Korea.

Note: Shaded areas represent the first quarter of 1997 to the first quarter of 2008, and the first quarter of 2007 to the fourth quarter of 2008.

16 percent in the run-up to the 1997 crisis to below 4 percent in 2006 (Chung 2007).

The transition from a repressive to a market-oriented financial system may not necessarily develop a buffer against the onslaught of external financial turbulence or improve distributive equity. However, it is almost a matter of faith that such a transition will improve the efficiency of the financial system in allocating capital across different firms and industries, especially compared to a state-controlled regime.

This and the two following sections throw light on whether Korea's experience with financial liberalization bears out the positive effects claimed for it. More specifically, they investigate whether financial liberalization has led to an increase in total factor productivity of firms and industries through improvement in the efficiency of the allocation of loanable funds at banks and non-bank financial intermediaries.

The evaluation begins with a brief survey of the literature on the effects of financial liberalization on financial development, efficiency improvements, and economic growth. Empirical studies attempting to analyze the finance-growth nexus need to begin with the measurement of the degree of market orientation of the financial system. Therefore, an index of financial liberalization is constructed. Three models of the behavior of banks and firms are then developed for an empirical estimation of the effects of financial liberalization at the firm and industry level.

The Literature

Early studies on financial development and economic growth, such as Gurley and Shaw (1955), Shaw (1973), and McKinnon (1973), identify potential channels through which financial liberalization would bring about diversification and improvements in the efficiency of the financial sector with an attendant positive effect on economic growth. According to their thesis, government controls on market interest rates and asset and liability management at banks and non-bank financial institutions, which constitute financial repression, cause stagnation in financial development and ultimately in economic growth. Greenwood and Jovanovic (1990) and Bencivenga and Smith (1991) concur by showing that financial intermediation in a liberal financial regime enhances efficiency of the economy and growth through better information processing and investment screening.

King and Levine (1993), conducting a cross-country regression analysis, and Levine, Loayza, and Beck (2000), performing country-level panel regression estimation, show that financial development spawns positive effects on economic growth. Beck, Levine, and Loayza (2000) find that expansion and efficiency improvements of financial intermediation produce positive effects on total factor productivity growth, although they have few long-term effects on investment and the savings rate. Favara (2003) disputes the findings of Beck, Levine, and Loayza (2000) in a study using cross-country panel data that suggest financial development does not necessarily promote economic growth.

Rajan and Zingales (1998) present evidence that industries differ on the degree of financial dependency on external financing, suggesting that the lack of an adequate provision of capital through financial markets implies that financially dependent industries are less able to take advantage of the potential growth opportunities presented by financial growth and development than industries requiring less external financing. They argue that, given the differences in external finance dependency, capital market development would result in differential rates of growth in different industries.

However, Fisman and Love (2003) show that growth opportunities, rather than external-finance dependency, better explain the growth of different industries, using the dataset of Rajan and Zingales (1998). Using firm-level data from 30 countries, Demirguc-Kunt and Maksimovic (1998) find that a wider access to external finance tends to encourage the long-run growth of firms.

Using panel data on a large number of firms from 13 developing countries, Laeven (2003) examines whether financial liberalization relaxes financial constraints on firms. He finds that small firms are more financially constrained than large firms before the start of liberalization but that afterward financial constraints on small firms are low, whereas they are higher for large firms. This is because large firms have access to preferential directed credit during financial repression.

Surveying the literature, Levine (2005) shows that finance has a positive causal effect on growth because it improves the allocation of capital by easing external financing constraints on firms and that countries with more efficient financial systems grow faster. Bekaert et al. (2006) also present a positive assessment, and a large number of empirical studies on the finance-growth nexus confirm Levine's view. However, there is also evidence from the experiences of emerging economies suggesting that the positive effect is not universal. Reasons for negative effects have been advanced by Stiglitz (2000) and FitzGerald (2006).

As for studies on the Korean experience, Kim (2003) considers five facets of financial liberalization to analyze the effect of financial liberalization on economic growth: changes in the regulation of, and government policy on, interest rates; the foreign exchange rate; the legal reserve requirement; capital account liberalization; and bank privatization. He uses a principal component analysis to create a single index representing the five facets. Kim concludes that financial liberalization in Korea has had a significantly positive impact on economic growth.

Shyn and Oh (2005) use Korean industry-level panel data from 1981 to 2001 to investigate the extent to which external-finance dependency and growth opportunities have contributed to the growth of Korean industries. Their results imply that both were instrumental to industrial development in the 1980s and growth opportunities played a dominant role in the 1990s.

Ahn et al. (2008) use Korean firm-level data from 1991 to 2003 to see if there was a differential effect of external financing on capital accumulation, research and development, and total factor productivity (TFP) growth before and after the 1997 financial crisis. Separate regressions on the subsamples of 1991–1996 and 1999–2003 show that the availability of external finance supported faster capital accumulation, but this was less so after the crisis. In contrast, the external finance effect on TFP growth was found to be relatively weak both before and after the crisis.

Financial Liberalization Index

Empirical examinations of the effects of financial liberalization on the economy need to begin with the identification and estimation of the variables measuring quantitative changes in the degree of deregulation and opening of financial markets. Since there is no generally accepted measure of financial liberalization, most studies develop indices that cover a number of aspects of financial reform. Following a similar approach, this study uses principal-component analysis to construct an index based on several measures reflecting changes in the financial system brought about by liberalization during 1990–2007.

The models are summarized below. Details of their construction are provided in Appendix 4.1. Their specification is summarized in

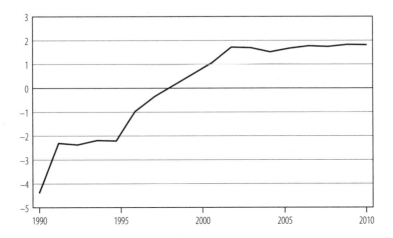

Figure 4.10 Financial Liberalization Index.

Note: This index is derived from six other indexes using principal component analysis. See discussion in the text and technical details in appendix 4.1.

Appendix 4.2; details are in Park and Park (2012a). Details of the estimation results are available from the author on request.

Six measures are used. The first four estimate changes in entry barriers, banking supervision, liberalization of capital flows, and deregulation of security markets. These are drawn from the IMF financial reform database. The fifth component is domestic financial deregulation. Interest rate decontrol is used as a proxy. The sixth component is a measure of the volatility of the nominal exchange rate. Since capital account liberalization and the adoption of a more flexible exchange rate system led to larger swings in the exchange rate than before, it captures the progress in financial market opening. Figure 4.10 charts the financial liberalization index from the principal component analysis.

Throughout the sample period, firms—in particular large ones—continued to rely less on traditional bank financing in favor of raising funds on the capital market. The ratio of direct financing (bond and equity) to total financing is used to examine the effect of the relative increase in capital market financing on firm efficiency. Changes in the ratio are shown in figure 4.11.

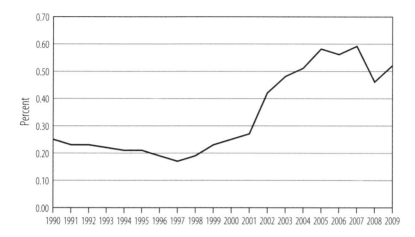

Figure 4.11 Direct Financing as a Percentage of Total Financing, 1990–2009. *Source*: Flow of Funds Tables, Bank of Korea.

Note: Direct financing includes bonds and equity.

Main Questions and Empirical Models

This section uses three linear regression models for firm-level and industry-level panel data for 1991–2007 to assess the impact of financial liberalization on the lending behavior of banks and non-bank financial institutions (NBFIs) before and after the 1997 crisis.

In estimating the three models, the sample of firm-level data is divided into two subgroups: firms listed on the Korea Stock Exchange (KRX) and the remaining firms. KRX firms are relatively more established and large due to the requirements for listing. The remaining-firm group is mostly small and medium enterprises (SMEs). The group includes KOSDAQ-listed firms, external audited firms, and firms under government supervision. (KOSDAQ is Korea's over-the-counter stock market.)

Three questions are posed. These follow, with a statement of the findings.

RATIONALIZATION OF BANK LENDING OPERATIONS Have banks and NBFIs rationalized their lending operations to allocate loanable funds more efficiently, taking into account a firm's and industry's fundamental characteristics such as return on assets (ROA) and value-added history more than before? Put differently, in the process of financial liberalization, have the individual firms and industries with a better ROA or value-added record become favored borrowers at financial intermediaries?

At the firm level, the findings suggest that financial liberalization allowed more room for — and generated incentives for — accommodating the loan demand of SMEs at banks and NBFIs, but it did not affect to any considerable degree the access of large and more established firms to indirect financing.

Overall, at the industry level the results suggest that financial liberalization had little bearing on the lending behavior of banks and NBFIs. These results contradict those of the firm-level analysis. One possible explanation for this disparity is that the magnitude of the positive effect of financial liberalization on the SME group may not have been large enough at the industry level to produce results similar to those of the firm-level analysis.

BANK LOANS AND PRODUCTIVITY Have firms and industries with greater access to indirect bank financing (or with the easing of external financing constraints) done better in improving their total factor productivity?

At the firm level, the findings suggest that SMEs were able to enhance their TFP growth by gaining greater access to indirect financing in the process of financial liberalization.

The relative importance of financial liberalization at the industry level may not have been large enough to produce results similar to those of the firm-level analysis. The results may be interpreted as implying that financial liberalization has not improved efficiency of lending by banks and NBFIs to foster an industry's subsequent TFP growth.

CAPITAL MARKET FINANCING AND TFP GROWTH Has the growing reliance on capital market financing by firms had any real impact on their productivity growth? Here, the hypothesis is that capital markets, as opposed to banks and NBFIs, are more efficient in picking out the more viable and potentially successful firms.

At the firm level, the findings indicate that the relative increase in capital market financing had little impact on firm TFP growth, and this insignificance was not related to financial liberalization during the sample period, implying that capital market financing is a good substitute for bank financing for larger firms in Korea.

Overall Results

Overall, the empirical results of this study do not support the findings of Levine (2005), Bekaert et al. (2006), Galindo et al. (2007), and others. At most, the results provide only weak and mostly indirect evidence of a positive effect of financial liberalization on enhancing the efficiency of firms and of industries. The results also reveal that a greater reliance on capital market financing relative to bank financing has had little effect on the productivity growth of either firms or industries.

One possible explanation for the weak evidence is the banking consolidation that has taken place since 1998. The consolidation has failed to nurture a competitive banking environment. Instead, it has created an oligopolistic market dominated by the four largest banks, which at the end of 2010 accounted for more than 73 percent of total bank assets.

At the same time, many of banks' blue-chip borrowers, large firms and *chaebol*, have migrated to capital markets and relied increasingly on internal financing. While losing some of their traditional favored borrowers, the large banks have chosen to diversify into consumer lending instead of searching for new potentially large corporate borrowers.

Further, as suggested by the results of this study, together with other circumstantial and anecdotal evidence, performance indicators such as return on assets (ROA) do not figure importantly in bank lending to different industries. For these reasons, banks have continued to operate in a business-as-usual environment where they have had few incentives to tighten their screening process.

On capital market financing, the firms in the sample are large listed ones with a high standard of disclosure and governance. Most are also the ones highly sought after by banks as long-term customers. They could easily continuously renew short-term loans from banks. They also can readily issue bonds with a three-year maturity. As far as these large firms are concerned, bank and capital market financing thus are good substitutes. This substitutability, together with the increase in internal financing, appears to be the reason the relative increase in bond and equity financing has not had much impact on firm productivity growth.

The Effects of Financial Liberalization on Income and Wealth Distribution

Since the 1997 crisis, the distribution of income measured by the Gini coefficient has become more unequal. The coefficient had risen from 0.283 in 1997 to 0.314 in 2008 before falling to 0.31 in 2011. Inevitably, questions have been raised as to whether the financial crisis and liberalization have in any way been responsible for the setback. There is no widely accepted theory on the effects of financial deregulation and market opening on distributive equity, and empirical studies remain ambiguous.

Intuitively, there are two conflicting effects that may render empirical studies inconclusive. One effect is associated with efficiency improvements from financial liberalization, which would tend to improve income distribution. At an early stage of financial development, a large segment of the population relies on informal financial markets for financing consumption and investment at a usurious cost of borrowing. Many of these borrowers—self-employed and small and medium firms—are able entrepreneurs, but they may have to forgo profitable business opportunities because they do not have ready access to banks and other financial intermediaries.

Relaxation of financial repression could bring these borrowers into the organized formal system of finance, assuming that financial intermediaries—once freed from government control—would be able to better screen creditworthy borrowers than before, and thus accommodate many of those entrepreneurs they had kept at a distance. The new borrowers will then benefit from the low cost and greater availability of organized finance, opening and expanding the opportunities to move up the ladder of distribution by earning more than before. However, with the passage of time this effect is bound to peter out. That is, at a certain stage of financial development following liberalization, the Kuznets cycle would set in, causing the distribution of wealth to widen.

A second effect is a negative effect to income distribution. The post-1997 deregulation of government controls on asset management opened wide the door for banks and NBFIs to increase consumer loans. Thus the proportion of household loans in total lending by these institutions more than doubled to 50 percent between 1998 and 2005.

However, it is not altogether clear whether this expansion helped many low-income households and self-owned small businesses borrow more than before for housing and real estate investments. When lending, banks and other financial institutions often discriminate against low-income households and small firms unable to provide real property collateral or keep compensating balances, and more so when they are dealing with new customers without established credit records. Even after deregulation, this practice may not have changed. If this were the case, most of the small and medium firms, and even new promising entrepreneurs, still would have been kept outside bank financing, whereas well-to-do households with collateral would have benefited from the surge in mortgage and consumer lending.

This lopsided access accorded to already high-income households at banks would, other things being equal, worsen the distribution of wealth. This was especially the case during the period of the real estate market boom, as increases in property prices allowed rich borrowers to obtain more loans to be invested in real estate and realize capital gains.

Income Distribution

Park and Park (2012a) empirically examined the relative significance of these two effects on income distribution in Korea. A rigorous study of this nature requires reliable data on measures of distributional equality and the asset composition of households in different income brackets. Unfortunately, these data do not exist. In order to overcome this limitation, this study adopts a two-step approach that poses the following two questions:

1. What change did financial liberalization bring about in the relative accessibility of households to bank loans across income quintiles during the sample period (1999–2008) when most financial reform measures were put into effect?
2. Did this change have any effects on household incomes in each income quintile?

The questions are analyzed in terms of individual household panel data from the *Korea Labor and Income Panel Survey* (KLIPS) spanning the period 1999 to 2008. Two empirical models are constructed. Their specifications are in Appendix 4.3. Estimation results are available from the author on request.

In addressing the first question, the study examines the extent to which financial liberalization, the level of which is quantified by an index, changed the ratio of loans to income (a measure of access to bank lending) of each household in different income groups during the sample period, controlling other determinants of household loans as specified in model 1. More specifically, the study investigates whether different amounts of bank loans were provided to different income groups throughout the liberalization process, leading to higher loan-income ratios in some specific income groups than in others.

An increase in the loan-income ratio in any given income group results from either a household decision to borrow more (an increase in demand)—assuming there are no borrowing constraints—or from the relaxation of credit constraints (an increase in supply), allowing households greater access to bank loans than before. It is not possible to make distinctions between these demand- and supply-side changes. However, it is reasonable to assume that the increase in the loan-income ratio was caused by changes in supply-side factors, given that banks ration credit among household borrowers in terms of their credit quality and collateral.

In order to answer the second question, the study estimates an equation (model 2) in which household income is regressed against the loan-income ratio (lagged one year) along with a number of instrumental variables for individual households in four income brackets. In combining the estimation results of the two questions, one can make inferences regarding the effects of financial liberalization on income distribution.

The authors show that increases in the loan-income ratio were uneven across different income groups and that households in higher income quintiles gained greater access to bank loans than those in lower brackets. Further, households that were able to borrow more from banks increased their earnings more than those with more limited access to bank lending. Combining these results, the authors conclude that financial liberalization was likely to have caused deterioration of income distribution during the sample period.

Wealth Distribution

An empirical study (Kim 2010) examines the effects of the expansion of consumer loans following financial liberalization on the distribution of wealth among different income groups of households by comparing the distribution of wealth for two sample years: 2000 when financial reform was launched, and 2006 when most of the reforms were completed. The data are from the 2000 National Survey of Household Income and Expenditure and the 2006 Survey on Household Wealth compiled by Korea's National Statistical Office.

Household wealth consists of financial and real assets. Financial assets include bank deposits, stocks, bonds, and net equity in life insurance and pension funds. Real assets include residential housing, commercial real estate, and land. The 2000–2006 period saw a large increase in the nominal value of both wealth and income per household. However, there was a huge difference between the growth of wealth and income. Wealth grew 143 percent, whereas income increased merely 25 percent. This difference is accounted for by a real estate boom that inflated the value of housing and other real estate. The expansion of consumer loans fed the boom, which in turn further fed into the demand for mortgage loans.

On the asset side, households displayed a strong preference for bank deposits and contractual savings instruments: their share in total financial assets rose from 57.8 percent to 61.2 percent over the six-year study period. The proportion of households with a stock portfolio did not change, although the share of stocks in total financial assets fell from 8.4 percent to 6.0 percent between the two sample years.

On the liability side, high-income households accumulated more debt, mostly for financing investments in housing and other types of real estate by bank loans, whereas low-income households reduced debt.

The share of aggregate financial assets belonging to the highest 20 percent wealth group fell (56.8 percent to 53.2 percent), whereas the share of the lowest 20 percent group rose slightly (from 9.1 percent to 9.4 percent). For real assets, the opposite was the case: the share of the highest 20 percent group rose (63.8 percent to 69.2 percent), whereas the share of the lowest 40 percent fell (from 6.2 percent to 4.8 percent).

In Kim's study, wealth distribution is measured by the ratio of the asset share of the lowest 40 percent to that of the highest 20 percent wealth group (decile distribution ratio), Gini coefficient, and Theil's L index. (Theil's L index, also known as the general entropy measure with parameter o or $GE(0)$, is defined as: $GE(0) \equiv 1/N_{i} \cdot \sum^{N}_{i=1} \log(\mu/y_{i})$, where y_{i} is total wealth of household i, μ is total wealth per household, and N is the total number of households in the economy.)

The results of the author's estimation show that the decile distribution ratio (DDR) estimate was lower, and the Gini coefficient and Theil's L index were larger in 2006 than in 2000, suggesting that wealth distribution deteriorated between the two sample years.

Theil's L index for wealth distribution can be expressed as a weighted average of the indices for individual components of wealth. This decomposition measures the contribution of each component to changes in the inequality of wealth distribution. The analysis shows that much of the worsening in inequality came from an increase in inequality in the distribution of residential housing.

Evaluation and Effects

This chapter has analyzed the background and evolution of financial reform for market deregulation and opening since the early 1980s with a view to assessing its effects on growth, efficiency, equity, and financial stability in the Korean economy. At the outset it was noted that Korea would not on its own have undertaken a financial reform as extensive as the one mandated by the IMF at the time of the 1997 crisis. There was domestic opposition to, and doubt about the effectiveness of, the IMF program, which had been prepared quickly and without much scrutiny of the reform capacity of the country at a time when the country was deep in a crisis. Nevertheless, it has been steadfastly carried out— notwithstanding intermittent relapses.

Evaluation of Financial Reform

The reform has involved deregulating interest rates, adopting a free-floating exchange rate, overhauling the system of risk management and governance at financial institutions, and revamping the financial market infrastructure, as well as creating an independent and unified financial regulatory agency. More importantly, reform has dismantled the industrial policy regime of a developmental state characterized by a collusive arrangement among the government, *chaebol*, and banks. It was expected that these institutional and structural changes would put Korea on a new and rapid growth path with stability.

However, contrary to early expectations, a decade and a half after the 1997 crisis, Korea has yet to regain its pre-crisis dynamism of rapid growth and has endured a marked deterioration in distributive equity. Korea has also suffered a series of financial market turbulences, including the 2008 liquidity crisis, raising the specter of failure of the reform in laying the foundation for financial stability. In particular, the slow-down in growth has been a disappointment, as it was believed that the reform would strengthen overall economic fundamentals to improve efficiency and resilience to withstand both domestic and external shocks to the economy. However, there was much more to the slowdown in growth than the impact one way or the other of financial liberalization.

One may argue that the disappointing economic performance simply reflects the reality that Korea still has some distance to travel before completing the reform it embarked on. This view may not be as persuasive as it appears, given the fact that, among the crisis-hit countries in East Asia, Korea stands out as having been most successful in complying with the economic reforms required by the IMF policy conditionality.

An alternative explanation, which this chapter subscribes to, is that some of the causes of market failure in finance—information asymmetry, pro-cyclicality in lending, collective action problems, and the market's excessive pessimism and exuberance—have also been liable for the poor performance. To be sure, an efficient system of financial regulation could ameliorate the significance of these imperfections, but as shown later, only to a limited extent.

Effects on Economic Efficiency and Growth

Financial liberalization may spur economic growth in transforming a repressive to a market-oriented system if it improves the efficiency of investment across different sectors of the economy or increases the quantity of saving and investment. On the former, most empirical studies do find measurable efficiency improvements; on the latter there is no clear evidence. Further, a review of the raw data for the post-crisis period in Korea from 1998 to 2010 does not show any positive association between financial liberalization and the level of saving and investment as a proportion of GDP.

The empirical estimation of efficiency, although suffering from a lack of needed data, provides some, but only weak, evidence of a contribution from financial liberalization to more robust total factor productivity at the firm and industry levels. This weak evidence is consistent with another estimation result showing that financial liberalization has done little in the way of changing the behavior of banks and other financial institutions in their loan allocation.

The same empirical examination also finds that financial market deregulation has increased the relative importance of capital markets in corporate financing, but the expansion of debt and equity financing does not appear to have exerted any positive impact on the efficiency of listed firms or nonfinancial industries. One possible explanation for this result may be the sharp increase in the share of internal financing at large listed firms during the sample period.

Effects on Distribution of Wealth

The effects of financial market liberalization on the distribution of income and wealth of a country depend on the degree of diversity, depth, and sophistication of its financial system. The issue is an empirical one. This study presents some preliminary evidence showing that a large increase in the availability of mortgage and consumer loans at banks following the reform has widened the gap in wealth between high-income and low-income household groups.

This growing gap appears to have resulted from the preference accorded to rich household borrowers with real assets (property) as collateral at banks and other financial institutions. This preference allows rich households to come into the markets for housing and other types of real estate as speculative investors using borrowed funds rather than as consumers of housing and other real estate services. This advantage in bank financing gives already-rich families opportunities to amass larger capital gains during real estate booms. The index of a proxy for housing prices has displayed considerable fluctuations over the years, but between 1990 and 2010 it soared by more than 250 percent, making rich households richer.

Effects on Financial Stability

Freed from government control and operating in a more competitive environment, banks and other financial institutions need to improve their risk and capital-adequacy management. Changes in interest rates and the foreign exchange rate are supposed to speed and smooth adjustments to shocks emanating from both domestic and foreign sources, thereby helping ensure financial stability. But one does not find any evidence supporting such an outcome for Korea: in the years following the 1997 crisis, it succumbed to another major crisis in 2008 and two minor ones.

In both the 1997 and 2008 crises, one of the causes of the financial breakdown was contagion from crises erupting elsewhere: the Thai crisis in 1997 and the US subprime meltdown in 2008. Some of the domestic factors that made Korea susceptible to and deepened the crises were much the same, and the patterns of recovery were similar. Capital flight triggered by ill-informed foreign investors overreacting to crises elsewhere was the immediate cause of both Korean crises.

In 1997 the rigid exchange rate system was blamed for the massive capital outflows, but a flexible exchange rate system did not prevent or mitigate the reversal in flows in 2008.

In both crises, a large depreciation did not generate any expectation of appreciation; instead, it shifted the exchange rate onto an implosive path as the panic triggered destabilizing speculation in the foreign exchange market. As the 1997 crisis unfolded, Korea depleted almost all of its reserves. Afterward, realizing that the international community and IMF would not come to the rescue again, or would come with the wrong conditions, Korea started building its foreign exchange reserves.

At the end of 2007, Korea held $260 billion in foreign exchange reserves. To many experts, this was excessive. But it turned out to be not enough to keep the speculators at bay. If there is a lesson to draw from the 2008 liquidity crisis, it is that no amount of foreign exchange reserve will guarantee emerging economies immunity from financial crisis, and that when a financial crisis is caused by market overreaction, it cannot be resolved without the intervention of a lender of last resort who can provide reserve-currency liquidity.

Korea's experiences with the crisis episodes underscore the difficulty of small emerging economies in moderating and adjusting to a high degree of volatility of capital flows even when the exchange rate is freely floating. This inherent difficulty stems from—in a literal sense—the big fish in a small pond problem. To large foreign private and institutional investors, exposure to an individual emerging economy such as Korea often accounts for a very small share of their total investments. But to a small emerging economy with shallow and illiquid domestic financial markets, their investments are often large enough to overload the country's limited absorptive capacity. In many cases, their investments in the local financial markets and changes in their portfolios determine the level and the direction of change in the exchange rate. When they pull out for whatever reasons, nothing short of direct capital controls could stop a runaway depreciation.

Evaluation of Financial Regulations

In the aftermath of the 2008 global financial crisis, there has been a growing movement led by the G-20 toward strengthening financial regulations at the global level for the prevention and better management of future financial crises. Emerging economies, such as Korea, have taken steps to accommodate new regulatory proposals, such as Basel III, and to restructure their financial regulatory systems. In this regard, the analyses in this chapter cast some doubt as to whether reinforcing and expanding the scope of both micro- and macro-prudential regulations could help arm emerging economies with more effective tools to ward off future financial crises.

When a financial crisis is of domestic origin—as in the credit card and savings bank debacles—with few consequences on capital account transactions, it can be resolved by domestic regulatory and liquidity interventions. In contrast, however, financial regulations are mostly ineffective in mitigating—let alone preventing—capital account crises, as shown by the 1997 and 2008 cases.

The credit card lending boom-bust was a classic example in which a combination of moral hazard and laxity in regulation escalated an insolvency problem in a small financial industry into a crisis, threatening the stability of the entire financial system. The boom-bust could have been prevented had a tighter regulatory system governing the practices of the credit card industry been installed. However, the regulatory apparatus—however sophisticated it may be—is of no avail if regulators are corrupt or easily succumb to political influence to refrain from exercising regulatory authority. This was what came out of the savings bank scandal in 2011.

The savings bank crisis shows how susceptible a financial system can be to collusive behavior tainted with corruption among the regulators, the regulated, and politicians when the incentives for regulatory forbearance are combined with moral hazard in banking. Many in Korea believed that democratization and market liberalization, together with various checks and balances created over the past two decades, rooted out much of the corruption in the banking sector, the business community, and the public sector. The savings bank crisis in 2011 shattered this idyllic perception. In fact, bankers, regulators, and politicians were conspiring together to falsify the books and conceal losses to keep zombie savings banks in operation.

On managing capital account crises, a study of Korea's regulatory reform shows that there is a limit to how much micro- and macroprudential regulations can safeguard banks and other financial institutions against a reserve currency liquidity crisis, unless they are deprived of their asset transformation function altogether. (On macro-prudential regulations in Korea, see Park 2010.) As banks rely on short-term funding for their long-term lending and investments, they are automatically exposed to maturity mismatch and, hence, potentially to a liquidity crisis, which often provokes a bank run.

In emerging economies, banks active in international financial intermediation are open to another risk that can undermine their soundness. This is currency mismatch—banks financing local currency lending by borrowing in foreign currencies. Various regulatory restrictions may not be effective in ameliorating the mismatch because banks entrenched in long-term relationship banking find it difficult to comply with the restrictions. If strictly enforced, there is the danger that restrictions could limit the scope of bank asset-liability management, thereby undermining competitiveness in international financial intermediation vis-à-vis banks from advanced or reserve-currency countries that are not subject to similar constraints.

When a sudden reversal in capital flows occurs, even well-regulated and sound banks in emerging economies are likely to face solvency risk as they are denied access to external wholesale funding markets. This risk is one of the main reasons why many emerging economies hold "excessive" foreign exchange reserves and may need to intervene in the foreign exchange market and impose capital controls.

Since holding large amounts of reserves in emerging economies is costly and could exacerbate global trade imbalances, constructing a global liquidity safety net that could meet the short-term reserve currency liquidity needs would serve as a more effective system of safeguarding against reserve-currency liquidity crises in emerging economies.

Conclusion

On reviewing financial developments in Korea since the late 1990s, casual observers may find it difficult to assess the benefits of financial liberalization. Since financial reform got under way after the 1997 crisis, Korea has suffered through a series of financial turbulences. At this writing, it is enduring uncertainties and financial market instability caused by the deepening euro-zone crisis, has yet to recover from the busting of a real estate market boom, and is in the midst of resolving a savings bank crisis with the prospect of more bankruptcies of these institutions to come in the near future.

Moreover, it is difficult to gauge efficiency gains; in fact, Korea has lost much of its pre-crisis dynamism. This is evidenced by a GDP growth rate that has been about 4 percent per annum on average for the past 10 years, less than half of what had been achieved during the preceding decade. Worse yet, the slowdown in growth has been compounded by deterioration of income distribution and the hollowing out of the middle class, causing polarization of income earners and social unrest.

All of these developments could not, and should not, be blamed on financial liberalization and market opening. However, the Korean experience suggests that there is a limit to which a small emerging economy could open its financial sector. Once opened, it appears the financial market can become a playground for international investors: a large number of large international banks and other non-bank financial institutions move in out of a relatively small financial sector at a moment's notice whenever they see favorable or unfavorable market developments, thereby playing havoc with the financial industries.

As Kose et al. (2010) argue, the disappointing outcome could be laid on undertaking reforms before establishing threshold conditions supportive of an orderly process of financial liberalization. In this regard, Korea may have failed to establish an efficient and independent system of financial regulation that could have safeguarded stability and soundness of the financial system by preventing the buildup of systemic risk. The credit card and savings bank crises, together with the 2008 liquidity crisis, all point to regulatory failure to mitigate excessive leverage and risk taking at banks and other non-bank financial institutions, exacerbating adverse internal and external shocks to the financial system.

More worrisome has been the pervasiveness of regulatory forbearance and corruption that have undermined the reputation and credibility of regulators. The regulatory system has also been open to political pressure and lobbying of the financial industries it regulates. The problems Korea has encountered in its financial regime transition may not have been unique. They may reflect some of the travails of liberalization to which a small opening economy is exposed when it integrates itself into the global financial system.

However, overall, this assessment does not mean Korea should and can move back to the repressive and closed regime of the pre-1997 crisis years. Such retrogression would be self-defeating, as it would incur an enormous cost Korea can hardly afford.

What is needed at this stage of development is for Korea to fortify its financial system to spare itself the vagaries of international financial markets. To this end, it needs to construct an efficient system of both micro- and macro-prudential regulations and install a regime of capital controls and foreign exchange market interventions to better counter the high degree of capital movements, together with securing access to short-term reserve-currency liquidity through participation in international cooperative arrangements to prepare for an unexpected reversal in capital flow.

Appendix 4.1: Constructing a Financial Reform Index

This study uses a six-component index to measure financial reform. The composite index equally weights the components.

Abiad et al. (2008) created a financial reform index by summing seven indices: credit controls, interest rate controls, entry barriers, banking supervision, privatization, international capital flows, and security markets.

However, three of these are not used here for Korea. The interest rate controls index exhibits an unrealistic downward movement after 2000, and the credit controls index does not vary after 1990. Further, although the privatization index seems to capture the flow of privatization—the index has the value 2 for the pre-1997 period, and 0 thereafter—conceptually it does not seem a suitable measure of the degree of financial liberalization.

The four IMF measures used thus are entry barriers, banking supervision, international capital flows, and security markets. These are all measured on a scale of 0 to 3, 3 being the highest degree of liberalization.

For the fifth measure, domestic financial deregulation, interest rate liberalization is used as a proxy. The measure starts at 1 for 1991–1992 and then increases incrementally in steps of 0.5 for the 1993–1994, 1995–1996, 1997–2004, and post-2005 periods. It is reasonable to assume that full interest rate liberalization was completed during the post-2005 period, so the measure rises to 3, its highest level.

The sixth measure, exchange-rate volatility, is constructed by estimating a series of annual standard deviations of the rate of change in the monthly nominal effective exchange rate obtained from BIS for 1990–2007 (excluding the currency crisis period of 1997–1998). For normalization, this annual series is adjusted by subtracting its sample mean and then dividing the resulting series by its sample standard deviation. Values range between −1 and +2.

Appendix 4.2:
Specifications of Impact of Liberalization Models

Model 1

The first model is designed to address firm-specific and industry-specific rationalization of bank lending—that is, to answer the first question. It is specified as:

$$d\ln(loans)_{i,t} = \alpha_0 + \alpha_1 * X_{it\text{-}1} + \alpha_2 * finlib_t + \alpha_3 \\ * X_{it\text{-}1} * finlib_t + Z_{it} + \upsilon_i + \nu_t + \varepsilon_{it} \tag{1}$$

The dependent variable—$d\ln(loans)_{i,t}$—is the rate of growth of total loans extended by both banks and NBFIs. The variable $finlib_t$ is the financial liberalization index at time t. $X_{it\text{-}1}$ is the rate of return on assets (ROA) of firm i in year $t-1$ (the growth of value-added of industry i) and represents firm (industry) i's main past-performance characteristic.

In this specification, the regressor, $X_{it\text{-}1}$, represents an independent effect of past performance on loan acquisition.

The interaction term ($X_{it\text{-}1} * finlib_t$) captures the extent to which financial liberalization has changed the effect of past performance on acquiring loans. If this latter term is significant and positive, then it suggests financial liberalization prevailed on banks and NBFIs to consider a firm's (industry's) past performance more than before in allocating loans. Z represents a vector of control variables. Variables υ_i and v_t stand for firm-fixed (industry-fixed) effects and year-dummies.

Model 2

The model for analyzing the second question—the contribution of loans by banks and NBFIs to a firm's (industry's) total factor productivity (TFP) growth—takes the form:

$$
\begin{aligned}
d\ln(TFP)_{i,t} = {} & \beta_0 + \beta_1 * d\ln(loans_{i,t\text{-}1}) + \beta_2 * finlib_t \\
& + \beta_3 * d\ln(loans_{i,t\text{-}1}) * finlib_t + \delta Z_{it} \\
& + \upsilon_i + v_t + \varepsilon_{it}
\end{aligned}
\tag{2}
$$

The dependent variable is a firm's (industry's) TFP growth $(d\ln(TFP)_{i,t})$. The regressor, $d\ln(loans_{i,t\text{-}1})$, captures an independent effect of past loan growth on TFP growth.

The interaction term $(d\ln(loans_{i,t\text{-}1}) * finlib_t)$ measures the role of financial liberalization in influencing contribution of loans to firm (industry) productivity. If this term is significant and positive, it suggests that financial liberalization has been instrumental in effecting a larger contribution of loans of banks and NBFIs to TFP growth of firms (industries). In other words, the interaction term could be understood as measuring the significance of the effect of past loan growth on TFP growth.

Model 3

The third model for analyzing the effect of change in the structure of financing on a firm's efficiency is:

$$
\begin{aligned}
d\ln(TFP)_{i,t} = {} & \rho_0 + \rho_1 * d\ln(loans_{i,t\text{-}1}) + \rho_2 * finlib_t \\
& + \rho_3 * d\ln(loans_{i,t\text{-}1}) * finlib_t + \rho_4 * shdirect_{i,t\text{-}1} \\
& + \rho_5 * shdirect_{i,t\text{-}1} * finlib_t + \psi Z_{it} + \upsilon_i + v_t + \varepsilon_{it}
\end{aligned}
\tag{3}
$$

Shdirect is the share of direct financing in total financing of an individual firm. In this specification, $shdirect_{i,t\text{-}1}$ captures the effect of the structural change in a firm's financing method on its productivity (TFP) growth, whereas $shdirect_{i,t-1} * finlib_t$ measures how much financial liberalization has changed the effectiveness of the direct financing on improving firm productivity.

Industry-level analysis for this model is not conducted due to the lack of relevant direct-financing share data.

Data Description and Regressions

This study uses 33,162 annual observations of 6,233 firms in the KIS-VALUE database for the 1990 to 2005 period. The KIS-VALUE database, compiled by NICE Information Service, provides financial and non-financial data for listed and externally audited firms. Financial companies and the financial crisis period from 1997 to 1999 are excluded from the sample.

The bank financing variable (*loans*) is the sum of short-term and long-term loans from banks and non-banks. Data are in table 4.8.

TABLE 4.8
Summary Statistics and Definition of Variables: Firm-Level Data

Variable	Description	Obs	Mean	Std	Min	Max
$d \ln(tfp)$	Growth rate of TFP	32,881	0.004	0.104	−0.497	0.497
$d \ln(loans)$	Growth rate of external financing	32,881	0.053	0.358	−1.000	1.000
ROA	Return over asset	32,873	0.065	0.077	−0.653	0.971
finlib	Financial liberalization index	32,881	0.792	0.268	0.323	0.991
rnd_sales	Ratio of R&D to sales	32,881	0.01	0.06	−0.04	4.24
ln(assets)	Log of total assets	32,881	24.10	1.36	19.54	31.80
liab_eq	Ratio of liability to equity	32,771	6.53	262.02	−1547.40	39,200.84
shdirect	Share of direct financing	32,881	0.29	0.31	0.00	1.00

Note: All variables except for *finlib* are firm-level annual frequency data;. *finlib* is a year-specific variable.

TABLE 4.9
Summary Statistics and Definition of Variables: Industry-Level Data

Variable	Description	Obs	Mean	Std	Min	Max
$d \ln(tfp_i)$	Growth rate of TFP	218	0.007	0.034	−0.126	0.198
$d \ln(loans_i)$	Growth rate of external financing	218	0.055	0.138	−0.393	0.456
$d \ln(va_i)$	Growth rate of value-added	218	0.067	0.101	−0.409	0.421
finlib	Financial liberalization index	218	0.889	0.184	0.349	1.000
rnd_va_i	Ratio of R&D to value-added	218	0.035	0.039	0.000	0.182

Note: All variables except for finlib are industry-level annual frequency data; finlib is a year-specific variable.

Industry-Level Data Description and Regressions

The data are from the annual industry panel data set at the two-digit level from 1990 to 2007. The financial crisis period of 1997–1999 is excluded. Data are in table 4.9.

Appendix 4.3: Specifications of Income Distribution Models

Model 1

A reduced form equation on the determination of the loan-income ratio for individual households (question one) is specified as follows.

$$\ln(loan\_inc)_{it} = \alpha_0 + \alpha_1 * finlib_t + \sum_j \alpha_2 j * quint_{i,t}^j * finlib_t$$
$$+ \sum_j \alpha_3 j * quint_{i,t}^j + \gamma' Z_{it} + u_i + \varepsilon_{it}$$

Controlling many plausible factors that may influence the household's loan-income ratio (loan_inc), the model includes a financial liberalization index (finlib) and its interaction term with quintile income group dummies (quint_j) to detect whether there was any change in the loan-income ratio in each income group throughout the financial liberalization process.

The list of control variables (Z) in the empirical models includes a dummy variable for owning real estate (*asset_p*), a dummy for owning a house (*live_own*), a log of financial assets (*finasset*), the age of the head of household (*hage*), a quadratic term of age (*hage$_2$*), the education attainment level of the head of household (*hedu*, scale from 2 to 9), and the sex of head of household (*hsex*), the number of family members (*member*), a dummy for living in Seoul (*seoul*), and a dummy for living in a metropolitan area (*met*).

All regressors are one-year lagged to limit the endogeneity problem. The sample excludes extreme outliers. (Observations with loan-income ratio of greater than 10 are excluded.)

For a robustness check, a loan access dummy is also considered as an alternative for the dependent variable. Tobit and random-effect Tobit models are used for estimating the equation with the loan-income ratio as the dependent variable. In the formulation where a loan access dummy is the dependent variable, random-effect probit models are chosen for estimation.

Model 2

In the model specification of the second question, the log of household income ($\ln inc$) is the dependent variable. The log of the loan-income ratio ($\ln loan\_inc$) enters as a regressor—the main variable of interest—along with a number of instrumental variables.

A reduced form equation for the household income is:

$$\ln(inc_{it}) = \alpha_0 + \alpha_1 * \ln(loan\_inc)_{i,t} + \gamma'Z_{it} + u_i + \varepsilon_{it}$$

Controlling other factors that may influence household income [$\ln(inc)$], the model postulates that changes in household income are positively related to changes in the loan-income ratio a year later. The variable $\ln inc$ is the log sum of income plus 1. The log sum of incomes from the periods t, $t+1$, and $t+2$, plus one more variable, $\ln(inc_3)$, was also considered as an alternative dependent variable. The results are qualitatively the same and available on request.

The list of control variables (Z) includes a dummy variable for owning real estate (*asset_p*), a log of financial assets (*finasset*), the age of the head of household (*hage*), a quadratic term of age (*hage₂*), the education attainment level of the head of household (*hedu*, scale from 2 to 9), and the sex of head of household (*hsex*), a dummy for self-employed (*job_own*), and the housing price index (*housingpr*).

References

Abiad, Abdul G., Enrica Detragiache, and Thierry Tressel. 2008, December. "A New Database of Financial Reforms." IMF Working Paper 08/266.

Ahn, Sanghoon, Joon-Ho Hahm, and Joon-Kyung Kim. 2008. "External Finance and Productivity Growth in Korea: Firm Level Evidence Before and After the Financial Crisis." *KDI Journal of Economic Policy* 30 (2): 27–59.

Allen, Franklin, and Douglas Gale. 2007. *Understanding Financial Crises.* Clarendon Lecture in Finance. Oxford University Press.

Bandiera, Oriana, Gerard Caprio Jr., Patrick Honohan, and Fabio Schiantarelli. 2000. "Does Financial Reform Raise or Reduce Savings?" *Review of Economics and Statistics* 82 (2): 239–63.

Bank of Korea (BOK). Financial Assets and Liabilities Outstanding, various years.

Beck, Thorsten, Ross Levine, and Norman Loayza. 2000. "Finance and the Sources of Growth." *Journal of Financial Economics* 58 (1): 261–300.

Bekaert, Geert, Campbell R. Harvey, and Christian Lundblad. 2006. "Growth Volatility and Financial Liberalization." *Journal of International Money and Finance,* 25 (3).

Bencivenga, Valerie R., and Bruce D. Smith. 1991. "Financial Intermediation and Endogenous Growth." *Review of Economic Studies* 58 (2): 195–209.

Chung, Kyuil. 2007. "Decrease in Household Savings Rate and Effectiveness of Monetary Policy." *Economic Papers*, Vol. 10, The Bank of Korea.

Demirguc-Kunt, Asli, and Vojislav Maksimovic. 1998. "Law, Finance and Firm Growth." *Journal of Finance* 53 (6): 2107–37.

Favara, G. 2003. "An Empirical Reassessment of the Relationship Between Finance and Growth." IMF Working Paper 03/123.

Fisman, Raymond, and Inessa Love. 2003. "Financial Dependence and Growth Revisited." NBER Working Paper 9582.

FitzGerald, Valpy. 2006 March. "Financial Development and Economic Growth: A Critical View." Background Paper for *World Economic and Social Survey* 2006. UN Development Policy and Analysis Division.

Galindo, Arturo, Fabio Schiantarelli, and Andrew Weiss. 2007. "Does Financial Liberalization Improve the Allocation of Investment?: Micro-Evidence from Developing Countries." *Journal of Development Economics,* 83 (2), 562–87.

Ghosh, Swati R. 2006. *East Asian Finance: The Road to Robust Markets.* The World Bank.

Greenwood, Jeremy, and Boyan Jovanovic. 1990. "Financial Development, Growth and the Distribution of Income." *Journal of Political Economy* 98 (5): 1076–107.

Gurley, John G., and E.S. Shaw. 1955. "Financial Aspects of Economic Development." *American Economic Review* 45 (4): 515–38.

Jeong, Hyung-Kwan. 2009, June. "The Procyclicality of Bank Lending and Its Funding Structure: The Case of Korea." Paper presented at the 2009 BOK International Conference.

Johnson, Chalmers. 1982. *MITI and the Japanese Miracle: The Growth of Industrial Policy, 1925–1975.* Stanford University Press.

Kang, Taesoo, and Guonan Ma. 2007. "Recent Episodes of Credit Card Distress in Asia." *BIS Quarterly Review* (June): 55–68.

Kim, Han-Ah. 2003. "The Relationship Between Economic Growth and Financial Liberalization and Development." *KDIC Financial Review* 4 (2): 5–30. (In Korean.)

Kim, Jun-Kyung. 2010. "Expansion of Consumer Credit and the Distribution of Household Wealth." Unpublished manuscript, Korea Development Institute.

King, R.G., and Ross Levine. 1993. "Finance and Growth: Schumpeter Might Be Right." *Quarterly Journal of Economics* 108 (3): 717–37.

Kose, M. Ayhan, Eswar Prasad, Kenneth Rogoff, and Shang-Jin Wei. 2009. "Financial Globalization: A Reappraisal." *IMF Staff Papers* 56 (1): 8–62.

Kose, M. Ayhan, Eswar Prasad, Kenneth Rogoff, and Shang-Jin Wei. 2010. "Financial Globalization and Economic Policies." In Dani Rodrik and Mark Rosenzweig, eds., *Handbook of Development Economics*, vol. 5, 4283–4362.

Laeven, Luc. 2003. "Does Financial Liberalization Reduce Financing Constraints?" *Financial Management* 32 (1) (Spring): 5–34.

Levine, Ross. 2005. "Finance and Growth: Theory and Evidence." In Philippe Aghion and Steven Durlauf, eds., *Handbook of Economic Growth*. Elsevier.

Levine, Ross, Norman Loayza, and Thorsten Beck. 2000. "Financial Intermediation and Growth Causality and Causes." *Journal of Monetary Economics* 46: 31–77.

McKinnon, R. 1973. *Money and Capital in Economic Development.* Brookings Institution.

Padoa-Schioppa, Tomasso. 2003. "Central Banks and Financial Stability: Exploring the Land in Between." In Vitor Gaspar et al., eds., *The Transformation of the European Financial System*, 269–310. European Central Bank.

Park, Jungsoo, and Yung Chul Park. 2012a. "Financial Liberalization and Income Distribution in Korea: Evidence from Household Data." Unpublished manuscript.

Park, Jungsoo, and Yung Chul Park. 2012b. "Has Financial Liberalization Improved Economic Efficiency in Korea?: Evidence from Firm-Level and Industry-Level Data." Paper presented at the 15th KEA International Conference, June 20.

Park, Kang H. 2011. "What Happened to Efficiency and Competition after Bank Mergers and Consolidation in Korea?" *KDI Journal of Economic Policy* 33 (3) (March): 33–55.

Park, Yung Chul. 1998. *Financial Liberalization and Opening in East Asia: Issues and Policy Challenges*. Korea Institute of Finance.

Park, Yung Chul. 2010. "Global Economic Recession and East Asia: How Has Korea Managed the Crisis and What Has It Learned?" Bank of Korea Working Paper.

Rajan, R.G., and L. Zingales. 1998. "Financial Development and Growth." *American Economic Review* 88 (3): 559–86.

Rodrik, Dani, and Andres Velasco. 2001. "Short-Term Capital Flows." In Boris Pleskovic and Joseph E Stiglitz, eds, *Annual World Bank Conference on Development Economics 1999*. World Bank.

Shaw, Edward S. 1973. *Financial Deepening in Economic Development*. Oxford University Press.

Shyn, Yong-Sang, and Wankeun Oh. 2005. "Financial Dependence, Growth Opportunity, and External Finance and Productivity Growth in Korea: Industrial Growth in Korea." *Kyungjehak Yeonku (Journal of Korea Economic Association)* 53 (3): 49–76. (In Korean.)

Stiglitz, Joseph E. 2000. "Capital Market Liberalization, Economic Growth and Instability." *World Development* 28: 1075–86.

Yun, S. 2004. "Impact of Direct Regulations on the Korean Credit Card Market and Consumer Welfare." Bank of Korea Economic Papers 42.

CHAPTER FIVE

Banking, Capital Flows, and Financial Cycles

Common Threads in the 2007–2009 Crises

YOUNG-HWA SEOK AND HYUN SONG SHIN

FINANCIAL GLOBALIZATION has a mixed record. This chapter seeks to make sense of the reasons for this and to diagnose the specific factors involved in the boom-bust cycles associated with rapidly increasing capital inflows.

The global financial crisis that began in 2007 engulfed not only the advanced economies, but it also spread to emerging markets that were not directly implicated in the erosion of lending standards and other practices associated with the crisis. Open economies in Asia felt the impact of the spreading crisis beginning in the fourth quarter of 2008, evoking memories of the dark days of the Asian financial crisis of 1997. Some countries, such as Korea, were harder hit than others following the bankruptcy of Lehman Brothers in September 2008. Their experiences revealed that the hard-won improvements in financial resiliency since the Asian financial crisis were not enough to forestall liquidity crises when the impact was felt globally.

For observers of the emerging-market crises of the 1990s, events since 2007 have a very familiar ring. Emerging economy policy makers have learned to be wary of financial booms riding on the back of easy credit conditions, ample liquidity, and ballooning current account deficits.

The common thread that ties together the lessons from the Asian financial crisis of 1997 and the 2007–2009 global crisis is that the financial system is prone to the propagation and amplification of boom-bust cycles. Rather like a tropical storm over a warm sea, financial crises appear to gather more energy as they develop. Financial crises can almost be defined as episodes where the proper allocative role of prices breaks down.

Arguments for the benefits of financial globalization rest on capital inflows allowing an emerging economy to supplement its own domestic savings in financing investment, thereby lowering the cost of capital and boosting investment. However, experience shows that capital inflows also fuel permissive domestic liquidity conditions that fuel housing booms and build vulnerability to crises.

The chapter's organizing theme is the role of financial intermediaries, especially banks, in the propagation of financial cycles. The 2007–2009 crisis has shown that the banking sector can play the role of the engine that drives the cycle.

Within the context of our organizing theme, we discuss four specific episodes that illustrate the general workings of the propagation mechanism. These are:

- The liquidity crisis in Korea in 2008 in the aftermath of the failure of Lehman Brothers;
- Japan's experience in the 1980s prior to the bursting of the stock market and real estate bubbles;
- The US financial crisis of 2007–2009, and the role of the "savings glut" of surplus countries in the emerging world;
- The European crisis that began in 2010, which combines a sovereign-debt crisis with a banking crisis.

The chapter proceeds as follows. We begin with a review of the merits of financial globalization, especially the effects of unhindered capital flows. Then we analyze the consequences to the financial system as a whole of the balance sheet management done by financial intermediaries. We apply our insights to the four episodes listed above. We conclude by analyzing the implications for policy. We stress the importance of macro-prudential policies—that is, policies concerned with the resilience of the financial system as a whole—and review the tools available. In particular, we look at policies intended to neutralize the effects of capital inflows when monetary policy is constrained.

Revisiting the Merits of Financial Globalization

The 2007–2009 crisis has reopened the fundamental debate on the merits of financial globalization and the desirability of completely unhindered capital flows into emerging countries. (Or, more accurately, the question hinges on the merits of private-sector capital inflows, since countries can run current account surpluses and be subject to surges of capital inflows into the private sector. The gap is made up by the buildup of official reserves.)

The wave of financial globalization that started in the 1980s led to rising cross-border financial flows among high-income economies and between high-income and emerging economies.

Financial globalization was spurred by liberalization of capital controls that rested on the strong presumption that such liberalization would result in two types of economic benefits. First, there was an expectation of improved allocation of capital across countries. That is, capital would flow from the advanced economies to emerging economies that had higher rates of return on capital. Second, there was an expectation of improved risk-sharing among countries. The strong presumption was that these benefits were likely to be large, especially for developing countries that tend to be relatively capital poor and have more volatile income growth.

The simplest theoretical basis for such thinking is the benchmark one-sector neoclassical growth model where financial globalization leads to flows of capital from capital-rich to capital-poor economies, driven by the higher returns to capital in the latter group. The textbook model predicts that these flows should complement the limited domestic saving in the capital-poor economies and reduce their cost of capital. In so doing, capital inflows should increase investment and, hence, growth.

In addition to the quantitative impact of capital inflows on investment, certain types of financial flows were expected to have indirect—collateral—benefits. First, capital flows could be accompanied by technology spillovers and serve as a channel for the spread of good governance practices and managerial and organizational expertise. Second, financial flows might help foster specialization by allowing more efficient sharing of income risk globally, thereby allowing greater productivity growth. Third, monitoring by investors in international capital markets was thought to promote better discipline of government macroeconomic policies, such as ensuring that governments pursued sustainable fiscal policies and enlightened prudential policies with respect to their domestic financial institutions. Such indirect benefits of financial openness were also thought to contribute to enhanced growth.

However, even before the 2007–2009 global crisis and the European crisis that began in 2010, the case for the benefits of financial globalization was vulnerable. Indeed, the studies that preceded the crises had painted a mixed picture of the benefits of financial globalization for emerging economies.

Perhaps the most comprehensive study of the evidence up to 2006 is Kose, Prasad, Rogoff, and Wei (2006), who provide a careful review of the literature. Their conclusion was that the cross-country evidence on the growth benefits of capital-account openness was inconclusive and lacked robustness.

Prasad, Rajan, and Subramanian (2007) and Gourinchas and Jeanne (2007) also found little evidence in favor of the economic growth benefits of foreign capital. Their work indicated that countries that grew more rapidly were those that relied less on foreign capital, and foreign capital tends to go to countries that experience low productivity growth.

The trauma of the 2007–2009 crisis has reinforced doubts about supposed benefits of greater financial openness. Indeed, the two countries that managed to weather the crisis with the least negative impact, China and India, maintained substantial controls on capital flows, and otherwise have been the most cautious in pursuing openness.

The evidence on the benefits of better international risk sharing was similarly suspect, again, even before the crisis. Kose, Prasad, and Terrones (2003) found that during the 1990s, average declines in output growth volatility were smaller for emerging markets than for either high-income or low-income (developing) economies. More importantly, they found that the ratio of consumption growth volatility to income growth volatility actually *increased* during the period of globalization for emerging-market economies. What was notable was not only that the volatility of consumption rose but that it increased by more than income volatility. This finding runs counter to the presumed theoretical benefit of financial integration allowing countries to share income risk so as to smooth consumption.

These findings, as well as cases of large economic costs due to crises, such as Korea in 1997, suggest the need to revisit the assumptions underlying the arguments for increased financial liberalization, and in particular, the key plank in the argument that low savings and the weakness of the domestic financial system in channeling resources for investment is the key impediment to economic growth and development. This financing constraint on investment is the reason why, in the textbook model, greater access to international capital and improved financial intermediation provide a boost to domestic investment and growth along with better consumption smoothing.

However, the balance sheets of Asian companies reveal that lack of funds has not been the primary constraint on investment. As noted by Park (2006), most East Asian economies were growing at rates much higher than the rest of the world, so these economies did not have to liberalize their capital accounts to attract more capital inflows. That is, a lack of funding was not the primary constraint holding back investment expenditure.

Indeed, for both advanced and emerging economies, corporate investment is well known to use a "pecking order" of funding categories in which firms favor internal funds over external funds. The cross-section empirical study by Beck, Demirgüç-Kunt, and Maksimovic (2002) shows that the bulk of investment in developing countries is self-financed through retained earnings or the family savings of owners and partners.

Instead of financing real investment, surges in capital inflows in periods of plentiful global liquidity are associated with a boom in consumption and household debt that fuels asset price booms, especially in residential housing. The pattern was well recognized even before the latest boom-bust cycle. Calvo, Leiderman, and Reinhart (1996) noted that the early 1990s saw a surge in capital inflows to Latin America and Asia, and observed that much of the surge was associated with more permissive global liquidity conditions. The Thai property boom in the mid-1990s is perhaps emblematic of such a case, where the boom in capital inflows was intermediated by local finance companies.

From a longer perspective, the surges in capital flows to emerging market countries in the 1920s and 1978–1981 were associated with increased consumption and asset price booms, which were then followed by subsequent capital outflows and economic crises.

Table 5.1 shows that, for a sample of emerging markets, the vast majority exhibits positive correlations between US interest rates and domestic

TABLE 5.1

Correlation between US Real Interest Rates and Domestic Investment (as percentage of GDP)

1990–2006	1985–2006	
0.67	0.28	Argentina (1993–2006)
0.23	…	Bolivia
0.28	0.40	Brazil
0.59	0.04	Chile (last year 2005)
−0.57	−0.66	China
0.10	0.03	Colombia
−0.56	−0.67	India (last year 2005)
0.48	0.43	Indonesia
0.43	0.22	Malaysia
0.05	−0.08	Mexico
0.69	0.43	Peru
0.60	0.22	Philippines
0.33	0.00	South Korea
0.16	0.03	Thailand
0.64	0.26	Turkey
0.58	0.10	Uruguay

Source: Rodrik and Subramanian 2009.

investment. This suggests that their investment rates tend to fall when US interest rates are low and external liquidity is plentiful. If the binding constraint on domestic investment were the lack of funding, then one would have expected exactly the opposite sign—that investment would be high when external funding conditions are more permissive.

It is also notable that the only two countries for which the correlation is negative and sizable are China and India, the two countries that have been most cautious in their approach to financial globalization.

Drawing any implications based on correlations is fraught with difficulties for the usual reasons of endogeneity or common causes. The point is merely that the outward evidence does not conform to the textbook effects.

Volatility and Composition of Capital Flows

As an entry into our organizing theme that financial intermediaries, especially banks, play a major role in the propagation of financial cycles,

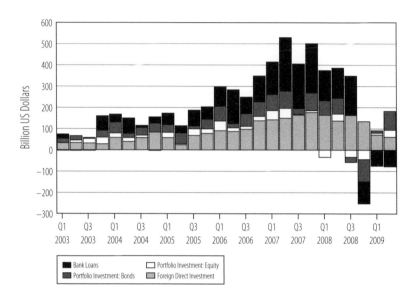

Figure 5.1 Composition of Capital Flows to Emerging Economies, 2003–2009.
Source: IMF Global Financial Stability Report, April 2009.

Note: Quarterly data.

consider the composition of capital flows to emerging economies from 2003 to the end of 2009, that is, the period just before and after the Lehman bankruptcy.

Figure 5.1 shows the markedly different patterns in the components. Foreign direct investment (FDI) is quite stable over the period, even during the fourth quarter of 2008 in the immediate aftermath of the Lehman bankruptcy. Portfolio equity flow is somewhat more volatile, showing a reversal during the fourth quarter of 2008.

Although the exact classifications between FDI and portfolio flows can be difficult (especially when capital controls rely on this distinction, as in Brazil currently), the most volatile components can be seen to be those associated with debt—in particular, portfolio bond flows and bank debt. Bank debt, in particular, shows a very sizable reversal in the last quarter of 2008 during the height of the financial distress and deleveraging by global banks.

The observation that debt flows are more volatile than other types of flows and are easily reversible in times of crises has been made many times. Moreover, it has been recognized for some time that short-term bank loans to developing countries are pro-cyclical, increasing during booms and rapidly decreasing during economic slowdowns (World Bank 2000). Sudden reversals of international capital flows are more likely in countries that rely relatively more on debt flows, including bank loans, and less on FDI (Wei 2006).

Park (2006) notes that foreign lenders' inadequate steps in managing risks involved in lending to East Asian economies precipitated the confusion and panic in financial markets of the 1997–1998 crisis countries. Specifically, many small foreign banks will leave a market when they see leader banks making a hurried exit, believing that these large institutions know what they are doing.

The literature on early warning systems to financial crises that emerged after the Asian financial crisis also pointed to the role played by high levels of short-term external debt denominated in foreign currency in heightening vulnerability to financial crises (see Berg, Borenzstein, and Pattillo 2004).

Financial Intermediation

Financial intermediaries often take a back seat in aggregate macroeconomic models. Here, we redress the balance and explore the extent to which banks and other intermediaries play the role of the engine that drives the financial cycle.

Figure 5.2 depicts a stylized credit system, which channels savings from *ultimate savers*—the household sector—to *ultimate users* such as nonfinancial firms or young households who wish to borrow to buy a house.

The funding has two possible routes. Funds can be granted directly. For example, households buy corporate bonds and equity issued by nonfinancial firms directly. Alternatively, funds can be placed indirectly through the financial intermediary sector, which collects funds from the household sector in order to lend to or invest in the ultimate user.

In a world where the Modigliani and Miller (MM) theorems hold, we can separate the decision on the size of the balance sheet (selection of the projects to take on) from the financing of the projects (composition of liabilities in terms of debt and equity). In textbook discussions of balance sheets, the set of positive net present value (NPV) projects

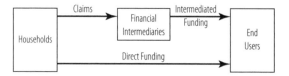

Figure 5.2 A Stylized Financial System.

is taken as given. In such a setting, the size of the balance sheet is fixed and is determined exogenously. In determining the relative mix of equity and debt, the focus is on the liability side. Even when the conditions for the MM theorems do not hold, the textbook discussion starts with the assets of the firm as given, in order to focus on the financing decision alone.

Leverage and Asset Growth

The distinguishing feature of banking-sector assets is that they fluctuate over the financial cycle. Credit increases rapidly during the boom but increases less rapidly (or even decreases) during the downturn. Some of the variation in the size of banking assets could be accounted for by fluctuations in the size of the pool of positive NPV projects, but some fluctuation almost surely is due to shifts in bank willingness to take on risky positions over the cycle.

Figure 5.3 uses Barclays, a typical global bank, to illustrate how much a change in balance sheet size was financed through equity and how much through debt. (A similar picture holds for US investment banks and, albeit in less stark form, other intermediaries. For example, Shin and Shin (2010) exhibit similar evidence for Korean banks.)

What is especially notable is how, during 1992–2010, the risk-weighted assets (RWA) of the bank (the assets of the bank weighted by Basel capital risk weights, which in turn determines the overall capital requirement for the bank) barely changed, even though the raw assets changed by several hundred billion pounds. Rather, assets expanded or contracted dollar for dollar (or pound for pound) through a change in debt.

Another striking feature of such an analysis, especially as regards US investment banks, is that leverage is pro-cyclical in the sense that

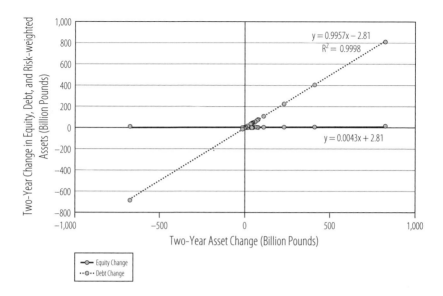

Figure 5.3 Barclays Bank Two-Year Change in Assets, Equity, Debt, and Risk-Weighted Assets, 1992–2010. *Source*: Bankscope. (Bankscope is an electronic global database of bank financial statements, ratings, and intelligence.)

leverage is high when balance sheets are large, and leverage is low when balance sheets are small. This is the opposite relationship to that for household balance sheets, whose leverage is high when balance sheets are small. For instance, if a household owns a house financed by a mortgage, leverage falls when the house price increases. This is because the increase in equity is relatively greater than the increase in assets.

Thus, unlike the textbook discussion of the Modigliani-Miller theorem, it is equity that seems to play the role of the exogenous variable, and total assets (the size of the balance sheet) is the endogenous variable that is determined by the willingness of banks to take on risky exposure.

Figure 5.4 is a stylized depiction of the consequences of balance sheet management during a boom. Suppose the initial balance sheet of the banking sector is as depicted on the left of the figure. Now suppose there is a positive shock to the price of the assets already held by the banking sector. We envisage an increase in the expected return from the assets. Since the banks are leveraged, there is a mark-to-market increase in the capital position of the banking sector. The middle

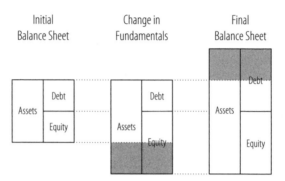

Figure 5.4 Increased Credit Supply from Intermediary Balance Sheet Management.

Note: Shaded areas in Change in Fundamentals represent an increase in the market value of Assets and concomitant increase in Equity. Shaded areas in the Final Balance Sheet represent new borrowing and new lending made possible by the increase in equity.

balance sheet shows the effect of the improvement in fundamentals that comes from an increase in asset values, but before any adjustment in the portfolio is made.

Although the liabilities of the banks will also change in value due to marked-to-market effects of debt, they will be small, so we approximate the effect by assuming that there is no change in debt value. Thus, the increase in asset value flows through entirely to an increase in equity. Any accumulation of profits will have a similar effect in expanding bank equity. Moreover, since the bank is leveraged, the percentage increase in the value of equity is much larger than the percentage increase in the value of assets.

The increase in equity relaxes the capital constraint (for instance, by relaxing the value-at-risk [VAR] constraint), and the intermediary can increase its lending or the holding of risky securities. The new balance sheet has assets large enough to make the capital constraint bind at the higher equity level, with a higher fundamental value.

In other words, after the positive shock to asset values, bank balance sheets have strengthened, in that capital has increased. There is an erosion of leverage, leading to spare capacity on the balance sheet in the sense that the bank has the capacity to extend new loans or purchase more securities. The demand response is upward sloping. The right-hand balance sheet in the figure illustrates the expansion of lending that comes from the increased capacity on banking sector balance sheets.

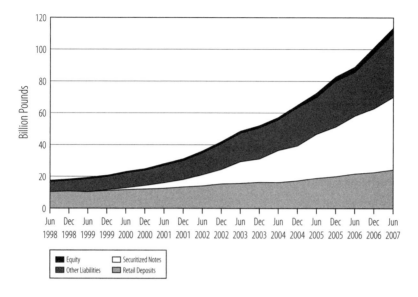

Figure 5.5 Composition of Northern Rock Liabilities, June 1998–June 2007. *Source*: Annual and interim reports of Northern Rock as reported in Shin (2009).

Note: Data are semi-annual.

The key question is what happens on the liability side of the expanding balance sheet—that is, how the increased lending is financed. When assets are expanding rapidly during a lending boom, deposit funding does not grow fast enough to fund the increased lending. Other sources of funding must then be tapped—hence, the new borrowing shown in the lower right corner of the final balance sheet.

Figure 5.5 is an illustration of the types of additional funding used to finance new lending. It shows the composition of liabilities for Northern Rock plc, a UK bank that failed in 2007, an event that heralded the global financial crisis. In the nine years 1998–2007, Northern Rock's lending increased 6.5 times. This increase far outstripped the increase in retail deposits (the bottom band). Wholesale funding enabled the increase in lending.

Northern Rock was an outlier in its use of capital-market funding, but the whole UK banking sector drew increasingly on wholesale funding (see Shin [2009] for further discussion). Northern Rock was the most vulnerable to the deterioration of funding conditions, but not uniquely so. Crucially, Northern Rock was vulnerable even though indicators of asset quality (such as nonperforming loans) were good. Also, its Basel capital ratios were healthy. The problem was the fragility of the liability side of the balance sheet.

This observation leads very naturally to situations where a banking crisis occurs in conjunction with a currency crisis—the twin crises in emerging economies.

Twin Crises as a Banking Sector Phenomenon: Korea

When rapidly increasing bank assets outstrip the funding available from retail depositors, other sources must then be tapped. In the aggregate (when cross-claims across banks are netted out), the total credit extended to non-bank borrowers must be funded from either domestic or foreign creditors. That is, the growth of bank lending results in either greater lending and borrowing between the intermediaries themselves or the sucking in of foreign debt.

When cross-claims between domestic banks are netted out, the ultimate creditors are either domestic claim holders (such as a households) or foreign creditors. (Institutions such as pension funds and mutual funds are not leveraged and hence may be seen as an extension of the household sector for this exercise.)

For the banking system as a whole, reliance on short-term foreign currency–denominated liabilities plays an important role. Shin and Shin (2010) discuss in detail the importance of foreign currency–denominated liabilities of the banking sector in propagating crises. We summarize the key points here, using Korea as an example.

Figure 5.6 plots the foreign currency–denominated liabilities of Korean commercial banks from 1995 to 2009, further classified as short- or long-term liabilities. It is noticeable that before each crisis episode (1997 and 2008) short-term foreign-currency liabilities increased rapidly and then fell sharply with the onset of the crisis. The pattern depicted is strongly suggestive of an increase in bank balance sheet totals in periods of financial boom, which is then reversed with the onset of the crisis and associated deleveraging by the banks.

Figure 5.7 plots the foreign currency–denominated liabilities of the Korean branches of foreign banks. Although the foreign branches played a relatively minor role in the 1997 crisis, they played a much more substantial role during the 2008 crisis. Indeed, the absolute value

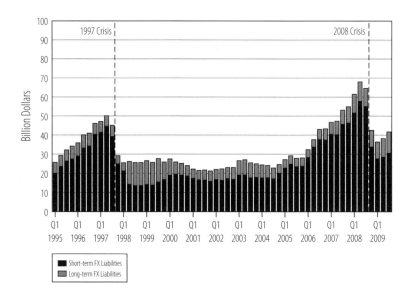

Figure 5.6 Foreign Currency Liabilities of Korean Commercial Banks, 1995–2009.
Source: Bank of Korea series on liabilities of Korean banking sector.

Note: Quarterly data.

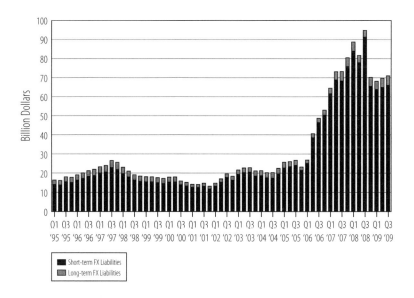

Figure 5.7 Foreign Currency Liabilities of Foreign Bank Branches in Korea, 1995–2009. *Source*: Bank of Korea series on liabilities of Korean banking sector.

Note: Quarterly data.

of foreign currency–denominated liabilities of foreign bank branches ($90 billion) was larger on the eve of the Lehman crisis than that of Korean commercial banks ($60 billion), and had increased much more.

Foreign bank branches raise funds either from their home offices through the interoffice account or by borrowing unsecured in the interbank market. They then enter the foreign exchange swap market in Korea, selling dollars to buy won on the spot market and simultaneously buying dollars in the forward market. Before the swap matures, foreign banks hold Korean government bonds, Bank of Korea bonds, and other fixed-income instruments denominated in won. They thus engage in a "carry trade," lending at the higher Korean interest rate by borrowing at the lower dollar or yen interest rate.

Although local banks also held dollar assets, such assets were claims on Korean firms, and hence not usable to meet maturing dollar liabilities. Nonfinancial firms in Korea had dollar receivables, such as the receivables of the shipbuilders, but they were long-term dollar receivables. By hedging the exchange rate risk in these long-term dollar receivables, the nonfinancial companies could transfer to the banking sector the long-term dollar claims, but the banks then would engage in maturity transformation by borrowing short in dollars. In this way, although the currency mismatch could be eliminated, there was still a maturity mismatch.

Figure 5.8 shows capital flows into and out of Korea in the equity sector (that is, traded stocks), decomposed into flows associated with domestic investors and foreign investors. In the early part of the sample, equity flows were small. However, 2007 saw substantial outflows, both for domestic and foreign investors. Note that the largest outflows occurred before the onset of the most severe episode of the crisis, that is, before the Lehman failure in September 2008.

Figure 5.9 shows the net capital flows in equity and the banking sector. In the six months beginning with the Lehman bankruptcy, the main cause of the overall capital outflow was banks pulling out funds. Equity actually saw *net inflows* beginning the month after the Lehman bankruptcy. This is because for four months repatriations by Korean investors who sold foreign equity holdings exceeded withdrawals from Korea by foreign investors who sold Korean equities. Then foreigners became a source of equity inflow.

Provided the exchange rate is allowed to adjust, equity outflows are not the main culprit in the draining of foreign currency reserves. During a crisis, stock prices fall, and there is a steep depreciation of the domestic

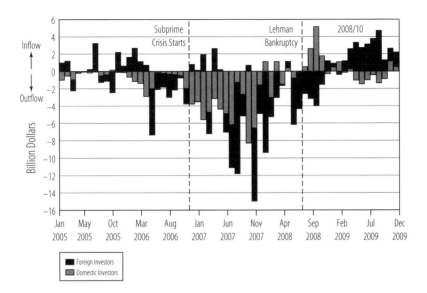

Figure 5.8 Portfolio Equity Flows in Korea, 2005–2009. *Source*: Bank of Korea balance of payments series as reported in Shin and Shin (2010).

Note: Monthly data.

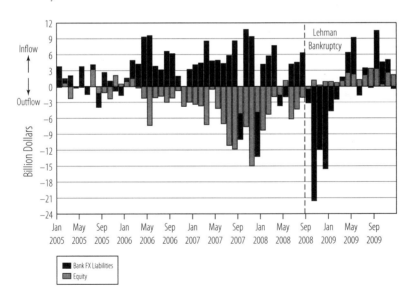

Figure 5.9 Net Capital Flows of Equity and the Banking Sector. *Source*: Bank of Korea balance of payments series as reported in Shin and Shin (2010).

Note: Monthly data.

currency. Foreign investors thereby suffer a "double whammy" if they withdraw from the stock market. Conversely, Korean equity investors gain on the currency shift, mitigating their stock market losses.

However, the banking sector is different. First, foreign currency liabilities of the banks have a face value that must be met in full, and the face value is in foreign currency. For both reasons, the deleveraging of the banking sector is associated with precipitous capital outflows. Second, deleveraging sets off amplifying effects through price changes.

Leveraged institutions are vulnerable to erosion of their capital, and hence engage in substantial adjustments of their assets even to small shocks. The feedback loop generated by such reactions to price changes amplifies shocks. The result is figure 5.4 in reverse.

Korea's foreign exchange reserves fell from over $240 billion to $200 billion during the fourth quarter of 2008—that is, in the wake of the Lehman collapse. The $49 billion outflow in the banking sector more than accounts for the overall decrease. The bank sector's outflow was $21.6 billion in October, $11.9 billion in November, and $15.5 billion in December.

Figure 5.10 shows that the sharp depreciation of the won in 2008 coincides with deleveraging by the banking sector. From stronger than 900 won/dollar in early 2007, the won weakened to near 1,500 during the fourth quarter of 2008.

The reason for the association between banking sector deleveraging and currency depreciation lies in the mutually amplifying effect of price changes and balance sheet adjustment during periods of crisis. For a bank that has engaged in the carry trade of financing the holding of won-denominated securities with short-term US dollar funding, the depreciation of the won entails losses on its portfolio in dollar terms, cutting into the capital base of the bank. The response of the bank is to cut back its exposure by selling assets and repaying the dollar debt. However, widespread selling of won assets and repayment of dollar debts results in further depreciation of the currency, putting further pressure on the exchange rates and asset prices.

Differences Between 1997 and 2008

Although there are common threads between the crises of 1997 and 2008, there are also notable differences. In 1997 the currency mismatch was on bank balance sheets and resulted from lending to large nonfinancial corporations, the *chaebol*. The hope of avoiding interruption in

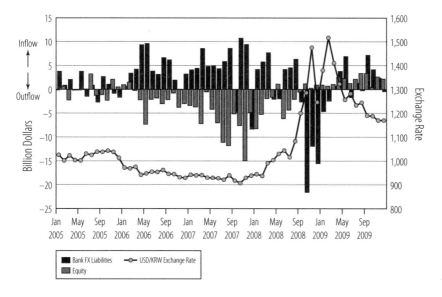

Figure 5.10 Exchange Rate and Capital Flows of the Banking Sector. *Source*: Bank of Korea balance of payments series as reported in Shin and Shin (2010).

Note: Monthly data.

the management of family-controlled businesses, together with under-development of domestic capital markets, made the *chaebol* reluctant to issue equity. This caused *chaebol* to be highly leveraged: the average debt-to-equity ratio of the 30 largest reached more than 380 percent in 1996, four times as high as that of Taiwan (Park 1998).

In contrast, in 2008 the mismatch arose from the selling of long-dated dollar receivables of the shipbuilders and other exporting firms. The banks, who bought the long-dated dollars as forward contracts, hedged the currency exposure by taking on short-term dollar-denominated debt. The large volume of dollar-forward contracts sold by exporting firms accounted for a substantial portion of the increase in short-term foreign currency–denominated liabilities in the banking system.

Japan's Experience from the 1980s Bubble Years

The 1980s bubble in Japan is linked with financial development and liberalization, especially that associated with the securities markets as a funding source. The development of a Japanese corporate bond market started in the late 1970s, but strict qualifying standards meant it was initially off limits to most firms. In 1979, the issuing of unsecured bonds and convertible bonds was permitted, but the criteria were so stringent that only two companies qualified (Toyota Motor Corp and Matsushita Electric Industrial Co Ltd). (For more detail on Japanese financial development generally, see Hoshi and Kashyap [2004]. Hattori, Shin, and Takahashi [2009] examine Japan's 1980s experience in light of the broad financing trends at the time.)

Significant government deficits caused by the oil shocks led the Japanese government to issue government bonds and relax restrictions on corporate debt issuance. During the 1980s the corporate bond market became increasingly accessible: by 1988 the number of firms qualifying for unsecured straight bonds was around 300, whereas the number qualifying for convertible bonds was around 500 (Hoshi and Kashyap 2004, 229–30). Also, starting in 1987, the issuing of commercial paper (CP) and related unsecured short-term liabilities was permitted for Japanese firms for the first time.

As a result of the opening of market-based funding for nonfinancial companies, the relationship between the banking system and the nonfinancial company sector underwent a fundamental shift in the late 1980s. A subset of nonfinancial companies—especially large manufacturing firms—ceased to rely on bank financing and tapped the capital markets instead.

Even more significantly, the nonfinancial companies that had good access to market financing raised surplus funding from the markets and then deposited the surplus in the banking system. This was profitable because, as a result of financial liberalization, time deposits that paid high rates of interest had been introduced in 1985. In effect, the nonfinancial companies transformed their role vis-à-vis the banking system. They went from being *debtors* to the banks to becoming *creditors* to the banks.

From the banks' point of view, such a development was a double blow. They not only lost their traditional customers—corporate borrowers—they had to deploy the funding newly acquired from corporate deposits. Hence, the banks were faced by a great imperative to expand lending to new borrowers.

Many nonfinancial firms became de facto financial intermediaries. This was part of a phenomenon known as *zaiteku* (*zaimu tekunorojii*), using capital for financial and real estate investment rather than for activities more directly related to a company's business. For a brief period in the late 1980s, the financial assets of nonfinancial companies overtook their financial liabilities.

The enhanced access to the capital market by nonfinancial corporations raised fundamental issues to do with the appropriate size of the banking sector. When nonfinancial firms can tap capital markets, the banks suffer a diminished role. From a financial system perspective, the capacity of the banking sector to supply funds ought to shrink to take account of the loss of its borrowing customers. However, such shrinkage is likely to be very difficult to engineer, especially in a period when liquidity conditions are permissive and buoyant real estate markets allow the impression of profitable lending opportunities. Such was the case in Japan in the 1980s.

The funding opportunities of nonfinancial corporations have also improved in other Asian countries. In Korea, the holding of liquid assets by manufacturing firms has increased in the years following the 1997 Asian financial crisis. Thus, large manufacturing firms in Korea had liquid assets that grew from just over 100 trillion won in 2001 to over 300 trillion won in 2009.

The increase in liquid assets held by nonfinancial corporations is mirrored in the composition of banking sector assets. There is a shift to household mortgages and other loans at the expense of corporate loans. In 1999 commercial bank lending to households in Korea was only half that to corporations, but it began to increase at a much faster pace, so that by 2005 it exceeded lending to corporations. After the 2007 crisis, banks increased their concentration on corporate lending due to stricter restrictions on household mortgages.

The paradox of financial liberalization is that as nonfinancial corporations have greater access to the capital market, the banking sector loses its previous rationale as an intermediary for the corporate sector and has to rely on lending to households, especially mortgage lending. Such lending will be associated with an increased amplitude of housing booms and busts and with increased consumption rather than with investment.

In this respect, Japan's experience in its bubble years of the 1980s holds great general importance for financial system development in countries at an earlier stage of financial development.

The European Crisis

Although the eurozone crisis is sometimes portrayed purely as a sovereign debt crisis that is due to prolonged fiscal profligacy, the facts suggest otherwise. Figure 5.11 shows the government budget balance of Ireland, Spain, and Germany, together with the average budget balance for the countries in the eurozone as a whole, for 2002 through 2006.

The picture painted is of countries witnessing rapidly improving budget balances, with Ireland and Spain moving into surplus and Germany and other euro countries seeing a decline in their deficits. By the end of 2006, Ireland had a budget surplus of 3 percent of GDP and Spain a surplus of 2 percent. This is a hardly consistent with commentaries emphasizing fiscal profligacy and chronic budget deficits.

Figure 5.12 shows the debt-to-GDP ratio for Ireland, Spain, Germany, and the EU average over the same five years. Spain and Ireland each had a ratio that was declining—and actually was lower than Germany's. Before the onset of the crisis, Ireland had outwardly sound public finances, with no hint of the trouble that awaited it.

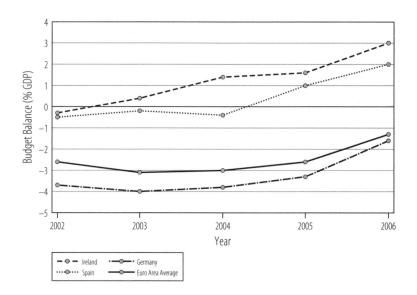

Figure 5.11 Government Budget Balance: Ireland, Spain, and Germany. *Source*: European Commission AMECO database. The portal is http://ec.europa.eu/ economy_finance/ameco/user/serie/SelectSerie.cfm.

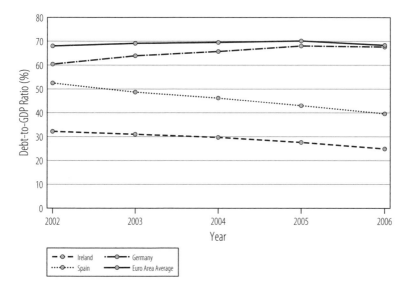

Figure 5.12 Debt-to-GDP Ratios: Ireland, Spain, and Germany *Source*: European Commission AMECO database, http://ec.europa.eu/economy_finance/ameco/user/serie/SelectSerie.cfm.

To understand Europe's current predicament, one needs to grasp the role played by the banking sector in financing the housing bubble. Sovereign risk alone does not explain why Spain, for instance, was one of the first countries to be drawn into the crisis, before other countries with much higher debt-to-GDP ratios. More significant is the silent run on the European banking system.

Figure 5.13 plots the cross-border assets and liabilities of eurozone banks in domestic currency, so that after 1999, the series denotes cross-border euro-denominated lending and borrowing by eurozone banks.

The figure shows that cross-border banking within the eurozone experienced explosive growth, especially after around 2003. This set off property booms in those countries that were recipients of the new cross-border lending. In Spain, the share of construction in GDP rose from less than 8 percent at the end of the 1990s to 12.3 percent in 2007. Meanwhile, residential house prices rose roughly threefold from 1995 to 2007. Ireland's housing boom was, if anything, more dramatic. Financing the housing booms in Ireland and Spain induced capital flows through the banking sector.

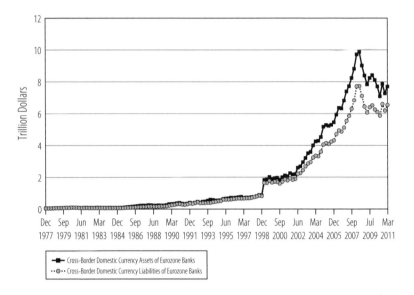

Figure 5.13 Cross-Border Domestic Currency Assets and Liabilities of Eurozone Banks. *Source*: BIS Locational Banking Statistics, Table 5A (Currency breakdown of reporting banks' international positions: External positions vis-à-vis all sectors). Most recent and some historical data for this series are available at http://www.bis.org/statistics/bankstats.htm.

The consequence for borrowers in countries that underwent property booms, such as Spain and Ireland, was that they were borrowing in increasing amounts from other European banks, as shown in figures 5.14 and 5.15.

Compared to other dimensions of economic integration within the eurozone, cross-border takeovers in the banking sector remained the exception. Herein lies one of the paradoxes of eurozone integration. The introduction of the euro meant that "money" (bank liabilities) was flowing freely across borders but that the asset side remained stubbornly local and immobile. It is this contrast between the free-flowing liabilities but localized assets of European bank balance sheets that has been a key contributing factor in the European crisis.

The banking flows that funded the property booms in Ireland and Spain were mirrored by their ballooning current account deficits, as shown in figure 5.16.

This perspective of the cross-border banking glut sheds much light on the current state of affairs in Europe. The European crisis carries

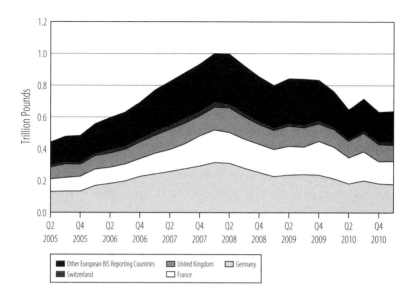

Figure 5.14 Foreign Claims of European BIS-Reporting Banks on Counterparties in Spain. *Source*: BIS Consolidated Banking Statistics, Table 9D (Foreign claims by nationality of reporting banks, ultimate risk basis). Most recent and some historical data for this series are available at http://www.bis.org/statistics/consstats.htm.

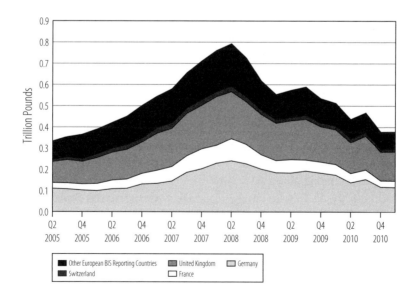

Figure 5.15 Foreign Claims of European BIS-Reporting Banks on Counterparties in Ireland. *Source*: BIS Consolidated Banking Statistics, Table 9D (see fig. 5.15).

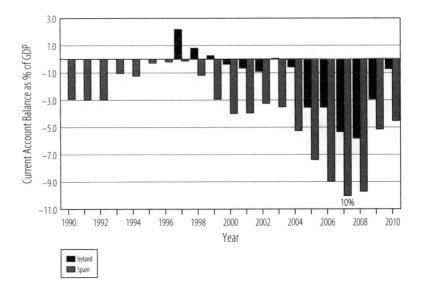

Figure 5.16 Current Account Balance of Ireland and Spain as a Percent of GDP. *Source*: IMF International Financial Statistics.

the hallmarks of a classic "twin crisis" that combines a banking crisis with an asset market decline that amplifies banking distress. In the emerging-market twin crises of the 1990s, the banking crisis was intertwined with a currency crisis. In the European crisis of 2011, the twin crisis combines a banking crisis with a sovereign debt crisis, where the mark-to-market amplification of financial distress interacts to worsen the banking crisis.

The analogies between the European crisis of 2011 and the emerging economy crises of the 1990s also extend to the policy prescriptions, both preventive and remedial. Mitigating the risks of crises entails an approach to financial regulation that has broad macro-prudential goals in sight. It is here that an emerging-market perspective is especially useful. We return to this issue in the policy section.

Securitization and Global Imbalances

The role of financial intermediaries in the financial cycle is perhaps best exemplified by the experience of the United States in the 2007–2009 global financial crisis. This is the first post-securitization crisis in which the traditional distinctions between banking and capital markets have been pushed aside. Indeed, capital market developments have been key to understanding banking sector distress and the progression of the financial crisis through its various stages. To explore the issues further, consider two pieces of received wisdom concerning securitization—one old and one new.

The old view emphasized the positive role played by securitization in dispersing credit risk, thereby enhancing the resilience of the financial system to defaults by borrowers. However, the current crisis has somewhat tarnished this positive image, and it has given way to a less sympathetic view.

The new view is unsympathetic of securitization, emphasizing the multilayered agency problems at every stage of the process. (See Ashcraft and Schuermann [2008], who detail specific agency problems at seven points in the securitization chain.)

We can dub this less charitable view the "hot potato" hypothesis, and it has figured frequently in speeches on the credit crisis given by central bankers and other policy makers. The mantra is that there is always a greater fool who will buy the bad loan. The hot potato is passed along until someone ends up suffering the eventual loss.

It is clear that final investors who buy claims backed by bad assets will suffer losses. However, it is important to draw a distinction between selling on a bad loan and issuing liabilities backed by bad loans. By selling a bad loan, you rid your balance sheet of the bad loan. In issuing liabilities backed by bad loans, you do not get rid of the bad loan. Instead, you borrow by putting up the hot potato as collateral.

In issuing liabilities backed by bad loans, the hot potato is sitting in the financial system, such as on the books of special-purpose vehicles (SPVs).

Although SPVs are legal entities separate from the large financial intermediaries that sponsor them, the intermediaries have exposure to them from liquidity enhancements and various forms of retained interest. Thus, far from passing the hot potato to a greater fool, the large financial intermediaries keep the hot potato. In effect, the large financial intermediaries are the last in the chain. They are the greatest fool.

Although the final investors will end up losing money, the financial intermediaries that hold the bad loans are in danger of even greater losses. Since the intermediaries are leveraged, they are in danger of having their equity wiped out.

Indeed, of the approximately $1.4 trillion total exposure to subprime mortgages, around half of the potential losses are borne by leveraged US financial institutions, such as commercial banks, securities firms, and hedge funds (Greenlaw et al. 2008). Foreign leveraged institutions are another one-sixth. Thus, leveraged financial institutions will have some dollars in losses.

Leveraging to a Tipping Point

There is an even less benign interpretation of securitization that has affinities with our earlier discussions on the dynamics of financial intermediaries themselves. Recall that the accounting identity for total credit is:

Total Credit = Total Equity of Banking Sector
+ Liabilities to Non-bank Domestic Creditors
+ Liabilities to Foreign Creditors

In a boom when credit is growing very rapidly, the growth of bank balance sheets outstrips the growth in the pool of retail deposits, so additional funding must be tapped. Securitization is one way to tap additional creditors. By bundling loans into securities, it becomes much easier to borrow by pledging the security in a collateralized borrowing arrangement, such as a repurchase agreement (repo).

The greater demand for securities backed by mortgages can be seen directly as a demand for greater leverage in the intermediary sector. In this way, securitization allows the banking system to tap new creditors. The new creditors who buy the securitized claims include pension funds, mutual funds, and insurance companies, as well as foreign investors such as foreign central banks. Foreign central banks have been a particularly important funding source for residential mortgage lending in the United States.

As recently as the early 1980s, conventional banks were the predominant holders of household mortgages. However, the growth of government-sponsored enterprises (GSEs) such as Fannie Mae (Federal National Mortgage Association) and Freddie Mac (Federal Home Loan Mortgage Corporation), as well as the "private label" mortgage securitizations, meant that market-based intermediaries became the dominant players in the mortgage sector (see Shin 2009).

As balance sheets expand, new borrowers must be found. When all prime borrowers have a mortgage, but still balance sheets need to expand, then banks have to lower their lending standards and lend to subprime borrowers. The seeds of the subsequent downturn in the credit cycle are thus sown. When the downturn arrives, the bad loans are either sitting on the balance sheets of the large financial intermediaries or they are in SPVs that are sponsored by them. This is so because the bad loans were taken on precisely in order to utilize the slack on the intermediaries' balance sheets. Although final investors will also suffer losses, the large intermediaries are more exposed in the sense that they face the danger of seeing their capital wiped out.

The severity of the credit crisis of 2007–2009 lies precisely in the fact that the bad loans were not all passed to the final investors. Instead, the "hot potato" sat inside the financial system, on the balance sheets of the largest, and most sophisticated, financial intermediaries.

Demand Pull or Supply Push

The expansion of credit to US households driven by the expansion of intermediary balance sheets has implications for the debate on global imbalances and the "savings glut" hypothesis. In a well-known 2005 speech, Federal Reserve Bank chair Ben Bernanke highlights the desire by savers in emerging market countries who demand US assets as a vehicle for their saving. In a similar vein, Cabellero, Farhi, and Gourinchas (2008) have argued that the shortage of high-quality assets in emerging market countries has increased demand for US securities. For both Bernanke and Caballero et al., the increased foreign holdings of US debt is seen from a "demand pull" perspective. The greater demand for US securities pulls US securities out of the United States and into foreign hands.

But the fastest growing component of US debt securities going into the crisis was the "capital market" component, which consisted of securities issued by private-label asset-backed security (ABS) issuers. It is not obvious why foreigners should express such a strong preference for such securities when the backing assets are subprime mortgage pools.

This indicates a need to complement the demand pull story with a supply response from US debtors. That is, there is a "supply push" perspective in which greater holding of US debt securities is explained by the momentum of rapidly growing balance sheets in the residential mortgage sector that searches for funding sources. Under this story, the US current account deficit is explained by the US housing boom.

The distinction between gross capital flows and net capital flows is important, as emphasized by Borio and Disyatat (2011). The balance of payments sheds light on net capital flows but may not be so informative about gross flows. In the case of securitization and mortgage lending in the United States, the role of European banks must be considered. European banks raised large amounts of wholesale funding in the United States by issuing certificates of deposit (CDs), commercial paper (CP), and repos to prime money market funds, and then redirected much of this funding back to the United States by buying mortgage-related securities, thereby funding mortgage lending in the United States. (See Baba, McCauly, and Ramaswamy [2009], who document that 40 percent of the assets held in US prime money market funds were liabilities of European banks.)

The role of the European banks in intermediating dollar funding from US savers to US borrowers was important in determining the overall credit availability condition in the United States and entailed large gross capital flows. However, in net terms, the borrowing by European banks was canceled out by the lending by European banks, leaving a roughly balanced net position. Hence, the balance of payments statistics did not reflect the substantial role played by European banks.

The study by Gete (2008) is the closest in spirit to the hypothesis explained here. However, for Gete the housing boom is explained by a preference shift toward housing, rather than being a financial market phenomenon. But Gete does document cross-country evidence that suggests that countries experiencing housing booms are those that have experienced the largest current account deficits.

Looking at changes in the percentages of foreign holdings of US debt securities held by foreigners provides further insight. Overall, during the five years 2002–2007, the foreign share increased 2.6 times. The "capital market" component increased over 29-fold (computed by the authors from the US Treasury TIC database.)

The capital market series includes mainly the liabilities of private-label securitization vehicles. This means the series includes the asset-backed securities (ABS) issued by the ABS-issuer sector of the economy. The largest component of ABS in the years just before the crisis was securities backed by subprime mortgage assets (such as collateralized debt obligations [CDOs] based on subprime mortgages).

These findings suggest the need to complement the "savings glut" hypothesis advanced by Bernanke (2005), Caballero et al. (2008), and others. According to the savings glut view, it is the excess savings of residents in some emerging market countries, and the shortage of high-quality assets in these countries, that increased the demand for US securities as a vehicle for saving.

For the savings glut camp, increased foreign holdings are seen from a "demand pull" perspective. The greater demand for US securities pulled US securities out of the United States and into foreign hands. In the popular press, such an account can easily turn into a blame game in which foreign investors are blamed for causing the asset price bubble in the United States (see, for instance, *NY Times* 2008).

However, the greatest increase in foreign holdings of US debt securities has been of asset-backed securities issued by private-label securitization vehicles. The bulk of these were ABS built on subprime mortgages. It is difficult to see why foreigners in search of high-quality assets were expressing such a strong preference for securities backed by subprime mortgages.

The savings glut hypothesis is built around an accounting identity and so does not do a good job of indicating the underlying economic mechanism that explains the changes in aggregate quantities.

Our discussion suggests that the savings glut hypothesis for the global imbalances must be complemented with a supply response on the part of the debtor sectors in the United States. Any explanation of global imbalances must account for the fact that the largest increase in debt securities held by foreigners is for securities issued by private-label mortgage pools, the bulk of which contain low-quality subprime assets.

All this suggests that an examination of the causes of global imbalances is incomplete without looking into the role of housing policy in the United States, including monetary policy's role in the housing boom.

Indeed, instead of the "demand pull" perspective, there is a "supply push" perspective in which greater holding of US debt securities is explained by the momentum of rapidly growing balance sheets in the residential mortgage sector, which was searching for funding sources. Under this alternative story, the US current account deficit is explained by the US housing boom and the imperative to increase the size of financial sector assets as a whole. To that extent, the role of loose US monetary policy in fueling the housing boom is an important part of the overall discussion surrounding global imbalances.

Implications for Bank Regulation

The analysis and historical evidence presented in this chapter suggest the need for macro-prudential regulation—regulation concerned with the resilience of the financial system as a whole. However, under its current agreed form, the centerpiece of the capital and liquidity framework for banks known as Basel III is almost exclusively micro-prudential in its focus, concerned with the solvency of individual banks.

A well-designed macro-prudential policy framework encompasses a system of early warning indicators that signal increased vulnerabilities to financial stability and a set of associated policy tools that can address the increased vulnerabilities at an early stage.

Instead, Basel III is a strengthened common equity buffer of 7 percent together with new liquidity requirements and a leverage cap, to be phased in over an extended timetable running to 2019.

The elements that are most promising in living up to the macro-prudential aims of regulatory reform—the countercyclical capital buffer and the capital surcharge for systemically important financial institutions (SIFIs)—have proved the most controversial and in mid-2012 had yet to be fully agreed on and implemented. The language of Basel III is revealing, with repeated references to greater "loss absorbency" of bank capital. However, achieving greater loss absorbency by itself is almost certainly inadequate in achieving a stable financial system for two reasons:

- Loss absorbency does not directly address excessive asset growth during booms.
- Preoccupation with loss absorbency diverts attention from the liability side of bank balance sheets, and from vulnerabilities related to reliance on unstable short-term funding and short-term foreign currency debt.

Excessive asset growth is at the core of increased financial sector vulnerabilities. The challenge is knowing when asset growth is "excessive."

Simple rules of thumb such as the ratio of total credit to GDP may be useful, but more promising are measures derived from the liability side of banking-sector balance sheets.

The ratio of noncore to core liabilities of the banking sector may be especially useful in gauging the stage of the financial cycle. Monetary aggregates and other liability measures of the banking sector may also be useful. Whereas the traditional role of monetary aggregates has been through their effect on inflation, their macro-prudential role has to do with the behavioral and stability properties of such aggregates.

The legal form of a claim may not coincide with the behavioral properties of the claim. For instance, household deposits have empirical traits that differ from interbank deposits, even though the legal forms of the claims are identical.

Measures of cross-exposures across intermediaries (such as CoVaR) may be useful complementary indicators, bearing in mind that cross-exposures themselves are pro-cyclical, and track noncore liabilities.

Agreements on banking regulation by the Basel Committee are positive steps forward in establishing stability in the financial system, but because effectiveness of such policy can be different depending on economic stage and conditions, regulators need to find ways to adopt policies that are more suitable to their region.

For example, although bank capital requirements are often viewed simply as a buffer against loss, another important role is to restrain excessive asset growth during financial booms. In a boom, when credit growth outpaces the pool of deposits, other sources of funding must then be tapped to fund the increased asset growth of banks and other intermediaries. In advanced countries, the gap is made up by wholesale bank funding such as securitized notes and repos. For emerging countries that operate with open capital markets, the growth in bank assets is fueled by short-term funds raised in foreign currency, so that the downturn in the cycle manifests itself as twin crises in which a banking crisis and currency crisis reinforce each other. The Asian financial crisis of 1997 and the turmoil in global financial markets in the last part of 2008 are glaring instances of the vulnerability.

As seen from the experience of Ireland and Spain, the bursting of a housing bubble can have very large negative consequences for public finance. As output slumps and economic activity falls during the crisis, both the fall in net receipts and the increased expenditures to meet the crisis can lead to very rapid deterioration. The country can move from what appears to be a very healthy budget surplus and negligible debt to very large deficits and ballooning debt.

Macro-Prudential Policy Tools

Macro-prudential policy tools aim to lessen the buildup of vulnerabilities to financial instability. The primary aim of macro-prudential policy is to secure financial stability by leaning against permissive financial conditions (should they be deemed excessive), and to lean against excessively rapid loan growth by the banking sector.

There are many ways to group macro-prudential tools. One useful way is to distinguish among *bank capital-oriented tools* that limit loan growth through altering incentives of banks, asset-side tools that limit bank loan growth directly, and *liability-side tools* that limit vulnerability to liquidity and currency mismatches. We look at these in turn.

Bank Capital-Oriented Tools

Capital requirements that lean against the credit or business cycle — that is, rise with credit growth and fall with credit contraction — can thus play an important role in promoting financial stability and reducing systemic risk. This is because bank balance sheet management is inherently pro-cyclical, making a boom and bust more likely. The rise in asset values that accompanies a boom results in higher capital buffers at financial institutions, supporting further lending in the context of an unchanging benchmark for capital adequacy. In the bust, the value of this capital can drop precipitously, possibly even necessitating a cut in lending.

The framework for counter-cyclical capital buffers as envisaged in the Basel III framework has focused on the ratio of credit growth to GDP. There are two preconditions for the successful implementation of such counter-cyclical measures. First, the quantitative signals that trigger actions must reflect accurately the features (such as excessively loose lending conditions) that are being targeted by policy makers. Second, the implementation procedure should be such that policy makers can move decisively and in a timely manner in heading off the buildup of vulnerabilities. We have already commented on the first point, so here, we focus on the second.

If the triggering of the counter-cyclical capital requirements is predicated on the exercise of discretion and judgment by the authorities, the political-economy problems associated with the exercise of such discretion put the authorities under pressure from market participants and other interested parties.

The political-economy problem is similar to that of central banks that tighten monetary policy to head off property booms. Since there are private-sector participants (such as construction companies and developers) who are beneficiaries of the short-term boom, they can be expected to exert pressure on policy makers or engage in general lobbying. The political-economy problems will be more acute if there are controversies on the exact stage of the financial cycle or on the degree of conclusiveness of the empirical evidence invoked by the policy authorities.

Thus, the accuracy of the quantitative indicators and the political-economy problem are very closely related. One of the disadvantages of the counter-cyclical capital buffer is that it relies on triggering additional capital requirements in response to quantitative signals. Although such quantitative measures are relatively straightforward in simple theoretical models, there may be considerable challenges in the smooth and decisive implementation in practice.

FORWARD-LOOKING PROVISIONING Forward-looking provisioning requires the buildup of a loss-absorbing buffer in the form of provisioning at the time of making a loan. It shares similarities with the counter-cyclical capital buffer. However, there is a key difference in the accounting treatment of provisioning and equity. That difference has a potentially crucial effect on bank behavior.

By insisting on forward-looking provisioning, the bank's equity is reduced by the amount of the provision. For bank management that targets a specific level of return on equity (ROE), removing some of the capital base can play an important role in reducing the pressure to grow the balance sheet during a boom. To the extent a bank uses its capital as the base on which to build its total balance sheet, the size of the base affects the size of the balance sheet. During a credit boom, a buildup of assets using debt financing contributes to a buildup of vulnerabilities. Inhibiting equity growth reduces the buildup of assets, and thus the need for debt.

Although forward-looking provisioning has been important in cushioning the Spanish banking system from the initial stages of the global financial crisis, there is a question mark on whether building loss-absorbing buffers, by itself, can be sufficient to cushion the economy from the bursting of a major property bubble, as Spain has discovered.

CAPS ON BANK LEVERAGE Caps on bank leverage may be used as a way to limit asset growth by tying total assets to bank equity. The rationale for a leverage cap rests on the role of bank capital as a constraint on new lending, rather than on the Basel approach of bank capital as a buffer against loss.

The main mechanism is the cost of bank equity, which is regarded by the bank as being a more expensive funding source than short-term debt. By requiring a larger equity base to fund the total size of the balance sheet, the regulator can slow asset growth.

The experience of Korea holds some lessons in the use of leverage caps. In June 2010 the Korean regulatory authorities introduced a new set of macro-prudential regulations to mitigate excessive volatility of foreign capital flows. Specific policy measures included explicit ceilings on the foreign exchange derivative positions of banks, regulations on foreign currency bank loans, and prudential regulations for improving the foreign exchange risk management of financial institutions.

These measures were intended to limit short-term foreign currency–denominated borrowings of banks, and did so by requiring banks to put up more equity capital if they chose to increase volatile debt. Korea's leverage cap on bank foreign-exchange derivative positions introduced in June 2010 saw some success in limiting the practice of banks hedging forward dollar positions with carry trade positions in won funded with short-term US dollar debt.

Asset-Side Tools

Asset-side tools act directly as brakes on bank asset growth, counteracting the superficial and transitory strength of individual bank capital ratios inflated by higher profitability during booms or temporarily depressed measures of risk.

LIMITS ON BANK LENDING When monetary policy is constrained, administrative rules that limit bank lending, such as caps on loan-to-value (LTV) ratios and debt-service-to-income (DTI) ratios, may be useful. LTV regulation restricts the percentage of the value of the collateral asset that can be lent. DTI caps operate by limiting the debt service costs of the borrower to less than some fixed percentage of verified income.

Conceptually, it is useful to distinguish two motivations for the use of LTV and DTI. The first is consumer protection, where the intention is to protect household borrowers who may take on excessively burdensome debt relative to their reasonable means to repay it from wage income. This is not relevant for macro-prudential policy, so it is not discussed here.

The macro-prudential rationale for imposing LTV and DTI caps is to limit bank lending so as to prevent both the buildup of noncore liabilities to fund such loans and to lean against the erosion of lending standards associated with rapid asset growth.

Although LTV caps are familiar, the use of DTI caps is less widespread. For Korea and some Asian economies such as Hong Kong, the use of DTI has been an important supplementary tool. DTI rules have the advantage that bank loan growth can be tied (at least loosely) to wage growth in the economy. Without this fundamental anchor, an LTV rule by itself will be susceptible to the amplifying dynamics of a credit boom, which interacts with an increase in the value of collateral assets during a housing boom. Even though the LTV rule is in place, if house prices are rising sufficiently fast, the collateral value will rise simultaneously, making the constraint bind less hard.

CAP ON THE LOAN-TO-DEPOSIT RATIO   A cap on the loan-to-deposit ratio limits credit growth by tying it to the growth of deposits. Korea provides an example of its use. In December 2009 Korea's supervisory authority announced it was reintroducing the loan-to-deposit ratio regulation that had been scrapped in November 1998 as a part of deregulation. With the regulation, the ratio of won-denominated loans to won-denominated deposits should fall to below 100 percent by 2013. However, the banks anticipated the cap and began reducing their LTV ratios.

Because the deposit base constitutes the baseline, the definition of what qualifies as deposits has strict guidelines. For instance, negotiable certificates of deposit (CDs) are not included in the measure of deposits in the denominator in computing the ratio.

One potential weakness of the regulation is that the rule does not apply to the Korean branches of foreign banks. Since foreign bank branches supply a substantial amount of foreign exchange–denominated lending to Korean banks and firms, the exemption leaves a gap in the regulation. However, a loan-to-deposit cap is not particularly applicable to foreign bank branches because, by their nature, they rely mostly on funding from home offices or wholesale funding, rather than on local-deposit funding.

For domestic banks, a loan-to-deposit ratio cap has two effects. First, it restrains excessive asset growth by tying loan growth to the growth in deposit funding. Second, there is a direct effect on the growth of noncore liabilities, and hence on the buildup of vulnerabilities that come from the liability side of the balance sheet.

At the theoretical level, a loan-to-deposit cap can be seen as a special case of a noncore liabilities levy (discussed below) where the tax rate is kinked, changing from zero to infinity at the threshold point. However, the comparison with the noncore liabilities levy is less easy due to the fact that the loan-to-deposit cap applies only to loans, not total assets or total exposure (including off balance sheet exposures).

Liability-Side Tools

Liability-side tools address the buildup of systemic risks through currency and maturity mismatches, as well as the underpricing of risk on global capital markets. These tools distinguish between core liabilities (traditional retail deposits) and noncore liabilities (other funding sources). The stock of noncore liabilities reflects the stage of the financial cycle and the extent of the underpricing of risk in the financial system.

NONCORE LIABILITIES LEVY A levy or tax on noncore liabilities can mitigate pricing distortions that lead to excessive asset growth. The Financial Stability Contribution (FSC) recommended to G20 leaders by the IMF in June 2010 is an example of such a corrective tax (IMF 2010). The levy on noncore liabilities has several features that affect overall financial stability.

First, the base of the levy varies over the financial cycle. The levy bites hardest during the boom when noncore liabilities are large. This means the levy acts as an automatic stabilizer even if the tax rate itself remains constant. Given the well-known political-economy challenges to the exercise of discretion by regulators, the automatic feature may have important advantages.

Second, the levy addresses financial vulnerability while leaving unaffected the essential functioning of the financial system—channeling core funding from savers to borrowers. By targeting noncore liabilities only, the levy addresses externalities associated with excessive asset growth and systemic risk arising from the interconnectedness of banks. In other words, the levy addresses the "bubbly" element of banking sector liabilities.

Third, the targeting of noncore liabilities can be expected to address the vulnerability of emerging economies with open capital accounts to sudden reversals in capital flows due to deleveraging by banks. Indeed, for many emerging economies, the levy on noncore liabilities could be aimed more narrowly at foreign currency–denominated liabilities only. Shin (2011) discusses some of the potential advantages of a levy on noncore liabilities of this sort.

The revenue raised might be used for a market stabilization fund, but the amount collected is a secondary issue. The main purpose is to align incentives. A good analogy is with traffic congestion charges: the main purpose is to discourage cars from entering an area, thereby alleviating the externalities associated with congestion. In the same way, the noncore liabilities bank levy should be seen primarily as a tool for aligning the incentives of banks more closely to the social optimum.

MACRO-PRUDENTIAL LEVY In December 2010 Korea announced it was introducing a macro-prudential levy aimed at the foreign exchange–denominated liabilities of banks—both domestic banks and the branches of foreign banks. Implementation began in August 2011. The rate for the Korean levy has been set at 20 basis points for short-term foreign exchange–denominated liabilities of up to one year, falling to five basis points for liabilities exceeding five years. The proceeds are held in a special account of the already existing Exchange Stabilization Account, managed by the Finance Ministry. The proceeds may be used as part of the official foreign exchange reserves.

There is a key difference between Korea's macro-prudential levy and the outwardly similar levy introduced by the United Kingdom. In the UK case, the revenue goes into the general fiscal account of the government and hence can be regarded as a revenue-raising measure. In contrast, the Korean levy has its revenue ring-fenced for specific use in financial stabilization.

UNREMUNERATED RESERVE REQUIREMENTS Perhaps the best known traditional form of capital control has been unremunerated reserve requirements (URR), where the central bank requires importers of capital to deposit a certain fraction of the sum at the central bank. The prevalence of the URR owes in large part to the fact that the central bank has been in charge both of prudential policy and macroeconomic management, and the central bank normally has had discretion to use URR policies without going through the legislative procedures associated with other forms of capital controls, such as levies and taxes. (Ostry et al. [2011] has a comprehensive discussion of the experience of countries in their use of URRs.)

Most central banks impose some type of reserve requirement for deposits, especially when the deposits are under government-sponsored deposit insurance. The rationale is as an implicit insurance premium paid by the bank in return for the deposit insurance.

The macro-prudential motivation for URR is to impose an implicit tax on those components of financial-intermediary liabilities other than insured deposits that are likely to impose negative spillover effects. Introduction of a reserve requirement for the non-deposit liabilities of banks would raise the cost of non-deposit funding for banks and thereby restrain the rapid growth of such liabilities during booms. In this respect, a reserve requirement on non-deposit liabilities has a similar effect to a tax or levy on such liabilities.

A COMPARISON OF URR AND AN EXPLICIT TAX Although the URR is an implicit tax on a balance sheet item, the implied tax rate itself will vary with the opportunity cost of funds, and hence on the prevailing interest rate. The variability of the implicit tax rate necessitates some adjustment of the reserve rates, and the requirements will need to be raised to a high level when interest rates are low. This is a disadvantage of the URR relative to other measures.

Another issue is the challenges to managing the central bank's balance sheet as a consequence of URRs. The reserves would have to be held on the central bank's balance sheet as a liability, with implications for the fluctuations in the money supply in line with the private sector's use of non-deposit liabilities, and the selection of counterpart assets on the central bank's balance sheet.

There are also differences in the revenue implications between the reserve requirement and a levy or tax. A reserve requirement raises revenue to the extent that the net income on the assets held by the central bank that is funded by the reserves is positive. Hence, the bigger the interest spread between the asset and liability, the larger the income.

There is one advantage of the reserve requirement that is not shared by the levy: the banks have access to a liquid asset in case there is a liquidity shortage or run. In this respect, the reserve requirement has some of the features of the Basel III liquidity requirement on banks (Basel Committee on Banking Supervision [BCBS] 2010).

Another disadvantage of the reserve requirement is that it applies only to banks, rather than to the wider group of financial institutions that use noncore liabilities. When faced with the possibility of arbitrage, or with structural changes that shift intermediation activity from banks to the market-based financial intermediaries, the reserve requirement is less effective than a tax.

The time delay in implementing the macro-prudential levy in Korea offers useful lessons on the relative merits of unremunerated reserve requirements and levies or taxes. The legislative process required to implement a levy can entail considerable delays in the introduction and effectiveness of the policy. In the case of Korea, the initial discussions concerning the levy began in February 2010, but the announcement of implementation came only in December 2010. The legislative hurdles were cleared in April 2011, for implementation after August 2011.

When the external environment is changing rapidly, such long delays make introduction of a levy cumbersome and impractical as the first line of defense. However, as in Korea's case, alternative measures that rely on existing legislation or other temporary measures can be used until the longer term measures come into force.

In practice, the choice between URR and levies or taxes is driven by practical reasons such as administrative expediency rather than by principle. Typically, the central bank is the best established policy institution that has direct contact with the financial markets and institutions. The long established status of the central bank in most countries explains why URRs have been more prevalent than levies or taxes.

There are, however, exceptions to this. In Brazil, an inflow tax (IOF) was introduced in 1993, and the legislation has been in effect since. Although the rate has been set at zero at times, the infrastructure has been available as circumstances have demanded.

342 Banking, Capital Flows, and Financial Cycles

Unlike a tax, a URR can usually be removed (or set to zero) more easily because the budget is not directly reliant on its revenues. For a similar reason, the macro-prudential levy set by Korea has been designed so the revenue does not have any budgetary implications, precisely in order to forestall potential political-economy concerns.

Conclusion

This chapter delved into the workings of financial intermediaries and how the inner logic of the balance sheet management and risk control of financial intermediaries can set in motion amplifying forces for financial booms and busts.

The forces that drive the behavior of financial intermediaries are quite general and apply to advanced countries as well as to emerging countries. As the 2007–2009 global financial crisis has demonstrated, the mechanics of the boom-bust cycle played out even more potently in the capital markets of the advanced countries than in the emerging countries. Indeed, one of the lessons of the crisis is that the forces behind financial instability (in particular, the role of global banks) that were familiar to emerging countries' policy makers were made more familiar to advanced country policy makers, too.

We now return to the question of the benefits of financial globalization and the belief that capital inflows allow an emerging country to supplement its own domestic savings in financing investment, lowering the cost of capital and boosting investment and growth.

The evidence is mixed at best, with the greater weight pointing to capital inflows fueling permissive domestic liquidity conditions that fuel housing booms and consumption. The experience of Japan in the 1980s also rests on the role of intermediaries, although the channel was through the corporate sector acting as financial intermediaries that drew market-based finance and supplied financing to the banking sector. In all cases, the vulnerability stems from the potential for excessive growth of assets funded with short-term debt, with a substantial part being denominated in a foreign currency.

A reassessment of the rules of the game in international finance has been given further momentum by the simmering crises in the advanced economies in Europe. The framework outlined in this chapter should prove useful in understanding the current European predicament and forging tools useful for strengthening and stabilizing the global and national financial systems.

Acknowledgments

The authors thank Kazumasa Iwata, Ed Lincoln, Hugh Patrick, and Yung Chul Park for their comments on earlier versions of this chapter.

References

Adrian, Tobias, and Hyun Song Shin. 2008. "Financial Intermediaries, Financial Stability and Monetary Policy." Paper for the Federal Reserve Bank of Kansas City Symposium at Jackson Hole.

Adrian, Tobias, and Hyun Song Shin. 2009. "Financial Intermediaries and Monetary Economics." Draft chapter for the *Handbook of Monetary Economics.*

Adrian, Tobias, and Hyun Song Shin. 2010, December. "Liquidity and Leverage." Federal Reserve Bank of New York Staff Report 358. Revision of May 2008. Also in *Journal of Financial Intermediation* 19 (3): 418–37.

Agrawal, Amol. 2010. "Using Leverage Ratio—Differences Between Canada and US." Mostly Economics blog. http://mostlyeconomics.wordpress.com/2010/02/06/using-leverage-ratio-%E2%80%93-differences-between-canada-and-us/ (accessed September 17, 2012).

Ashcraft, Adam B., and Til Schuermann. 2008 March. "Understanding the Securitization of Subprime Mortgage Credit." Federal Reserve Bank of New York, Staff Reports 318.

Baba, Naohiko, Robert N. McCauley, and Srichander Ramaswamy. 2009. "US Dollar Money Market Funds and Non-US Banks." *BIS Quarterly Review*, March, 65–81.

BCBS = Basel Committee on Banking Supervision. 2010 December (rev June 2011). *Basel III: A Global Regulatory Framework for More Resilient Banks and Banking Systems*. Bank for International Settlements.

Beck, Thorsten, Asli Demirgüç-Kunt, and Vojislav Maksimovic. 2002, October. "Financing Patterns Around the World: The Role of Institutions." World Bank Policy Research Working Paper WPS2905.

Bernanke, Ben S. 2005, March. "The Global Saving Glut and the US Current Account Deficit." The Sandridge Lecture, Virginia Association of Economics, Richmond, Virginia.

Berg, Andrew, Eduardo Borensztein, and Catherine Pattillo. 2004. "Assessing Early Warning Systems: How Have They Worked in Practice?" IMF Working Paper 04/52.

Borio, Claudio. 2009 May. "The Financial Crisis of 2007-?: Macroeconomic Origins and Policy Lessons." Presentation at the G-20 Workshop on the Global Economy, Causes of the Crisis: Key Lessons.

Borio, Claudio, and Piti Disyatat. 2011, May. "Global Imbalances and the Financial Crisis: Link or No Link?" BIS Working Papers 346.

Borio, Claudio, and Haibin Zhu. 2008. "Capital Regulation, Risk-Taking and Monetary Policy: A Missing Link in the Transmission Mechanism?" BIS Working Papers 268.

Brunnermeier, Markus, Andrew Crockett, Charles Goodhart, and Avinash Persaud. 2009. *The Fundamental Principles of Financial Regulation.* Geneva Report on the World Economy 11. Centre for Economic Policy Research.

Caballero, Ricardo J., Emmanuel Farhi, Pierre-Olivier Gourinchas. 2008. "An Equilibrium Model of 'Global Imbalances' and Low Interest Rates." *American Economic Review* 98 (1): 358–93.

Calvo, Guillermo A., Leonardo Leiderman, and Carmen Reinhart. 1996. "Capital Flows to Developing Countries in the 1990s: Causes and Effects." *Journal of Economic Perspectives* 10 (2): 123–39.

Dooley, Michael, David Folkerts-Landau, and Peter Garber. 2003. "An Essay on the Revised Bretton Woods System." NBER Working Paper 9971.

Gete, Pedro. 2008. "Housing Markets and Current Account Dynamics." Working Paper, University of Chicago, Booth School of Business.

Gourinchas, Pierre-Olivier, and Olivier Jeanne. 2007, November. "Capital Flows to Developing Countries: The Allocation Puzzle." CEPR Discussion Paper DP6561 http://ssrn.com/abstract=1140088 (accessed August 5, 2012).

Greenlaw, David, Jan Hatzius, Anil Kashyap, and Hyun Song Shin. 2008. "Leveraged Losses: Lessons from the Mortgage Market Meltdown." *US Monetary Policy Forum Report 2.*

Hattori, Masazumi, Hyun Song Shin, and Wataru Takahashi. 2009 May. "A Financial System Perspective on Japan's Experience in the Late 1980s." Bank of Japan, Institute for Monetary and Economic Studies, Discussion Paper 2009-E-19. Paper presented at the 16th Bank of Japan International Conference, May 27–28, Tokyo, Japan.

Hoshi, Takeo, and Anil Kashyap. 2004. *Corporate Financing and Governance in Japan: The Road to the Future.* The MIT Press.

IMF = International Monetary Fund. 2010, June. "A Fair and Substantial Contribution by the Financial Sector." Report by the IMF to the G20.

IMF = International Monetary Fund. 2011, February. "Recent Experiences in Managing Capital Inflows—Cross-Cutting Themes and Possible Policy Frameworks." Strategy, Policy, and Review Department, in consultation with Legal, Monetary and Capital Markets, Research, and other Departments.

Kose, M. Ayhan, Eswar S. Prasad, and Marco E. Terrones. 2003. "Financial Integration and Macroeconomic Volatility." IMF Staff Papers 50, Special Issue.

Kose, M. Ayhan, Eswar Prasad, Kenneth Rogoff, and Shang-Jin Wei. 2006. "Financial Globalization: A Reappraisal." IMF Working Paper 06/189.

Lynch, Kevin G. 2009, May. "Public Policy Making in a Crisis: A Canadian Perspective." Government of Canada, Privy Council Office.

New York Times. 2008. "The Reckoning: Chinese Savings Helped Inflate American Bubble." December 26.

Ostry, Jonathan D., Atish Ghosh, Karl Habermeier, Marcos Chamon, Mahvash S. Qureshi, and Dennis B.S. Reinhardt. 2010. "Capital Inflows: The Role of Controls." IMF Staff Position Note 10/04.

Ostry, Jonathan D., Atish Ghosh, Karl Habermeier, Luc Laeven, Marcos Chamon, Mahvash S. Qureshi, and Annamaria Kokenyne. 2011. "Capital Inflows: The Role of Controls." IMF Staff Discussion Note 10/06.

Park, Yung Chul. 1998. "The Financial Crisis in Korea and Its Lessons for Reform of the International Financial System." In Regulatory and Supervisory Challenges in a New Era of Global Finance, Jan Joost Teunissen, ed. FONDAD (Forum on Debt and Development).

Park, Yung Chul. 2006. *Economic Liberalization and Integration in East Asia: A Post-Crisis Paradigm.* Oxford University Press.

Prasad, Eswar, Raghuram Rajan, and Arvind Subramanian. 2007. "Foreign Capital and Economic Growth." *Brookings Papers on Economic Activity.*

Prasad, Eswar, Rogoff Kenneth, Wei Shang-jin, and M. Ayhan Kose. 2003. "The Effects of Financial Globalization on Developing Countries: Some Empirical Evidence." IMF Occasional Paper 220.

Rodrik, Dani, and Arvind Subramanian. 2009. "Why Did Financial Globalization Disappoint?" IMF Staff Papers 56, pp 112–38.

Shin, Hyun Song. 2009. "Reflections on Northern Rock: The Bank Run that Heralded the Global Financial Crisis." *Journal of Economic Perspectives* 23 (1): 101–119.

Shin, Hyun Song. 2010. *Risk and Liquidity*, Clarendon Lectures in Finance, Oxford University Press.

Shin, Hyun Song. 2011. "Macroprudential Policies Beyond Basel III." Princeton Policy memo.

Shin, Hyun Song, and Kwanho Shin. 2010. "Procyclicality and Monetary Aggregates." NBER Discussion Paper 16836.

Wei, Shang-Jin. 2006. "Connecting Two Views on Financial Globalization: Can We Make Further Progress?" *Journal of the Japanese and International Economies* 20 (4): 459–81.

World Bank. 2000. "The Benefits and Risks of Short-Term Borrowing." In *Global Development Finance*, 77–95 (chap. 4).

Index